Tariq Ali was born in Lahore
1943 and was educated at Punj
Oxford. He is the author of
world politics and biography,
and *Streetfighting Years: An A*
Howard Brenton, he has wr
Iranian Nights and *Moscow (*
is also published by Picador.

Tariq Ali produced *The Bandung File* for four years and is currently the producer of the arts series, *Rear Window*, on Channel 4.

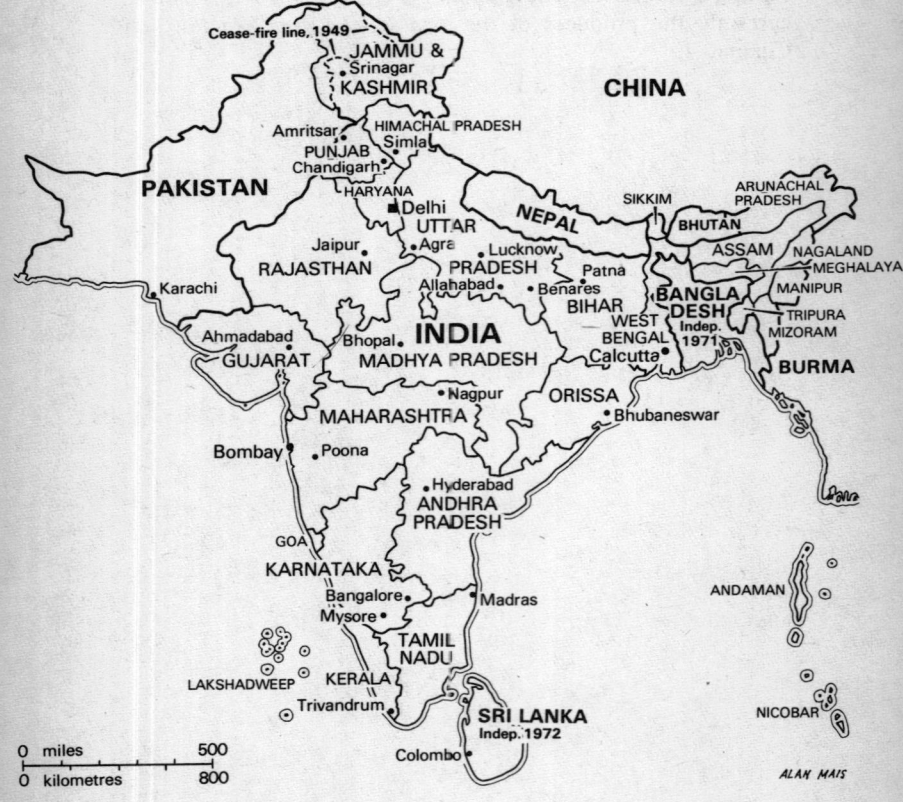

Tariq Ali

The Nehrus
and the Gandhis

AN INDIAN DYNASTY

published by Pan Books
in association with Chatto and Windus

For
Chengiz, Natasha and Susan,
who all helped in their different ways

First published 1985 by Pan Books Ltd

This revised edition published 1991 by
Pan Books Ltd, Cavaye Place, London SW10 9PG
in association with Chatto & Windus Ltd

1 3 5 7 9 3 6 4 2
© Tariq Ali 1985, 1991

ISBN 0 330 324527

Printed and bound in Great Britain by
Cox & Wyman Ltd, Reading

This book is sold subject to the condition that it
shall not, by way of trade or otherwise, be lent, re-sold,
hired out or otherwise circulated without the publisher's prior
consent in any form of binding or cover other than that in which
it is published and without a similar condition including this
condition being imposed on the subsequent purchaser

Contents

A chronology	vii
What's past is prologue	ix
The politicians	xi
The parties	xv

FOUNDING FATHER
Jawaharlal Nehru, 1889–1964 — 1

1 Early years, 1889–1912	3
2 Marriage, politics and prison, 1912–26	18
3 Gandhi versus Nehru, 1926–36	31
4 War, repression and independence, 1937–47	60
5 Prime Minister of India, 1947–64	78

MOTHER INDIRA
Indira Gandhi, *née* Nehru, 1917–84 — 111

1 Daughter and mother, 1917–47	113
2 Daughter and father, 1947–64	131
3 Indira independent, 1964–74	145
4 Empress of India, 1974–79	178
5 The last years, 1980–84	209

THE BROTHERS GANDHI
Sanjay, 1946–80; Rajiv, 1944–1991 — 261

1 The nation's grandchildren	263
2 Sanjay and Maneka, 1974–80	275
3 The birth of a dynasty: Captain Rajiv	287
4 The assassination of Rajiv Gandhi	301
Books and magazines consulted	325
Index	326

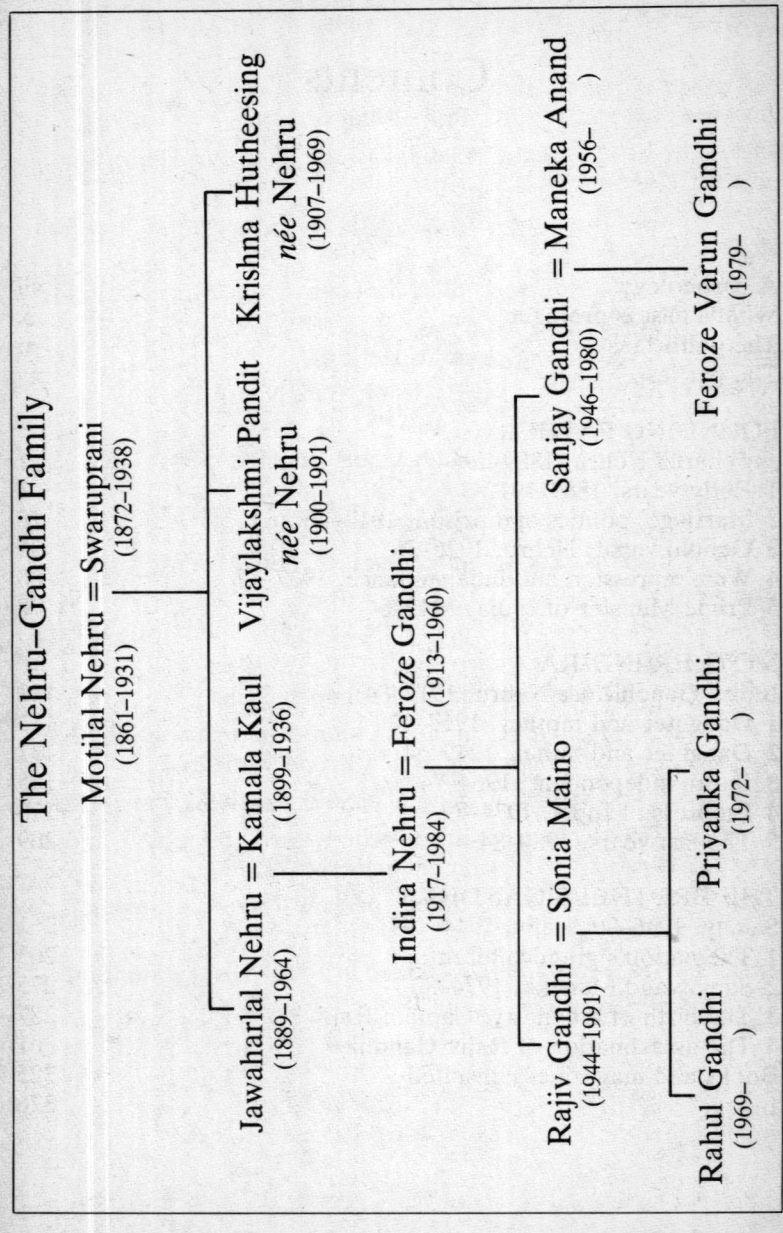

A chronology

15 August, 1947: India wins independence. Jawaharlal Nehru takes charge as the country's first Prime Minister.

30 January 1948: Mahatma Gandhi assassinated by a Hindu fanatic in New Delhi.

27 May 1964: Nehru dies at the age of 74. Succeeded by Lal Bahadur Shastri.

24 January 1966: Indira Gandhi sworn in as Prime Minister, following Shastri's death at Tashkent.

March 1971: Indira wins general elections.

December 1971: War with Pakistan. Bangladesh appears on the world map.

12 June 1975: Allahabad High Court convicts Mrs Gandhi on charges of electoral malpractice.

26 June 1975: National emergency declared in India.

March 1977: Janata Party wins general election. Morarji Desai new Prime Minister.

January 1980: Indira Gandhi and the Congress win back power in new elections.

23 June 1980: Sanjay Gandhi, 33, dies in plane crash.

31 October 1984: Indira Gandhi, 67, shot dead by two Sikh bodyguards. Rajiv Gandhi sworn in as new Prime Minister.

December 1984: Rajiv wins general elections with huge majority.

December 1989: Congress fails to win majority in polls. National Front forms minority government under V. P. Singh.

April 1991: New polls scheduled for May following downfall of Chandra Shekar's government.

21 May 1991: Rajiv Gandhi, 46, killed in bomb blast at public meeting near Madras. Tamil extremists suspected.

What's past is prologue

Fifteen hundred years ago, the theatre critics of ancient India devised a strict set of rules which were intended to determine the quality, effect and impact of the compositions produced by Sanskrit playwrights. The criteria devised were such as to be easily grasped by the audiences, for the aim was not to restrict the output of criticism by confining it to a tiny elite, but to ensure the exact opposite. Anyone could evaluate and judge the performance for themselves.

To that end the unbending dramaturgs of old defined eight formal categories or flavours: marvellous, romantic, comic, sorrowful, violent, heroic, terrifying and repulsive. The success or failure of a play depended on the ability of the writer and actors to evoke the emotions that flowed directly out of these flavours: wonder, love, mirth, grief, fury, resoluteness, fear and revulsion. Since those who came to watch had assimilated the principles of criticism they could collectively judge the merits or demerits of a particular performance. A wrong gesture or facial expression, the tiniest flaw, and heads began to shake.

The plays had either a straightforward historical theme or were a combination of history and mythology as contained in the epics of Hinduism, the *Ramayana* and the *Mahabharata*. These were familiar to most and therefore it was the ability to project the flavours that became decisive in evaluating the show. Even today, in the southern state of Kerala, the *Kathakali*, an ancient dance and mime act accompanied by drums and cymbals, is enacted before extremely critical audiences. The play lasts for several hours and depicts the loves and intrigues of the ancient gods of Indian mythology. Any mistake here and the more discerning critics in the audience can be observed whispering to their neighbours.

In a somewhat unorthodox fashion, all these flavours are

present in the political dramas that have galvanised contemporary India. The founding fathers of our dynasty are shadowed from beginning to end by wonder, love, mirth, grief, fury and resoluteness. There is one important difference. All the leading actors, bar one, have belonged to a single family. The Nehrus of Allahabad. They have dominated the stage ever since India became independent in 1947, and for the preceding two decades. The sole outsider was Mahatma Gandhi. Interestingly enough, he requires a special flavour and a related emotion: cunning and foxiness.

The audience in this play is not just a collective critic, but also the cast. It is an epic with millions of extras, constantly on the increase; at the end they number 730 million. They can all be accommodated because India, after China, is the largest stage in the world. The cast of millions speaks eight major languages, worships a wide variety of deities in temple, mosque, church, *gurdwara* and private altar.

Then our scenario is complete. The props are all in place. The actors are waiting for the show to begin.

The Politicians

Sheikh Abdullah: Leader of the Kashmir National Conference, who led a radical struggle during the 1930s for a 'New Kashmir'. Ally of Congress and opposed to Pakistan, but toyed with idea of an independent Kashmir. Imprisoned for many years by his old friend, Nehru, after independence. Founder of Kashmir's own mini-dynasty. His son Farooq was chosen to succeed him after he died in 1982. Family wars followed and in 1984 Indira Gandhi replaced Farooq with his brother-in-law G. M. Shah.

L. K. Advani: 63-year-old leader of the BJP. Once a journalist, now the Hindu fundamentalist candidate for Prime Minister.

Maulana Abul Kalam Azad: 1888-1958. Leading Muslim Congressman. Strongly opposed to the 1947 partition and violently opposed to Jinnah's Muslim League. Close friend of Nehru and served as Minister of Education in Nehru governments till his death in 1958.

Jyoti Basu: Veteran Bengali Communist. Knew Indira Gandhi in Britain when he was a fellow-student of Feroze Gandhi at London School of Economics. Currently heads the Communist-led coalition in West Bengal.

Subhas Chandra Bose: A Bengali leader of the Congress left, he was a strong opponent of Gandhi but his brand of radical, ultra-nationalism led to a liaison with Britain's strongest enemies, Nazi Germany and fascist Japan, during the Second World War. In 1942 he founded the Indian National Army from Indian prisoners of war in Japanese camps. He died in a plane crash in August 1945.

Chandrashekhar: Once a 'Young Turk' in the Indira Congress, now Leader of the Janata Party and principal opposition spokesman.

Morarji Desai: A leader of the Congress right. Served as Finance Minister in Nehru Cabinets, but removed in 1960s. On Shastri's death, Desai opposed Indira for Congress leadership, but was defeated. Subsequently he left Congress and became a leader of opposition coalition. In 1977 he became the first opposition Prime Minister, but fell as a result of internecine squabbling in 1979.

Feroze Gandhi: 1913–60. A Congress activist from his student days in Allahabad. Greatly inspired by Kamala Nehru in early 1930s. Studied at the London School of Economics. Married Indira in 1941. Became a Congress Member of Parliament for Rae Bareilly after independence and a fierce critic of corruption. Separated from Indira in 1948. No relation of Mahatama Gandhi.

Indira Gandhi née **Nehru:** 1917–84. Only child of Jawaharlal and Kamala, born in family home in Allahabad. Became President of Congress Party in 1959. A member of short-lived Shastri Cabinet in 1964. Following Shastri's death, she was elected Leader of the Party by Congress parliamentarians. Prime Minister of India from 1967–77, defeated by Janata coalition in 1977, but re-elected in January 1980. Assassinated by her Sikh bodyguards in November 1984.

Maneka Gandhi: 1956– . Sanjay's widow. When her attempts to step into her husband's shoes were thwarted by her mother-in-law, she left the family home and formed a new party in opposition to the Congress. One child, Feroze Varun.

Rajiv Gandhi: 1944–1991. Older son of Feroze and Indira, educated at Doon School and Cambridge. Served as a pilot in Indian Airlines for over ten years. Married Sonia Maino, an Italian. Two children: Rahul and Priyanka. Entered politics after his brother's death in 1980, became Prime Minister on the day his mother was assassinated in 1984. Was elected Prime Minister in the December 1984 elections.

Sanjay Gandhi: 1946–80. Younger son of Indira and Feroze Gandhi. Became famous in India when he set-up a factory to produce a small car. Later entered politics and intended to succeed his mother. A hated figure during the emergency of 1975–7. Died piloting his own plane in 1980.

Krishna Hutheesing née **Nehru:** Jawaharlal's younger sister.

Mohammed Ali Jinnah: 1875–1948. A distinguished Bombay lawyer and moderate constitutionalist politician. Described as 'ambassador of Hindu-Muslim unity' in 1916. Left Congress because of opposition to Gandhi's civil disobedience and joined communalist Muslim League. Spent five years (1931–5) in Britain in self-exile, then returned to lead the League and fight for a religious division of the sub-continent. Became first Governor-General of Pakistan in August 1947 and died a year later.

K. Kamaraj: A Congress leader and Chief Minister after 1947 of Madras State, now Tamil Nadu. Kamaraj devised the plan whereby veteran ministers gave up their jobs in the government and built a regenerated Congress instead. He also became head of a group of power-brokers known as 'The Syndicate' who ensured Indira's election to the Congress leadership in 1967. She defeated them in the party in 1969. Kamaraj's power declined when he was displaced in his own state by the DMK.

E.M.S. Namboodiripad: Veteran leader of Indian communism. Acquired fame when the communists won the state of Kerala in 1950. He became Chief Minister till he was removed from office by Nehru government.

Jawaharlal Nehru: 1889–1964. Motilal's only son. Educated Harrow and Cambridge. Trained as a lawyer, but became a full-time nationalist politician in 1920s. Married Kamala Kaul in 1916. Elected first prime minister of free India and won two consecutive general elections, remaining in office for seventeen years.

Kamala Nehru née **Kaul:** 1899–1936. From a Delhi family of Kashmiri immigrants. Married Jawaharlal at age of sixteen. Became active in Congress politics and went to prison. Died of tuberculosis in Switzerland in 1936.

Motilal Nehru: 1861–1931. An extremely successful Allahabad lawyer and *bon viveur*. Married Swaruprani. Initially a supporter of the British Empire, he gradually moved towards nationalism. President of All-India Congress in 1928. Founder of Nehru dynasty. Of Kashmiri Brahmin stock.

Vijaylakshmi Pandit née **Nehru:** Jawaharlal's younger sister.

Sardar Vallabhai Patel: Senior Congress leader in pre-independence period and a protegé of Mahatma Gandhi. Strongly opposed to Nehru's socialism. Became Home Minister in first Nehru government. Maintained a strong grip on Congress Party and often clashed with Nehru, who disliked him intensely. With his death in 1950, Nehru dominated the Party as well as the government.

Rajendra Prasad, Sarvapelli Radhakrishnan, Zakir Hussein, V. V. Giri, Fakhrudin Ali Ahmed, Zail Singh: Presidents of India (a largely titular post) from 1950–85. Prasad, the first president, was a deeply religious man and was often subjected to tongue-lashings from Nehru on this question. Giri was a trade-unionist, Zail Singh a Congress politician and the others were all scholars and educationalists.

Lal Bahadur Shastri: A Congress leader from Uttar Pradesh. An able organiser in the pre-1947 period, he served as Home Minister in Nehru's Cabinet after independence. In 1963 he resigned from the government as part of the Kamaraj Plan, but Nehru invited him back into the Cabinet in 1964. After Nehru's death, the Congress unanimously chose Shastri as his successor. He became India's second prime minister in June 1964, but died shortly afterwards, after signing a Peace Treaty with neighbouring Pakistan in the Russian city of Tashkent in January 1966.

Bal Gangadhar Tilak: 1864–1920. A leading West Indian journalist and politician, who typified the early pre-Gandhian militancy of the Congress. His main moderate rival was G. K. Gokhale, who was amongst Gandhi's first patrons in India.

Atal Behari Vajpayee: Leader of the BJP, an extreme right-wing communalist party. Vajpayee is an effective tribune. Served as Foreign Minister in the opposition Cabinet from 1977–9.

The Parties

Akali Dal: The Party of Immortals. Founded in 1920 by Sikhs in order to wrest control of the Sikh temples from corrupt and unaccountable priests. Gradually became the politico-religious voice of a substantial layer of Sikhs. Main regional opponent of the Congress in the Punjab.

Communist Party of India: Communist groups began to form in the 1920s, but a unified and national CPI took shape at end of the Second World War. CPI's legality during the years following USSR involvement in the war saw a massive growth in its numbers. It was banned in the years immediately following independence, but emerged as the major opposition party in Parliament after the first general elections. It remained a strong force till the split in 1964 when the Communist Party (Marxist) – CP(M) – was born. Both parties are today strong in Kerala. The CP(M) dominates West Bengal.

Dravida Munnetra Kazhagam (DMK): The regional party of the Tamil people in Tamil Nadu, whose capital is Madras. It was strongly anti-Brahmin (upper-caste Hindus) and defended the rights of the 'Dravidian peoples of the south' against the 'Aryans of Northern India'. It has ruled Tamil Nadu since 1967, though a number of major splits have weakened its initial impact.

Hindu Mahasabha: A Hindu revivalist organisation founded in 1923 and affiliated to the Congress until 1933, when it split, claiming the latter was 'appeasing the Muslims'. Its most influential leader was V. D. Savarkar, who emerged as the principal ideologue of Hindu communalism.

Indian National Congress: Founded in 1885 by an Englishman, Allan Hume, to press for more Indian representation on nominated councils. Remained an instrument of India's professional middle classes until advent of Mahatama Gandhi, who made it a mass organisation. From 1933–6, Nehru argued for transforming Congress into a socialist party, but was defeated by Gandhi. Congress dominated India until 1969, when it began to split into competing factions. The bulk of the organisation, however, stayed with the Nehru dynasty.

Janata Party: Formed in 1977 to contest post-emergency elections as a coalition of dissident Congress members and the Jan Sangh. Split in 1980. Now led by Chandrashekhar. Has no fundamental differences with Congress, but strongly opposed to dynastic politics.

Jan Sangh: Organisation of the People, founded by S. P. Mookerji in 1950, after he left the Nehru Cabinet in the same year. Denounced by Nehru as 'an illegitimate child of the RSS'. Mookerji was succeeded by Vajpayee, who had been his secretary. The Jan Sangh merged with the Janata Coalition after the emergency. After the 1980 elections it re-emerged as the Bharitya Janata Party (BJP).

Muslim League: Founded in 1906 as the result of a British initiative. Its stated aim was to inculcate in Indian Muslims 'a sense of loyalty to the Empire'. Utilized by Jinnah in late 1930s as a rival to Congress with active British encouragement and support. Became major party in post-partition Pakistan, but began to disintegrate after Jinnah's death in 1948. Still strong in Southern Indian state of Kerala, but nowhere else in the entire sub-continent.

Rashtryiya Swayamsevak Sangh (RSS): It literally means National Volunteer Corps. Was set up in 1925 by Mahasabha's most diehard elements. Denounced by Nehru as the 'Indian version of fascism'. The RSS was structured like the early Nazi stormtroopers in Germany, with a hierarchical chain of command and an infallible leader. It was banned for a few years after two of its members had killed Mahatama Gandhi.

Telugu Desam: The latest regional sub-nationalist party formed in 1982 by dissident Congressmen in the southern state of Andhra Pradesh. It won the state elections in 1982 under the leadership of an ageing actor, N. T. Ramarao (NTR).

Unionist Party: An inter-communal party of Muslim, Hindu and Sikh landlords which ran the Punjab during the 1930s. It defeated both Congress and League in the 1935 elections.

FOUNDING FATHER
Jawaharlal Nehru
1889–1964

1
Early years
1889–1912

The old Indian city of Prayag dates back to AD 600. Its importance lay in its situation. It was at the confluence of the two sacred rivers, the Ganga and the Jamuna (Ganges and Jumna) and ancient folklore had added a third river, the Saraswati, which existed only in the imagination. The Emperor Harsa had made Prayag one of his capitals. It was here, in the seventh century AD, that he built an enclosure where treasure was distributed to the needy every five years. Yet in those days life, even for the upper castes, could not have been all that satisfactory. Many people came to Prayag, stood beneath the old fig tree, and committed suicide by jumping into the waters of the combined Ganga-Jamuna. The Patal Puri temple, now under the ground, was a major centre for worship in those times.

Prayag, like many other centres of the ancient world, had fallen into ruin and decay for many centuries. The Mogul Emperor Akbar, had visited the confluence of the rivers and built a new city, Allahabad (literally the 'city of God'). The Ganga is a liquid history of India. It was this river that the Aryans saw in 3500 BC and marvelled at its magic. In Indian mythology, the river Ganga fell on the matted head of the god Shiva, the latter being an obvious representation of the Himalayan mountain-range. The Greek invasion of India under Alexander was stopped by the Indian ruler, Chandra Gupta, not far from modern Allahabad.

It was a city of its own special smells, receiving pilgrims from all over the country, who came to cleanse themselves spiritually and physically in the holy river. Like all British Indian cities, Allahabad was divided into the old quarters and the modern 'civil lines'. Cities within cities. In the old section were the common people, the bazaar, the noise and bustle of everyday life as it is lived by the bulk of the urban population. The smells of the country were never far from these old cities, which did not simply harbour the poor. Some rich Indians also preferred to live near these smells than the antiseptic 'civil lines'. The Nehrus had first lived in the old part of Allahabad, known as Cheoki. Then they had moved to the English part of town, which was most aptly described many years later by one of its inhabitants, Jawaharlal Nehru:

> It is in these civil lines that the English officials and businessmen, as well as many upper middle-class Indians, professional men, officials, etc., live. The income of the municipality from the city proper is greater than that from the civil lines, but the expenditure on the latter far exceeds the city expenditure. For the far wider area covered by the civil lines requires more roads, and they have to be repaired, cleaned-up, watered, and lighted; and the drainage, the water supply, and the sanitation system have to be much more widespread. The city part is always grossly neglected, and, of course, the poorer parts of the city are almost ignored; it has few good roads, and most of the narrow lanes are ill-lit and have no proper drainage or sanitation system. It puts up with all these disabilities patiently and seldom complains; and when it does complain, nothing much happens. Nearly all the Big Noises and Little Noises live in the civil lines.

There was a lot of noise in one house in the civil lines in Allahabad on the day that Jawaharlal Nehru was born. It was 14 November 1889. Some months after his birth, he was weighed in a ceremony which involved using wheat and rice, instead of weights, on the scales. The foodstuffs were then distributed amongst the poor. The older Nehru got, the larger the crowd that gathered outside his house for a free treat.

The family was descended from Kashmiri Brahmin stock, the highest of high-caste Hindus, and was reasonably well-off. It is likely that they would have stayed in the north, had it not been for the changed fortunes of one of their forebears, Raj Kaul. The year was 1716. The once-mighty Mogul Empire was already beginning to decay, but the Emperor could still dispense patronage. The ruler of the time, a characterless prince named Farrukhsiar, had invited Kaul to move to Delhi. The immigrant from Kashmir was provided with land and a house adjoining a canal. The Urdu word for canal is *nehar*. The Kauls must have become known to other court retainers as *neharis* (the ones from the canal) and, presumably, they obliged their Delhi acquaintances by altering their name to Kaul-Nehari. The process is not dissimilar to that inflicted upon immigrants from continental Europe to Britain or the United

States. So, as Oppsbaum could become Hobsbawm, Kaul became Kaul-Nehari, then Kaul-Nehru, till ultimately the 'Kaul' was dropped completely. Its obliteration did not indicate any hostility to the past. The past was Kashmir, and its citizens have always insisted that Kashmir is heaven on earth. The Nehrus would never forget their Kashmiri origins. Their social circle was, initially, composed of other high-caste Brahmin émigrés from Kashmir.

India in 1889 was relatively quiet, undergoing its own version of the *belle époque*. Political activity, to the extent that it existed, was concentrated in the three presidency towns: Calcutta, Bombay and Madras. The growth of an Indian middle class, however, meant that activities were beginning elsewhere in the country. The Indian National Congress had been founded in 1884 by an Englishman named Hume, with the aim of encouraging Indians to press the *raj* for democratic reforms which would enable Indians to participate in the politics of their country. Political India saw this as an opening, and many Indian lawyers joined its ranks. By the time Jawaharlal was born, the Congress had grown in size, but was still a long way from any involvement with the ordinary people. These people, we should not forget, comprised the overwhelming majority of the population.

Jawaharlal (his name means 'precious stone') was the son of his father's second wife. Motilal had been married at the age of twenty to a Kashmiri woman from Lahore, but she died soon after giving birth to a son, who soon followed his mother. Motilal married again. His choice this time was a fifteen-year-old girl, also from Lahore, named Thussu. After her marriage she changed her name to Swaruprani and moved into the Nehru household, which was still presided over by Motilal's ageing mother. Relations between Swaruprani and her mother-in-law were not friendly. Differences often arose, and the daughter-in-law patiently gave in on every occasion. After the birth of Jawaharlal both his parents were adoring and over-protective. It was from his mother that Jawaharlal used to hear endless talk about Kashmir. Its cuisine was the best in the world. Its women were the most beautiful in all India, more like the fairies from beyond the Caucasus mountains. But above all there was its remarkable climate and scenery.

'Kashmir,' Swaruprani used to tell the three-year-old Jawaharlal, 'is the marvellous mountain region in the north of India. The mountain-tops there are covered in white snow, and down below are beautiful fields of tulips and other flowers, but most of all tulips. We Kashmiris have always been a proud and ancient people.'

Motilal Nehru had inherited a lucrative legal practice from his elder brother. He was usually extremely busy, and Jawaharlal's first ten years were spent largely in the company of tutors, governesses, servants and his mother. Motilal had abandoned the traditional rites of Hinduism but Swaruprani was an orthodox Brahmin. She did not speak any English and insisted that Jawaharlal mimic her religious beliefs and rituals. With his father's encouragement, the young Nehru mocked his mother's superstitions. He developed an insolence which both amused and pained her.

Jawaharlal's childhood was secluded. He was an only child for eleven years, and he spent his time almost exclusively in the company of adults. The family house in Allahabad, Anand Bhavan (House of Happiness), was a large, rambling Victorian mansion encircled by wide verandas. There was an imposing set of columns, arches and balconies, with carefully designed terraces. The house was topped with a cupola. Below its canopy there was a viewing platform. Here on a summer's evening, just after sunset, a visitor could get a phenomenal view of the rose-garden, the neatly trimmed lawns, the closely shaved croquet lawn and tennis court. The House of Happiness also possessed a swimming pool, which was considered a remarkable innovation in Allahabad. This triumphant display of wealth was lit up every evening by large floodlights. The entire neighbourhood was thus aware that Motilal's practice was flourishing.

The atmosphere in the house was distinctly Victorian. The widow at Windsor had been dead for a few years, but it always took British India a decade or more to adjust to the changes back home. Nehru's English tutor was a young man named F. T. Brooks. He was a protégé of Annie Besant, a fiery Irishwoman who had made her name by campaigning against poverty in the East End of London. Together with Bernard Shaw, she was a member of the Fabian Society, and a close friend of the atheist British Member of Parliament, Charles Bradlaugh. There was, however, another side to the tempestuous Annie Besant. She was also a mystic, heavily influenced by the theosophical doctrines of Madame Blavatsky, which had created a stir in India with their talk of extraterrestrial phenomena, divine revelations and fulfilled prophecies. Brooks was also a theosophist, and his beliefs left a mark on his young pupil. On one occasion when Brooks was holding forth on the joys of the 'Great Spirit', Jawaharlal saw a deep frown developing on his father's forehead. Motilal stopped Brooks in midstream.

'I realise, Mr Brooks, that you could develop a rich imagination in my son. Well, there's no harm in that. However, I would prefer my son to learn to be guided in life not so much by emotion as by reason, so that his imagination will not prevent him from seeing reality.' Brooks had no alternative but to concur.

Motilal Nehru, like many liberal Indians of his standing, was a member of the Indian National Congress. These were still early days, but already the schism between moderates and extremists that would run through the organisation's later history was discernible. The moderates were led by G. K. Gokhale and Dadabhai Naoroji. They restricted their demands to social reforms: they wanted to end child marriages, caste exclusiveness (but not the caste system as such) and the ban imposed on the remarriage of widows. The extremists were led by Tilak, a fiery orator, who was in favour of street activities to challenge the colonial powers. He did not want Congress to become a party of 'beggars', reduced to pleading, protesting and appeasing. These debates were held largely in private houses, and the young Jawaharlal used to observe his father and his friends with wonder and amazement.

Occasionally his father would laugh loudly as he downed his claret. Jawaharlal recalled rushing to his mother the first time he saw his father drinking red wine, and shouting that Father was drinking blood. There is little doubt that Motilal was the dominant figure in his son's life. A jovial authoritarian with a foul temper, he would not tolerate any challenge to his authority, and none was possible. For Jawaharlal this was the most stultifying aspect of early life. It was a form of solitary confinement.

This enforced solitude compelled Nehru to develop a passion for reading which stayed with him till the end of his life. He became a voracious reader, devouring everything in sight: Lewis Carroll, Rudyard Kipling, Conan Doyle, Scott, Dickens, Thackeray and, slightly later, H. G. Wells' romances. The influence of Brooks had affected him deeply. Could theosophy possibly hold the key to the universe, he wondered? The answer was a strong rejection, but something stayed behind. From now on he was troubled by a recurring dream.

> I dreamt of astral bodies and imagined myself flying vast distances. This dream of flying high up in the air (without any appliance) has indeed been a frequent one throughout my life; and sometimes it has been vivid and realistic and the countryside seemed to lie underneath me in a vast panorama. I do not know how the modern interpreters of dreams, Freud and others, would interpret this dream.

Nehru was approaching adolescence. The dream could easily have denoted his awakening sexuality, but it persisted far beyond this time. In the dream itself he was always flying 'without appliances', like the ancient gods of Greek and Hindu mythology. Like the gods, too, he observed the vast panorama below him. This flying dream could, therefore, just as easily have been about power and political landscapes.

It is strange how flying preoccupied the Nehru family. Jawaharlal later observed Count Zeppelin landing his machine at Tempelhof field in Berlin. Both he and Motilal stared in amazement at this new advance in science and technology. In later years flying played an important part in the lives of both his grandsons. Sanjay Gandhi died piloting a private plane which escaped his control and crashed down in a field in the centre of Delhi; his elder brother, Rajiv Gandhi, an experienced airline pilot, was to abandon flying in order to join his mother in the political arena.

Much more revealing than Jawaharlal's dream, in many ways, is an actual incident which he described in his autobiography. On this occasion he does not refer to Freud, not because the inferences are obvious, but because what occurred was commonplace in an urban upper-class Victorian establishment in British India. Nonetheless it left a feeling of fear in the young boy's mind.

> One of my earliest recollections is of his temper [Motilal's], for I was the victim of it. I must have been about five or six then. I noticed one day two fountain-pens on his office table and I looked at them with greed. I argued with myself that father could not require both at the same time and so I helped myself to one of them. Later I found that a mighty search was being made for the lost pen and I grew frightened at what I had done, but I did not confess. The pen was discovered and my guilt proclaimed to the world. Father was very angry and he gave me a tremendous thrashing. Almost blind with pain and mortification at my disgrace I rushed to my mother, and for several days various creams and ointments were applied to my aching and quivering little body.
>
> I do not remember bearing an ill-will towards my father because of this punishment . . . my admiration and affection for him remained as strong as ever, but fear formed a part of them. Not so with my mother.

I had no fear of her, for I knew that she would condone everything I did, and, because of her excessive and indiscriminating love for me, I tried to dominate over her a little.

Family life has traditionally been seen as a refuge from the pain and cold of the world that lies outside. There is, of course, more than a kernel of truth in this belief. But there is another side, described above by Jawaharlal. Motilal Nehru was not sadistic or cruel by temperament. He adored his only son. The violence inflicted on the young boy was, in fact, part of an older tapestry. The family reproduces, in its own unique fashion, the relations of authority that exist in society as a whole. The subordination of women is the most notorious aspect of this process, but there is another, equally crucial, dimension: the ritual socialisation of men. Male initiation rites stretch back to the dawn of history. The father-son relationship enshrines and symbolises male domination. Violence is always there, lurking in the background, sometimes hidden, sometimes openly practised. The bruises inflicted are often invisible. Even when the actual pain has gone, the suppressed anger and resentment can stay with the victim for the rest of his life. The effects, naturally, vary from one individual to another. Jawaharlal's attachment to his father was genuine, but it could not have been free of ambiguity.

In 1905, Jawaharlal was fifteen years old. He now had a four-year-old sister, Vijaylakshmi, whom he adored, but who was, alas, too young to be a companion. He continued his intense bouts of reading and followed the newspapers carefully. The phenomenal Japanese victory against Tsarist Russia had excited his latent nationalism and filled his head with all sorts of ideas. In Tsarist Russia, two men, a generation older than Jawaharlal, were also savouring the defeat of the autocracy. Lenin and Trotsky understood very clearly that this defeat had sounded the death-knell of tsarism. The Russian people observed that the Tsar was not invincible and celebrated this new realisation by attempting to overthrow him. 1905 witnessed a failed revolution. In reality it was an elaborate and important dress-rehearsal for the thunderclap that shook the whole world twelve years later. Between Nehru and the Russian revolutionaries there was a crucial difference on the level of perception. It was not simply that the Russians were older in years. It was that they rejoiced at the epochal Japanese sea-victory at Tsushima precisely because they were *not* nationalists.

In the same year Jawaharlal's whole world was altered. A loving mother and an anxious father were to subject their fifteen-year-old 'precious stone' to the rigours and humiliations of an English public school, that stern parent to so many temporary orphans. Motilal and Swaruprani believed that this was the best possible thing for their son. They felt that it was a real honour for a young Indian boy to obtain a place at one of England's most privileged schools. Jawaharlal could not be sent just anywhere. He went to Harrow, a school established in 1572 for the children of England's aristocracy. It had provided the British Empire with four prime ministers: Pitt, Palmerston, Baldwin and Winston Churchill.

Swaruprani was pregnant again and unwell, and Motilal had business in Paris, so the family went to France for a short time before returning to India. In a letter to his son from France, Motilal explained how he felt.

> In you we are leaving the dearest treasure we have in this world and perhaps in other worlds to come . . . It is not a question of providing for you as I can do that, perhaps from a single year's income. It is a question of making a real man of you, which you are bound to be. It would be extremely selfish, I should say sinful, to keep you with us and leave you a fortune in gold with little or no education . . . I never thought I loved you as much as when I had to part from you.

Jawaharlal's response was equally explicit. 'My dear Father, how I wish to be near you again. I wish the days would pass quicker and bring the happy day when I shall see you again . . . '

The Nehrus returned to India without Jawaharlal. Soon afterwards Swaruprani gave birth to a son, whose birthday was the same as Jawaharlal's. The elder brother was thrilled beyond belief, but by the time his congratulatory letter reached his parents, the newborn infant was dead. Motilal was shaken. Swaruprani was desolate. They now treasured their only son more than ever before.

Jawaharlal found life at Harrow difficult and painful. In photographs of him at this stage of his life he appears uneasy in the school uniform, clutching his boater self-consciously, and there is rarely a smile on his face. Above all, he was incredibly lonely. Matron, the only female figure in the institution, was no substitute for an Indian mother. In his autobiography there are odd sentences which describe his feelings: 'I was never an exact fit'; 'I was left a little to myself'; 'Always I had a feeling that I was not one of them'.

This was a time when racism and anti-semitism were common in all public schools — it was, after all, the heyday of the Empire. For a short time Nehru affected anti-semitism in order to become a member of the pack. He does not describe any actual incident, but the shame-faced description in his memoirs clearly indicates that he felt it was an easy way to try and ingratiate himself with his contemporaries. The pressures towards conformity and uniformity were much stronger in those days. Nehru found comfort in literature and history. He played cricket, but preferred the discipline of chess. When he left Harrow a couple of years later, he was delighted — it was the same joy that he would experience in years to come whenever he was released from British prisons in India. School tradition, however, compelled him to feign grief on departure; he even managed to squeeze out a few tears. The ordeal was at last over.

He did not see Harrow again till he was Prime Minister of free India and was invited to visit his old school. It could have been his incurable sentimentality that made him accept the offer, but it could also have been the desire to have his revenge. An interesting photograph records the visit. Jawaharlal, immaculately garbed in his Indian clothes (tight-fitting trousers, long coat and a cotton cap) can be seen walking through rows of cheering Harrovians, waving their top-hats and singing 'For He's a Jolly Good Fellow'. Nehru's raised hand acknowledges their cheers, but he does not look at them. It is almost as if he is thinking of his past receptions and is pleased at having turned the tables at long last.

During his years at Harrow, Jawaharlal kept himself fully informed of what was happening in India. He got regular clippings from the Indian press and followed political developments closely. The interest was still academic, but it was strong. Even as a child, Nehru used to listen avidly to his male cousins telling stories of their encounters with the ruling race. He was delighted whenever a visiting cousin described a triumph, for life in India, even for privileged Indians, was not without its dark side. In many aspects of everyday life there was social apartheid determined by race. Nehru, despite his sheltered upbringing, was not oblivious to these realities. His tutor, Brooks, had often railed against the racism and philistinism of his fellow Englishmen, and Nehru had thus acquired an early taste for political confrontations, even though he could not fully understand why things were as they were. His father never discouraged a critical awareness, but he did not want

Jawaharlal to get too involved in 'extremist politics' in England. He must, stressed Motilal, remain loyal to the Empire.

This loyalty was soon to become extremely strained, even for Motilal himself. Lord Curzon, the Viceroy of India, who was almost a law unto himself, had decided to partition the large and politically conscious province of Bengal. His motives were clear. He regarded the Bengalis as an infernal nuisance, saw that the rest of India constantly looked towards Bengal for political leadership, and observed that the natives in this region tended to regard themselves as the moral, intellectual and cultural equals of the British, if not their superiors. Curzon's sword cut Bengal in two, but the division was designed to separate Muslims from Hindus. Curzon played on the fears of the downtrodden Muslim peasants and was open about his hostility to the Bengalis as a race. The result was political mayhem. The Bengali intelligentsia raised the flag of revolt, and resistance took the shape of boycotting British goods, which were burnt in bonfires throughout the province.

Indian nationalism was now aroused as never before. The Bengal partition was discussed throughout the country by moderates and extremists. They agreed that the decision was wrong, but disagreed on the methods necessary to reverse it. Motilal denounced talk of self-government as a delusion. Tilak, the leader of the extremist branch of Indian nationalism, spearheaded the *swadeshi* movement, which demanded the Indianisation of industry and was, as a result, supported by numerous Indian capitalists, who chafed at the controls utilised by the colonial powers to limit their enterprises. Jawaharlal followed all this from his English public school. His sympathies were with the extremists, despite his father's numerous letters painting a vivid picture of their iniquities. In 1907 the Congress met in Surat for its annual convention. There was a split between Tilak and Gokhale and their respective followers. Jawaharlal wrote to his father supporting Tilak. Motilal was so shocked that he became slightly ill as a result.

In Britain, the Liberal Party had won a landslide victory in 1906, and among the first acts of the new government was the dismissal of Lord Curzon. The Viceroy had only inflamed patriots by his arrogance and contempt. In a letter to a close friend Curzon wrote what he said repeatedly in public.

> You can scarcely have any idea of the utter want of proportion, moderation or sanity that characterises native agitation in this country.

Starting with some preposterous fiction or exaggeration, the Bengali, after repeating it a few times, ends by firmly believing its truth. He lashes himself into a fury over the most insignificant issues, and he revels in his own stage thunder in the happy conviction that owing to circumstances of the case it can provoke no reply.

A few weeks later, Curzon told students at Calcutta University, probably the most politically conscious group in the country, 'I hope I am making no false or arrogant claim when I say that the highest ideal of truth is to a large extent a Western conception.' The Liberal administration in London removed Curzon without ceremony. His replacement, Lord Minto, was a very different sort of person. He was far more willing to listen to native complaints and much more responsive to the moderates and their demand for reforms. Minto and Lord Morley, who was the British Secretary of State for India, prepared a set of reforms. These included a system of elections to Indian legislative councils (which had consisted until now of nominees chosen by the Viceroy, and had occupied a purely advisory role in any event). The sting, however, lay in the tail. The system of elections was governed by the principle of 'separate electorates' for Muslims. In other words, there were to be seats specially reserved for Muslims that could not be contested by candidates of any other religion. This was a more subtle approach than that of Curzon, but the end result was the same, to divide Hindu from Muslim. A leaflet was circulated in Bengal under the title 'Who Governs Us?' Someone sent this to young Nehru in England, and he read it with increasing emotion, for it corresponded to his own nationalistic urges. The following passage excited him greatly.

> Can these thieves really be our rulers, these thieves who have destroyed our handicrafts, taken their work away from our weavers and blacksmiths, who import an innumerable multitude of goods, produced in their own country, and sell them through our own people in our bazaars, stealing our wealth and taking life from our people? Can those who pillage the harvest of our fields and doom us to hunger, fever and plague really be our rulers? Can foreigners really be our rulers, foreigners who impose on us ever more taxes? Brothers, the more patient you are, the more strongly will these perfidious people oppress you. We must stand on our own feet and search: are there no means of deliverance? We are brothers, all of us on earth. They grow fat on our money, without working. They drink our blood. Why do we endure it?

Jawaharlal now believed that it should not be endured for much longer. His father's letters were always welcome, but they were beginning to annoy him politically. In one of these Motilal complained bitterly at the change which was transforming students in India from passive recipients of education to active participants in their country's political life.

Wrote Motilal to his son,

> They have of late developed a remarkable aptitude for rowdyism, and no sober and serious thinker can ever expect to secure an uninterrupted hearing from an audience composed of this element. Tilak was here the other day especially to address the students. He inculcated all his wild and revolutionary propaganda and succeeded to such an extent that the students of the Muir College have assumed an attitude of open defiance to the more moderate leaders of these provinces. Sundarlal and Malaviya [two moderate Congressmen] are openly abused. I have so far escaped but cannot be safe much longer as my views are even more moderate than those of the so-called moderates.

Jawaharlal expressed some sympathy for the problems his father had to confront, but he could not totally conceal his real sympathies. 'Rowdyism is, of course, a most undesirable thing, and yet it smacks of the West and shows a certain amount of independence.'

Nehru's thoughts were divided between the troubles back home and his forthcoming entry to Cambridge University. He wanted to enter the coveted ranks of the Indian Civil Service, but Motilal had other ideas. From Allahabad, he argued that Jawaharlal should think of law as a future career. Two Nehru cousins had already returned home from England and joined the Civil Service, so there was nothing new for Jawaharlal to do in that particular quarter. Jawaharlal must follow Motilal into the legal profession. Allahabad High Court without a Nehru? The very idea was unthinkable.

It was not a question of sentiment alone. Motilal had a lucrative practice and he wanted his son to inherit the fruits of his hard work. Reluctantly, and against his better judgement, Jawaharlal agreed once again, but insisted on studying for a natural sciences tripos at Cambridge. At university he was much happier than he had imagined possible. At Trinity College he was given the worst possible room — dark, with semi-obscured windows and looking on to an inner courtyard. He didn't mind too much. He was eighteen years old and life was becoming enjoyable.

In 1907, the student Nehru, in the company of his cousin Brijlal

Nehru, visited Ireland for the first time. They spent more than a month there, and Nehru's sympathies were totally with the Irish. He could not but notice the similarities between India and Ireland. The enemy, in both cases, was the same Empire and he observed with delight that Sinn Fein (the Irish nationalist organisation) was arguing about tactics in the same way as Congress was in India. But in Ireland it was the extremist wing that was triumphant. He wrote excitedly to Motilal: 'Have you heard of the Sinn Fein in Ireland? It is a most interesting movement and resembles very closely the so-called extremist movement in India. Their policy is not to beg for favours, but to wrest them by force.'

At Cambridge, Jawaharlal, while studying the natural sciences (geology, botany and chemistry), pursued his extracurricular interests relentlessly. The study of history and literature continued unabated. He read much of Bernard Shaw and discovered Havelock Ellis. In public he preferred to listen rather than talk, though he enjoyed debates. He joined Trinity's debating club, 'The Magpie and the Stump'. Here, he tells us, 'there was a rule that a member not speaking for a whole term had to pay a fine'. Nehru regularly had to pay fines. Even in later life he spoke in a quiet and modest style, shunning the tricks of the trade.

There were, of course, other Indian students at Cambridge. For the first time, Jawaharlal had a large circle of acquaintances who were not related to him in any way. He discerned two trends amongst his fellow students from India. There were the 'parlour-firebrands', most of whom ended up in the service of the British state in India, and there were others, less forthcoming, but more committed in their beliefs — young men who were not dissimilar to Jawaharlal in temperament and style. Amongst them he found warmth and friendship and a few remained close friends for the rest of his life.

After Cambridge, Nehru moved to London and joined the Inner Temple. His head assimilated jurisprudence, but his heart was indifferent. It was a chore and he did his duty, commenting later that 'law studies did not take up too much time and I got through the Bar examinations, one after the other, with neither glory nor ignominy'. During this last phase in London, he spent some time enjoying the delights of life in London before the First World War. He met some of his English acquaintances from Cambridge, and together they indulged in various escapades, including gambling, wild bouts of drinking, sex, and crazy spending sprees. Motilal, who had to foot the bills, called his son to order from distant Allahabad. It was hardly necessary. Nehru *fils* had got fed up with the life he was leading and had called a halt to his own excesses. He was now worried about the prospect of an arranged marriage.

Ever since his arrival in Britain in 1905, Jawaharlal had not been able to resolve the battle between tradition and modernism on the front of personal relations. His head was full of modern ideas, but his heart? He was not sure about this at all. Before he left India his mother and aunts had told him explicitly that they would forgive all his sins in advance, provided that he never fell in love with or married an English woman. They filled his head with images of vampires prowling the streets, just waiting to pounce on innocents like himself. What had struck him as odd, even then, was that his father, supposedly a modern man, had reinforced these strictures. Motilal was subsequently to emphasise his views on this question even more strongly. He confessed to his son that he found the very notion of 'mixed breed' or 'Eurasian' children repugnant. He warned Jawaharlal that if such a dread event were to occur he, Motilal, would not be able to feel affectionate towards his own grandchildren.

Jawaharlal had not challenged these ideas, but had, nonetheless, been somewhat puzzled. Why, he had wondered, were they going on in this fashion? He was still an adolescent and, in any event, his mind was full of other images. He thought, as boys of that age do, about the beautiful Kashmiri girls he had met at parties. The 'accidental' touching of arms or shoulders, or sometimes even hands, had been an intense pleasure. It had left behind a lingering sensation which multiplied in the imagination and became unforgettable. Under pressure Jawaharlal had agreed, before leaving India, that he would marry a Kashmiri girl regardless of her caste. Inter-caste marriages were not permitted by Hinduism.

Jawaharlal had been at Harrow for barely a year when his parents had started to search for a bride. During the last two years of his life in England, 1910–12, he had become increasingly fretful about the very thought of marriage. He had a number of affairs but, feeling his father watching from afar, had always prevented them from becoming too serious. Soon the exchanges with his parents on this question became frequent and sharp. Missives flowed regularly from London to Allahabad, and back again.

Nehru wrote to his mother, Swaruprani: 'There should be no

marriage without mutual love. I consider it a crime and a ruination of one's life if one has to marry merely for the sake of creating children'.

Nehru wrote to his father, on receiving a photograph with whose subject it was hoped he might fall in love:

> There is not an atom of romance in the way you are searching out girls for me and keeping them waiting till my arrival. The very idea is extremely unromantic. And you constantly expect me to fall in love with a photograph. The days for that are gone by. The girl whose photograph you sent me is very probably a nice person, but I can hardly say I am enamoured of her from the photo.

Sensing a battle, Motilal increased the pressure. He withdrew that particular photograph, but began to extol the virtues of a twelve-year-old he had found in Delhi. Her age was regarded as being only a minor problem. A *hakim* (traditional Indian physician) had convinced Motilal that she was an ideal match for Jawaharlal and that the age difference was perfect for reasons of health. It would keep Jawaharlal's blood pressure stable. Nehru was worn out by this transcontinental battle. He now tried to postpone any decision. In his last letter from abroad he wrote:

> As regards the Delhi girl, surely she is too young for me. I am nearly ten years her senior and that is rather a big difference. I could not possibly marry her until she was eighteen or nineteen and that is six or seven years hence. I would not mind waiting as I am not in a matrimonial state of mind at present.

In the summer of 1912, Jawaharlal Nehru was called to the Bar. A few weeks later he left for India, a 'self-sufficient pedant', as he observed with irony many years later.

2
Marriage, politics and prison 1912–26

Jawaharlal was greeted on his return by an impatient family. He had a new sister, Krishna, whom he had never seen, and his mother had not seen him for many years. Her son had become a man. His features had begun to take the form they would retain for the rest of his life. His hair, never thick at the best of times, had thinned considerably, bringing his forehead into sharp prominence. The family was waiting at Mussoorie, a summer resort in the Himalayan foothills, where they spent the summer when the suffocating heat of Allahabad became intolerable. For the first weeks after his arrival Jawaharlal was lionised. The whole family listened with amazement to his stories. Only Motilal, equally charmed, felt it necessary to interrupt the monologues with a few sharp questions. In return Jawaharlal questioned them at length about everything: gossip about the family, common friends, politics, till he had had his fill and began to think of his future.

Before anything else (such as marriage) could be discussed, Jawaharlal was installed in his father's legal practice. He worked diligently, studying his briefs carefully, questioning clients with a detail that would intimidate the civil servants of India in years to come. His style was self-effacing. He was initially extremely shy in court, but gradually he mastered the art, never giving way to histrionic displays. Motilal watched carefully, but did not interfere. He was extremely proud and happy that Jawaharlal was settling down. When the young Nehru was paid his first fee, a cheque for five hundred rupees, Motilal was exultant. 'The first fee your father got was only five rupees. I wish I were my son instead of being myself.'

Jawaharlal could not have returned the compliment. He found the atmosphere of the courtroom and its surroundings stale and soul-destroying. He did not find the profession particularly stimulating, and the monotonous routine of everyday life was becoming unbearable. Whether he visited the Bar library or the club, he met the same old bores, 'discussing the same old topics, usually connected with the legal profession, over and over again. Few experiences are more dreary than sitting with highly-placed officials and listening to their unending talk about promotions, leave rules, transfers and little tit-bits of Service scandal.' There were times when he felt that the stuffiness would kill any spark of life in himself.

He decided to attend the Bankipur session of the Indian National Congress in December 1912. Tilak was in prison and his followers stayed away from the session. The delegates were all moderates, mainly from the property-owning classes. Nehru was not amused by their dandified European suits or their self-parodying mannerisms which aped European conventions. He disliked the monolithic nature of the Congress, and the fact that there was no political tension, no debate. It was more a social gathering of like-minded friends and he was not sparing in his criticisms to his father: 'A fashionable society! Spare-time amusement for armchair politicians!' Motilal asked him to be more tolerant, but his pleas fell on stony ground. What shocked Nehru was that these 'johnnies' were so far removed from Indian realities that they could not even contemplate self-government.

In despair he returned to his books, his oldest companions. He read and re-read Bertrand Russell's *Religion and Science* and *A Free Man's Worship*. The militant atheism of this ruling-class rebel appealed to Nehru deeply, and he often wondered how Russell, a scion of one of the oldest ruling families in Britain, had become an atheist, a pacifist and a socialist. Together with his reading, Nehru was following the world situation closely. The Italian attack on Turkey had alienated Indian Muslims, since the Caliph, or Khalifa, the titular head of the House of Islam, was also the ruler of the Ottoman Empire. The Italo-Turkish war soon spread and the Balkan Wars of 1912–13 broke out.

Indian Muslims were for Turkey. They raised money to despatch a medical mission, but hardly had they done so when the war began to escalate. From a struggle for mastery in the Balkans it became the First World War, a vicious and bloody struggle for colonies and raw materials between the mightiest imperialist nations of the world. India was inevitably drawn into the conflict. It was, as Lord Curzon had tactfully remarked, the 'Queen on the English chessboard'. Many Indians, not surprisingly, sympathised with Germany. This was not because they had any illusions about the Kaiser. For the Muslims, it was simply because Germany was Turkey's ally, and for the rest it was an expression of the old nationalist motto: 'The enemy of my enemy is my friend'. Jawaharlal was not very interested in the conflict as such, but his sympathies for French people and their culture made him feel that it was they who were suffering the most.

Many moderates of the Congress called for Indians to support England in the war. They hoped that loyalty would be rewarded by more reforms. Even the veteran extremist, Tilak, called for support for Britain after having spent six years in prison.

India did its duty. Cannon-fodder was supplied in plenty. Over a million Indians fought in the Middle East, Africa, Iran and Afghanistan. Raw materials from India were loaded on to ships and sent to Europe: manganese ore, mica and saltpetre were sold at ridiculously low prices. India's fledgling capitalists grew rapidly during this period. Jamshedjee Tata supplied the rails for constructing railways on the Near-Eastern front, thus laying the foundations of Indian heavy industry after independence. The famine-stricken peasants saw wheat, rice, jute, tea and copra produced by their hard labour being despatched to England at the cheapest possible rates, while taxes in India were doubled. Lord Birkenhead later admitted these realities when he said, 'Without India the war would have been immensely prolonged, if indeed without her help it could have been brought to a victorious conclusion.'

In response, Annie Besant, ever the ardent nationalist, exclaimed, 'If a mushroom nation like the Boers, who fought the British, were deserving of freedom, the Indians, who were fighting for Britain, now deserved their freedom.' There was no reply from the India Office, so Besant and Tilak founded Home Rule Leagues in April 1916. Their model was the Irish, who were also fighting for 'home rule', by which they meant an independent parliament to determine the future of their country. Jawaharlal joined both the Leagues. At last there was some political organisation in which he could be active. The British authorities were, initially, somewhat complacent. They imagined that the Leagues would be an exclusively urban middle-class phenomena which would not pose any threat to the stability of the political order. Tilak, however, opened up the Leagues to peasants, workers and tradespeople. Many of the new intake were utterly hostile to the impotent constitutionalism of the Congress. There were a number of clashes between the militant home rulers and colonial troops. On at least three recorded instances, the nationalists succeeded in snatching arms and the colonial authorities panicked. Tilak was by now too popular, and the British understood that to arrest him would provoke a massive reaction. Instead they arrested other leaders of the Home Rule League, including Annie Besant, and debarred students from attending any meetings or assemblies organised under the auspices of the League.

Politics in India were beginning to develop a new pace. The repression unleashed against the Leagues resulted in a new division amongst the Congress moderates. Motilal Nehru was shocked by the arrest of Annie Besant, whom he knew well. She had often stayed at Anand Bhavan in Allahabad and was regarded as a friend of the family. Motilal now joined the Home Rule League and stated that the moderates were incapable of ever leading India to *swaraj* (self-government). He nonetheless maintained a clear distance between himself and the more radical sections of the League, those under the inspiration of Tilak.

In the middle of all this, the question of Jawaharlal's marriage was once again raised. Both his parents were insistent in their belief that their son needed a wife. Jawaharlal was now twenty-six. The girl from Delhi, Kamala Kaul, was sixteen. She was, like the Nehrus, a Kashmiri Brahmin. Orthodoxy, at least, would be satisfied. Jawaharlal felt he was trapped. There was no escape and reluctantly he agreed to the marriage. The element of love, which he had previously insisted was an essential part of marriage, was undoubtedly missing. Jawaharlal's younger sister, Krishna, described Kamala Kaul thus: 'She was sixteen and very lovely; slim and rather tall for an Indian girl, with the typically fair skin of Brahmins of Kashmiri descent. Her hair was dark brown and she had large brown eyes and a very gentle disposition . . . she was one of the most beautiful women I knew or ever had known.'

The wedding itself was an elaborate affair which lasted for nine days in Delhi, where a 'Nehru wedding camp' was erected around the bride's house; festivities then continued for several weeks at Anand Bhavan in Allahabad. On the first evening after the marriage, the young couple walked outside to try and find the pole star, which according to an ancient Hindu custom was a symbol of constancy. Jawaharlal was undoubtedly buffeted by contradictory pressures throughout this period. His recently acquired cosmopolitanism, his hostility to the retrogressive aspects of tradition and his deep-rooted rationalism must have rebelled against the farce that was about to be enacted. Kamala had no choice in the matter. She, like other young women of her time, obeyed her parents. Jawaharlal could have fought back, but he chose not to do so: it would have meant a serious break with his father and a split with his mother, and he could not bear the thought of upsetting them. His father was now moving closer to him politically and he could well have felt that the sacrifice being demanded of him was not too great. Whatever else happened, family unity would be preserved. He does not discuss these dilemmas in his autobiography. The internal torment is completely suppressed There is no other explanation for the fact that in a 600-page book, the chapter on his marriage is just two pages long. Even this must have been painful for him. The chapter in question is headed 'My Wedding and An Adventure In The Himalayas'. The actual reference to the nuptials consists of two sentences: 'My marriage took place in 1916 in the city of Delhi. It was on the *Vasanta Panchami* day which heralds the coming of spring in India.' This must surely rank as the shortest-ever description of a crucial personal event in the annals of autobiographical literature. Kamala is not even named. Later, after her death, he paid her a handsome tribute and, realising his omissions, dedicated the autobiography to her memory.

Meanwhile the First World War was coming to an end, but before it was over something dramatic occurred in Russia: the Revolution. A year later the Kaiser and his allies, including Turkey, had been defeated. The two events were, in their different ways, to galvanise Indian politics. The Russian Revolution was, of course, a universal event. Indian nationalists were excited beyond belief. They read with bated breath Lenin's announcement that the infant Soviet state had renounced all Tsarist claims to the territories of other nations. They were thunderstruck when Trotsky, the new Foreign Minister, opened the doors of the Chancery and published the secret protocols of the imperialist states, revealing plans for dividing the world after the war. In this exciting month baby Indira made her appearance and her father, henceforth, always teased her about the fact that she was as old as the Russian Revolution.

It was the second event that affected India most immediately. Indian Muslims were outraged at the treatment being meted out to

Turkey; the overthrow of the Caliph was regarded as imperialist perfidy of the worst sort. The Khilafat Movement was started to mobilise Indian Muslims against the British and thereby pressure the latter into restoring the Caliphate/Khilafat to its former glory. This marked the first real awakening of India's giant Muslim population. Their target was British power, since it was the same power in Europe that had overthrown the head of Islam. Though, in fact, few Indian Muslims had ever thought twice about the Caliph or his activities, once he was overthrown he became a symbol. His fall was seen as an affront to world Islam.

The Congress, which had shed some of its moderates, took an important step by allying itself with the Khilafat Movement. The man chiefly responsible for this decision was Mahatma Gandhi. He perceived that Hindu-Muslim unity was crucial if a fully *national* movement was to be constructed. The real issue was soon provided by the colonial government. The Montagu-Chelmsford Report proposed in 1918 a further set of reforms for India, but these were far removed from self-government.

The Congress met in emergency session in Bombay in September 1918 to consider the proposals. It was split once again. The moderates wanted to accept the offer. A large majority was for total rejection. Both Nehrus were, for once, on the same side. On their return to Allahabad, Motilal began to finance an independent newspaper to oppose the influence of the moderates, which was exercised through *The Leader*.

Jawaharlal now formally ended his days as a lawyer and decided to work full time in politics. There was no shortage of money, but Nehru's tastes, by this time, were hardly extravagant. The entire family lived at Anand Bhavan so there was no problem as far as financial security was concerned. On 18 March 1919, the Rowlatt Acts, which gave the colonial administration unlimited powers of detention and repression, were approved by Britain. Gandhi proposed that the new laws should be resisted by a general strike and 30 March was named as the day of action, which Gandhi said should be devoted largely to prayer and fasting. At the last minute the Congress foolishly delayed the strike and set a new date, 6 April, for the action. In several major cities, however, the people decided not to wait. In Delhi and Allahabad, Lahore and Multan (as well as many smaller towns), there were strikes, followed by demonstrations and meetings.

Within a few days, a creeping general strike had paralysed

political India. The worst clashes took place in the Punjab, where troops were used and martial law was declared. The whole of the Punjab had become a large prison encampment. Stories were circulated in the rest of the country of how the British authorities were humiliating and torturing the nationalists in the Punjab.

The British Government felt compelled to set up an official commission of inquiry, headed by Lord Hunter. The composition of the committee, five Englishmen and three Indians who were nominated by London appeared to nationalist India to merely be rubbing salt in the wounds. Congress asked that one representative from its ranks be seated on the committee, that all witnesses should be heard and legal procedures followed. If this was rejected, said Jawaharlal Nehru, then India would boycott the commission. It *was* rejected, and the Hunter Commission was, in return, boycotted by the Indians. Congress set up its own team of investigators, whose task was both to collate facts and to collect food and money for the victims of the repression.

The Congress Inquiry Team consisted of Gandhi, Motilal Nehru, C. R. Das (a leading lawyer from Calcutta) and two lawyers from Bombay. The younger Nehru was assigned to assist Das in the town of Amritsar. He arrived there at nine o'clock one morning and toured the city in the company of local Congress supporters. He was told of how the strike had spread rapidly. Striking workers had headed for the post office, the bank, the railway station and shops. Slogans had suddenly appeared on walls exhorting Hindus, Muslims and Sikhs to 'unite and kick out the European monkeys'. The city had been in the hands of the people by ten o'clock in the evening. It was then that General Dyer had arrived and occupied Amritsar.

Witnesses described to Nehru the humiliations they had suffered, and he was deeply shocked by their accounts. During one skirmish, an English missionary woman doctor had fallen off her bicycle and suffered some injuries; General Dyer decided to punish the whole town for this indignity. He established a 'retribution post'; for ten whole days every Indian who passed the post had to crawl on his belly and endure the jibes and abuse of the soldiers.

Three days after Dyer's men moved in, on 13 April 1919, the massacre in the Jallianwalla Bagh (a walled garden with only one exit) took place. Twenty thousand people had gathered there to listen to speeches against the Rowlatt Acts and demand the release of imprisoned nationalist leaders. At the peak of the meeting, forty soldiers entered the packed square and assumed menacing positions. When the officers ordered them to fire, they did so, and killed hundreds in the process. The meeting had included large numbers of children and many of them lay dead with one or sometimes both parents. Escape had been impossible. Nehru wept many times in Amritsar as he heard the same stories over and over again. The city was traumatised. Later, Jawaharlal recorded his own view: 'I realised then, more vividly than I had ever done before, how brutal and immoral imperialism was and how it had eaten into the souls of the British upper classes.'

Officialdom stated that 379 had died and 1,200 had suffered injuries during the massacre; unofficial sources multiplied both figures by three. India was stunned. Trauma soon gave way to rage. Dyer, treated as a hero by the British in India, was unrepentant. He casually informed the Hunter Committee:

> I fired and continued to fire until the crowd dispersed, and I considered this as the least amount of firing which would produce the necessary moral and widespread effect it was my duty to produce if I was to justify my action. If more troops had been at hand, the casualties would have been greater in proportion. It was no longer a question of merely dispersing the crowd, but one of producing a sufficient moral effect from a military point of view not only on those who were present, but more especially throughout the Punjab.

In private, British officers boasted about the affair as they celebrated the gunning down of unarmed civilians. Nehru overheard them himself, when he was travelling on a night train from Amritsar to Delhi, and he wrote about the incident in his autobiography.

> The compartment I entered was almost full and all the berths, except the upper one, were occupied by sleeping passengers. I took the vacant upper berth. In the morning I discovered that all my fellow-passengers were military officers. They conversed with each other in loud voices which I could not help overhearing. One of them was holding forth in an aggressive and triumphant tone and soon I discovered that he was Dyer, the hero of Jallianwalla Bagh, and he was describing his Amritsar experiences. He pointed out how he had the whole town at his mercy and he had felt like reducing the rebellious city to a heap of ashes, but he took pity on it and refrained . . . I was greatly shocked to hear his conversation and to observe his callous manner. He descended at Delhi station in pyjamas with bright pink stripes, and a dressing-gown.

The butcher of Jallianwalla Bagh and the future Prime Minister of India travelling, even sleeping, in the same compartment was one of history's more grotesque ironies. For Jawaharlal, whose temper could be as sharp as his father's, it must have taken an incredible effort to remain silent. The humiliation of being forced to say nothing in such circumstances must have brought home the innumerable mental agonies that are inflicted upon the citizens of a subjugated nation.

In 1920 the Congress launched a Non-Cooperation Movement. Motilal was now to get rid of his European clothes, boycott the courts and agitate for self-government. The movement was a response by Gandhi and the Congress to the angry mood of the people, for the events in the Punjab had resulted in a massive shift of opinion. Popular anger and outrage had spread, but Gandhi wanted a movement which was strictly non-violent. He was determined to build a bridge between those who favoured some form of armed struggle and those who saw the future as being determined by a slow process of reform. Gandhi agreed with the militants that the people had to be mobilised on the streets, but, he insisted, in a non-violent fashion and largely for the purpose of offering themselves for arrest. He told the moderates that this action was essential pressure to win an escalating series of demands, which would be crowned with self-government. Some, like the Bombay lawyer Mohammed Ali Jinnah, now left the Congress. Jinnah was later to build the Muslim League as a communal counter to the Congress, but he left at this stage because, as Nehru correctly observed, 'He could not adapt himself to the new and more advanced ideology, and even more so because he disliked the crowds of ill-dressed people, talking in Hindustani, who filled the Congress. His idea of politics was of a superior variety, more suited to the legislative chamber or to a committee room.'

Jawaharlal Nehru now started travelling throughout the country, but he decided to make his first contribution to the Non-Cooperation Movement in his own home province. He spoke at countless meetings, met peasants and workers, enthused students, persuaded government employees to quit their jobs. All his time was now taken up by active politics and he delighted in the work.

> I became wholly absorbed and wrapt in the movement, and large numbers of other people did likewise. I gave up all my other associations and contacts, old friends, books, even newspapers, except

insofar as they dealt with the work in hand. I had kept up till then some reading of current books and had tried to follow the developments in world affairs. But there was no time for this now. In spite of the strength of family bonds, I almost forgot my family, my wife, my daughter . . .

In an effort to outflank the Congress, the Viceroy invited Edward, the Prince of Wales at the time, to visit India. It was thought that loyal India would welcome the young Prince and demonstrate to the world that Congress was a tiny minority. The Congress Working Committee met in November 1921 and Jawaharlal was extremely vocal in defending the resolution which demanded a total boycott of all the festivities that were being planned to welcome royalty. When Edward arrived in Bombay on 17 November 1921, there was a large demonstration and street clashes. Calcutta and Allahabad, by contrast, became ghost towns and the overwhelming majority of Indians stayed at home. The future Duke of Windsor was greatly irritated and the Viceroy was determined to teach the protesters a lesson. Large-scale arrests began while the Prince was still in India, shooting tigers with the native princes, and in December 1921 both the Nehrus, father and son, were imprisoned. Both refused to collaborate with the court. Like the Irish, they did not recognise the right of the court to try them. It must have been a truly novel experience for Motilal, himself a distinguished lawyer who had appeared in courts of law as a barrister for almost three decades, now to be engaged in boycotting the same institution. Motilal and Jawaharlal were sentenced to six months' imprisonment each and locked up in Lucknow prison. It was here that they got the news of the incidents at Chauri Chaura.

The village of Chauri Chaura was close to Gorakhpur. During the course of a demonstration, the police had used revolvers and guns to fire at the peasants. The enraged crowd had then chased the police back to the police station. Once the police had barricaded themselves inside, the peasants had set the small building on fire. The policemen had burnt to death. Three Congress volunteers had been arrested. They were two Hindus and a Muslim: Bhagwan Ahir, Rampati Chamar and Abdullah Julaha. They were tried at the Allahabad High Court, where the Nehrus had practised before the boycott. The judges sentenced them to death and they were hanged. No money was collected for their families. They became forgotten names, never to be remembered in the Congress list of martyrs. No tears were shed on their behalf by Gandhi or the Congress Working Committee.

After the Chauri Chaura incidents Gandhi unilaterally called off the movement, and the Congress Working Committee was, as usual, persuaded by him. Jawaharlal was extremely angry. 'Were a remote village and a mob of excited peasants in an out-of-the-way place going to be allowed to put an end, for some time at least, to our national struggle for freedom?'

The village may have been remote, but what troubled Gandhi was the general trend. He was extremely worried lest the movement get out of control and, instead of moving down the prepared channel of non-violence and nationalism, overflow into something very different. Gandhi knew that if peasant struggles became dominant and the workers started agitating for class demands, the nationalist movement would be seriously weakened. He calculated that it was far better to call it off rather than permit it to get out of control. In Chauri Chaura, it was this aspect of peasant spontaneity that had upset Gandhi.

During the Chauri Chaura case, the Allahabad court judges had explained that the Congress cry for self-government had only raised the hopes of the peasants for a millenium 'in which taxation would be limited to the collection of small cash contributions or dues in kind from fields and threshing floors and in which the cultivators would hold their lands at little more than nominal rents'. These were perfectly reasonable demands, but they had not been articulated by Gandhi. That was how the peasants viewed independence. Gandhi had been concerned with other problems. When he had spoken at a large peasant rally in Gorakhpur, prior to the Chauri Chaura incident, he had merely advised peasants to impose social self-discipline. Gandhi had asked them to implement four nos: no more gambling, no more drinking, no more smoking *ganja* and no more whoring. In return he had offered nothing.

Jawaharlal was released on 3 March 1922; Motilal on 6 June 1922. Jawaharlal, however, was, re-arrested and sentenced to eighteen months' imprisonment on 19 May 1922, charged with 'incitement to rebellion'. He used the dock as a platform to denounce the *raj*:

> Intimidation and terrorism have become the chief instruments of government. By these methods they seek to keep down a people and suppress their disaffection. Do they imagine that they will thus instil affection for themselves in the people or make them loyal instruments

of their imperialism? Affection and loyalty are of the heart. They cannot be purchased in the market place, much less can they be extorted at the point of a bayonet.

His health had begun to deteriorate. He was troubled by chest pains and insomnia. He treated himself by giving up smoking and developing a daily routine of yoga exercises, including the head stand. He also changed to a vegetarian diet. The net result was a rapid improvement in his health. Once he felt relaxed again, he resumed his reading. During the day he studied history: Carlyle, G. M. Trevelyan, Wells, Blunt, Ruskin and Romain Rolland all kept him busy. During the autumn evenings he concentrated on literature. He read the poetry and fiction of the Bengali writer, Rabindranath Tagore, Shakespeare and Bernard Shaw, Victor Hugo and Edgar Allan Poe and Fitzgerald's translation of Omar Khayyam. Then he returned to the Romantic poets, reading and re-reading Byron, Keats, Tennyson and Shelley. Shelley made a particular impression and Jawaharlal would often quote lines from the poet in later years. Shelley remained a friend for life.

Nehru was released on 31 January 1923, after having spent eight months in prison. The reason for his release was fairly obvious. The nationalist movement had petered out and it was pointless to keep Jawaharlal in prison any longer. He had been isolated from politics at a critical stage. After his release he plied Motilal with question after question and then, exhausted, sat back to contemplate the grim realities. He was fully convinced that the movement was finished. He now understood the iron law that determines the rise and fall of large mass movements. On the upswing, people are prepared to accomplish miracles. They learn things very rapidly, assimilate new ideas quickly and can even politically overtake a leadership which appears to them cautious and conservative. Once the movement is past its peak without achieving success, then a lot depends on the political organisation. If, like Congress, it is incapable of holding things together, then people get demoralised, feel leaderless and slip back into apathy.

Jawaharlal was determined not to let his mood be swayed by the decline of the movement. Political education remained a necessary prerequisite. He was disgusted by the factional squabbling inside the Congress and he decided to resume contact with the mass of the people. He was arrested in the town of Jaito in the princely state of Nabha on 21 September 1923. The British had sought to safeguard the loyal princes by allowing them to ban all politics in their principalities. This time he was handcuffed and taken to the local prison which was known for its bad conditions. 'In Nabha jail we were all three kept in a most unwholesome and insanitary cell. It was small and damp, with a low ceiling which we could almost touch. At night we slept on the floor and I would wake up with a start, full of horror, to find that a rat or a mouse had just passed over my face.' He was tried and sentenced to a further thirty months' imprisonment, but the Nabha authorities suspended his sentence and expelled him from the state. On his return home he fell seriously ill. The family doctor in Allahabad diagnosed typhoid. Nehru was too ill to attend the conference of the provincial Congress, but his speech was circulated to the delegates. In this written statement he declared that the only meaningful goal for Congress was total and complete independence.

Jawaharlal Nehru realised better than most leaders of India's nationalist movement that the struggle would have to be resumed sooner or later. There could be no drawing back. Moreover, colonialism would not concede anything unless concerted pressure was consistently applied. Without struggle there could be no independence. This was Nehru's creed, but he wondered what would happen if Gandhi repeated his action of 1922 and called off the movement after some aberration. One way of dealing with Gandhi would be to build a movement that he could not turn back. Another strategy might be to confront him personally and try and work out what he really wanted. Without ruling out the first possibility, Nehru met Gandhi at Juhu, a seaside suburb of Bombay. On a personal level the meeting was perfect. Politically, Jawaharlal was disappointed. Gandhi had not cleared up any doubts.

Towards the end of 1925, Kamala Nehru gave birth to a son prematurely. Little Indira had a brother at last. But the child died after two days and Kamala became seriously ill herself, suffering from tuberculosis. The doctors recommended a trip abroad and the high mountain climate of a Swiss sanatorium. Neither Motilal nor Jawaharlal had any doubt that she should go abroad for treatment. In March 1926, Kamala, Jawaharlal and nine-year-old Indira sailed for Europe from Bombay.

3
Gandhi versus Nehru 1926–36

Jawaharlal Nehru was about to confront the most crucial decade of his political life. The decisions which were taken during these years shaped Indian politics for the foreseeable future. Jawaharlal was faced with agonising choices. He had to think and rethink his political strategy. He embarked on a struggle against Gandhi to win the soul of the Congress, and upon the outcome of this battle depended the future of the sub-continent.

In Europe, the Nehrus made straight for Geneva, rented a cheap apartment some distance from the centre and settled down for a long stay. Kamala began her long treatment. Jawaharlal, who had got used to a certain style and tempo of political work, hated idleness. Leisure activities appeared to him as an indulgence he could ill afford. He learnt to ski and skate in no time, as was his wont, but he was restless. Finally, in the early summer, his youngest sister, Krishna, arrived in Geneva. This gave Jawaharlal the opportunity to travel to other parts of Europe and meet émigré Indians, some of whom were politically active in those days.

With the approach of winter, Kamala's condition worsened, and the doctors recommended that she be taken to a sanatorium in the mountains in Montana. Money became a problem, and they were forced to sell Kamala's jewellery as Jawaharlal refused to countenance borrowing any money. Motilal, when he learnt of his son's plight, sent some funds. Kamala, Krishna and Nehru went to Montana; Indira was sent to a Swiss school.

As soon as Kamala's health improved, Nehru went off to Berlin to meet expatriate Indians. It was here that he met a number of communists. One of them, Virendranath Chattopadhyaya (Chatto for short), made a powerful impression on him. They would sit up till the early hours discussing the situation in Germany, in the USSR, in China and then return to the question of India. Chatto was a Marxist. He had little time for Gandhi and explained at length to a patient Jawaharlal that the only solution for India was revolution. There is no other way, he insisted, to modernise that country – moral exhortations could not destroy the caste system. Jawaharlal found these talks intellectually stimulating and a complete contrast to the convoluted rhetoric of the Congress Working Committee.

It was Chatto who informed Nehru that a conference was to be held in Brussels to set up a League Against Imperialism. He strongly recommended that Nehru attend. Jawaharlal was too disciplined a member of Congress to take such a step without consulting his fellow leaders. The invitation was despatched to Congress, and the Gaukhat session agreed unanimously that a delegate should attend on their behalf. Jawaharlal was nominated and sent a cheque for £500 for his expenses. He arrived in Brussels on 6 February 1927, and threw himself into the organisation of the conference. He wrote articles for the radical press and drafted a resolution on India, which ended with the words: '... this Congress further trusts that the Indian national movement will base its programme on the full emancipation of the peasants and workers of India, without which there can be no real freedom.'

Ten days of conference routines exhausted Nehru. He wrote to a friend that the food was terrible and he had no time to rest. Nonetheless the conference was, in some ways, an important influence on Nehru. He observed at first hand the weakness of European solidarity with the colonial nationalist movements, but he also met fellow nationalists and radicals from the Arab world, Africa and Indo-China. Jawaharlal was introduced to a young Vietnamese called Nguyen Ai Quoc. This young man avoided public appearances, and exhibited an obsession that foreign intelligence agencies were following him, but he left a good impression on Jawaharlal. The two were to meet in Delhi in 1954, when Nehru was Prime Minister of India and the Vietnamese President of North Vietnam, but travelling under another name – Ho Chi Minh.

Nehru's report to the Brussels Conference had worried the Congress leadership. They felt that he was coming too much under the influence of the Comintern, and Motilal, who shared their fears, left for Europe to make sure that this was not the case. Father and son met in Venice for their summit conference. Jawaharlal did not conceal his move to the left, but he assured his father that he had not become an agent of Moscow. Motilal was convinced. His son then persuaded him to accept a Russian invitation to attend the tenth anniversary celebrations of the Revolution in November 1927. The Nehrus boarded a train at Berlin and left for Moscow. They had missed the celebrations, but observed the new country with some fascination in the short time available to them. They could only stay in Moscow for three days. They took in as much as they could and then, their minds full of their impressions of the Soviet Union, began the journey back to India.

The boat carrying them docked at Madras in South India in December. A Congress session was already taking place and Jawaharlal went straight to the conference, where he immediately introduced a resolution demanding total independence from the *raj*. Much to his surprise, it was carried. The main discussion was about the forthcoming Simon Commission, a group of seven Englishmen who were being sent to India to examine the political system and recommend what changes, if any, were necessary. Nehru was not surprised that there were Labour MPs on this body: he had no illusions about Labour's complicity with imperialism. What annoyed him was that Labour had not insisted that there should be Indian representation on the commission. One of the Labour MPs was a man called C. R. Attlee, who had been educated at a public school established by the East India Company and was probably seen as having an 'Indian connection'. Congress decided to boycott the commission. Political India followed suit. Wherever the commission went it was greeted by thousands of demonstrators. People who could not speak a word of English learnt three words that winter and spring: '*Simon go back.*' The authorities were furious at this reaction. They decided to embark on a show of force. In Lucknow, Jawaharlal Nehru led a massive demonstration when the commission visited the city. Instead of the Commissioners they were met by a mounted police charge. As the horses pushed into the demonstrators, foot police charged at the completely peaceful crowd and rained truncheon blows on any and every head. Nehru was angry. 'I thought,' he later wrote, 'how easy it would be to pull down the police officer in front of me from his horse and to mount up myself, but long training and discipline held and I did not raise a hand, except to protect my face from a blow. Besides, I knew well enough that any aggression on our part would result in a ghastly tragedy, the firing at and shooting down of large numbers of our men.'

Nehru was badly beaten up that day and he fell to the ground, bleeding and almost unconscious. In Lahore a young British police officer attacked Lala Lajpat Rai, a venerated elder statesman of the nationalist movement. He, too, fell to the ground. A few days later he died. The entire nationalist movement was shocked. Lajpat Rai had been a much loved figure. Two activists, Bhagat Singh and Batukeshwera Dutt, constructed some homemade bombs and planted them in the Legislative Assembly on 8 April 1928. The bombs exploded harmlessly and Bhagat Singh declared that the aim had been to 'wake up India and to avenge the death of Lajpat Rai'. He could have added that the intention had also been to send John Simon and his gang back to London.

Bhagat Singh had imagined that the bombs would spark off a general uprising throughout India. This was a grave miscalculation. He was tried and sentenced to death. Jawaharlal Nehru went to see him in prison and wrote that 'Bhagat Singh had an attractive, intellectual face, remarkably calm and peaceful. There seemed to be no anger in it.' In prison Bhagat Singh spent his time reading. He also wrote a short pamphlet entitled, 'In Defence of Atheism'. He studied the two Russians whose names were synonymous with the Revolution, Lenin and Trotsky, and wrote to his friends that he had come to the conclusion that terrorism was wrong. India needed something far more subtle. Nonetheless he refused to say so publicly and would not appeal to the Viceroy for mercy. Better, he thought, to die without shame. And he did. Within the Congress Party, the students and peasants wanted a campaign to save Bhagat Singh's life. He had become a national hero overnight and balladeers composed song after song dedicated to him, but Gandhi refused to plead his case. Everywhere people began to ask why Gandhi did not lift a finger to save him. Why did the apostle of non-violence, the saint who forgave all sinners, not try and protect an individual from the violence of the state?

There were answers to all these questions. Nehru, above all, understood Gandhi's motives. The great man was a ruthless politician. He had a fixed notion as to how independence could be won and he would tolerate nothing that stood in the way of that. For Gandhi, right from the beginning, a negotiated settlement for British withdrawal was the only possible exit route. This meant a peaceful transition to independence. On this question Gandhi was completely dogmatic.

Jawaharlal had been plagued by doubts even before his last trip to Europe, and the discussions he had initiated with friends abroad had clarified his views. He was becoming increasingly apprehensive of the growing religious divisions in the sub-continent. He was developing an alternative strategy to that of the Congress leaders, who usually followed Gandhi without much thought. Jawaharlal began to ask himself the following question: how do we prevent our movement from being seen by Muslims as a Hindu movement? In Berlin, Chatto had been scathing about Gandhi's use of mystical Hindu imagery. This was pandering to centuries of backwardness, he had argued. How could the people ever be united around religious symbols, however well intentioned? Jawaharlal, a diehard rationalist, agreed on these points without difficulty. He had thought deeply about all these problems and had come to the conclusion that the Congress was, in many ways, an extremely defective political organisation, a cross between a movement and a political party. And Gandhi? Jawaharlal thought more about this man than anyone else in India. He had imaginary debates with him. He saw him as 'a great peasant with a peasant's view of things and with a peasant's blindness in relation to some ideas of life. Perhaps in any other country he would be out of place just now, but India, evidently, still understands, or at least values people of an oracular-religious cast, who talk of sin, salvation and non-violence . . . ' This assessment was only partially correct. Gandhi was not so much a peasant as a fox. He was an extremely shrewd and intelligent political leader. He had outwitted Jawaharlal on many questions, but the issues which made him uneasy concerned the relationship between nationalism and class struggle. Whenever Jawaharlal asked whether the peasant and the landlord, the worker and the capitalist saw freedom in an identical fashion, the only replies he got were couched in a language that was drenched in mysticism.

The response to the Simon Commission had convinced London that cosmetic measures were no longer sufficient. They were now prepared to consider more substantial reforms. The Viceroy invited Gandhi for talks. These were successful and a round table conference was organised in London. In 1931, India went to London — but which India? There were many representatives of the Indian nobility, splendidly attired in their brocades and jewellery; there were the loyal knights of the Empire, Indians who had served the *raj* and were now searching for a place in the sun; and there was Gandhi, representing the Congress. His goat and his loincloth became the subjects for numerous music-hall jokes and political insults (Winston Churchill denounced him as a 'half-naked fakir'), but despite the ribaldry it was Gandhi who dominated the conference. The rest was just window-dressing. The 1931 conference marked the first real discussions about the future of India between the British and the Indian National Congress. India was, of course, a sub-continent of cultural, political and religious diversity, but during the 1930s it was Gandhi who symbolised the India that lay beneath the surface.

Mohandas Karamchand Gandhi was born in 1869 in Porbander, Gujarat, into a family of traders, middle-caste Hindus. The word *gandhi* literally meant grocer, which had been the family trade many generations ago. Gandhi's grandfather, however, had progressed. He had served as prime minister to the ruler of Porbander, a small dot of a state in Western India (now Gujerat). The post was hereditary. Gandhi's father, Karamchand, had inherited the prime ministership and it had then passed on to his brother. In 1888 Gandhi had left to study law in England, where he had flirted with agnosticism and behaved as a typical late-Victorian man and enjoyed himself enormously. An acquaintance who had run into him in London's Piccadilly Circus reported that he was 'a nut, a masher, a blood — a student more interested in fashion than his studies'. It is one of the most sympathetic descriptions of Gandhi written. In 1891 he returned to India and was a total failure as a lawyer and teacher. His family began to despair of him, and there was universal relief when he was offered a job with a trading firm in South Africa which required a young legal assistant.

In 1893 he left for South Africa, where he was to spend the next twenty years of his life. Gandhi rethought many of his previous beliefs and certainties. He became enamoured of Tolstoy and began a correspondence with him from which emerged the political tactics he would deploy against mighty enemies. He began to campaign against the stifling restrictions imposed on Indians by South Africa. Success in this field was to become his most formative experience. Gandhi's initial actions were informed by a faith in the benefits of Empire, his sole objection being that all its subjects were not treated in the same manner. Gandhi explained his own behaviour with a refreshing honesty and never attempted to conceal his past, in sharp contrast to some of his disciples. Thus he wrote candidly that:

> Not only did I offer my services at the time of the Zulu revolt, but before that, at the time of the Boer War, and not only did I raise recruits in India during the late war [First World War], but I raised an ambulance corps in 1914 in London. If, therefore, I have sinned, the cup of my sins is full to the brim. I lost no occasion of serving the [British] Government at all times. Two questions presented themselves to me during these crises. What was my duty as a citizen of the Empire, as I then believed myself to be, and what was my duty as an out-and-out believer in the religion of *ahimsa* — non-violence?
>
> I know now that I was wrong in thinking I was a citizen of the Empire. But on those four occasions I did honestly believe that, in spite of many disabilities that my country was labouring under, it was making its way towards freedom, and that on the whole the Government from the popular standpoint was not wholly bad . . . Holding that view, I set about doing what an ordinary Englishman would do in the circumstances.

In South Africa, something else happened to Gandhi. He developed a revulsion against European civilisation. Not so much the Empire, but industrialisation, which he began to regard as the root of all evil. During a brief trip to London in 1909 he noted that in the West there was no longer any time for prayer. The pace of life had become too fast. He continued to emphasise strongly that his hostility was not to Britain, but to modern civilisation; he considered it necessary to overthrow the 'whole machinery' of industrialised societies. He went so far as to write: 'If British rule was replaced by Indian rule based on modern methods, India would be no better, except that she would then be able to retain some of the money that is drained away to England; but then Indians would only become a second or fifth edition of Europe or America.'

Gandhi began to advance an image of a utopia, which he claimed lay buried in India's past. He began to idealise the prehistory of Hinduism, in which it is impossible to disentangle facts from mythology. Nehru regarded this as a reactionary utopia and dismissed Gandhi's hatred of urban civilisation as an eccentricity. It was, in fact, much more than that, and it began to dominate his politics so strongly that he increasingly appeared to be a mongrel offspring of Victorian liberalism and Indian mysticism.

Gandhi returned to India in 1915, when he was forty-six years old. For a year he simply met people, travelled and observed India. He was presented soon after his arrival with the Kaiser-i-

Hind Gold Medal by Lady Willingdon, who described him as 'the well-known South African leader, who has now returned to India, where he is regarded almost as a saint'. Only four years later, Lord Willingdon described the same man as 'honest, but a Bolshevik and, for that reason, very dangerous'. The Lord and Lady were both wrong. Gandhi became a decisive link between the old and the new India, between the peasants and the colonial state, between Jawaharlal Nehru and India's strong capitalist class. He was the man who held the whole act together. It would have been impossible to find another like him. He took the village to the metropolis and, in the process, became the country's leading power broker. His fads and fallacies were indulged only because his political abilities were immense. Amongst his contemporaries, he could even laugh at himself. Sarojini Naidu, a distinguished poet and a leader of the Congress, did not care much for the saintly image. For her, Gandhi was neither Jesus nor Buddha, but Mickey Mouse. That was her name for him, used half-affectionately, half-mockingly, and the man responded generously. But he was probably not very amused when the poet told the Congress High Command in his presence on one occasion that 'it is costing us a lot to keep Gandhi in poverty'.

Gandhi's significance lay in his consummate skills as a politician and leader of the masses. The attempts, old and new, to portray him as a saint without earthly desires, a sun without black spots, an infallible leader hovering above the more sordid aspects of politics, are not convincing. Gandhi both reflected and abrogated the aspirations of the poor peasants, as we have already observed in Gorakhpur and Chauri Chaura. He regarded himself as an indispensable mediator on every possible front, and this determined the twists and turns of his political tactics. When the mist created by the clouds of incense that surround his name is cleared, he appears as a political leader with a confessional bent. Religion was, according to Nehru, the Achilles' heel of the Mahatama, and this created obstacles for all those who were attempting to articulate a *secular* nationalism. Gandhi was far removed from the crude communalism of the Hindu Mahasabha (a religious-political organisation which claimed to defend Hindu interests) or the crazed politics of other religious sects. He was a deeply tolerant man. Nonetheless it was his insistence on using religious symbolism to appeal to the peasantry that made a secular path more difficult to find. Four years after his return from South Africa, he defined his credo in a letter to an Englishman:

> My bent is not political, but religious, and I take part in politics because I feel that there is no department of life which can be divorced from religion and because politics touch the vital being of India almost at every point. It is therefore absolutely necessary that the political relation between Englishmen and ourselves should be put on a sound basis. I am endeavouring to the best of my ability to assist the process.

This remarkable candour needs to be further amplified. The 'sound basis' to which Gandhi referred meant two things: an orderly and planned British withdrawal from India *and* an economic continuity in the post-withdrawal period. Thus, at a fairly early stage, Gandhi established the limits of the great game. Not that he observed all the rules himself: he flouted many of them with impunity and displayed a panache more suitable to the age of television and media stardom. His importance, for India and Britain, lay in the fact that he had agreed to play the game in the first place. The one occasion when he wavered in this resolve was 1942, but that was a temporary lapse (as we shall see later) and he was soon back on course. In the late 1920s and 1930s, as he was preparing to outflank and outmanoeuvre Nehru, his strategy could be summed up in a sentence. The problem with the colonial state is that it is colonial; the task therefore is to Indianise it. No more, no less.

The British were sometimes confused by his change of tactics, much like an opposing cricket captain is puzzled when his opponent changes from pace bowling to slow-arm googlies, but they understood perfectly well his importance if they were to decide on a peaceful transition to independence. In 1921, Lord Reading, the Viceroy of India, sent to the Secretary of State in London a despatch which sums up, in a way, the attitude of the *raj* to Gandhi:

> There is nothing striking about his appearance. He came to visit me in a white *dhoti* (loincloth) and cap, woven on a spinning wheel, with bare feet and legs, and my first impression on seeing him ushered into my room was that there was nothing to arrest attention in his appearance, and that I should have passed him by in the street without a second look at him. When he talks the impression is different. He is direct and expresses himself well in excellent English with a fine appreciation of the words he uses. There is no hesitation about him and there is a ring of sincerity in all that he utters, save when discussing some political questions. His religious views are, I believe, genuinely held, and he is

> convinced to a point almost bordering on fanaticism that non-violence and love will give India its independence and enable it to withstand the British Government. His religious and moral views are admirable . . . but I confess that I find it difficult to understand his practice of them in politics. To put it quite briefly, he is like the rest of us, when engaged in a political movement he wishes to gather all under his umbrella and to reform them and bring them to his views. He has consequently to accept many with whom he is not in accord, and has to do his best to keep the combination together.

This was a fairly shrewd assessment. The British knew exactly what they were doing in India, and also that they could not stay there for ever. Gandhi appealed to them immensely because he was not in the least bit interested in any real socio-economic alternative. In brief, he was hostile to socialism in any shape or form. This did pose certain problems for him. He knew that the big landlords, who dominated Northern India in particular, were aligned with the British. They had their own landlords' associations, created to defend their interests as a class. In some cases they had even joined forces and formed a political party. The Unionist Party in the Punjab reflected the union between Muslim, Hindu and Sikh landlords, who had closed ranks against the moneylenders, the peasants, the nationalists and the communists. It was an extremely successful operation, one of the few instances of communal harmony on a political level. These landlords were not ignorant men. They foresaw that the *raj* would be compelled to deal with the nationalists and they merely wanted to ensure that when the time came, veteran loyalists such as themselves would not be ignored in the final settlement. They had, after all, staked their lives (and, one might add, made their fortunes) defending the *raj*. They wanted to make sure that both these gains were preserved in the future.

Gandhi attacked the landlords, but rarely did he defend the class interests of the poor peasants. Since the Chauri Chaura incident he had retreated even further. Times had changed. What he had intended in the early 1920s was to fire a few shots across the bows of the *raj* and force them to a compromise. The movement had, alas, begun to go in other, more dangerous directions. He had halted it then, but the result had been a defeat and it had taken six years to revive the masses. If something similar were started again (and he now felt that a last push was vital) then Congress unity was all-important. The umbrella under which he had assembled them all must not be seen to leak. If the movement began to get out of control and Jawaharlal, in one of his romantic moods, decided to put himself at the head of it, then things could get out of hand. This is how Gandhi thought. He knew that Jawaharlal's support was an indispensable ingredient for his own political strategy. This became an obsession with him in this period.

The contrast between Nehru and Gandhi, these two giants of India's nationalist movement, could not have been greater. The first was a Kashmiri Brahmin who had discarded every religious inhibition. The older man was a Gujerati *bania* (trading caste), who had toyed with doubt, but then re-embraced orthodoxy. Nehru, a product of Harrow and Cambridge, was tempered by his lengthy stays in numerous British prisons; Gandhi was a product largely of Hindu India, but had learnt his politics through his South African experiences. Gandhi regarded religion as crucial to everyday existence. Nehru saw it as India's deadliest enemy, containing the seeds of destruction. This confrontation between modernism and tradition would have been completely academic if the British imperialists had fulfilled the hopes of Karl Marx and John Stuart Mill. Both Marx and the utilitarians believed that the British would 'regenerate India', transform the countryside, establish new modes of communication and push through universal education. The British consciously decided not to alter the rural landscape of India. To do so, they believed, would rapidly create the conditions for their own removal from the region. Lord Macaulay, in his minute of 1834, made it clear that there was no question of mass education. Instead, the priority was to create 'a class who may be interpreters between us and the millions we govern . . . Indian in blood and colour, but English in taste, in opinions, in morals and in intellect'. And this is what happened.

Political India was, for a long time, confined to the three towns where the British had first impressed their mould: Calcutta, Bombay and Madras. The new Indian middle classes dominated civil society, regardless of the social and racial apartheid imposed by their rulers. They were moderates in the main — men like the young Motilal Nehru — and they hoped that by remaining moderate they would, one day, get some degree of self-government. Not as much as Australia and Canada, perhaps, but at least fifty per cent. They were all fifty per-centers. Initially they had been bemused by Gandhi. Why did he spend so much time in the countryside, they asked each other? They could not even invite him for a drink, let alone to make a four at bridge. Their attitude towards the man who, if the truth be told, was doing his utmost to preserve their futures, was one of utter contempt. In a bid to please they joined their English superiors in making jokes about him, or, when the English made the jokes (as was often the case), they made sure that they laughed the loudest. In the end they realised the true worth of Gandhi and belatedly, half-sheepishly, they embraced him. Then they looked around and discovered in Jawaharlal Nehru their new *bête noire*. These people were the children of Macaulay, but even their numbers were beginning to diminish as the students of the following generations began to discover new heroes and treated their ability to read English as a springboard to learning about rationalism, freedom, democracy and, yes, socialism.

Gandhi said that India had had enough of westernism and education. It was time to call a halt. He forgot that he himself had only read the *Gita* and other holy texts for the first time in English. In fact he forgot many things. Nehru was an ardent exponent of universal education. He wanted every Indian to read Bertrand Russell. Gandhi demanded a return to Rama Rajya, supposedly an early Hindu paradise on earth. He was explicit about this belief. He wanted a society without machines and with a non-industrial village as its central unit. How, replied Jawaharlal, could India possibly revert to a primitive agricultural state? Nehru agreed that industrialisation on the pattern of the West could be disastrous, but he believed that with properly planned development India could be far better off than ever before.

Nehru rejected the Western model of capitalism. In this he was not alone, for the American stock market crash of 1929 had rocked Europe and America and the result had been massive unemployment and unbelievable hardship for working people. Nehru wanted a total regeneration of India. He realised that the battle had to be fought on two fronts simultaneously — not only against British imperialism, but also against the force of Indian conservatism — for he knew that reaction and religion always marched together. He had been under strong attack by Hindu communalists for not paying any attention to the scriptures and for speaking Urdu laced with references to Persian poetry. Jawaharlal had decided by now that he was not going to remain on the defensive, let alone offer any conciliatory crumbs to the reactionaries. He was angry and he was determined to hit back.

Nehru never tolerated fools, but when stupidity was combined with irrationality, then scorn, sarcasm and contempt poured out of him like hot lava. Gandhi did not even try to contain the torrent, but sought instead to pacify the victims of Nehru's wrath. On one occasion during this period, when Nehru was visiting Gandhi and his wife Kasturbai, the latter, knowing that Nehru was about to be arrested, said affectionately, 'God preserve you!' Nehru laughed and replied: 'Where is *he*, Ba? He seems to be permanently asleep!' Gandhi, listening from a distance, chuckled sagely and told his wife that arguments on this subject were simply useless. Jawaharlal was too set in his ways.

On the subject of industrialisation, however, Gandhi did argue, but there was no budging Nehru. He would often quote Marx to the effect that:

> The bourgeoisie, in its reign of barely a hundred years, has created more massive and more colossal productive power than have all previous generations put together. Subjection of nature's forces to man, machinery, application of chemistry to agriculture and industry, steam navigation, railways, electric telegraphs, clearing of whole continents for cultivation, canalisation of rivers, whole populations conjured out of the ground — what earlier century had even an intimation that such productive power slept in the womb of social labour?

Gandhi would argue back, describing the destruction of the soul. 'Mysticism,' Nehru would reply. They would agree to differ.

Motilal Nehru had presided over the Congress in 1928. In the following year, Gandhi insisted that Jawaharlal should succeed his father. His motives were far removed from any thought of dynasticism; Gandhi wanted Jawaharlal fully integrated in the Congress High Command because he felt that this was the best way of keeping some control over his activities and preventing too much of a drift to the left. It would not be an easy task. Jawaharlal reluctantly accepted the post, but decided to make as sharp a presidential address as circumstances would permit. In the event, the speech aroused India and created panic in London.

The session at which Nehru made his inaugural address took place in Lahore. It was December, when the weather is at its best, with clear blue skies, warm days, cold nights and an atmosphere free of dust. Nehru received a hero's welcome when he arrived in the city to preside over the session. His speech was the most radical and uncompromising ever to be made by a president of the Indian National Congress, before or since. In Lahore that year, Congress declared itself to be seeking full independence. Even the delegates were stunned. Had Jawaharlal gone too far, they asked each other? All eyes were on Gandhi. He confirmed that this was indeed the new Congress line: no more talk of reforms or self-government, but a fight for total independence. But Gandhi could not and did not endorse the social content of Nehru's speech, for he had not stopped at calling for independence. Instead he had lectured the delegates on the need to eradicate poverty and class inequalities, proposed workers' control of industry and the granting of land to the tillers. 'I am a socialist and a republican,' he had stated in his quiet but firm way, 'and am no believer in kings or princes or in the order which produces the modern kings in industry, who have even greater power over the lives and fortunes of men than even the kings of old, and whose methods are as predatory as those of the old feudal aristocracy.'

Nehru also explained his attitude to non-violence and here, too, the contrast with Gandhi was clear: 'The Congress has not the material or the training for organised violence, and individual and sporadic violence is a confession of despair . . . But if this Congress, or the nation at any future time, comes to the conclusion that methods of violence will rid us of slavery then I have no doubt that I will adopt them. Violence is bad, but slavery is far worse.'

After they had got over the initial shock, the delegates applauded for a long time. The students, in particular, were enthused as they had never been before. At midnight on 31 December 1929, the Indian National Congress unanimously voted to fight for complete independence. Many years later, when he revisited Lahore for the last time in his life (it was then a Pakistani city), Nehru recalled the 1929 Congress with some emotion. He said: 'If we did not actually gain independence in that year, at least our hearts became free.'

The Congress also voted to declare 26 January as Independence Day and called on people throughout India to take a pledge to fight until total independence had been achieved. Motilal Nehru, accordingly, called on all Congressmen to resign from the Legislative Assembly and the provincial legislative councils.

After the triumph at Lahore, the Nehrus returned to their native Allahabad. Here Jawaharlal observed the annual Magh Mela, a

Hindu festival, and watched thousands of worshippers making their way to the holy river Ganges. The sight did not particularly please him.

> How amazingly powerful is that faith which had for thousands of years brought them and their forebears from every corner of India to bathe in the holy Ganges! Could they not divert some of this tremendous energy to political and economic action to better their own lot? Or were their minds too full of the trappings and traditions of their religion to leave room for other thought? I knew, of course, that these other thoughts were already there, stirring the placid stillness of ages.*

A new wave of civil disobedience was personally launched by Gandhi. He decided to defy the Salt Act, which protected the British monopoly on salt production. On 11 March 1930, at Dandi on the Indian Ocean, Gandhi went to the sea and symbolically extracted a tiny amount of salt from the water, watched by thousands of peasants. This gave the green light to the peasantry to boycott salt in the shops and prepare their own. Nehru insisted that this was not enough and that the struggle should be further accelerated. The Viceroy, Lord Irwin, ordered mass arrests. During the first four days of April 1930, Jawaharlal Nehru addressed twenty-two meetings attended by almost a quarter of a million people. He proclaimed that what was taking place was a national liberation struggle and 'He who is not for us is a rebel against his own country.' His mother, wife and two sisters decided to join the movement in Allahabad, Kamala displaying a talent for organisation which took her husband completely by surprise. He was, of course, thrilled, but had little time to talk to her or anyone else, for on 14 April 1930, Nehru was once again arrested and taken to Naini prison. He was sentenced to six months in jail for breaking the Salt Act. The movement had, by now, become truly national. In Peshawar, on the frontier with Afghanistan, the police used machine guns against demonstrators; in Bombay there were massive strikes and giant demonstrations; in Calcutta the police attacked the 'illegal' salt factories; in every village there was a manifestation of anger against the British.

The British Viceroy, Irwin, was a deeply religious man. He told journalists that before declaring the Congress Working Committee

---

* The classical German philosopher, Immanuel Kant (1724–1804), had a slightly more earthy explanation of religious emotions: 'If it goes behind,' he said, 'it becomes an F., if it goes upward it becomes religious inspiration.'

illegal he had prayed to God for help. Gandhi, who also communicated with the Supreme Being, commented wrily: 'What a pity God gave him such bad advice.' Gandhi himself was arrested on 5 May. Motilal, after consulting his son in prison, donated his house, Anand Bhavan, to the Indian National Congress, renaming it 'Swaraj Bhavan' (Independence House). During the civil disobedience that followed it was used as a hospital for injured Congress volunteers. Motilal bought a smaller house in the neighbourhood, and this became Anand Bhavan. He, too, was arrested, on 30 June 1930, so Gandhi and both the Nehrus were once again in prison, together with virtually the entire national and provincial leadership of the Congress.

In prison it was damp. The rainy season had begun and Motilal's asthma grew worse; he found it difficult to breathe on certain days. His son cared for him, but conditions were difficult. The movement outside showed few signs of abating and Motilal could well have died in prison, had it not been impossible for the *raj* to keep them in prison indefinitely. Using Indian intermediaries, Lord Irwin re-opened discussions with Gandhi and the Nehrus in prison, and Nehru agreed to the talks, under pressure from Gandhi, provided that it was recognised that India had the right to secede from the Empire. Congress agreed to suspend the movement if all political prisoners were released and all viceregal decrees withdrawn. The talks soon came to an end.

Motilal's health deteriorated still further, and he was released on 8 September. On 14 October Jawaharlal was set free. He returned to Allahabad and found Kamala alone, because the rest of the family had taken Motilal to Mussourie to convalesce. On seeing Jawaharlal for the first time in months, Kamala wept uncontrollably. One had tried to be brave, but it was no use. She had missed him a great deal. Being parted from him had been an unbearable agony. Kamala Nehru loved her husband a great deal. But after only one day at home, Nehru was on the road again, to attend a peasant gathering, and then to see his father in Mussourie. This time it was his mother who shed tears of joy. The family had not been together like this for a very long time. That day Jawaharlal played with his daughter, and the evening was spent having a lengthy and intimate discussion with Motilal. Father and son were now extremely close to each other and their conversation covered almost everything: family business, personal matters, politics and the future. Jawaharlal was not aware of it at the time, but this was to be the last occasion of its kind. He did see his father again, but under different circumstances, and they were not able to talk.

After leaving Mussourie, Jawaharlal and Kamala returned to Allahabad in order to participate in a peasants' conference. On his arrival he was handed an official notice which forbade him to make any public speeches. He defied the injunction. On 19 October 1930, he addressed the peasants and suggested that they stop payment of all rents and taxes. On his way home with Kamala, he was arrested once again, and this time he was sentenced to two years' solitary confinement. The charge was 'incitement to rebellion'. On 14 November, Jawaharlal's birthday, there were meetings all over India to demand his release. It was during this spell inside that Nehru wrote his famous letters from prison to his daughter, sharing his knowledge of the world with her. He heard on New Year's Day (1931), that Kamala too had been arrested and had declared that she was proud to follow in her husband's footsteps. On 26 January the Indian nationalists commemorated the first anniversary of Independence Day and meetings throughout the land pledged to carry on the struggle till the end.

London, fearing that the situation might get out of control, decided to exert all possible pressure for a new set of talks. An order was issued releasing the Congress leaders. Jawaharlal returned home to find his father on his deathbed. Motilal was taken to a hospital in Lucknow, much against his will, and he died there on 5 February 1931. His body was wrapped in the Congress tricolour and placed on a sandalwood pyre on the banks of the Ganges; Jawaharlal raised the torch and set the wood alight.

Motilal's death had not been unexpected, but it was nonetheless a sad blow. As time had passed father and son had moved towards each other both personally and politically. Jawaharlal's growing prestige in India had delighted Motilal. In his last years he would not listen to any criticism of his son, despite the fact that he did not always agree with Jawaharlal himself. Their relationship had slowly, but perceptibly, altered over the years. There was no authoritarianism any more. Father and son had become friends, able to discuss almost everything with each other. This had imparted a mutual dependence on each other, which both had valued enormously. Motilal's death left a space that could not be filled by anyone else. Gandhi was a godfather of sorts, but even he could not replace Motilal. His name had meant 'Red Pearl'.

Jawaharlal would never find another.

Another blow was on its way. Gandhi had agreed to talks with the Viceroy, which had taken place on 17 February 1931, in Delhi. Gandhi had agreed to visit London as the sole representative of the Congress and argue the case for independence, but Congress had obtained nothing in return. Jawaharlal was both angry and depressed. He stated that it amounted to a betrayal of all those who had fought continuously for a whole year. Gandhi attempted to utilise his personal standing and regard for Jawaharlal to calm his fears. When the Karachi Congress approved Gandhi's decision, Jawaharlal decided that the time had come to go on holiday with his family. He would never get any peace in India, so they went to Ceylon, the beautiful island of which Bishop Heber had said 'the prospect pleases, only man is vile'. The Nehrus had their rest, but Jawaharlal's mind was restless. He argued ceaselessly with Gandhi in his head, thinking of the replies he should have given. He was coming to the conclusion that a fight with Gandhi was now inevitable. The old man was politically backward and acted too individualistically; as for his views on social aspects of life, the less Jawaharlal thought about them the better.

Nehru returned to India in time to see Gandhi depart for the Round Table Conference in London. The movement had not stopped, especially in the countryside, but Gandhi's decision to open talks had encouraged a wave of terrorism in Bengal. Young men had decided that their political frustrations needed to be expressed somehow. The authorities were continuing to use harsh methods in dealing with peasant unrest. Hundreds of tenants were being evicted from their land for non-payment of dues. On 16 October a cable was despatched to Gandhi in London advising him that the situation in the United Provinces was critical, but Gandhi replied that he was helpless and advised the Congress to take whatever measures it deemed necessary.

In December 1931, Gandhi returned from London empty-handed. There was still unrest in many parts of India and the British were worried that Gandhi's presence might spark off a new set of disturbances. Nehru was confined by a new order to Allahabad. He refused to accept the restriction and boarded a train for Bombay to attend a Working Committee meeting. The train was stopped and Nehru was arrested, together with other Congress leaders. Gandhi appealed to the Viceroy for a meeting to discuss the crisis. The Viceroy refused. The Congress now called for a resumption of civil disobedience, but the response was limited. Nehru was tried and sentenced to two years in prison. Mass arrests followed, including Gandhi and Vallabhai Patel, a leader of the Congress right. The authorities now became much more vindictive. Nehru's two sisters were arrested; Swaraj Bhavan and Nehru's car were seized.

In prison, Jawaharlal resumed his studies. It was, he wrote, 'the best of universities, if only one knows how to take its course'. He had always been deeply attached to nature. In prison he sometimes used to jump up and down just so that he could see trees and the sky. In his latest quarters in Dehra Dun, he could actually see a lot of what Oscar Wilde had referred to as 'that little tent of blue which prisoners call the sky.' In fact 'The Ballad of Reading Gaol' had become one of Jawaharlal's favourite poems, reminding him vividly of the aesthete and writer whose works he had enjoyed so much at Cambridge. When he was not thinking about the future or world history he became increasingly lyrical:

> The moon, ever a companion to me in prison, has grown more friendly with closer acquaintance, a reminder of the loveliness of the world, of the waxing and waning of life, of light following darkness, of death and resurrection following each other in interminable succession. Ever changing, yet ever the same, I have watched it in its different phases and its many moods in the evening, as the shadows lengthen, in the still hours of the night, and when the breath and whisper of dawn bring promise of the coming day.

The news from the outside was beginning to alarm him considerably. He noticed that random incidents were taking place, but there was no organisation to unite the struggle. Once more he despaired of his own party. In April 1932 he received a communication from Allahabad which frightened and outraged him. There had been a week of remembrance for the martyrs of Jallianwalla Bagh in the town. The Nehru women had participated. At the head of the demonstration, which was illegal, there was a frail old woman dressed in a white cotton sari. She was baton-charged by the police and received several blows to the head, until a police officer recognised her, lifted her from the ground, put her in a car and drove her home. The woman was Swaruprani. For days Jawaharlal paced up and down in his cell, fearing the worst. Appreciating his agony, his mother decided to visit him in prison. He was relieved that she was not dead, but this relief gave way to anger as he saw her bandaged head. He did not say anything to her, but the incident cast serious doubts, for him, on Gandhi's policy of non-violence.

> How would I have behaved if I had been there beside my mother? Would I really not have beaten off the policeman's hand, have taken his blows myself, but stood aside until the suffering of the old, helpless woman softened the heart of the scoundrel who was beating her unmercifully?

In general, this spell in prison made Jawaharlal much more critical of the Congress strategy than ever before. He thought that the wheel had now turned full circle and that the pattern of alternately applying pressure and submitting to compromise had to be drastically altered. What was needed was a one-way process: relentless pressure leading to ultimate victory. Gandhi's failure to wrest any real reforms in London confirmed Nehru in his new ideas.

On 30 August 1933, Nehru was released from prison. He went straight to Poona, where Gandhi was resting. The two men talked for several hours, and Nehru confessed his worries and fears. Unless the people know what we are fighting for, they will begin to get tired, he told Gandhi. The old man tried to calm him down. 'Why run so far ahead?' he asked. 'For me it's enough to take one right step for each given moment.' Jawaharlal had explained his ideas patiently, stressing the key importance of educating the masses, making them self-sufficient. He now told Gandhi bluntly that Congress must announce its intention of ending class privileges in free India. Gandhi did not disagree, but repeated that 'It must be by conversion, not compulsion.' Nehru began to despair. There was not a single instance in history, that he could recall, where the owners of property had voluntarily given up their privileges. This conversation, like many others between Gandhi and Nehru, ended not because they had reached agreement, but because of the pressure of other priorities. Gandhi was biding his time. He was aware that in London the government had published a White Paper on India, which offered provincial autonomy. Jawaharlal had dismissed the whole business in a very peremptory fashion, but Gandhi reserved his judgement.

Jawaharlal had kept abreast of events in the rest of the world. He had observed the rising tide of fascism with growing dismay, and the inability of the Western politicians to resist Mussolini, Hitler, and soon, Franco, merely strengthened his socialist convictions. It was fortunate for the British that the Indian

Communist Party was totally dependent on Moscow. It adapted to every twist and turn. Moscow had still not been able to decide whether or not the Indian National Congress was an anti-imperialistic organisation; whether or not the Indian bourgeoisie was capable of resisting Britain; whether it should fight alongside the national movement or fight behind its back. If the Indian communists had formulated a coherent line of advance, if they had linked arms with the Congress in the late 1920s or 1930s, it is possible that history might have taken a different course. Nehru was extremely sympathetic to Marxism at this stage, but not so much to Moscow. The most radical phase of Nehru's political career was the period between 1932 and 1936. This was also the period of the Stalinisation of the USSR and the world communist movement. Nehru, not unnaturally, reacted against this rather sharply. He had four major objections to Moscow. He did not like the regimentation then being imposed in the USSR; he was strongly opposed to that country's lack of individual and cultural freedoms; he was alienated by the semi-religious nature of the dogmatism espoused by the Comintern and unimpressed by the failure of Indian communists to think independently. He was close to many individual communists and never doubted their sincerity. He enjoyed talking and arguing with them, but it was their collective voice which failed to convince him — not because it was occasionally too shrill, but because it was too dependent on the mood in the Kremlin. Thus in his most radical political phase Nehru never had much time for the local Communist Party.

In 1933, Nehru wrote a pamphlet entitled 'Whither India?' His reply to this question was clear: 'Surely to the great human goal of social and economic equality, to the ending of all exploitation of nation by nation and class by class, to national freedom within the framework of an international cooperative socialist world federation.' Yet what was being proposed by the British authorities was something completely different, many worlds removed from Nehru's dreams, hopes and desires. In 1935 the British Parliament passed the Act of India, which was designed to begin the process of self-government. The Act offered provincial autonomy on the basis of an adult franchise throughout India, excluding the Princely States. The centre would remain firmly in British hands. What was being offered was power-sharing and the underlying implication was that if Indian nationalists accepted this carrot, chewed it carefully and digested it slowly, then more carrots might be on the way. Gandhi was in favour of immediate acceptance. Jawaharlal was for instant refusal. On this there could be no compromise between them: either one or the other had to give way. Nehru stated that 'the federal structure was so envisaged as to make any real advance impossible, and no loophole was left for the representatives of the Indian people to interfere with or modify the system of British-controlled administration. Any change or relaxation of this could only come through the British Parliament.' In brief, sovereignty lay outside India and for that reason the 1935 Act was unacceptable. Congress had only one option: a total boycott.

Nehru's position was supported by the Congress left, but he was by now in prison again and unable to campaign effectively for his views. He was released only because Kamala was again ill and Nehru was permitted to go to Europe and see her in the sanatorium in Germany. Meanwhile, Nehru had now finished the draft of his *An Autobiography*, which had been composed entirely in prison. Indira was a growing woman and it was time for her to go to university. Mother and daughter left for Europe. On his release from prison Jawaharlal rushed to Germany to join them. His face filled with pain when he saw Kamala. There was little hope. It was obvious that she was dying. She did not want them to stay with her. She virtually pushed Jawaharlal to go and find a publisher for his book and settle Indira in a university, and on this occasion he obeyed her. Indira Nehru found a place at Badminton School in Bristol and subsequently at Somerville College, Oxford; the Bodley Head agreed to publish *An Autobiography*. Just as it was going to press, Kamala died peacefully. It was February 1936. Nehru's memoirs were reprinted nine times that year and on a dozen other occasions subsequently. In another book he wrote what was, in effect, his obituary of Kamala Nehru, *née* Kaul:

> She never entirely lost that girlish look, but as she grew into a woman her eyes acquired a depth and a fire, giving the impression of still pools behind which storms raged . . . She was an Indian girl and, more particularly, a Kashmiri girl, sensitive and proud, childlike and grown-up, foolish and wise. She was reserved to those she did not know or did not like, but bubbling over with gaiety and frankness before those she knew and liked. She was quick in her judgement and not always fair or right, but she stuck to her instinctive likes and dislikes. There was no guile in her. If she disliked a person, it was obvious, and she made no attempt to hide the fact. Even if she had tried to do so, she would probably not have succeeded . . .

While he was in London the news was conveyed to him that he had been elected President of the Congress for 1936. The session was due to open in Lucknow in April. The Congress socialists, a party within the Congress, urged Nehru to be careful. Subhash Chandra Bose, an extremely popular Bengali leader of the Congress left, warned him that he was expected to make the Congress right palatable to India but that, instead, he should fight for boycott, prevent office-acceptance and take Congress in a new direction. There was widespread talk amongst all sections of Indian society, claiming that Gandhi had rented Nehru to kill the cobra of socialism. Jawaharlal was aware of all these facts. He argued his alternative to the 1935 Act in cogent fashion. What India needed, according to him, was not power-sharing, but a constituent assembly elected by *all* the people of India. Accepting the 1935 Act meant a long-term collaboration with imperialism. A constituent assembly meant fighting the British for freedom and democracy. The Act meant accepting the continuation of British rule and British control at the centre. A constituent assembly meant Indians determining their own future. The time had come to reject all compromise. Office-acceptance would be 'a pit from which it would be difficult for us to come out.' Nehru would argue his case time and time again. Which assembly are you talking about? they would inquire. Where is it, Jawaharlal? He would accept that it was not something the British would hand to the movement on a plate. It was a realisable goal provided that Congress was prepared to fight and mobilise the people towards that end. It was only when the British were confronted with 'at least a semi-revolutionary situation' that India would get its own sovereign assembly. Gandhi and the Congress right were, not surprisingly, unconvinced. At one stage Nehru talked publicly about a split, but always drew back in time.

At the Lucknow Congress he made a strong speech, spelling out his estimate of the situation but it was destined, as far as socialism was concerned, to be his swan-song.

> I am convinced that the only key to the solution of the world's problems and of India's problems lies in socialism, and when I use this word I do so not in a vague humanitarian way but in the scientific, economic sense. Socialism is, however, something even more than an economic doctrine; it is a philosophy of life and as such also it appeals to me. I see no way of ending the poverty, the vast unemployment, the degradation and the subjection of the Indian people except through

socialism. That involves vast and revolutionary changes in our political and social structure, the ending of vested interests in land and industry, as well as the feudal and autocratic Indian states system.

At Lucknow, Jawaharlal moved two separate resolutions, the first rejecting the 1935 Act, the second demanding collective affiliation of workers' and peasants' organisations to the Indian National Congress. Both were decisively defeated. Jawaharlal sulked in his tent. Gandhi humoured him, indulged him, flattered him and left him with no option but to split or to accept a forced marriage with the Congress right. Many Congress socialists left the party in disgust. Jawaharlal was now the prisoner of men with whom he had fundamental differences, but he had decided that the unity of the movement could not be broken. That had become an end in itself.

Jawaharlal had, till now, been the proud and self-confident defender of socialism. He had spoken to millions and perfected the art of communicating with mass audiences. On one occasion he had forced his audience to think for themselves. They had been chanting *Bharat Mata ki jai* ('Long Live Mother India'). Jawaharlal had told them to stop. There was silence. Then he asked them a question: 'What is Mother India? What does it mean to you?' At first they were dumbfounded. Were they not there to listen and acclaim their leaders? Now they had a strange leader! He wanted to hear *them* talk. Nehru insisted on a reply, and gradually some sections of the largely peasant audience began to touch the earth on which they sat and murmur: 'Here it is. This is Mother India!' Nehru listened to a number of variants of the same reply. Then he interrupted them again and said: 'No, you are wrong. It is not the earth that is Mother India. It is *you*, all of you together, *you* are India.' They had cheered him then for a long time.

Yes, he had almost stormed the heavens that day. He had demonstrated to thousands of Congress activists that there was no half-way house between imperialism and independence; no staging post between capitalism and socialism; no god in heaven or on earth; and he had said clearly and unequivocally that communalism, be it Hindu or Muslim, was a vice exploited by perverted minds; he had defended Marx against Gandhi and Gandhi against Lord Lothian. Above all, his voice had been the clearest in defending rationalist values. Now with India at the most crucial crossroads he would, in effect, end his crusade and accept Gandhi as the leader who could be questioned, but who must, in the end, be obeyed. Jawaharlal had not yet changed his theories, but he had altered his practice. The two always catch up with each other sooner or later and it is usually practice that becomes all-powerful.

In a letter from Naini jail to his youngest sister, Krishna Hutheesing, in 1930, the imprisoned Jawaharlal had written about his vision of the future. He told her that he was thinking a lot about 'a magic city, full of dream castles and flowering gardens and running brooks, where beauty and happiness dwell and the ills that this sorry world suffers from can gain no admittance'. Only then could the everyday life of the people 'become one long and happy endeavour, a ceaseless adventure, to build the city of magic and drive away all the ugliness and misery around us'. At the Lucknow Congress that dream came to an end. Nehru would still believe that it had only been temporarily postponed, but history was to refute this illusion in a cruel way.

He returned to London, met friends and acquaintances, including a young South Indian radical, Krishna Menon, founder of the India League, friend of the publisher Allen Lane and inspirer of Pelican Books as a cheap paperback series designed to enhance a critical awareness. With Menon, Nehru talked endlessly about Spain. He was so involved in the Spanish Civil War that he actually flew to Barcelona and saw the fighting. On his return he spoke at Hyde Park on the situation in Spain. Michael Foot, then a young socialist, remembers being taken to the meeting by Krishna Menon to hear Nehru speak. Foot recalls Nehru as being extremely 'sober, warm, very effective without a trace of demagogy'. Nehru loathed the appeasers in London. Unlike British politicians he had no time for fascism. Both Mussolini and Hitler wanted to meet him, but he was curt, even contemptuous in his refusal. This was only a few years after the great enemy of Indian independence, Winston Churchill, then a backbench Conservative MP, had boasted to Italian journalists that 'if I had been an Italian, I am sure I would have been wholeheartedly with you from start to finish in your triumphant struggle against the bestial appetites of Leninism'.

Nehru was saddened by this trip to Europe. He saw that the lights were beginning to go out again and war loomed on the horizon. In Stalin's Russia, the purges were starting in earnest. Europe seemed about to be plunged into darkness. In an odd way this gloomy forecast confirmed him in his decision not to break with Gandhi. He simply did not have the energy to build a socialism that was independent of Moscow, Gandhi and virtually everyone else. Unity seemed more important than ever before.

He returned home to campaign in the first elections held under the provisions of the 1935 Act. An openly communal organisation, the Muslim League, had entered the fray. It claimed to represent India's Muslim populations, and although Nehru dismissed these claims somewhat arrogantly, facts were there and could not easily be conjured away. Communalism was becoming an important factor in Indian politics. That it was ugly was indisputable. That it needed to be resisted in the name of secular and rational values was crystal clear. The question that had to be answered, however, was why all this was taking place. Nehru and most of the Congress High Command had one answer: it was a consequence of the 'divide and rule' strategy deployed by the British rulers. They recalled Curzon's division of Bengal. United India had managed to reverse that anomaly: it would do so again. This response was convenient and had the additional merit of simplicity, but it was not totally satisfactory. The British, of course, made use of communal polarisations, and even helped to provoke them, but these divisions, alas, had deeper roots.

The virus of communalism was not the result of perfidy on the part of any single person. Mahatma Gandhi's hostility to Hindu-Muslim clashes was genuine and he expressed it in very strong language. He was sickened by religious polarisations. The Muslim League leader, Mohammed Ali Jinnah, was not a religious leader – he was secular, some said even an agnostic. For him Islam was a useful weapon with which he could carve out an independent political base for his followers, for he thought that they would never get a fair deal from Congress. The problems did not lie at the level of personalities, but in the orientation of the Congress after the Lucknow session in 1936. Hindus of various castes, denominations and classes represented an overwhelming majority in India. Their religious leaders openly stated that majority rule meant Hindu rule, something that had not existed in the subcontinent for several centuries. Jawaharlal's approach, rejected by Gandhi and the Congress majority, was the only one capable of resisting communal pressures and creating the basis for a composite nationalism. If Congress refused to acknowledge that class divisions were of key importance, that Hindus and Muslims from the same social groups had equivalent interests to defend against other Hindus and Muslims, then it was utopian to expect the majority of Indians to grasp this undeniable fact spontaneously and to mobilise themselves without any leadership. They would do so, sporadically, in the years that followed, but without support from the leaders of either Congress or the Muslim League. Nehru had pointed out on many occasions that pure nationalism was insufficient. History was now, in its twisted and inimitable fashion, beginning to vindicate that approach. In brief, once Congress had decided that competition was justified, then it became difficult to unite all Indians under its banner. Jinnah told the Muslim peasants that in Hindu-dominated India, they would be eaten alive by the Hindu moneylenders; he told the Muslim landlords that without British protection they would be overwhelmed by the Hindu capitalists; he told the Muslim traders and merchants that they needed a Muslim chamber of commerce or else the competition with the Hindus would destroy them completely.

Nehru was shocked by this development. He became increasingly implacable in his hostility towards the League, but he was to discover that it was virtually impossible to defeat its influence as long as the Congress was controlled by men like Vallabhai Patel, Rajendra Prasad and the industrialist G. D. Birla, and all three in their turn functioned in the shadow of Gandhi.

He had not much time to think about these dilemmas, because the 1937 elections were taking place and Congress had agreed to participate. It was farewell to all thought of a constituent assembly. From July 1936 to February 1937, Jawaharlal Nehru visited every single province in the country. He travelled over 50,000 miles and his transport varied from train to car to bicycle to bullock-cart. It was in this period that he truly discovered India. He wrote in awe of how it reminded him of 'some ancient palimpsest on which layer upon layer of thought and reveries had been inscribed, and yet no succeeding layer had completely hidden or erased what had been written previously'.

He was, in particular, staggered by a recent discovery by archaeologists. In 1925 the remains of an ancient civilisation, which later became known as the Indus Valley Civilisation, had been discovered in Sind. Before the discovery, the British engineers constructing the Lahore to Multan railway line had been using a unique form of ballast: bricks dating back to 3000 BC. They were stopped in time and the foundations of the ancient city of Harappa were laid bare. Its twin city, Mohenjo-Daro (Mound of the Dead), was discovered some miles away on the old course of the mighty river Indus.

Nehru stood silently on a mound near Mohenjo-Daro and studied the ruins. This particular discovery had pleased him enormously, for what had been uncovered was a pre-Vedic civilisation, far more advanced than its successors. Religious orthodoxy would have to be revised; history would have to be re-assessed. He listened in wonder as the archaeologists described what they had discovered. Mohenjo-Daro was a model of town planning, with an advanced sewage system, water-wells for the public on the neatly constructed streets and clear social and class divisions. This had been amongst the earliest manifestations of organised living on our planet. As he observed the old city he probably thought of the similarities with the modern world. Europe was about to erupt in a new war. Some of the characteristics of these old civilisations did not appear too remote — their modernised facsimiles continued to haunt the present. Wars, famines, palace intrigues, class struggles, religious oppression, torture, expansionist empires, death, destruction, superstition, ritual and gods had formed a continuous mosaic for almost five thousand years. The long and complex evolution of India had started in the third millenium BC. It had been coloured by repeated conquests and displacements, which had formed the variegated landscape of the country. Was this history of strife at last coming to an end? Nehru did not stop thinking about these matters. Later, in prison for the last time, he gave all these themes a shape in his *Discovery of India*.

The election campaign had educated him in more ways than he had thought possible. The total electorate numbered thirty million (excluding the princely states, where democracy was not yet permitted). Fifty-four per cent had actually voted. Out of 1,585 seats in eleven provinces, the Congress had won 711 seats and obtained an overall majority in six provinces. The Punjab had resisted the nationalist upsurge. The Unionist Party held the province in its grip, an indication that communalism could be resisted. If Muslim, Hindu and Sikh landlords could work together, then surely their tenants could do as well, albeit in a different organisation.

Nehru was overjoyed by the results. What pleased him of all was that the predominantly (ninety per cent) Muslim Pathans of the North-West Frontier province had voted overwhelmingly for the Congress. So much, he thought, for the Muslim League. There was an added irony in this instance. The writers and ideologists of the *raj* had always idealised the 'wild' Pathans of the Frontier. In Kipling's works they had always been portrayed as a 'manly, lustful, warrior race' who had from 'earliest infancy been accustomed to look on battle, murder and instant death'. The Pathan satisfied all the fantasies of men brought up in the hothouse climate of the English public school. They were always counterposed to the 'weak, effeminate, bespectacled, intellectual' Bengalis. What a blow, then, that these living embodiments of *machismo* had voted for Mahatma Gandhi. In the aftermath of these victories, Nehru sat back, for a while, and rejoiced.

4
War, repression and independence 1937–47

Congress had won the election. It had campaigned on a platform which had included some radical promises, especially in relation to the peasants. It had pledged that it would not tolerate any interference from the British governors in those states where it had formed an administration; it would not collaborate with the federal provisions of the 1935 Act; it would never provide sustenance to the occupying power. A new dispute had flared within the upper reaches of the Congress. Should they accept office in conditions where they could not accomplish much? Nehru argued strongly that they should utilise the legitimacy gained by the election results to demand total independence. Gandhi opposed this line of thought, backed by the Congress establishment. Nehru succumbed; Gandhi won.

Congress chief ministers were accordingly sworn in by the British governors. Friendly relations between the two developed rapidly in some provinces. Nehru's sister Vijaylakshmi became the first woman minister in India, when she accepted a post in the ministry in the United Provinces. Jawaharlal observed that power had virtually become an end in itself. He saw how other factors were beginning to operate simultaneously. Power, even on a provincial level, meant patronage. Patronage meant competition. Competition encouraged communal and caste rivalries. Rivalries led to discrimination. Within the first six months of forming governments, there was an unmistakably nasty odour in the air.

The Muslim League had only won 109 of the 482 seats allotted to the Muslims; it had obtained an insignificant 4.8 per cent of the total Muslim votes. It now began to use the Congress monopoly of power and the failure to fulfil promises to provoke communal fears amongst the Muslim middle and lower classes. The League was a motley collection of small landlords, would-be entrepreneurs, city lawyers and bandwagon petit bourgeois. It had been set up on a

British initiative in 1906 and its founders had pledged their unswerving loyalty to the Empire. Jinnah, the smart Bombay lawyer and one-time Congressman, was beginning to change this image. Sarojini Naidu had once called him the 'ambassador of Hindu-Muslim unity', but that had been in 1916. Now the old ambassador had other dreams. He had been happiest in a court of law and even his opponents acknowledged his brilliance as a lawyer. Now he had to learn the direction of Mecca and call the faithful to arms. Once he had said that all religious communities could live in peace in one India. Now he stressed the divisions between Hinduism and Islam, which, it should be added, had never affected him or innumerable peasants in the immediate past. 'The Hindus worship the cow,' he had shouted. 'We eat it.' Evil winds had begun to blow in northern India: the first serious Hindu-Muslim riots had already taken place in Cawnpore in 1930 – 66 people had died – and in 1937 the League had won a number of critical by-elections. Jawaharlal was in a despairing mood. He wrote to Gandhi, complaining about this new breed of Congress ministers:

> They are trying to adapt themselves far too much to the old order and trying to justify it. But all this, bad as it is, might be tolerated. What is far worse is that we are losing the high position that we have built up, with so much labour, in the hearts of the people. We are sinking to the level of ordinary politicians.

Jawaharlal had been President of the Congress for two consecutive years. Gandhi had insisted on the second term, arguing that it would be foolish to break the continuity in the middle of an election campaign. The third year had now begun. It was 1938 and a 'draft Nehru' campaign had already started. The Congress left saw in him the only chance of preventing too sharp a swing to the right. In November 1937, however, the Calcutta *Modern Review* published an anonymous article which had argued that men like Nehru, despite their obvious talents, were endangering democracy:

> Caesarism is always at the door, and is it not possible that Jawaharlal might fancy himself as a Caesar? By electing him a third time we shall exalt one man at the cost of the Congress and make the people think in terms of Caesarism . . . In spite of his brave talk, Jawaharlal is obviously tired and stale . . . we have a right to expect good work from him in the future. Let us not spoil that and spoil him by too much adulation and praise . . . We want no Caesars!

This article caused a furore. The left were livid, the right smiled complacently. Who was responsible? Many accused the British and the Congress right, others even pointed the finger at Gandhi. The editor of the *Modern Review* swore that there had been no author's name on the article and that he had published it to provoke a debate. Jawaharlal could hardly keep a straight face when confronted with the anger of his friends. He confessed that he was the author and that he believed in every word that had been published. There was no way in which he was going to preside over the Congress for a third year. Over the last two years he had succeeded in making it a mass organisation. Its membership jumped from half a million to five million. He knew that he was encircled by the right within the leadership, but he had discovered a new maxim: 'A bad peace is better than a good quarrel.' He wanted a rest.

His mother, Swaruprani, had died in January, from a brain haemorrhage. She had not recovered from a series of strokes suffered two years earlier. Jawaharlal was at her bedside and she died in his arms. His parents and his wife were now all dead; his last link with the past was broken. He decided it was time to strengthen his links with the future.

His daughter was at Oxford and he had conveniently received a letter from Krishna Menon in London, inviting him to come and address a number of meetings. He attended the 1938 Congress session, spoke briefly about the need to defeat imperialism and explained to the delegates the world situation. Another leftist, Subhash Chandra Bose, was elected President (against Gandhi's wishes) and Jawaharlal departed for Europe. The trip was necessary, he confided in friends, so that he could 'freshen up my tired and puzzled mind'.

He spent five months in Europe, where fascism was growing stronger with every passing day. He spent some time with Indira and met her friends, but his mind was on the changing map of Europe. He had long discussions with Menon, who henceforth became a close family friend and later Defence Minister in free India. What disgusted Nehru most on this visit was the abandonment of Spain to the fascists. He was in Paris in 1938 when Chamberlain and Daladier signed the Munich Accords, surrendering Czechoslovakia to Hitler. Nehru described these politicians as 'Hitler's messenger boys' and expressed his views in a forthright fashion to a journalist: 'Peace at any price — at the price of the blood and suffering of others, the humiliation of democracy, and the dismemberment of friendly nations. Even so, it is not peace but continuous conflict, blackmail, the rule of violence, and ultimately war.'

In Europe he had also read about the events in China in some detail. Reports from the old Celestial Empire had become extremely interesting. He heard of a legendary retreat (known since as the Long March) undertaken by communist partisans to escape the brutal encirclement of the nationalist Chiang Kai Shek. He read of Mao Zedong, the author of a little-known study entitled *An Investigation Into the Peasant Movement at Hunan*, who had become a famous partisan leader and had built a base in Yenan. He heard of the Japanese occupation of China and mused grimly on the tragedies that were being piled on the head of China's peasants. The Japanese were not offering any equivalent of the 1935 Act, but drowning the country in blood, like General Dyer in Amritsar.

Nehru's hostility to fascism ran very deep. When he returned to India with Indira in November 1938 he was preoccupied with the thought of the impending catastrophe. He had been greatly struck by a remark of Trotsky's, which he now pondered over and would later repeat in his books: 'It is clear', Trotsky had said, 'that the twentieth century is the most disturbed century within the memory of humanity. Any contemporary of ours who wants peace and comfort before everything else has chosen a bad time to be born.' Nehru was convinced that a victory for Hitler in Europe would spell disaster for the entire world. He was not in the least impressed by Hitler's use of an old Hindu symbol — the swastika — or his glorification of the Aryan race, from which most Hindus trace their descent. Nehru spoke at numerous meetings in India to explain the struggles in Spain and China. The Congress sent food and medical aid to Barcelona, but by the time it arrived Franco had virtually entered the city. A team of Indian doctors was also despatched to the liberated area of Yenan in China to provide relief to the communist resistance. In the summer of 1939 a letter from Yenan arrived in Allahabad, addressed to Jawaharlal Nehru. It read:

> We wish to inform you that the Indian Medical Unit have begun their work here and have been very warmly welcomed by all members of the Eighth Route Army. Their spirit of sharing hardships with us has made a profound impression on all who come in contact with them. We take

this opportunity to thank your great Indian people and the Indian National Congress for the medical and material aids that you have given . . . accept our thanks, well-wishes and heartiest greetings.

The signatory was Mao Zedong.

In early 1939 a new session of Congress was planned. Bose decided to run again as the standard-bearer of the left. Nehru tried to dissuade him, but failed. Gandhi declared his outright opposition. Bose defied the party leadership and won. He declared that Congress should begin an immediate mass struggle for total independence and give the British an ultimatum to get out of India. He went further and charged that many Congress leaders were in cahoots with colonialism — the reference to Gandhi was unmistakable. The Congress session was the rowdiest ever. Upon Bose's election, twelve members of the Working Committee resigned. The only surprise was Nehru. He knew that to back Bose at this stage would mean a split and Nehru was not prepared to go on without Gandhi. He offered to mediate between Bose and Gandhi, but Bose now mistrusted Nehru because he had resigned with the right and Gandhi was not really interested in a compromise. He saw Bose as a real threat and refused to work with him. The session was dominated by abuse. Bose himself was ill and he felt that he was being destroyed by the Congress Party's two most important leaders. He then took everyone by surprise and resigned as President and from the Working Committee. Who was to replace him? Gandhi proposed Nehru; Nehru proposed Abul Kalam Azad; someone proposed Patel. Finally Rajendra Prasad, a party functionary, devoid of talent, was elected to replace Bose. Nehru refused to serve on the Working Committee. He had been completely alienated by the feuding and abuse.

He left India again, this time for a visit to China to meet both the nationalists and the communists and discuss with them the anti-Japanese struggle. He arrived at Chungking and met Chiang Kai Shek, who advised him to do a deal with the British and, to Nehru's amusement, boasted of how democratically the areas under his control were governed. Nehru was about to leave for the communist capital in Yenan, when he received a cable from the Congress President. Hitler had invaded Poland and war had been declared. They wanted Jawaharlal back immediately.

On his way back Nehru's head was full of conflicting emotions. He wanted the defeat of fascism, but he did not want a subjugated India to be used once again as cannon-fodder in Europe. If the

British wanted India as an ally, he would support them provided that they made *immediate* preparations for the transfer of power. These views were encapsulated by him in an emergency resolution and accepted unanimously by the Congress Working Committee on 14 September 1939, though not without debate. Gandhi and Bose had put forward other propositions. Gandhi had argued that neither Britain nor India should take part in the conflict because 'violence, even in the defence of justice, had almost outlived itself'. He had gone so far as to address an open appeal to the people of Britain advising them to oppose Hitler's violence by 'spiritual force'. Subhas Bose, who had been especially invited to the meeting, demanded that a new civil disobedience movement be launched against the British. Nehru's anti-fascist position was carried, but both Bose and Gandhi were unhappy.

A week later, the Viceroy, Lord Linlithgow, met leading politicians for 'frank and free discussions'. Congress despatched Nehru. As he was starting to detail the Congress view, the Viceroy asked him to calm down. 'A little more slowly, Mr Nehru,' he said with sarcasm. 'My slow Anglo-Saxon mind cannot keep pace with your quick intellect.' The outcome was not so positive. On 18 October 1939, the Viceroy made some weak, wishy-washy proposals promising 'dominion status' at an unspecified future date, but introduced a sinister undertone to the statement by insisting that power could not be handed over until the religious minorities (i.e. the Muslims) were satisfied with the constitutional arrangements. Jawaharlal was livid. He saw in this statement a clear example of the 'divide and rule' psychology and he decided to appeal directly to Jinnah:

> I do not know what you and your colleagues in the Muslim League will decide, but I earnestly trust that you will also express your strong disapproval of the Viceroy's statement and refuse to cooperate with him on the lines he has suggested. I feel strongly that our dignity and self-respect as Indians have been insulted by the British Government. They take us for granted as hangers-on of their system, to be ordered about when and where they will.

Jinnah was cool and unresponsive. For him the Congress's difficulties were the League's opportunities. When Gandhi appealed to him a few months later for a united effort on behalf of India against the British, Jinnah replied that there were two nations in India, one Hindu and one Muslim. They had separate interests and the League was committed to a separate Muslim nation, Pakistan (Land of the Pure). The Congress leaders now asked all Congress ministers to resign with immediate effect in protest against the Viceroy's statement. This decision made the League virtually indispensable for the British during the war years. They were used in every possible way and the British supplied funds for the League's newspaper *Dawn* in this period. When the Congress ministers resigned, Jinnah and the League called on Muslims to observe 'Deliverance Day' in celebration of the event. The politics of the future had begun to acquire a cruel permanence.

Not all the Congress ministers resigned happily. Quite a few provincial chief ministers had developed a close working relationship with the British governors, civil servants and military officers. The resignation of the ministers was portrayed with a remarkable accuracy in Paul Scott's fictional *Raj Quartet*. The first ten pages of the *Day of the Scorpion*, the most evocative in the entire quartet, open with a British governor pleading with a Congress chief minister not to resign. The following extract conveys a flavour of what took place at the time:

. . . 'your party, Mr Kasim, yesterday committed high treason by conspiring to take steps calculated to aid and comfort the King-Emperor's enemies. And the big question in my mind is why is it still your party, Mr Kasim? What official policy or policies has it adopted or pursued in the last three years that you have honestly felt to be either wise or expedient?'

'Perhaps none,' Kasim said.

'I want you on my executive council,' the Governor said. 'If it were constitutionally possible for me to re-establish autonomy in this province I know whom I'd invite to head the administration. Short of that I want you *in*, I want to use your talents, Mr Kasim.'

'It is very kind of you, Sir George. I am immensely flattered.'

'But you refuse, don't you? You refuse to resign. You insist on going to jail. Forgive me, then. I hope you don't feel insulted. That wasn't my intention.'

Kasim made a gesture of dismissal. 'Please. I know this.'

The Governor sat down, took off his spectacles and played with them as before, but with both hands, leaning forward, with his elbows on the desk. 'Waste!' he exclaimed suddenly. 'Waste! Why, Mr Kasim? You agree with everything I've said, but you don't even ask for time to consider my suggestion. You reject it out of hand. Why?'

'Because you only offer me a job. I am looking for a country and I am not looking for it alone.'

'A country?'

'To disagree about the ways of looking for it is as natural as you say it is to squabble about how power will be divided when it is found. And as you say, I have disagreed many times about these ways, and people have many times expected me to resign and change my political allegiance. And if ways and means were all that mattered I expect Congress would have seen the back of me long ago. But these are not what matter, I believe. What matters is the idea to which the ways and means are directed. I have pursued this idea for a quarter of a century, and it is an idea which for all my party's faults I still find embodied in that party and only in that party, Governor-ji, nowhere else. Incidentally, I do not agree with you when you speak of Indian independence having become a foregone conclusion. Independence is not something you can divide into phases. It exists or does not exist. Certain steps might be taken to help bring it into existence, others can be taken that will hinder it doing so. But independence alone is not the idea I pursue, nor the idea which the party I belong to tries to pursue, no doubt making many errors and misjudgements in the process. The idea, you know, isn't simply to get rid of the British. It is to create a nation capable of getting rid of them and capable simultaneously of taking its place in the world as a nation, and we know that every internal division of our interests hinders the creation of such a nation. That is why we go on insisting that the Congress is an All India Congress. It is an All India Congress first, because you cannot detach from it the idea that it is right that it should be. Only second is it a political party, although one day that is what it must become. Meanwhile, Governor-ji, we try to do the job that your Government has always found it beneficial to leave undone, the job of unifying India, of making all Indians feel that they are, above all else, Indians.'*

The job of unifying India was the dream of every nationalist. At a time when it appeared to be nearing fulfillment, the British authorities decided to play the Muslim card. Jawaharlal had failed to understand that Jinnah's support would grow, yet he should have realised this better than most other Congress leaders. In a letter to Jinnah, he freely confessed that: 'My own mind moves on a different plane and most of my interests lie in other directions. And so, though I have given much thought to the problem and understand most of its implications, I feel as if I was an outsider and alien in spirit.' It was to escape this 'alien' atmosphere within the Congress itself that Jawaharlal had gone to Europe, then

---

* This passage is, in some ways, the crux of what Scott is saying. It was not shown in the television series because the Indian government, which approves all scripts being filmed in India, refused to sanction this section.

China and returned home only to face the special difficulties caused by the war.

In July 1940 the Congress met at Poona and Nehru's position was reconfirmed: India would fight fascism, but only as a independent state. Nothing else would even be considered. Churchill, now Prime Minister of England, sent a negative response. Congress could no longer delay the protests. Gandhi, realising that if a popular movement were unleashed, it might be impossible to control the direction it took, gave orders that only *individual* acts of civil disobedience were to be carried out. In other words it was to be a token movement. On 30 October 1940 Jawaharlal addressed a rally at Gorakhpur and was delighted to hear their chants: they were now prepared to die in order to win independence. Within hours of his speech he was arrested and charged with 'anti-government propaganda'. He was sentenced to four years' imprisonment and despatched to Dehra Dun. He knew the prison there very well. In an epilogue to *An Autobiography* he wrote:

> The years I have spent in prison! Sitting alone, wrapped in my thoughts, how many seasons I have seen go by, following one another into oblivion! . . . How many yesterdays of my youth lie buried here; and sometimes I see the ghosts of these dead yesterdays rise up, bringing poignant memories, and whispering to me, 'Was it worthwhile?' There is no hesitation about the answer. If I were given the chance to go through my life again, with my present knowledge and experience added, I would no doubt try to make changes in my personal life; I would endeavour to improve in many ways on what I had previously done, but my major decisions on public affairs would remain untouched.

Jawaharlal was by now inured to prison life. He started each day by exercising, then he turned to gardening, digging the hard earth to plant flowers and vegetables. When the weather was inclement he became a weaver, spinning cloth at his wheel. In the evening he read, took notes and read again, till it was time to extinguish the lamp and retire.

He was in prison when he heard of the German attack on the USSR, which obliterated overnight the unpleasant memories of the Molotov-Ribbentrop agreements. The Japanese had began their march towards India. On 4 December 1941, Nehru and the other imprisoned Congress leaders were released. The British needed their collaboration and hoped that the changed circumstances might lead to an acceptable compromise.

Three days after Nehru's release, he read of the Japanese attack on Pearl Harbor and the destruction of the American fleet stationed at that port. This time he did not celebrate, as he had done in 1905, for he perceived Japan as a fascist and imperialist nation. He had seen first-hand examples of Japanese atrocities in China and he did not want them repeated in India. The more ardent nationalists in the Congress, such as Bose, did not see the situation from an international point of view. For them 'the enemy of our enemy is always our friend', regardless of any other considerations. Winston Churchill was under strong pressure from the American President Franklin D. Roosevelt to resolve the crisis in India, and Roosevelt himself favoured a rapid transition to Indian independence. The Atlantic charter of August 1941 had declared that people throughout the world had the right to choose their own government; in September, Churchill barked that this charter did not apply to India! The advance of the Japanese, however, compelled the British War Cabinet to make one last effort. Sir Stafford Cripps, once the leader of the Labour Party's left wing, was sent to India with promises relating to the future. Nehru was shocked that Cripps, who knew the situation well, had come as Churchill's messenger-boy with no real power to negotiate a meaningful settlement. Nonetheless the Congress leaders spent many hours talking to him. Nehru told Cripps that if the Japanese invaded India, Congress would lead a guerrilla war against the invaders. Passive resistance would fail miserably. Cripps failed to convince anyone inside the Congress that they should help the war effort unconditionally and he left for London empty-handed. Gandhi's acerbic comment on the Cripps proposals reflected Indian opinion. 'It was,' the cunning old man said, 'a post-dated cheque on a bank that is obviously failing.'

Gandhi, however, sharply reprimanded Jawaharlal for talking about forming partisan groups to fight the Japanese. The Japanese, he said, were at war with Britain, not India. Nehru became extremely bitter at this stage, as he saw that nationalists of both the Congress right and left had almost exactly the same points of view. Vallabhai Patel and Bhulabhai Desai had convinced Gandhi that Britain was a declining power; the fall of Singapore had convinced many Indians that the British lion was no longer invincible. Gandhi did not want to be so completely identified with the British that it would make compromises with the Japanese impossible. From the extreme left-wing nationalists came a similar reaction. Nehru was horrified when Bose, who had disappeared from his Calcutta home in January 1941, suddenly surfaced in the German capital, Berlin. In March 1942 he broadcast over Berlin radio and told Indians that the Axis powers were enemies of the British and *ipso facto* friends of India. The logic was obvious. He called on Indian patriots to fight alongside Japan against the British throughout Asia. This propaganda was reproduced by Radio Tokyo, which now increased its broadcasts to India. Nehru knew Bose extremely well. He was aware that he was attempting to use inter-imperialist differences to the advantage of India. It was the logic of ultra-nationalism. Nehru did not sympathise with his tactics. For him there could be no alliance with any fascist state.

On 7 August 1942, the Congress Working Committee met for its most historic session. They demanded immediate withdrawal by the British and stated that if this demand was refused then a mass movement of civil disobedience would begin. The 'Quit India' resolution was accepted by a large majority. Two days later, at five o'clock in the morning, Jawaharlal Nehru was arrested once again. This time he stayed in prison for almost three years. He was taken to Ahmednagar Fort, a historic monument where, in the second half of the sixteenth century, Chand Bibi, the woman ruler, had resisted the might of the great Mogul Emperor Akbar. When the latter discovered who his opponent was, he halted the seige and concluded a lasting peace. The fort had been transformed into a prison by the British during the First World War. Gandhi, too, was now imprisoned, together with all the Congress leaders.

In the absence of their leaders, the Indian people decided to carry on the struggle. Massive demonstrations took place in every major town and hundreds of villages were declared 'disturbed areas' by the colonial authorities. British troops were used to quell the movement and there were incidents of strafing by aeroplanes. The official British figures admitted to only 60,000 arrests and 1,000 deaths; even this understatement indicated the scale of the revolt. Sober observers put the actual death toll at 10,000. Inside prison, Nehru vigorously defended the people against attacks from the Congress right. 'You talk a lot about anti-colonial campaigns,' he shouted at one stage. 'The people are carrying them out.' Gandhi's notion that the British would not resort to large-scale repression was seen to be completely false.

It was in prison that Jawaharlal read about the amazing Soviet victories at Stalingrad and Kursk, which had halted the Nazi war-machine. He read, too, of the Soviet sacrifices and compared them to the plight of India. For while Russians were dying in their millions resisting fascism, there was a terrible famine in Bengal. The size of this catastrophe was so large that news could not be suppressed. India, thought Jawaharlal, was being bled to death by imperialism. At the same time, Bose had declared a 'government in exile' and persuaded Indian prisoners of war in Japanese camps to fight under his command in the Indian National Army (INA). Hostility to the British was now so great that Bose became a popular hero overnight. INA units did engage the British in a number of conflicts, but most of them were either captured or killed. What interested Nehru was that Bose had succeeded in uniting Indians: the INA had included Muslims, Sikhs and Hindus who had forgotten their religious divisions.

Bose was killed in a plane crash in 1945. Jawaharlal expressed his sorrow in public. He had not agreed with Bose, but had never doubted his patriotism. He had regarded Bose as childish, very impressionable, but also deeply sensitive and burning with a nationalist fervour. He opposed all attempts to blacken his name and, in this, was supported by Gandhi and Abul Kalam Azad. When the British authorities decided to try the INA men for 'high treason', Nehru became a lawyer again and defended them in open court, arguing that they had been wrong, but they had been motivated by love of country and a desire to free it from the yoke of imperialism. There were massive demonstrations in Calcutta, Bombay, Madras and other cities against the INA trials in 1946. If the men had been sentenced to death, there would have been violence all over India. Instead they were sentenced to exile for life, but were all later granted an amnesty by a viceregal decree.

The temperature throughout the country was rising. In Britain a Labour government headed by Attlee was in power. Throughout 1946 India teetered on the brink of revolution. There were mutinies in the police and in the army, while on 19 February 1946, 20,000 naval ratings from eleven shore bases in Bombay and all the ships in the harbour hauled down the Union Jack. Some weeks prior to the incident, Commander King, the officer in charge of a shore-base, had addressed the ratings in intemperate language as 'You sons of bitches, sons of coolies, sons of bloody *junglees* (savages).' Within 72 hours the British colonial administration had lost control of the Royal Indian Navy. The strike had spread to 74 ships, 4 flotillas and 20 shore establishments. Admirals Godfrey and Rattray, the two senior-most officers in command of the navy, reported that there was a smell of 'revolution in the air'. On some ships the red flag had been hoisted with the inscription *Inquilab Zindábad* (Long Live Revolution). In Bombay a general strike in solidarity with the sailors had been largely successful, with British troops opening fire and killing dozens of workers. An interesting feature of the naval mutiny was that, like the INA, there was total solidarity on the part of the men: religious differences did not appear.

Direct repression could have been dangerous, since the Army had become unreliable, so the British pleaded with the Muslim League and the Congress to end the mutiny. Jinnah made a communal speech asking Muslim sailors to cease participating in the mutiny, but to no avail. It was when Gandhi and Patel asked the men to surrender that the Naval Strike Committee, feeling isolated, called a halt to the rebellion. They felt betrayed, but there was no other choice. The Indian poet Sahir Ludhianvi spoke of their bitterness in a Urdu lament composed for the occasion:

O, Leaders of our Nation
Lift your heads,
Look into our eyes,
Whose blood is this,
Who died?

You showed us the direction
You painted our destiny
You blew on the embers
Now you shrink from the flames.
You appealed for waves
And now seek shelter from the storm.

We understand all;
Hope now lies in compromise
Colonial pledges are very wise.
Oppression was just a fairy tale!
The foreigner's promises we must all, hail!
Yes, accept their protestations of love
When the people rise from below, we take fright above.
The old legacy will not die.

O Leaders of our Nation,
Whose blood is this,
Who died?*

The situation in India terrified London. In the same year a special Cabinet mission was despatched to prepare for British withdrawal. It proposed a loose federation. At one stage both Congress and League leaders accepted the Cabinet mission plan, and hopes were raised. Maybe India would remain one state. Then Jinnah declared that he would never place his trust in a 'Hindu dictatorship' and withdrew support. Congress followed suit and the League called for a Direct Action Day for a separate Muslim state, Pakistan. Communal rioting became more widespread. Both Gandhi and Nehru were heartbroken. Nehru was now ultra-sensitive to communalism within the Congress ranks. There were a number of quarrels between him and Vallabhai Patel, the veteran power broker, leader of the Congress right and not averse to using communalism when it suited his interests.

In the winter of 1945-6, the British government had organised elections in India to elect a constituent assembly and provincial legislatures. The Congress leaders had all been released as the war came to an end. They fought the elections in the full knowledge that the unity of India was dependent on Congress Muslims defeating League Muslims in the seats reserved specially for the Muslim minority. The results were unsatisfactory for both Jinnah and Nehru. Although Congress won an overall majority, as had been widely expected, in the central assembly Congress won 57 general seats, but not a single Muslim seat: all thirty had gone to the League. Jinnah was thus awarded recognition on a national level. In the provinces the situation was uneven — Congress was still the largest party in the Frontier province, whereas the League did not get an overall majority in any Muslim majority province.

On 16 August 1946, 5,000 people died in Calcutta as a result of the Muslim League's 'Direct Action Day'. Communal rioting spread rapidly to the whole of North India and it did not stop until after independence. It had claimed at least a quarter of a million lives: men, women and children. Indian slaughtered Indian. By the time Lord Mountbatten was sent to speed up the transition to independence, the violence had become uncontrollable.

---

* 'Whose Blood is This?' Lines on the Naval Mutiny, 1946, by Sahir Ludhianvi. Translated by the author.

He arrived in March 1947 with a simple mandate from Attlee, the British Prime Minister: Quit India. Mountbatten, the last Viceroy of British India, came with more plenipotentiary powers than any preceding consul. The die had now been cast; the unity of India would be broken. Mountbatten tried to revive the remnants of the Cabinet mission plan: a federation with a guarantee that Muslim majority regions could secede after a certain time if they were dissatisfied with the experience. It was too late. The blood that had been spilt had made an early reconciliation between the Muslim League and Congress impossible. The Muslim Congressmen, men of the calibre of Abul Kalam Azad (a distinguished theologian and scholar who understood more about Islam than Jinnah ever would), Rafi Ahmed Kidwai and others, were opposed to any deals with the League. Reluctantly and with great sadness, Gandhi and Nehru agreed to the partition of the subcontinent. Very few had believed that it would actually come to this. Even Jinnah had remained confused until the last moment, seeing the division as a separation rather than a divorce. He told friends that he still hoped to spend some time every year in his favourite Indian city, Bombay. He conceived of Pakistan as a mini-India with a sizeable minority of Hindus and Sikhs. When the details of partition were being discussed he objected to the division of Punjab and Bengal. Mountbatten later recalled:

> He (Jinnah) produced the strongest arguments why these provinces should not be partitioned. He said they had national characteristics and that partition would be disastrous. I agreed, but I said how much more must I now feel that the same considerations applied to the partitioning of the whole of India . . . Finally he realised that either he could have a united India with an unpartitioned Punjab and Bengal or a divided India with a partitioned Punjab and Bengal and he finally accepted the latter situation.

The last year of British occupation was a cruel one. Communal rioting took away much of the pleasure that would otherwise have marked the countdown to independence; the northern part of the sub-continent was torn by ugly conflicts. Nehru was far too intelligent to think that the fault lay entirely on one side. Jinnah had brought religion into politics in an opportunist fashion, but he alone could not be held responsible for the debacle: he had merely taken advantage of existing conditions. Congress could not be absolved, for it had played its part in creating the overall situation.

Although the political situation was disastrous, a more personal aspect of Jawaharlal's life suddenly became very important to him. He had always enjoyed the company of women. He felt more relaxed, less competitive and on his guard in their presence. Swaruprani, Kamala and even young Indira had prevented him from feeling too lonely or companionless, but now the first two were dead and Indira had married a man of her choice in 1942. Unlike Gandhi, Nehru did not believe that men and women should exercise strict sexual self-discipline, and he had publicly attacked Gandhi on these questions in sharp language. Gandhi had stated that 'any union is a crime when the desire for progeny is absent', 'the adoption of artificial methods [of birth control] must result in imbecility and nervous prostration', 'it is wrong and immoral to seek to escape the consequences of one's acts . . . It is still worse for a person to indulge his animal passions and escape the consequences'. Gandhi refused to accept the power of sexual attraction.

'But I am told that this is an impossible ideal,' he had remarked,

> that I do not take account of the natural attraction between man and woman. I refuse to believe that the sensual affinity, referred to here, can be at all regarded as natural; in that case the deluge would soon be over us. The natural affinity between man and woman is the attraction between brother and sister, mother and son, or father and daughter. It is this natural attraction that sustains the world . . . No, I must declare with all the power I can command that sensual attraction, even between husband and wife, is unnatural.

Jawaharlal was not amused by these eccentricities. He was concerned lest Gandhi's advice was followed and he challenged him directly.

> In these days of the Oedipus complex and Freud and the spread of psychoanalytical ideas, this emphatic statement of belief sounds strange and distant. One can accept it as an act of faith or reject it. There is no half-way house . . . I think Gandhi is absolutely wrong on this matter. His advice . . . as a general policy can only lead to frustration, inhibition, neurosis, and all manner of physical and nervous ills.

On the arrival of the Mountbattens, Nehru felt that these were two people to whom he could relate fairly easily. Mountbatten himself was far removed from the traditional viceregal model. He was sympathetic to nationalism and believed that India should have its freedom. It was Lady Mountbatten, however, who charmed Nehru and *vice versa*. Edwina Mountbatten came from a wealthy Jewish family. She had been radicalised during the 1920s and had made some financial donations to the extreme left in Britain. The contrast with the typical women of the *raj* could not have been greater. Edwina Mountbatten was radical, a freethinker, extremely hostile to any manifestation of racism, a great reader of books (including Nehru's *An Autobiography*) and a very independent person. The effect on Nehru was magical. It can be seen even in the official photographs of them together. There is a tenderness in his eyes which is unmistakable. There was no doubt about it whatsoever: Jawaharlal Nehru and Edwina Mountbatten had fallen in love with each other. She became and remained his closest personal friend for the rest of her life, but as the Viceroy's wife, she had to keep her emotions under control. Mountbatten as an individual was also charmed by Nehru and politically he had been won over to his side. Personal relations were complicated by political considerations of one sort or another — nonetheless, the close friendship between Jawaharlal and Edwina prospered, creating much talk and gossip amongst the Congress as well as the Muslim League. Everyone assumed political motives. They were wrong. All those who knew them well were later to admit that, personally, Jawaharlal had never been as happy in his whole life.

On August 14 1947, India became independent. So did Pakistan. Jinnah appointed himself Governor-General. India asked Mountbatten to be its first head of state, thus symbolising the elements of continuity in the transition to freedom. At midnight on 14 August 1947, the 182-year-old Empire came to an end. India's first Prime Minister, Jawaharlal Nehru, rose to his feet in the country's Constituent Assembly and stated simply, his voice choked with emotion, the words which are better known in India today than virtually any other speech of the time:

> Long years ago we made a tryst with destiny, and now the time has come when we shall redeem our pledge, not wholly or in full measure but substantially. At the stroke of the midnight hour, when the world sleeps, India will awake to life and freedom. A moment comes, which comes but rarely in history, when we step out from the old to the new, when an age ends, and when the soul of the nation, long suppressed, finds utterance. It is fitting that at this solemn moment we take the pledge of dedication to the service of India and her people and to the still larger cause of humanity.

The bloodshed of partition had, nonetheless, made it not purely an occasion of joy, but also of sorrow. Muslims from the north of India fled to Pakistan. Hindus and Sikhs from Pakistan fled to India. On the way, they killed each other. In the towns they were leaving for ever, they looted each other's houses, raped women, burnt children alive and shouted religious slogans. It was a cruel irony that in the months before independence the only guarantee of safety was a white face. These countless tragedies blighted the dawn of independence. In neighbouring Pakistan a radical poet, Faiz Ahmed Faiz, had written a poem, 'Dawn of Freedom', which became for many a necessary corollary to the 'tryst with destiny':

> This leprous daybreak, dawn night's fangs have mangled —
> This is not that long-looked-for break of day,
> Not that clear dawn in quest of which those comrades
> Set out, believing that in heaven's wide void
> Somewhere must be the star's last halting place,
> Somewhere the verge of night's slow-washing tide,
> Somewhere an anchorage for the ship of heartache.
>
> But now, word goes, the birth of day from darkness
> Is finished, wandering feet stand at their goal;
> Our leaders' ways are altering, festive looks
> Are all the fashion, discontent reproved;
> And yet this physic still on unslaked eye
> Or heart fevered by severance works no cure.
> Where did that fine breeze, that the wayside lamp
> Has not felt, blow from — where has it fled?
> Night's heaviness is unlessened still, the hour
> Of mind and spirit's ransom has not struck;
> Let us go on, our goal is not reached yet.

5
Prime Minister of India 1947–64

Jawaharlal Nehru was now approaching his fifty-seventh year. He was beginning the most important phase of his life. It would not be a heroic period but it would demand more from him and pose unpleasant choices, ultimately casting a shadow on his reign and bequeathing to India a troubled legacy.

The British had departed and the Mountbattens were soon to follow, but what was the shape of the country they had left behind?. Their most important gifts to the new India were the two institutions they had nurtured and developed for almost two centuries with a combination of paternal affection and discipline: the Indian Army and the Indian Civil Service. It was these that provided the infant state with an adult spinal chord. It was the Civil Service that was able to ensure a smooth transition to the new regime. It was the army which defended the new frontiers. The new state was therefore Indian in its colour, composition and make-up, but its pedigree was unmistakably British. As for the rest, Nehru thought, time alone would tell. The old India had not been changed that much by the British. Some of it, of course, couldn't have been. The hot sun, the thick palm forests, the paddy fields and tea plantations, giant trees which had been there since time immemorial, the mud-homes of the exhausted peasants, the temples and mosques, the gaudy religious icons of the south, all these seemed immutable. Not so, however, the rule of princes and maharajahs. The time for turbans bedecked with jewellery, elephants laden with multicoloured canopies and royal palanquins, the ostentatious display of gold and silver, guarded by spear and mace, rifle and machine-gun, were now over. The royal houses had served the British well. They had mocked and harassed the nationalists. Once the rulers acceded to India, and some did so more willingly than others, they would be democratised, brought into line and denied any special privileges.

The princely states had been carefully protected by the British. Professor Rushbrook Williams, who had often served as a go-between on behalf of the *raj* and the royal houses, had written in the London *Evening Standard* on 28 May 1930:

> The situations of these feudatory states, chequerboarding all India as they do, are a great safeguard. It is like establishing a vast network of friendly fortresses in debatable territory. It would be difficult for a general rebellion against the British to sweep India because of this network of powerful, loyal, native states.

In brief, it had been a fairly straightforward relationship. When they left, the British had insisted that the rulers of these princedoms retained the final veto as regards the future. They could accede to India, Pakistan or remain independent, though everyone knew that the last option was a non-starter. Nonetheless a great deal of intrigue had surrounded the final stages of decision-making. Nehru had bribed the princes by offering them a large, permanent state subsidy to help them live in the style to which the British had accustomed them. It would be left to his daughter, in the coming decades, to remove this, their last prop, and bring them down to earth.

Nehru had been forced to resort to violence in Kashmir and Hyderabad. The former had been the more serious, as Pakistani volunteers had been despatched by Jinnah to take Srinigar (the capital of Kashmir) before Indian troops could reach the valley. Kashmir was a princely state with a Muslim majority, but a Hindu ruler. In Sheikh Abdullah it had a talented and clever nationalist leader, who had associated himself and his organisation with the Congress throughout the pre-independence period. Abdullah was hostile to the Muslim League and was anxious for Kashmir to remain part of India, but no referendum was ever allowed. Once the unruly Pakistani volunteers had been defeated, India regarded Kashmir as its own, a vital ingredient of a secular state. However, the two new states had almost fought a war over this beautiful valley. Both their armies had, at that time, been headed by British commanders-in-chief. Whether they would have led their troops against each other on the orders of Pakistani and Indian leaders was never put to the test. A ceasefire was hastily organised and Kashmir, too, was divided, though the bulk of the valley (including the most populous and beautiful parts) stayed within India. The apostle of non-violence, Gandhi, had given his reluctant approval for troops to be used on this occasion. Gandhi held no official position in the Congress or the government. His influence, however, was phenomenal and Nehru consulted him on all major issues.

The most immediate problem confronting India continued to be communalism. As the new year of 1948 began it was estimated that there were almost half a million Hindu and Sikh refugees from Pakistan who had begun to settle in Delhi and its suburbs. They were bitter, angry, emotional and homeless, an easy target for the semi-fascist propaganda of the Hindu Mahsabha and the RSS (Rashtriya Svayam Sevak Sangh), two communalist groups that terrorised the Muslims of Delhi. The old imperial capital had a large Muslim population, many of whom were settled around Chandni Chowk (Moonlight Roundabout). It was from here that the Muslim Congress leader, Abul Kalam Azad, had appealed to Delhi's Muslims not to flee to Pakistan. He had spoken in chaste and simple Urdu, appealing to the traditions of old Delhi, reminding them of Akbar's reign, pleading with them not to leave their homes and telling them that *he*, Azad, would never leave Chandni Chowk for any so-called paradise.

As the RSS hoodlums began to organise pogroms to drive the Muslims away, Nehru exploded in anger at his Home Minister, who was supposed to be in charge of law and order. This was Vallabhai Patel, a traditionalist Hindu, susceptible to communalism, hostile to Nehru and a protegé of Gandhi. 'I will not tolerate Muslims being slaughtered as if they were animals,' Jawaharlal told Patel. The Home Minister replied that reports were exaggerated. Gandhi then stepped into the dispute. 'I don't live in China,' he said, reprimanding the man who owed him everything, 'but here in Delhi, and what's more I still have the use of my ears and eyes. If you are trying to persuade me not to believe my own eyes and ears, and to assure me that the Muslims have no cause for complaint, then obviously neither of us is going to convince the other.' In response Patel had remained silent.

On 12 January 1948, the seventy-eight-year-old leader announced that he was about to begin the sixteenth hunger strike of his life, this one directed against the violence in Delhi and, obliquely, the inefficiency of Patel. Nehru, Patel and Azad called on him to desist, but he refused to listen. Nehru was worried that the old man might die, since he was now at an age where regular sustenance was crucial. Patel said that his death would help nobody. When he stood up and indicated his desire to leave the room, Azad said that he should stay. Patel's self-control then disappeared: 'What use is it if I stay?' he said loudly. 'Gandhi won't listen to me. He seems to have decided to blacken the Hindus before the whole world. If that's his aim, then there's nothing for me to do here.' Angered by this crude display, Gandhi began his hunger strike on behalf of India's Muslims. For six days he ate nothing. As his condition deteriorated rapidly, India was stunned. Mass meetings were held in Delhi, where resolutions were passed accepting Gandhi's injunctions to cease all communal violence. On Sunday, leaders of the local religious communities met Gandhi and pledged to call a halt to the violence. Gandhi called off his fast and declared his intention of visiting Pakistan to pursue his call for peaceful co-existence. Two days later he was assassinated by a Hindu fanatic, a member of the RSS. While India waited for the assassin's name to be announced, the Muslims locked themselves in their houses. They were fearful that if the killer had been a lunatic Muslim, the ensuing bloodbath would be horrendous. Muslim India was saddened by Gandhi's tragic death, but it was relieved that the assassin was a member of the religious majority.

The death of Gandhi shocked India. Communalism subsided and the Home Minister was compelled to ban the RSS, though Patel's own role came under heavy fire. It fell to Nehru as Prime Minister to speak for India with tears in his eyes:

> The light has gone out of our lives and darkness reigns everywhere. I do not know what to tell you or how to say it. Our beloved leader, Bapu (father) as we called him, is no more. No more will we run to him for advice or seek solace from him, and that is a terrible blow, not to me alone, but to millions and millions in this land.
>
> The light has gone out, I said, and yet I was wrong, for the light that shone in this country was no ordinary light. The light that had illumined this country these many years will illumine it for many years to come, and a thousand years later that light will still be seen in this country and in the world.

In a very real sense, Nehru now felt alone. A number of close colleagues were still alive, Azad, Kidwai, Menon and others, men on whom he could rely, but there was no one left whom he regarded as superior, whose reprimands and advice he could accept. In later years, Indira, his daughter, was able to speak bluntly to him, but she lacked the authority of Gandhi and the experience of Azad. The Mountbattens, too, had left India, on 30

May 1948.

After the death of Gandhi, the only Indian known to the world was Nehru. His period as Prime Minister saw both events on the world stage, where he was to leave an indelible mark, and a series of domestic crises which signalled the beginning of the problems which still confront India. The Congress had been a movement, an umbrella uniting nationalists with differing views, who had agreed to set their differences aside until the British had been forced to leave India. Bose's followers had already split and formed the Forward Bloc, with a strong base in Bengal. Then Jayaprakash Narayan and other Congress Socialists left to found an independent socialist party. In West Bengal and what was soon to become the southernmost state of Kerala, many left-wing Congress members left and joined the Communist Party of India.

The CPI's position in 1947–8 was based on the slogan that the freedom obtained was a 'false freedom', that the Nehru government was a satellite of British imperialism and that communists must continue the struggle. The CPI leader, B. T. Ranadive (now an octogenarian theoretician of the CP(M)), had drafted theses advocating insurrection and armed struggle. They did so in some areas, like Telengana, Andhra, and West Bengal, but found themselves isolated and bereft of mass support. They remained underground and the Home Minister, Patel, did not permit his indulgence towards Hindu communalists to extend to India's communists. Large-scale arrests took place in the early years as many party activists were put behind bars. Once the CPI altered its position and decided to participate in the electoral process its members were released and restrictions on its activities removed. On occasion Nehru advised provincial Congress leaders not to treat the communists in too tough a fashion. They included in their ranks some of the most intelligent young people in the country and he did not want them to become permanently embittered.

Whereas Patel concentrated on the communists, Jawaharlal turned his fire on Hindu communalism. Gandhi's death had meant that the Mahsabhites and the RSS were on the defensive. Nehru was determined to give them no quarter. He declared that he regarded them as enemies of India and of himself; he would not rest till he had defeated them decisively. This battle occasionally reached into the heart of the Congress itself, as when Patel proposed an old Hindu communalist and bigot, P. D. Tandon, for the post of Congress president in 1948. Nehru supported the candidature of Kripalani, one of his own supporters. It was a close result and Tandon won by 1,306 votes to 1,092. Exactly a year later, Nehru, as Prime Minister, declared that he would not and could not serve on Tandon's Working Committee. His resignation forced Tandon to resign, thus weakening Patel's grip over the party machine.

In Parliament, Nehru was equally dominant, making use of every speech to educate his own party as well as the opposition. He supported a bill introduced by a private member which called for restricting parties whose membership excluded people on grounds of race, caste or religion. 'The alliance of religion and politics,' said India's Prime Minister, 'is a most dangerous alliance and it yields the most abnormal kind of illegitimate blood.' A couple of years later he repeated the message, after a Hindu communalist, S. P. Mookerji, had resigned in protest against Nehru's 'softness' towards Muslims. Once again he defended secular values:

> They put us in a position in which we have to say to people who are our fellow citizens, 'We must push you out, because you belong to a faith different from ours.' This is a proposition which, if it is followed, will mean the ruin of India and the annihilation of all that we stand for and have stood for. I repeat that we will resist such a proposition with all our strength, that we will fight it in houses, in fields and in market places. It will be fought in the council chambers and in the streets, for we shall not let India be slaughtered at the altar of bigotry.

There can be little doubt that it was Jawaharlal Nehru, more than any other political leader of the Congress, who fought for secular principles in post-independence India. His triumph was complete, or so he thought, when India adopted a new constitution and declared itself a republic on 26 January 1950. Its new constitution was the longest in the world, but more importantly it was totally secular in character. There was no state religion; there was a complete separation of state from religion; schools were to be run on secular principles; there were to be no taxes to support any religion. All citizens were equal before the law and anyone could hold the highest offices of state; religious liberties were guaranteed to individuals as well as associations. The preamble had a distinctly social-democratic flavour. It promised all its citizens: '*Justice*, social, economic and political; *liberty* of thought, expression, belief, faith and worship; *equality* of status and of opportunity . . .'

The Chinese Revolution was at this time less than a year old. Mao Zedong's armies had marched into Peking and proclaimed China a People's Republic in October 1949. China was not only the largest state in the world; it also shared a long border with India. There were many in Delhi, including some of Nehru's closest admirers, who looked longingly towards Peking. The Chinese Revolution had destroyed the old state, root and branch, and was constructing a new society. India had taken over the old colonial state and was attempting piecemeal reforms. The contrast was obvious. The preamble to the Indian Constitution had been written with the Chinese events in mind.

Domestic fronts

On the domestic front, the British had left behind a largely rural country. This was to remain one of the most serious indictments of imperialist rule in India. Even *The Times* had felt constrained to protest at the situation whereby Indian industry was deliberately being hampered. In an editorial on 12 September, 1882, the newspaper had commented:

> Government is such an extensive consumer . . . that if all its wants were supplied in the open market here, India's trade and industry would at least be fostered . . . But no. It would seem that one of the dearest privileges of the Secretary of State for India is to go shopping on behalf of his dependencies; the Viceroy dared not interfere with this.

During the First and Second World Wars, however, the British had permitted Indian industrialists to step up production and had lifted restrictions which prevented the growth of indigenous capital. India's fledgling entrepreneurs had grown by leaps and bounds. In 1927 they had set up the Federation of Indian Chambers of Commerce and Industry (FICCI) with members from different parts of the country and cutting across communal, caste and regional differences. Inside the FICCI were represented the shrewdest capitalists of the Third World. These men, and they were *all* men, were not, in their majority, weak-kneed agents of British capital, dependent on it for every crumb. They were independent in the sense that they had set up industries with their own capital. They resented the system of preferential tariffs imposed by the *raj* to aid British firms and prevent Indian capitalism from becoming too competitive. They saw themselves as 'national guardians of trade, commerce and industry' and in 1928 the FICCI President, Purshottamdas, declared bluntly: 'We can no longer separate our politics from our economics.' What did this mean? Purshottomdas amplified his position: 'Indian commerce and industry are intimately associated with and are, indeed, an integral part of the national movement — growing with its growth and strengthening with its strength.' The most farsighted and intelligent leader of FICCI, G. D. Birla, used his powers of persuasion to convince his fellow members that this was the only serious course for Indian capitalism. He stated that there was no way in which the British Government was going to discriminate against its own entrepreneurs and aid their Indian counterparts. Therefore, argued Birla, the only solution lay 'in every Indian businessman strengthening the hands of those who are fighting for the freedom of the country'.

From the 1930s onwards the Indian business community was solidly behind the Congress. They were extremely alarmed by Jawaharlal's socialist phase in 1933–6. A majority wanted to denounce him publicly and demand his removal from such a key position in the movement, but G. D. Birla convinced them that Gandhi would tame Jawaharlal. Moreover, he told them, as far back as 1936, that of all the Congress leaders only Jawaharlal was capable of leading India after independence. Birla's message was simple: Jawaharlal Nehru is the best leader we have. Patience was the virtue he preached to the FICCI faithful.

When Jawaharlal became Prime Minister he had already discussed the future economy of the country at length with J. R. D. Tata and G. D. Birla (the Indian equivalents of Ford and Rockefeller). Tata and Birla were in complete agreement with Nehru, as early as 1938, that economic planning was crucial in order to modernise the country. They agreed that the scale of investment required was beyond the capacities of the entire FICCI membership, and that the country needed a healthy dose of state capitalism to put the economy on its feet. There was no talk of 'socialism'. Jawaharlal had realised, in his sub-conscious if not explicitly, that when he agreed to the 1935 Act and the power-sharing exercise of 1937, the game was virtually over. India's political trajectory had determined its economic future, and it was by then impossible for Nehru to pursue 'scientific' or 'full-blooded' socialism and expropriate the 'kings of industry', even if he had been so inclined. A serious attempt on his part to do so would have led to his instant removal from the Congress leadership. Any revolt from below would have been dealt a severe blow by the recently acquired apparatus of the old colonial state. All sides were aware of these realities, although they were rarely discussed within the Congress.

We can perhaps conjecture that Jawaharlal still thought about the old days, especially when, as a member of the Delhi Gliding Club, he flew his glider high up towards the cooler currents in the atmosphere. He was flying, of course, with appliances, but what did he think of the panorama below? Was it ever going to change, or was the Indian peasant doomed to an eternity of suffering? Land reforms were promulgated, but even they did not fundamentally alter the countryside. Certain extra-economic powers exercised by landlords were restricted, the peasants were guaranteed certain rights to safeguard them against arbitrary evictions, rents were regulated, but none of this was enough to produce a new landscape. Land reforms had comprised a crucial section of Congress's political armoury prior to independence. It had declared that the land must belong to the tiller; rural debts should be written off for agricultural labourers and state-credit institutions generalised to replace the hated money-lenders. The aim was to wipe out all traces of landlordism and semi-feudalism. The reality had been different. Even though the measures had been promulgated, it had not been possible in most instances to implement them because the rural rich dominated the Congress machine at state levels. They resisted change. This did not mean that nothing had been done. Some of the large estates had been broken up, but the total impact of the reforms was much less than what had been planned. The Planning Commission had acknowledged as much in their draft outline for the Fourth Five-Year Plan:

> Substantial areas in some regions of the country are still cultivated through informal crop-sharing arrangements; there were ejections of tenants through the device of voluntary surrenders; the fair rent provisions were not enforced effectively in all cases; and the ceilings [on ownership of land – *author*] had been evaded through the well-known device of transfers and partitions and not much land was available for distribution to the landless.

In their classic study, *Land and Labour in India*, Alice and Daniel Thorner wrote: 'To put matters bluntly, the land reform legislation of India has been defectively conceived; bills with major loopholes have been presented to the legislatures, which in turn have seriously weakened the original bills by adding crippling amendments.' In effect the land reforms aided a particular stratum of rich peasants in the countryside. They were crucial intermediaries and extremely well represented in the Congress at regional and national level. They happily supported the curtailment of big landlords, but were opposed to cooperative farming, security of tenure for the poor peasants and even over-rigid limits on land ownership.

In the sphere of industry, too, the inequalities refused to disappear. New projects were undertaken, Congress leaders pledged that they were moving towards equality, albeit slowly, and Nehru himself began to speak increasingly of a 'socialist pattern of society'. When pressed he defined it as a 'middle path between orthodox practices of the communist and the capitalist countries' — an economy, in other words, that was neither fish nor fowl, but a hybrid. The men from the FICCI had no doubt as to the character of the economy: it was capitalism, aided by a strong public sector. For that reason they made sure that the coffers of the Congress were never empty. This is not to suggest that the state sector was subordinated to private capital: if anything, the large industrial houses were dependent on the goodwill of the state and its agencies. In 1951, Jawaharlal had given his active support to the Industries Act, which permitted the state to limit, regulate and control private industries. It established the Licensing Commission, making it compulsory for private entrepreneurs to obtain a licence before expanding an old industry or setting up a new one. In 1956, the Companies Act was passed, designed to curb monopolies. It was described by a foreign expert as 'one of the most detailed and stringent codes of business legislation to be found anywhere in the world'.

These new laws were designed to curb excesses. What happened, in reality, was that they increased the power of the civil servants, who had never in the past had the right to determine the life or death of a private firm. Not unnaturally this degree of power was open to underhand influences, and corruption reached astronomical levels even during Jawaharlal's lifetime. Monopolies could not be curtailed, and by 1961 an official Government commission revealed that 1.6 per cent of the country's companies owned 53 per cent of the total private capital, whereas 86 per cent of companies owned only 14.6 per cent of the capital. The Houses of Birla and Tata, veterans of the nationalist struggle, headed a list of twenty companies which dominated economic life in the country. Even within this twenty, the top four — Birla, Tata, Dalmia-Sahu and Martin Burn — controlled 25 per cent of all share capital and a major section of industry, trade, banking and the press. Professor Birman's study, 'Mysteries of the House of Birla', provided a detailed account of how the industrial giants operated in India. He stressed, in particular, corruption and bribery, fraudulent accounting, political and social liaisons, infiltration of religious charities, control of educational and cultural institutions, and so on.

Most of this was known to Jawaharlal. He realised that this was the price that had to be paid and concentrated his attention on what he believed were more pressing matters. In particular, he became obsessed with the question of national unity. The Congress had agreed long before independence that it would rearrange provincial boundaries along linguistic lines. This had been intended as a sop to the provinces and was designed to win nationwide support for the nationalist movement. After independence, Jawaharlal was extremely lukewarm, when not utterly hostile, to the idea. Within the Congress, however, even though Patel was very ill and soon to die, his followers were determined not to allow Jawaharlal to triumph on the question of linguistically determined provincial boundaries. His secularist offensive had been successful. On the 'language question' the old pledge must be redeemed. Rajendra Prasad announced an Inquiry Commission to study the demands from the provinces. From 1950 to 1956 there were demands for the establishment of provinces delineated by the Telugu, Malayalam, Marathi, Gujerati and Punjabi languages. The Bengali state of West Bengal already existed after partition. Gradually Nehru realised that the best way to prevent secessionism was to permit a certain degree of provincial and cultural autonomy. The new states of Andhra Pradesh (Telugu) and Kerala (Malayalam) were formed; Bombay was divided into two states, Maharashtra (Marathi) and Gujerat (Gujerati); and, after Nehru's death, the Punjab was divided into the Punjabi-speaking Punjab, peopled predominantly by Sikhs, and the supposedly Hindi-speaking Haryana, dominated by Hindus. This last was, in some ways, the most dubious of all the divisions and, as we shall see later, history's verdict would be unkind.

India was now paying the price of the educationally elitist policies of the British *raj*. For centuries, the country's diversity had not posed any challenge to the concept of one India. The ancient language of Sanskrit had united the Brahmin elites which, in effect, ruled the country. Sanskrit imagery and religious tales had found their way into even the remotest villages, and the non-Brahmins had accepted this cultural hegemony quietly. The Muslim invasions had ended the domination of Sanskrit, but without instituting a new all-Indian language. The courts spoke Persian, which was later transformed into a new hybrid language, Urdu, whose spoken version became known as Hindustani. With the British conquest and the contemporary European advance towards a new age of industry, science and technology, there was a real possibility of a total transformation of India, but, as we have already suggested, such a change would have threatened British power long before 1947. The result was that English became the language of the new elites, while in the provinces, regional languages experienced a certain resurgence. The reformers wanted more scientific knowledge, and Rabindranath Tagore, the Bengali winner of the Nobel Prize for Literature and a firm supporter of the need to learn English, bemoaned the fact that:

> We pass examinations, and shrivel up into clerks, lawyers and police inspectors, and we die young . . . Once upon a time we were in possession of such a thing as our own mind in India. It was living. It thought, it felt, it expressed itself. But it has been thrust aside, and we are made to tread the mill of passing examinations, not for learning anything, but for notifying that we are qualified for employment under organisations conducted in English. Our educated community is not a cultured community, but a community of qualified candidates.

There was, of course, a great deal of truth in Tagore's observation, but the fact remained that then, as now, the English language was the only medium in which a Tamil from Madras could converse with a Bengali from Calcutta, a Punjabi from Amritsar or a Malayalee from Trivandtum.* Nehru himself was a strong partisan of English as a modernising influence. In those days, Delhi schoolchildren used to recite, with more affection than malice, the following couplet:

---

* Satyajit Ray, the Indian film-maker, told an interviewer in July 1984 that he was thinking of making an English-language film consisting exclusively of Indians from different parts of the country and their attempts to communicate with each other.

A,B,C,D,E,F,G,
Ismeinsey nikalay Panditji
(Out of this came Panditji)

'This' was a reference to English education, and 'Panditji' was an honorary title acknowledging Nehru's high status as a Kashmiri Brahmin. Nehru did not prevent Indian universities from allowing students to take their exams in local languages, but he was not displeased when it was reported that in science and technology, the overwhelming majority expressed a preference for English.

Given that the situation in the countryside could hardly be described as a process of liberation for the peasantry, that in industry, Birla and Tata were decisive influences — and if one added to this the proximity and impact of the Chinese Revolution of 1949 — it was obvious that Congress would face its most serious challenge from the left. The only national challenge could have come from the Communist Party and it could have taken three possible directions: an attempt at insurrection or guerrilla warfare on the Chinese pattern; a combination of extra-parliamentary activities and participation in the electoral process, with the latter seen as a means of strengthening the former; and a clear-cut move towards electoralism. The first had been tried soon after independence, with the encouragement of Moscow, which saw everything in the context of the Cold War and believed that the Nehru Government was simply a creature of imperialism. This attempt had been defeated. The second option was rarely taken seriously; therefore, as India prepared for its first general elections under the new Constitution, India's Communist Party, again with nudging from Moscow, decided to participate in the electoral process.

The CPI had played a national role, but it had never become a national party. The reasons for this were rooted both in its formation and in its strategic and tactical mistakes in the colonial period. In the Hindi-speaking belt of Northern India, the party never struck deep roots. In Bombay it played a crucial part in helping to establish trades unions, but it never developed a corresponding political base. The three regions of the country where the CPI attracted a mass following were Andhra Pradesh, West Bengal and Kerala. There were a number of reasons for this, but the most pronounced lay in the tactics that had been adopted during the days of the *raj*. In all three regions, the local communists had worked within the framework of the Congress

Party and had been identified with the advances of nationalism. The Congress Socialist Party (the organised left within the Congress) had in these three places, at least, been virtually taken over and run by the communists. In Andhra and Kerala this had meant that it was the communists who had played a leading role in the nationalist movement. This prestige had enabled the local units of the CPI to get a head start over the rest of the country. In 1974, a veteran member of the CPI, K. Damodoran, confirmed to me during an interview that this was indeed the reason for the CPI's strength in his region, Kerala.

> While the CPI was in fact properly established in 1934–5 its development was uneven. For instance the first communist group in Kerala was organised only in 1937 by five comrades including Namboodiripad, Krishna Pillai and myself. We decided that we should not openly call ourselves the Communist Party but win ourselves a base inside the Congress Socialists. I think that we were correct, but this did not happen nationally. Accordingly we disseminated communist literature inside the Congress Socialist Party, which itself worked inside the Congress as an organised grouping. Our influence inside the Kerala Congress was not negligible: Namboodiripad, A. K. Gopalin, Krishna Pillai and, later, myself were all recognised leaders of the Kerala Congress and we held office on the leading committees. Utilising our positions in the Congress we organised trades unions, peasants' organisations, students unions, and associations of progressive and anti-imperialist writers. We organised a regular Communist Party in Kerala only at the end of 1939. It was our mass work coupled with the fact that we were identified with the nationalist aspirations of the people which undoubtedly played a significant role in ensuring that Kerala became one of the important strongholds of post-independence communism.

This is a far more convincing account of the CPI's regional strength in its strongholds of Andhra, Kerala and West Bengal than the arguments which explain virtually everything by the fact that particular leaders of the CPI belonged to particular castes. The question which arose was how the CPI would treat Nehru, and vice versa. The answer to this question could not simply be determined by the CPI. At that time hardly a single communist party in the world dared defy the instructions or known wishes of the Kremlin. In 1950 Moscow began to realise that India was not a country that could be characterised as a 'stooge of Western imperialism'. President Truman had realised this earlier, and treated India accordingly. The intensity of the Cold War in those days was such that Nehru's views on the world crisis were not easily comprehensible to either Washington or Moscow. Nonetheless the shift in Moscow's attitude affected the Indian Communist Party. It scaled down its extra-parliamentary activities in the countryside and the industrial regions and prepared itself to contest India's first general election.

Jawaharlal was not complacent on the electoral front. He knew that the communalist disease had afflicted members of his own Cabinet. One such, S. P. Mookerji, had resigned from the Cabinet and Congress and founded an openly communal party, the Bharatiya Jan Sangh. For Nehru these elections were an important test for his anti-communalist stance. Would secularism prevail or would Indian democracy collapse into chaos? The elections to the Lok Sabha (House of the People) and the state legislatures took place from October 1951 to May 1952. It was a unique experiment. With a total of 173,213,635 voters, India was the largest liberal democracy in the world. Congress was, not surprisingly, the largest political party in the country. It could, however, hardly be accused of suppressing pluralism. A total of 59 parties presented 17,000 candidates to contest almost 4000 seats in the national and provincial assemblies. The scale of the process was truly continental. The ban imposed on the RSS and the Hindu Mahasabha following Gandhi's assassination had been lifted in September 1949. It could not even be argued that Hindu communalism was being denied its freedom.

Jawaharlal threw himself into the campaign heart and soul. He was in his element when addressing public gatherings.

The relief at moving out of the South Block office was visible to everyone. This was also an opportunity to tour the country, meet old veterans of the movement, denounce communalism, explain why he thought the communists had no real solutions and listen to endless complaints. He was told of a number of instances of intercaste violence in the villages, where the upper-castes had murdered low-caste Hindus who had won elections to the local council. These were cases of Hindus killing Hindus. How he cursed the caste system! Gandhi had denounced the absurd practices of the system and its taboos, but never challenged the caste division as a whole. Nehru frequently did, arguing that it was a distorted, degenerate reflection of Hinduism's prehistory. Why should modern Indians observe prejudices which were over two thousand years old and whose causes were still a matter of dispute amongst historians? Time and time again he would shake his head in despair. The task was formidable. When friends pointed out that maybe the Chinese had the right idea as to how old customs could be rooted out, he would become reflective and then remark that India had chosen a different path and it was too late to think about the Chinese road.

The results were a gigantic triumph for the Congress. It won 364 out of 499 seats in Parliament and a majority in 22 out of 26 states (as they then were) and in the remaining four it was the largest party in the Assembly. The extreme right-wing Jan Sangh had won only three seats in Parliament and 35 in the provinces. This made the Communist Party the main opposition. It had won 16 seats in the centre and 106 in the states, though the majority of its votes had come from the south. Nehru felt vindicated: his policies had been given an extraordinary vote of confidence, and members of his party as well as the Congress High Command were under no illusions as to the influence of his personal appeal in obtaining this victory. Four years after independence, he had come to be regarded as indispensable. His enhanced prestige in the country meant that, from now on, he would increasingly get his own way on issues big and small inside Congress.

Foreign policy

Now that Nehru had obtained this confirmation of his popularity at home, he turned his attention to the crisis abroad. India's freedom had coincided with the irretrievable breakdown of the wartime alliance between the USA, USSR and Britain. Europe had been divided into power-blocs. Eastern Europe was undergoing a process of Stalinisation; Western Europe was under the domination of the United States. The use of nuclear weapons against Japan had been intended by the West as a show of strength to its one-time ally, Russia, and as a warning. The Japanese people had suffered and died for no fault of their own. The Chinese Revolution had occurred, changing the map of Asia and altering the relationship of forces on a global scale. Washington was outraged and the Cold War became a real war in Korea, where the West confronted the East. Imperialism now confronted the Chinese Revolution: Peking saw Western intervention in Korea as an undisguised attempt to quarantine its social upheaval. When the North Korean regime tottered in the face of a Western offensive, Peking sent in its army and drove back the troops of the Anglo-American alliance. The situation reached stalemate as Truman prevented General MacArthur from crossing the Yalu river, the frontier between Korea and China. Jawaharlal refused to back the West, but neighbouring Pakistan simultaneously moved towards the pro-American camp. Nehru did not believe that the Chinese Revolution could be reversed. If it had to be combatted, then the only way that could be done was to follow a progressive social and foreign policy.

In 1949, Nehru was invited to visit the United States. His sister, Mrs Pandit, was India's Ambassador in Washington at the time and he wrote to her:

> I think often, whenever I have the time to think, of this coming American visit. In what mood shall I approach America? How should I address people, etc? How should I deal with the government there and businessmen and others? Which facet of myself should I put before the American public — the Indian or the European, for after all I have that European or English aspect also? I shall have to meet some difficult situations. I want to be friendly with the Americans but always making it clear what we stand for. I want to make no commitments which come in the way of our basic policy. I am inclined to think that the best preparation for America is not to prepare and to trust to my native wit and the mood of the moment, the general approach being friendly and receptive.

In reality, Nehru had decided that he was not going to be cajoled by the Americans. He was friendly but firm in the United States, making it clear to his hosts that India's policy would be one of non-alignment. He told his hosts that they were wrong about China and that their re-armament programmes would hinder, not help, world peace; on his return he immediately pushed through India's formal recognition of the new China. Britain followed suit a month later. In retaliation the Americans wooed Pakistan and here they found a willing playmate, whom they armed and integrated in 1954 into their system of regional alliances.

In addition to his job as Prime Minister, Jawaharlal Nehru was also his country's Foreign Minister and Chairman of the Planning Commission. From 1951–4 he was also President of the Congress. Despite the fact that all his time was now taken up with the affairs of state, Jawaharlal found time to play with his grandchildren and supervise his niece's marriage. His daughter, Indira, was his official hostess, helping him in the arduous task of entertaining diplomats and travelling abroad. In addition to this, the Indian Prime Minister insisted on interviewing the top entrants to the Foreign Service and questioning them at length. These questions, in reality, formed an important part of the new civil servant's education. Simultaneously he corresponded every fortnight with the Congress Chief Ministers in the provinces in order to brief them on various issues of national, international or provincial importance.

This was a demanding schedule for any person. For a man who was now sixty, it must have been exhausting. His normal pattern of work took him from 7 a.m. till 2 a.m. the next day, with intervals for meals and yoga. During the summer months he rested for a short time in the afternoon. The only Cabinet minister with the authority to challenge Nehru's concept of the Prime Ministership was his old right-wing sparring partner, Vallabhai Patel. He declared that he disagreed with Nehru's view of the Prime Minister as someone with 'full freedom to act when and how he chooses'. Patel accused Nehru of behaving like a 'dictator' and insisted that the Cabinet's supremacy should be defended. During Gandhi's lifetime, Nehru had complained bitterly of Patel's ceaseless harassment and the old man had ruled that they should work together, but that if they were unable to do so Patel should leave quietly. Gandhi's assassination had led to a temporary truce, but Patel was constantly intriguing within the party organisation. His death on 15 December 1950 removed the last thorn from Nehru's flesh. He was now in total command of party and government.

His complete immersion in the affairs of state did not make him feel completely self-sufficient. He was often lonely, and at those times he thought more about Edwina Mountbatten than any other person. Her laughter and jokes had enlivened many an occasion. He used to recall her story about when she and her Lord had visited the Tsar in Russia. Mountbatten was a member of the English royal family and thus invited to many royal family gatherings, since Europe's pre-war rulers were close relations. The Tsar had invited his English cousins for some grand celebration in St Petersburg. The men of the party were provided with white chargers to take part in the parade. The organisers discovered that they were short of a horse and hurriedly obtained one from the circus. As the Tsar was acknowledging the march-past, he saw an English prince falling on his behind in front of the saluting base —

he had not been warned that the circus horse was trained to lift its right leg on hearing the national anthem! Nehru remembered, too, her last official banquet in Delhi, when it had fallen on him as India's Prime Minister to make the official farewell speech. After thanking her husband, he had turned to look at her and smiling, oblivious to everyone and everything else, he had made a lyrical farewell:

> The gods or some good fairy gave you beauty and high intelligence, and grace and charm and vitality — great gifts — and she who possesses them is a great lady wherever she goes. But unto those that have even more shall be given and they gave you something that was even rarer than those gifts — the human touch, the love of humanity, the urge to serve those who suffer and who are in distress. And this amazing mixture of qualities results in a radiant personality and in the healer's touch.
>
> Wherever you have gone you have brought solace, and you have brought hope and encouragement. Is it surprising, therefore, that the people of India should love you and look up to you as one of themselves, and should grieve that you are going? Hundreds of thousands . . . will be sorrowful at the news that you have gone.

The people of India had probably never loved Edwina, or certainly not as much as their leader did, and his sorrow at her departure must have exceeded that of anyone else. They still met regularly, or at least as often as circumstances permitted. Whenever Nehru visited Britain, which was once a year till 1956, he stayed at the Mountbatten country home, Broadlands, and called on Edwina often at her home in London's Wilton Crescent. A neighbour at the time, Jean Gowan, recalls that 'there was a lightness in his step and happiness was written all over his face. There were no two ways about it. They were in love. Oh yes! They were definitely in love.'

When Nehru could not be in Britain, Edwina used to turn up in Delhi. One of her visits coincided with that of the sculptor, Jacob Epstein, who was there to do a bust of Nehru. Edwina sat through the sessions observing the subject. When Nehru was called away on business, as he invariably was, she would turn to Epstein and ask: 'Do you not think that he is the most remarkable looking and beautiful man you have ever sculpted?' Epstein hated being questioned or talked to while at work and did not respond warmly. This became evident when he had finished the sculpture!

When Edwina died, in February 1960, Jawaharlal was heartbroken. His close friends recalled a sadness that was to stay with him till his own death. No one else could provide him with the intellectual and emotional satisfaction that he needed just like any other human being. His politics, his high standing in the three worlds of Asia, Africa and Latin America, was gratifying, but could never become, nor did he ever want it to, a substitute for Edwina.

In the great world outside the turbulence never seemed to subside, but Jawaharlal had carved a place for himself. His refusal to toe the American line in the Korean war enraged Harry Truman, but in Moscow and Peking there was genuine bewilderment. How could this happen? they asked each other. Was not India a thoroughly bourgeois country? Were not India's capitalists solidly behind Nehru? If even the British Labour Government was forced by economic realities to kow-tow to the Americans, how had Nehru managed to escape the net? Could non-alignment then be something real? These questions were not confined to the two capitals of world communism. They were whispered in other parts of Asia and Africa, where burgeoning nationalist movements were beginning to challenge colonialism. They were also discussed in Belgrade, where Josip Broz Tito had broken away from the tutelage of Stalin and was searching desperately for a half-way point where he could escape both the pressures of Moscow and the bribes of Washington. Without being fully aware of it himself, Jawaharlal fathered a new trend in world politics. With the overthrow of the decadent Egyptian monarchy in 1952, the Middle East witnessed the advent of Gamal Abdel Nasser, who was in a few years time to tell the 'British imperialists to choke in their rage' and nationalise the Suez Canal. In Tito and Nasser, Nehru was to discover two leaders who would remain lifelong political allies.

Nehru was, in some ways, the strongest of the three. This was not simply a question of his personality, but a reflection of the place that India occupied in the world. It was the second largest country in the world after China, but it would not, despite its social and economic system, be bound over to the West. There were two basic reasons for this independence. The first was that India was creating the economic infrastructure of a sizeable public sector; furthermore, the indigenous industrialists were firmly rooted in Indian realities, despite their links with the world market. What India possessed was a national bourgeoisie, in the real sense of the word. Messrs Tata, Birla and Dalmia did not want India's economy to be dominated by the United States or Britain. They knew, from previous experiences in the colonial era, what that had meant and they valued their independence. Thus when Nehru stated that India's foreign policy was in no way contradictory to its economic policy, he was simply stating the obvious. The second reason was geo-political. Even if India's independence of the West irked Washington, there was very little that could be done about it. The geographical distance was far too great, and India's sheer physical size was an undeniable factor. Interference in the affairs of continental giants such as Brazil and Argentina could not be repeated in India. At the same time it would have been counter-productive of the West to have imposed an economic blockade and not even John Foster Dulles, the hardline US Secretary of State in the Eisenhower period, was to recommend such a drastic course.

Nehru's foreign policy prospered. He followed India's official recognition of China by an invitation to Chou en Lai to visit India in 1954. The French occupiers of Vietnam had in that year suffered a crushing blow in the North Vietnamese town of Dienbienphu. The Indian press had highlighted the victory and Nehru had not concealed his pleasure at the French defeat. The Vietnamese could easily have followed through this victory and marched southwards, taking Hue and Saigon on the way, but they were prevented from doing so by their 'elder brothers', Moscow and Peking, who put pressure on them to attend a conference in Geneva in 1954 with France, Britain, China, the USSR and North Vietnam, with the USA present as observers. It was here that John Foster Dulles literally turned his back on Chou en Lai, when the latter had extended his hand to the American. The insult was noticed and commented upon throughout the world. Jawaharlal Nehru, to whom these gestures meant a lot, was furious with Dulles, and this influenced the decision to invite Chou to visit Delhi.

An Indian aircraft was despatched to Geneva to fetch the Chinese Prime Minister and his entourage, who arrived in Delhi on 25 June 1954. The weather was extremely hot, but that did not inhibit the crowds — people wanted to see a Chinese revolutionary. Like Nehru, the Chinese leader came from an upper-class background. He had spent his early life in France and was the only senior Chinese communist who had a cosmopolitan outlook. Mao had left China for the first time in 1949, and then only in order to sign an economic agreement with Stalin in Moscow. Chou had been trained in a very different school. He had seen his closest comrades massacred in cold blood; he had himself spent a large amount of time operating in the underground, when capture by Chiang Kai Shek's men would have meant instant death: these experiences had given him a ruthless edge. André Malraux's novel, *Man's Fate*, set in the Shanghai of 1927, has a central character who is based on Chou en Lai; he and Malraux, then a leftist, had met and become close friends at the time. Despite his ruthlessness Chou en Lai possessed considerable charm, which made him a diplomat's idol.

In India in 1954, he embraced and kissed Nehru, who responded equally warmly. 'The friendship of 960 million people,' declared Chou in public, having added up the populations of the two countries, 'constitutes a mighty force for peace in Asia and the world.' Nehru heartily concurred with these sentiments and the crowds which met Chou everywhere chanted '*Chini-Hindi bhai bhai*' ('Chinese and Indians are brothers'). Both leaders agreed to five basic principles of peaceful co-existence, known in India as *Panch Shila*: 1. mutual respect for each other's territorial integrity and sovereignty; 2. mutual non-aggression; 3. mutual non-interference in each other's internal affairs; 4. equality and mutual benefit; 5. peaceful co-existence.

In October of the same year, Nehru visited China and received an extremely warm reception. He met Chou, and together they discussed the Sino-Indian border, for Nehru had noticed that some Indian territory was marked on Chinese maps as being in China. Chou en Lai said that the maps pre-dated 1949 and had not been renewed after the Revolution.

Nehru also met, for the first time, Mao Zedong, the legendary guerrilla chieftain and tactician who had led the Long March of 1935 and reorganised the Party and Army before the great victory of 1949, as well as some of the other great military leaders who had liberated this vast country: Chu Teh, Ho Lung, and a younger man called Lin Piao. Jawaharlal was impressed and said so publicly, while making it clear that India, too, was determined to obliterate poverty and suffering — but in its own way. In a few years time Chou en Lai was to say that Nehru was the most arrogant man he had ever met, but on this occasion he never allowed a hint of this feeling to surface. Chou proclaimed the ancient trade and cultural links between the two countries, which stretched back over a thousand years; at a final press conference on 26 October, 1954, both sides declared that they agreed on most international questions, despite basic differences in approach.

Nehru's meeting with Mao was an eye-opener. The Chinese revolutionary, smoking non-stop, casually told Nehru that he (Mao) would never be intimidated by the United States or nuclear blackmail — even if a few million Chinese perished in the first attacks, there would still be enough left to finish off the Americans! Nehru was also taken aback by Mao's obsession with the old emperors of China. He told Nehru of Chin Shih Huang, the founder of the Chin dynasty in 22 BC, and commented at length on his virtues. But he burnt books, Nehru recalled. It may have been necessary for creating an 'ideological unity' at the time, Mao replied. Nehru, who hated blind glorifications of India's past and the use which the religious fanatics made of it, was shocked by these remarks, and he later told his colleagues in India that he detected a very strong and slightly unhealthy nationalist fervour in Mao, which was totally absent in Chou.

On his return to Delhi, Nehru began to work towards realising an old dream: a conference of newly-freed nations to discuss their futures. After intensive discussions and correspondence, the Indonesian city of Bandung was agreed as the venue for an unprecedented gathering of Asian and African heads of state and government. On 15 February 1955, Nehru flew to Cairo for a meeting with Nasser. There was complete accord between the two leaders. In April, the North Vietnamese leader, Pham van Dong, visited Delhi and agreed on the *Panch Shila* principles. On Delhi radio he broadcast to the Indian people, thanking them for their support in his country's long struggle for freedom. Later in the same month, Nehru and Nasser travelled in the same plane to Bandung. There was a small shadow hanging over the summit, a reminder that certain 'big' powers were displeased. An Indian aircraft, *Kashmir Princess*, was flying from Hong Kong to Jakarta, ferrying delegates from China and Vietnam to Bandung. The plane blew up *en route* and crashed into the sea; three crew members were the only survivors. Their account was clear: there had been two explosions in the baggage compartment. An investigation confirmed sabotage. The intelligence agents responsible were traced to Taiwan, but Washington refused to support Indian demands for extradition. The Bandung Conference, despite the use of Pakistan as a Trojan horse of the Pentagon, was a limited success, and the final document contained the five principles of peaceful co-existence. Nehru returned to Delhi completely exhausted, but pleased with the outcome. It was at Bandung that the non-aligned movement was born. The United States responded by stressing the key importance of SEATO —the South-East Asia Treaty Organisation — a defence umbrella which included Pakistan and Thailand together with Britain, France, New Zealand and Australia.

Nehru's next major visit abroad took him to the USSR. Moscow prepared for the visit by publishing a Russian-language edition of *The Discovery of India* with a special preface by Nehru, and marked his arrival in the capital by issuing the first volume of the collected works of Rabindranath Tagore. Jawaharlal spent most of the two-week trip seeing the country. He visited the Central Asian Republics and admired the architecture of Samarkand, a city well known to Babar, the first Mogul Emperor of India, whose forebears had ruled from here. He saw factories and museums. In Leningrad he insisted on a visit to the Hermitage and spent some time admiring the old masters, especially Leonardo da Vinci and Rembrandt.

His schedule was heavy. His entourage was exhausted, but Jawaharlal's schoolboy enthusiasms provided the drive. He wanted to see it all. On the political front, the visit was a great success. The new leaders of the country, and Khruschev in particular, made a positive impression on Nehru, and he saw for himself the post-Stalin thaw that was beginning to take effect in different spheres of life and activity. The long period of Indo-Soviet economic collaboration started during this visit and it soon escalated at a pace that surprised many people in India.

When Jawaharlal passed the age of sixty, he began to think of retirement. From 1954 to 1958, he raised the possibility in public four times. On every occasion there was a furore both within the Congress and in the media. Cynics began to say that the only reason he raised the issue was to be reassured that he was as indispensable and as much loved as ever. There may have been an element of truth in this, but there is little doubt that even though Jawaharlal was firm in his belief that only he could govern India satisfactorily, there was another side of him which wanted peace and rest in his last years. He was beginning to get tired. He felt extremely stale. 'Stale' was a word he used frequently. He was very attached to both his grandsons and he took a keen interest in horticulture, in addition to being an animal-lover. The Prime Minister's residence in Delhi was almost a private zoo. Lion and tiger cubs which he had been given as presents spent their formative years there, closely observed by Nehru, before being despatched to various zoos. And then, of course, there was Edwina. He undoubtedly felt that he didn't see enough of her and that as a private citizen he would have more time for leisure — after her death he never mentioned retirement in public, despite the fact that he was ill. Sometimes he would get fed up with the perennial question posed by the Indian press, 'After Nehru, Who?' On one occasion he said that if he resigned he, too, would find out the answer to 'that question'.

Indira was now beginning to play a greater role in the Congress Party than before. In 1959 she was elected President of the Congress, but there is no evidence that Nehru was responsible for her elevation. In fact he was a bit surprised. His enemies claimed that the reason he was refusing to name a successor was because he was grooming Indira for the job, but this was a calumny. The only occasion on which the question of Indira and the Government was raised was when some Congress leaders told him that she deserved a post in the Cabinet. 'Not while I am Prime Minister,' Nehru replied with some indignation. In fact, for a long time he would insist on paying her fare when she accompanied him on a visit to a foreign country. Caesar's daughter could not be above the law.

It was Jawaharlal who led the Congress when the second general election took place, from 25 February to 14 March 1957. Congress won a larger share of the popular vote — 46.5 per cent —from an electorate which had increased from 173 million to 193 million. Congress obtained 365 out of 500 seats in the Indian Parliament and held every state but one. This latter was Kerala, where the results created news throughout the world. The Communist Party had won the state and E. M. S. Namboodiripad became Chief Minister.

Nehru tried to dismiss the victory as a 'fluke' due to the bankruptcy and corruption of the local Congress administration. In fact it was the first sign that there was a growing discontent with Congress at the grassroots level. The CPI press exaggerated the victory by slogans such as 'After Nehru, Namboodiripad!', but there was no doubt that this victory made the CPI a national force. It had increased its strength in the national Parliament from 16 to 29 members and obtained just under 10 per cent of the votes cast, thus doubling their support since the previous election. Namboodiripad was drawing giant audiences throughout the country. The new Kerala government embarked on a series of reforms in the countryside and in education, but above all the CPI victory enthused the poor, who expected a lot. Poor workers were heard telling policemen on the streets: 'Now you daren't attack us because *our* government is in power. Namboodiripad is *our* leader. We are ruling.' However, most of the reforms were obstructed by the Civil Service under orders from the central government. The Congress was split on the subject. Nehru favoured a soft approach, but Indira favoured an open confrontation. The Chief Secretary was receiving orders directly from Delhi and the instruction was to keep a high profile. Meanwhile, Roman Catholic priests (Kerala has a relatively large Catholic minority) started public agitation against the plan to disestablish the schools and make all education secular. They were soon joined by Hindu communalists and gradually this issue united all opponents of the CPI. When the Namboodiripad government could not prevent the police from shooting at workers on strike in Quilon and actually defended the decision, their own supporters began to get disillusioned.

Jawaharlal visited Kerala for discussions with the CPI leaders. The first question he asked his opponents was characteristic: 'How did you manage to so wonderfully isolate yourself from the people in such a short space of time?' He then proposed that the Government should continue in office, pending a state election to renew its mandate. This was intended as a compromise. The other option was dismissed – an unhealthy precedent was about to be established. The Kerala unit of the CPI rejected this suggestion and, on Namboodiripad's insistence, demanded elections in every province including Kerala. Although the principle was correct, the CPI had made a tactical error. If they had agreed to the election, they would have been able, as the government of the day, to neutralise the use of the civil servants and the police against the CPI. Their refusal led to the arbitrary dismissal of the government by Presidential decree in 1959. The pretext was that there was a breakdown of law and order. The Congress President herself came to supervise its overthrow. It was Indira Gandhi. She stayed on to cement an electoral alliance between Congress and the local Muslim League in order to defeat the communists. Communalism was thus utilised officially by the Congress leaders. The CPI increased its popularity but narrowly lost the election. An unprincipled coalition then took office, setting the stage for the future of Indian politics.

In the international field, Nehru was most concerned with the Anglo-French-Israeli invasion of Egypt. He backed Nasser to the hilt and played an active role in mobilising world opinion against Britain's Sir Anthony Eden and the French socialist Premier, Guy Mollet. This was an interesting example of politics taking precedence over religion. The 'Muslim' State of Pakistan backed the West against its 'co-religionist' Egypt. India backed Nasser. Many children born that year of 1956 in Egypt were named after Nehru, a measure of the impact he had made on that beleaguered nation.

He was now at the peak of his popularity as a world statesman, respected in East and West. The lessening of the Cold War meant that liberal America could also begin to appreciate Nehru and now he began to be compared to Roosevelt (Franklin not Theodore) in sections of the American press. Washington's decision to distance itself from the Anglo-French adventure in Egypt also helped to enhance Jawaharlal's stature. He had been interested in world politics since his youth, and the world had moved a long way from the Japanese sea-victories against Tsarist Russia. Wars, revolutions, the end of empires, winds blowing change in different continents, had all transformed the world and Jawaharlal could pride himself in his expert knowledge of what was taking place in its most obscure corners. He was, therefore, particularly traumatised by the blow that was about to fall: war with China.

More books, monographs and articles have been written about the Sino-Indian dispute and war than on virtually any other aspect of Indian or Chinese foreign policy. There is a mountain of material containing everything about the dispute: descriptions of the Tibeto-Indian frontier; the character of the Indian town of Kalimpong (which the Chinese claimed was a CIA centre of operations); a detailed anthropological account of the Ladakh region, where the dispute centred, and a lot else besides. This vast literature is a cartographer's delight, for maps and borders and histories of old demarcation disputes colour the whole dispute — but how relevant is all this to what actually took place?

In 1959 there was a brief skirmish on the Sino-Indian border near Hotsprings in Ladakh, in which nine Indian policemen died. The USSR issued a rapid rebuke to unnamed parties pointing out that a conflict between an ally (China) and a friend (India) was both undesirable and unacceptable. A Sino-Indian correspondence commenced with both sides stating their case regarding the permanence of the McMahon Line (as the border was called, after the British official responsible for its demarcation). China claimed that territory which was on the Indian side of the Line was, in reality, Chinese territory. The main dispute concerned 16,000 square miles of uninhabited land in the north-eastern section of Ladakh, which was known as Aksai Chin, Lingzi Tang and Soda Plains. The area was devoid of vegetation and would in any case have been impossible to inhabit. The dispute generated a lot of heat on both sides: *Peking Review* published vituperative attacks on Nehru, the Indian press responded in kind. *Time* magazine commented sardonically that *India-China bhai-bhai* should now be altered to 'India-China bye-bye'! Chou en Lai and Chen Yi paid a last visit to Delhi in 1960, but the talks with Nehru and others were a failure. Both sides became more belligerent and Nehru warned China not to try and occupy Indian territory by force. On his return from China in 1954, Nehru had reported to his Cabinet that India need have no fear of Chinese communism, and that the threat, if any, might come from Chinese nationalism. He now appeared to have been proved right, but another interpretation of events is possible.

In 1960, two leaders of the CPI were in Hanoi as delegates to the Conference of the Vietnamese Communist Party. The Chinese delegation invited them to return to China for a lengthy discussion on the Sino-Indian border dispute, and they readily agreed. A special plane arrived and flew them from Hanoi to Peking, via Canton. In the Chinese capital they were immediately received by Chou en Lai. The room was full of maps, old and new, border treaties past and present and intricate details concerning both. One of the two India communists, K. Damodaran, described what took place:

> I said to the Chinese comrades: 'Legally, geographically, historically you may be correct. The question which concerns me is what political purpose does this dispute over uninhabited territory serve? You have come to an agreement with Pakistan and you have given up some land. Why not do the same with India? It will prevent the reactionaries from whipping up anti-Chinese chauvinism and it will strengthen the left movement in India. We will be able to demonstrate the superiority of the method by which socialist states settle border disputes. We could utilise this to strengthen the bond between the Chinese Revolution and

the Indian masses.' I explained that this had been Lenin's attitude when dealing with bourgeois governments such as Finland or even pre-capitalist monarchies such as Afghanistan. By doing so Lenin strengthened the Russian Revolution and its appeal to the broad masses. Immediately Chou said, 'Lenin did the correct thing.' But he explained it in terms of the Soviet state's isolation and the non-existence of a 'socialist camp'. I responded by arguing that while I did not have the texts on me there was considerable evidence to show that Lenin's motives were in reality to develop friendly relations with the peoples of these countries and not to allow the ruling classes to paint the Soviet Union as a big power gobbling up their countries. Finally Chou said that he could not agree and that we should agree to disagree on this point. I had an extremely soft spot for the Chinese comrades and their Revolution so I didn't want to leave matters there. I asked Chou: 'Is there any danger of the US imperialists attacking you through these disputed border territories?' He replied in the negative and said the threat was from the Nehru government and not from the Americans in this instance.

Chou en Lai was, alas, not being truthful. It is true that the Western powers attempted to use the Chinese take-over of Tibet as a pretext to weaken the Mao regime. It is also very likely that there were many CIA operatives based on the Indian side of the border. But India never threatened China militarily. The real reason for the Sino-Indian conflict related largely to the Sino-Soviet dispute. The Peking-Moscow war of words had begun in 1957, and by 1961–2 it had turned into a major schism. The Sino-Indian border conflict can therefore be seen as a side-show designed to demonstrate to Russia and the world that China was totally self-sufficient and independent. It was not *pure* nationalism, but a *sui generis* variety intended to damage Soviet strategy in the Third World, peaceful co-existence, and other aspects of Soviet policy. Mao was, in effect, acting upon an old principle which he had developed during his many years in the countryside and expressed as follows: 'Comrades, you should always bear your own responsibilities. If you've got to shit, shit! If you've got to fart, fart! Don't hold things down in your bowels, and you'll feel easier.' This line was clearly applied during the Sino-Indian conflict. If it had been unbridled nationalism, the Chinese would never have agreed to give up territory to Pakistan, then under the military dictatorship of General Ayub Khan. No, the Great Helmsman, casually described by a French president as the 'beacon of human thinking', was simply teaching the Russians a few lessons. The battles over Aksai Chin and Soda Springs were resumed with greater ferocity at the Ussuri River, the border between the USSR and China.

In 1962, some months prior to the actual conflict, Nehru had fought and won the third general election for the Congress Party. During the campaign his stance towards the Chinese had become somewhat bellicose. It was later argued that the Chinese acted to pre-empt an Indian forward trust. This was a false assessment. As late as 1962, the Indian General Thimmaya told a seminar in Delhi: 'As a soldier I cannot even envisage India taking on China in an open conflict on its own. It must be left to the politicians and the diplomats to ensure our security.' It was not a foolish point. The Sino-Indian border is 2,600 miles long.

Skirmishes began in September 1962. On 20 October the Chinese made an all-out attack on Indian positions and within a few days they had overrun the area. The Indian army retreated and large numbers of soldiers surrendered to the Chinese. The evacuation of Assam was considered, but rejected. On 21 November, the Chinese called a unilateral ceasefire and asked both sides to retreat behind a borderline which existed between the two countries on 7 November 1959. This meant in one sector the Chinese withdrawing fifteen miles north of the McMahon Line. The war was over. Its only purpose had been to humiliate the Indian government, force it closer to the United States and demonstrate to the Russians and the Third World the real nature of so-called non-alignment. Chou en Lai, in a bid to compete with Mao's earthiness, told visiting Pakistani army officers that China had never had any intention of occupying Indian territory. 'Why,' he is reported to have said, 'if we wanted to conquer India all we would need to do is march half our population to the top of the Himalayas, and, with their backs turned to their own country, they would all piss at the same time. The result would be floods in India for at least a year.' This story, often retold in Pakistan, may or may not be apocryphal, but it confirms the view that the conflict was essentially intended to do no more than display China's strength.

In India itself, Jawaharlal was initially extremely depressed, but soon recovered, though he had to sacrifice his Defence Minister, Krishna Menon, who had, in reality, not made any serious mistake. Nehru's mind wandered to Algeria, where the population was trying to drive out the French. 'A popular liberation struggle against colonialism,' he remarked, 'is the best possible tonic.'

He was now seventy-four years old. He had suffered a kidney disease in 1962 which had left him with a tiny stoop. In January 1964, while attending a Congress session in Bhubaneswar, he suffered a serious stroke. He kept with him a few lines from Robert Frost which he would take out and read at odd moments:

> The woods are lovely, dark and deep
> But I have promises to keep,
> And miles to go before I sleep,
> And miles to go before I sleep.

He had once described his father, when Motilal was ill and dying, as a 'mortally wounded lion'. Jawaharlal was now himself in that position. In these few remaining months he often thought of India, its people, its future, and of what his role had been. He often remarked to his sisters or to Indira that he was happiest when attacked by the right for being 'soft on socialism and communism' and by the left for being 'an agent of capitalism and reaction'. That, he would say, makes me feel I'm on the right course. In his inimitable romantic fashion, he left in his will a tribute to the Indian people, who had given him more trust and affection than he could ever have repaid. He also left strict instructions that he was not to be given a religious funeral. The old lion might have compromised with Indian capitalism, but he remained a firm atheist to the end, regarding religious communalism as a cancer that needed to be erased from India.

The end, when it came on 26 May 1964, was quick. Nehru went into a coma and died soon afterwards. Contrary to his instructions, his daughter overrode his will and organised a religious funeral.

In a lengthy and moving obituary, the one which would have pleased Jawaharlal the most, Bertrand Russell had made an insightful comment which summed up his views of a man he had greatly admired:

> Looking back I agree with those who say Nehru made a mistake in not dividing the Congress Party into its socialist and non-socialist components by retaining the Congress as his political vehicle. After the struggle for independence had been won, Nehru was hampered by the power of the right-wing, which increasingly came to dominate the Congress Party. This domination was only held in check by his own leadership and command over the population of India. The price, however, of having to reconcile the powerful economic forces which the Congress comprised with his hopes for democratic socialism, was

the emasculation of the latter programme. India has a slow growth rate and remains stricken with poverty and disease. Nehru's own efforts to alter this would have succeeded more had his party been forthrightly socialist with an opposition in Parliament representing the very forces which now dominate the Congress.

A caretaker Prime Minister was appointed by the President, a Mr G. Nanda. Some weeks later, the Congress Parliamentary Party met and elected Lal Bahadur Shastri as the Leader of the Congress Party and India's new Prime Minister.

EPILOGUE

Wrote Bertolt Brecht, the great German poet and playwright, from his American exile during the late 1930s and 1940s:

If the indispensable man frowns
Two empires quake.
If the indispensable man dies
The world looks around like a mother without milk for her child.
If the indispensable man were to come back a week after his death
In the entire country there wouldn't be a job for him as a hall-porter.

But what if the indispensable man has left behind him an equally indispensable daughter?

MOTHER INDIRA
Indira Gandhi, *née* Nehru
1917–84

1
Mother and daughter
1917–47

On 19 November 1917, twenty months after her marriage to Jawaharlal, the eighteen-year-old Kamala Nehru gave birth to a daughter. She was anxious to have her first child at home with her own parents in Delhi: custom demanded this, but there was an additional reason. She did not get on well with the Nehru women and felt that her own mother's presence would make the pains of childbirth, physical and psychological, a far more relaxed and bearable event. But Motilal would not hear of her departure. His first grandchild had to be born in Anand Bhavan. He was also genuinely fond of Kamala and she succumbed to his affectionate pressure.

On 19 November a Scottish doctor delivered a healthy baby with the words, 'It's a bonnie lassie!' Jawaharlal was delighted. Mother and child were both doing well. Swaruprani, however, could not conceal her displeasure. 'It should have been a boy,' she said without a smile on her face. Motilal leapt to the new-born child's defence. He turned angrily on his wife and said, in a loud voice: 'Have we made any distinction between our son and daughters in their upbringing? Do you not love them equally? This daughter of Jawahar, for all you know, may prove better than a thousand sons.' The tale may be apocryphal, but it was part of the Nehru family folklore well before Indira became a prominent person in her own right. A tiny question mark hangs over Motilal's own attitude. As Indira grew up her grandfather indulged her in thousands of ways, but at the time of her birth he may not have been totally satisfied. Could it be that secretly Motilal, too, had hoped for a grandson to continue the line? If this was ever the case, the old man, to his credit, never allowed it to show. The young granddaughter became an absolute favourite. Indira herself later recalled that during her early years she admired her grandfather much more than her father – one reason being that

Jawaharlal was hardly ever at home.

The house in which Indira grew up was the same one in which her father had spent his early life and where her two aunts, Vijaylakshmi and Krishna, had been born and nurtured. Yet in some ways it was very different. Her aunts remembered a home full of British and European influences. Their English governess, Cecilia Hooper, had lived there since 1906, leaving in the year of Indira's birth to go home and get married. The aunts still talked of the day when Motilal had been invited to attend the *durbar* or a public audience with the representative of the King-Emperor George V in Delhi in 1911. He ordered his clothes from London and insisted that Jawaharlal ensure that nothing went wrong. The young Nehru wrote from Cambridge to reassure Motilal that everything was under control:

> I suppose you want the ordinary levee dress with sword and everything complete. The shoes for the court dress will be made at Knighton's and the gloves at Travelette's . . . the hats I am sending ought to fit you. Heath's man has managed to fish out your old measures and cast, and he will shape your hats accordingly.

The photograph of Motilal which was taken on the occasion is a tribute to the skills of English tailoring.

Akbar of Allahabad (1846–1921), a reputable Urdu and Persian poet and wit, commented thus on the Indians who had dressed up to attend the Durbar:

> 'Tis they who've called the guests,
> 'Tis they who serve the drink;
> They're masters of the show,
> I only stand and blink.

The partition of Bengal, and later Gandhi, had changed all that. The house was now one where a symbolic bonfire of foreign clothes had been carried out. Western clothes had been abandoned and the white, home-spun *khadi* had replaced the tweeds, silks and brocades imported from abroad. Kamala felt a lot happier in the new atmosphere, at least in an aesthetic sense. She was never truly happy in Anand Bhavan. Indira's early years were spent in close proximity to her mother, towards whom she became extremely protective from a very young age. 'We were very close to each other,' she remembered many years later. 'I loved her deeply and when I thought she was being wronged I fought for her and quarrelled with other people.'

Vijaylakshmi, the eldest aunt, was particularly nasty to the new sister-in-law. She mocked Kamala's unfamiliarity with the Western style of Motilal's household; teased her maliciously because of her unsophisticated ways and constantly told tales about the young woman's 'blunders' to all and sundry. Kamala felt the torment much more because her husband rarely defended her against her detractors. If Jawaharlal, instead of listening to the inane prattling of Vijaylakshmi, had made it clear that he was not interested in her prejudiced gossip, Kamala would have been a lot happier. That was, in reality, the root of the problem. Jawaharlal never adjusted to his marriage, and relations were often fraught. Both husband and wife had sharp tempers. Both sulked a great deal and there were often days when they did not speak to each other. The only person apart from Indira, then still very young, who defended Kamala and talked to her a great deal was Motilal Nehru. Growing up in this atmosphere, where her mother was constantly unhappy, could not have been reassuring for young Indira. She grew up feeling insecure, not because she was unloved – the entire household, including her younger aunt and her grandmother, spoilt her considerably – but because of the lack of love between her parents. To Jawaharlal's surprise and pleasure, however, Kamala became a political ally long before Motilal. Indira explained her role in the Nehru household with some pride:

> Many people know the part which was played by my father and my grandfather. But in my opinion, a more important part was played by my mother. When my father wanted to join Gandhiji and to change the whole way of life, to change our luxurious living, to give up his legal practice, the whole family was against it. It was only my mother's courageous and persistent support and encouragement which enabled him to take the big step which made such a big difference not only to our family but to the history of modern India.

It would be false to imply that too much had changed in the lifestyle at Anand Bhavan. European clothes had been easily discarded, but Motilal was an ostentatious man who enjoyed his comforts. He was prepared to make a few token gestures, but was quite incapable of curbing his spending habits. In later years when both the Nehrus, father and son, were regularly arrested and fined, they would refuse, in accordance with Congress rules, to pay any fines to a British court whose very legality they questioned. On these occasions, the police would be sent to Anand Bhavan to sequestrate valuables in lieu of the fine. Indira, then five years old, hated this invasion and would shout and scream at the policemen. On one occasion she 'almost succeeded in chopping off an officer's thumb with a bread-slicing gadget'. In a BBC interview in 1971, she explained the constraints of that period:

> As a child, when the freedom struggle was on, the house was being constantly raided by police, our goods and chattels being confiscated, we were being arrested and having to hide contraband literature and I was all part of it. Yes, I was part of the processions and the meetings and it was an extremely insecure childhood. One did not know from day to day who would be alive, who would be in the house and what would happen next.

In the first phases of the nationalist movement, it was the men who were carried away to prison. With her father and grandfather both away, Indira became even closer to Kamala. There were now six women in the house, including Indira. The formidable Swaruprani often indulged Indira, but was cool and even hurtful to Kamala. She felt that Kamala was not good enough for her son and, in a way, she made her daughter-in-law the scapegoat for the trivial domestic problems which afflicted every such household. Swaruprani's constant companion was her own widowed sister. Together they shared each other's confidences and talked freely about 'family problems'; both were deeply religious and ate food cooked in a specially 'clean' kitchen, untainted by the meat which was a necessary part of every meal at Motilal's table. Then there were the two aunts. Krishna was fond of Indira and tolerant of her mother, but Vijaylakshmi treated Kamala with contempt and had no time for Indira, whom she regarded as a weak and ungainly child. In later years Indira would 'return the compliment'. She never forgot the treatment meted out to her mother by her aunt.

Kamala, lonely and miserable, retreated into religion. Indira was taught to appreciate Hinduism by her mother. She heard endless tales from the old Hindu classics, stories of wars, loves, adventures, which made an undoubted impact on her and left a permanent mark on her consciousness. Kamala, who had only received lessons in English after her engagement to Jawaharlal, ensured that her daughter was not simply interested in religion, but was also fluent in Hindi and felt at home in India, unlike her aunts who had been brought up in a completely English style. Perhaps Kamala felt that this was the best way of showing her resentment to Jawaharlal. In any event, the experience was important and, in later life, very useful to Indira. At the same time Kamala talked to her daughter about men and how they ran women's lives and had caused so much unhappiness. The only way women could challenge this was by being independent. Kamala was certainly bitter about her own experience, but she did attempt to generalise it and her daughter always valued the advice. She proudly confessed many years later that having seen her mother's unhappiness had made her determined never to be dependent on any man in the same fashion.

While Indira was growing up, the nationalist movement, too, was maturing. The house was full of politicians of one variety or another. As the movement gathered steam she felt neglected as it claimed first her father, then her grandfather and finally her mother and grandmother. By the time politics and prison had claimed her and her aunt, she was already deeply committed to the cause of nationalism.

Her formal education was episodic. From prison Jawaharlal wrote to Motilal:

> Kamala writes to say that Indu is becoming more and more intractable and pays no heed to any kind of study. I wish some arrangement could be made for her lessons. I am confident that I could have managed her easily but I am in barrack number four so some other arrangement must be thought of. I do not suppose that she will acquire much knowledge just yet but she must begin to acquire the habit of doing lessons. The longer this is delayed, the more difficult it will be for her and others. As it is she is past the age when she should have begun seriously.

In many ways Indira was experiencing a childhood very similar to that of her father. Kamala had not been able to provide more brothers and sisters; there had been two miscarriages. The problem of Indira's education was also compounded by the boycott strategy of the Congress. All government schools had to be shunned. Indira was sent to the Modern School at Allahabad, but Motilal decided that although it was a nationalist institution, it was simply not good enough for his granddaughter. He withdrew her from the school and despatched her to a private one, St Cecilia's, run by the three Cameron sisters. Jawaharlal insisted that St Cecilia's was part of the boycott. Motilal disagreed. Jawaharlal then complained to Gandhi, who wrote a letter to Motilal backing the son. Motilal exploded. He claimed that what Jawaharlal had told Gandhi 'was a tissue of lies from beginning to end', 'absolutely false' and that 'I was solely prompted by the desire to give Indira companionship of children of her own age'. Nonsense, replied Jawaharlal. It was pure snobbery and he, the girl's father, would not tolerate Indira being brought up by the three Camerons and becoming 'a little Miss Muffet'. Finally both sides compromised. The young girl was withdrawn from St Cecilia's, but she did not return to the Modern School; instead, private tutors were hired so that she could be educated at home.

By now Kamala had become involved in Congress politics and was regularly attending meetings and participating in processions. This was the happiest phase of her life. She felt free, independent and totally committed to a cause. All the petty squabbles and insults at Anand Bhavan seemed trivial by comparison. Unfortunately she became very ill at this time. Indira was eight years old, deeply attached to her mother, and now extremely concerned at the state of her health. The local doctors had diagnosed tuberculosis, in those days a much-feared infection and killer. The doctors advised a trip to Europe for further consultations and treatment. Motilal insisted that there was no other solution.

In March 1926, Indira accompanied her parents to Europe. The treatment took a year and a half to complete and Indira enrolled in a new school, the International School in Geneva, which was housed in a Swiss chalet and had a lovely view of the mountains. Indira was now with both her parents. Even though Kamala was ill, she was improving rapidly and the three of them were alone for the first time in Indira's nine years. Her father took her to school and brought her back. She described this time as one of the happiest in her whole life. She learnt French, music and skiing, and tried her hardest to live up to the school motto, which was simple and to the point: 'Do Your Best'.

When they returned to Allahabad in December 1927, Indira was sent to St Mary's Convent School, but a man was engaged to teach her Hindi at home. After a three-year stint with the nuns, she was sent to an experimental school at Poona but she was not happy there. Her grandfather was dead. Her mother was in a remote sanatorium, her father was in and out of prison, even her aunt had been arrested. Life seemed unbearable. Bereft of her relations and without any close friends, she often wept at night. The loneliness seemed intolerable. She was overjoyed when Nehru was released in 1933 and came to see her at school. She went home with him and both parents wondered where to send her next. Their choice was Santiniketan, an academy run by the philosopher-poet Tagore, who was an admirer of Jawaharlal. Both Jawaharlal and Kamala had visited Tagore and found his academy 'a breath of fresh air'. At Santiniketan, for the first time since Switzerland, Indira felt at peace with the world. The sweet sound of Bengali, the semi-idyllic tranquillity and the presence of Tagore were all enjoyable experiences. Tagore was then seventy-three and with his white locks and beard he appeared an awesome figure. Indira was reproached by the great man for avoiding his company, so she and her friends would sit at his feet, 'talk of diverse subjects, watch him paint. Often he would recite or read aloud'. She no longer felt lonely and these times became 'moments of supreme joy, memories to cherish'.

On his way to leave Indira at Santiniketan, Jawaharlal made a series of militant speeches in the Bengali capital of Calcutta. He was punished for this by another prison sentence. The charge this time had been sedition. Meanwhile, Kamala's condition had deteriorated once again and to Indira it seemed that her happiness was always to be circumscribed by worry. She thought a lot of her mother at this time, even more than before. The thought had occurred to her that Kamala did not have long to live. In May 1935 the doctors again suggested that Kamala should be taken to Europe immediately. Jawaharlal was still in prison and the authorities refused to release him unless he made a pledge not to intervene in politics, but his wife was adamant that he should not give any such undertaking, and Indira, now 17 years old, was asked to leave Santiniketan and take her mother abroad. She did so without question. Tagore wrote to Nehru:

> It is with a heavy heart we bade farewell to Indira, for she was such an asset in our place. I have watched her very closely and felt admiration for the way you have brought her up. Her teachers, all in one voice, praise her and I know she is extremely popular with the students. I only hope things will turn for the better and she will soon return here and get back to her studies.

This hope was not to be fulfilled.

Kamala died in Lausanne in February 1936. Jawaharlal was at her side, having been unconditionally let free some months previously. When Kamala died, Indira felt desolate. Her relationship with her mother had been very close. With Jawaharlal she could soar above mountains, but with her mother she had, in many ways, a more real bond. Mother and daughter had supported each other at difficult moments – Kamala had depended on Indira's love and affection in those unhappy early years at Anand Bhavan, and Indira had needed her mother's attention when Jawaharlal was inhaling the dust of India's numerous villages on political tours or writing his books in prison.

Kamala Nehru died at the age of thirty-six. Indira's epitaph came some decades later: 'I saw her being hurt and I was determined not to be hurt.' At the time, however, daughter and father consoled each other as Kamala was cremated in Lausanne. But Jawaharlal had to hurry back to India: the movement had little time for personal tragedies. In his absence, he had been elected President of the Congress, and there was no time to stay with Indira for even a short period.

Meanwhile, he decided that it would be far better for her to stay in Britain and go to school and university. The question of studying in the United States was considered, but the choice was left to Indira. She opted for Britain. She had no desire to be in a country where she had no friends at all. In Britain, a young student from Allahabad, Feroze Gandhi, was studying at the London School of Economics. Feroze had been a great admirer of Kamala Nehru, who had inspired him by her Congress activities to join the nationalist movement. He had been in and out of Anand Bhavan, ready to do whatever work was needed for Kamala, and he had visited her regularly in Europe when she lay dying. Kamala liked the young man. It was obvious that he had fallen in love with her Indu, and Kamala strongly approved, despite the fact that Feroze was not a Hindu, but a *parsi*. The *parsis* were believers in the ancient cult of Zoroaster, worshippers of fire. They had fled from Persia over a thousand years ago to escape persecution from Islam. A few hundred had landed in India, where they were promised a sanctuary. They remained a tiny but cohesive sect, largely as a result of marrying within their own community. Jawaharlal was not particularly keen on the young man, though not for religious or political reasons. He had no real reason for his disapproval, except a father's natural caution and over-protectiveness towards his daughter's first suitor.

Indira first went to boarding school in Bristol, after her father had returned to India. The place he had selected for her, after consultations with English friends, was Badminton School. This was a progressive institution, whose headmistress, Miss Beatrice

Baker, was a quaker, a socialist and a great supporter of the League of Nations. A fellow student of Indira's was the novelist Iris Murdoch.

She recalled that:

> It was a very left-wing school. Its academic courses were excellent, but it also generated an idealism amongst all of us. We all thought that we must fight for social justice. It was socialism of a sort, but a very liberal variety of socialism.

Iris Murdoch remembered Indira's arrival at the school:

> She was extraordinarily beautiful, but looked very frail. At times it was almost as if she would be carried away by the wind. She was a very dignified and aloof girl, but it was obvious to all of us that she was very unhappy and couldn't wait to get back to her country. She didn't like the school very much, and who can blame her. For a young girl brought up in India, it must have been awful to be confined to an English girls' boarding school, however progressive. She wasn't the only one in that situation. There were lots of other children of many nationalities and a number of Jewish refugee children. We knew that Indira had just lost her mother and that her father was being permanently locked up by the British in India. As a result everyone looked after her and even spoilt her, but it didn't work. She wanted to go back. We were later together at Somerville, but she didn't stay there long either...

Indira was far happier at Somerville College, Oxford, than at most of her schools. She loved the city of Oxford and concentrated on studying history and anthropology. For a time she was a member of the Labour Party. On one occasion she was asked by Krishna Menon, also a Labour Party activist, to come and read a message from Jawaharlal at a public meeting. When she arrived, she was told that she would be expected to say a few words on her own behalf. The thought terrified her and she confessed in a BBC interview much later: 'I just could not get anything out at all. And there was a drunk in the audience, at least I hope he was drunk, and he remarked, "She does not speak, she squeaks." Naturally the audience were in fits of laughter and that was the end of the speech.' Oxford was enjoyable, but she still longed for India. She wanted to participate in the movement, but equally important was the fact that Jawaharlal was now a widower. She felt that she should be at her father's side. Jawaharlal disagreed. He was now more concerned than ever that Indira should not lead a nomadic existence.

Jawaharlal saw himself as responsible for his only child's

education and he set about it in an unprecedented fashion. He spent most of his early years in prison writing letters to her about the history of the world, letters which were an incredible education for a young girl. They numbered two hundred in all and Nehru later described them as 'a rambling account of history for young people' when they were published as a book, *Glimpses of World History*, and read by many Indians of all ages. The aim was largely educational. But there was another reason for the letters to his daughter. He realised that he was, through no fault of his own, spending too much time away from her in prison. Through these letters he confessed to her, 'you shall silently come near me and then we shall talk of many things'.

Indira's attitude to her own education was somewhat cavalier. The constant moves from one place to another had, with the exception of Geneva and Santiniketan, made her feel that it was a waste of time. She genuinely believed that she had learned more about the real world from her father's letters than at Somerville College, Oxford. There was some justification for this view.

The principal of Somerville College was worried by Indira's constitution and advised Jawaharlal in a letter that he should not allow her to spend the winter in England. In the autumn of 1939 she caught a serious chill, which soon became pleurisy. An Indian doctor friend saw her, helped her recover and despatched her to Switzerland. After breathing the air in the Alps she returned through a now war-torn Europe to London, where the bombing raids had already begun. The news from India was that the Congress was refusing to collaborate with the war and was preparing itself for the last push towards independence. She decided to abandon Oxford and, linking up with the persistent Feroze, caught a slow boat to Bombay via the Cape of Good Hope. She arrived back in India in March 1941. Jawaharlal had allowed her to make her own choice. He felt that she was returning because of him and that she might regret the decision in the years to come. Nonetheless he did not interfere. There was another decision which had to be taken soon — that of her marriage. On this question Jawaharlal would interfere, but only for a short time. Here too the decision would be her own.

Her friendship with Feroze Gandhi had grown in Britain. He was a face from home. He had known and worshipped Kamala; he supported the more militant section of Congress. And he was in love with her. How did all this fit in with her ideas about herself?

At Anand Bhavan when she was eight years old, her grandfather had overheard her in conversation with her younger aunt. Krishna had observed her in the veranda, her arm stretched high above her head declaiming something which was inaudible. When Krishna asked what she was doing, Indira explained that she was pretending to be Joan of Arc, whom she admired greatly. Motilal laughed and then reported the incident to Jawaharlal, who was in prison. A few years later he reminded her of this childhood fantasy in the first of his two hundred letters from prison:

> Do you remember how fascinated you were when you first read the story of Joan of Arc and how your ambition was to be something like her. . . ? Often we may be in doubt as to what to do. . . One little test I shall ask you to apply whenever you are in doubt. . . Never do anything in secret or anything that you would wish to hide. For the desire to hide anything means that you are afraid, and fear is a bad thing and unworthy of you. . .

Indira Nehru was about to put these principles to the test. The adversary, in this instance, was her father. She had got on very well with Feroze in London, but he wondered whether the affection would remain once they were in India. Until she was nineteen she rejected the idea of marriage. It did not appeal to her. It could have been the Joan of Arc fantasy; it could have been memories of her mother's unhappiness; possibly a combination of the two. But Feroze persisted. She finally agreed and pledged that she would marry him regardless of what her father or anyone else said or thought. Four decades later she described her feelings at the time:

> One reason for choosing Oxford was that Feroze was in England. I considered him more as a friend; it was a link with the family and India . . . I had met Feroze in Allahabad when he joined the movement . . . He had proposed to me already before I went to Santiniketan, but I had said no. He told my mother about this. Because I had not spoken to my parents, I was very upset that he should have. . .
>
> I had gone first to Paris and Feroze joined me there. That's when I finally said yes, on the steps of the Montmartre. But we didn't tell anyone.

Feroze wondered whether, once in India, Indira would become a Gandhi or remain a Nehru. Indira herself confided to friends, 'I don't like Feroze, but I love him.' It was an interesting remark and probably true. There was a certain class difference between them. She came from a wealthy urban background; he was from a petit-bourgeois family. His sister, Tehmina, was personal assistant to a schools inspectress. Feroze never attempted to hide his origins, nor was he ashamed of them, although his aggressiveness when the question sometimes arose indicated a resentment which was understandable. Kamala had liked his openness, his self-confidence and his sense of fun. Indira herself was very different in temperament from her husband-to-be. Her childhood experiences had created in her a certain reserve which never disappeared; a self-protective mechanism had made her a natural introvert. She also shared some of her father's patrician aloofness. She was a Nehru, and nobody was allowed to forget the fact.

Both Indira's aunts had married outside the narrow circle of Kashmiri Brahmins, and two of her cousins were subsequently to marry Muslims and one a Hungarian Jew, without any disapproval from the family. Why then were the Nehru aunts so taken aback by Indira's choice? Their objections were not based on Feroze's religious background as a *parsi*. They were offended by the fact that he came from a lower social class than themselves — it was snobbery at its worst. If Feroze had been from the Tata family (who were *parsi* millionaires) there would have been no problem as far as Vijaylakshmi and Krishna were concerned. Interestingly enough, Indira's maternal grandmother expressed no objections. Her attitude was simple: since neither Feroze nor Indira regarded religion as paramount, Feroze's non-Hinduism did not matter.

But what about Indira's father? Where did he stand on the matter? Jawaharlal was an atheist, with a strong streak of paganism, and religion meant nothing to him except countless horrors. When his younger sister, Krishna, had married a non-Brahmin, some eyebrows had been raised, but Jawaharlal had defended her vigorously in a letter to Gandhi:

> I would welcome as wide a breach of custom as possible. The Kashmiri community — there are exceptions, of course, in it — disgusts me. It is the very epitome of petit-bourgeois vices, which I detest. I am not particularly interested in a person being a Brahmin or a non-Brahmin or anything else. As a matter of fact, I fail to *see the relevance of all this; one marries an individual*, not a community.

Yet Jawaharlal did object to his daughter's marriage to Feroze, although his feelings were not articulated as crudely as the shock-horror response of his sisters. He had thought a great deal about the matter. He remembered how he had been compelled by Motilal and Swaruprani into an early marriage. True, this time it was Indira who was insisting, but was she completely sure of herself? He argued, as fathers often do, that Indira should meet other men. After all, she had only just returned from a long stay abroad, where loneliness had driven her and Feroze together. She might discover someone she preferred. When this attempt to divert his daughter failed, Nehru reminded her gently that the difference in backgrounds (a code-word for class) between her and Feroze might lead to real problems. She was accustomed to a comfortable life. Could he, in other words, keep her happy? Indira was indignant. She replied that her mind was made up, that shortage of money simply did not matter as their politics were similar and would help sustain them in difficult times and that she was not going to tolerate any more nonsense!

Her father's last request on this matter was that she discuss the affair with Gandhi. She did so, but the old fox, seeing how determined she was, did not attempt to dissuade her. He merely asked to see Feroze, who shared a surname with him. Having looked the young man over and obtained from him an assurance that he would not marry Indira against her father's will, Gandhi dismissed the couple. When both remained adamant, Jawaharlal had no choice but to capitulate and give his approval.

Feroze and Indira wanted the wedding to be a quiet and private affair. The press, however, leaked the news a month before the wedding. Orthodox Brahmins raised a furore. How could a Nehru girl be permitted to marry a fire-worshipper? It was an insult to Hinduism and should be stopped. This would encourage 'permissiveness' and laxity on the part of other Hindus. Nehru was admonished to set a proper example to the nation. He did, in the shape of a press statement outlining his view of the matter:

> A marriage is a personal and domestic matter, affecting chiefly the two parties concerned and partly their families. Yet I recognise that in view of my association with public affairs, I should take my many friends and colleagues and the public generally into my confidence.
>
> I have long held the view that though parents may and should advise in the matter, the choice and ultimate decision must be with the two parties concerned. The decision, if arrived at after mature deliberation, must be given effect to, and it is no business of parents or others to come in the way. When I was assured that Indira and Feroze wanted to marry one another I accepted willingly their decision and I told them that it had my blessing.
>
> Mahatama Gandhi, whose opinion I value not only in public affairs but in private matters also, gave his blessings to the proposal.

The opposition was far from satisfied. Gandhi had to take up the cudgels himself in response to a series of abusive letters that he had received in connection with this marriage. He replied to his correspondents publicly:

> His (Feroze's) only crime in their estimation is that he happens to be a *parsi*. I have been, and am still, a strong opponent of either party changing religion for the sake of marriage... In the present case there is no question of change of religion. The public knows my connection with the Nehrus. I also had talks with both the parties. It would have been cruelty to refuse consent to their engagement. As time advances such unions are bound to multiply with benefit to the society. At present we have not even reached the stage of mutual toleration. . . . I invite the writer of abusive letters to shed your wrath and bless the forthcoming marriage. Their letters betray ignorance, intolerance and prejudice — a species of untouchability, dangerous because not easily to be so classified.

There was a distinctly bizarre flavour to all these events. India's two most important political leaders had been compelled, at a politically critical moment, to expend part of their energy on justifying the decision of two people to marry each other. It was a sign of a much deeper malaise, though few recognised it as such at the time, but Jawaharlal's worst fears were confirmed. Religious prejudices still took precedence, in the minds of most Indians, over any other consideration. Moral exhortations alone, even from such respected preachers as Gandhi and Nehru, could not act as an effective antidote to the depth of such prejudice. India would soon learn these bitter lessons in some of the most violent episodes in her recent history.

No such thoughts were permitted to mar the wedding day. It was 26 March 1942, almost exactly a year since Feroze and Indira had returned from London. Anand Bhavan was decorated modestly and the guest list was limited. Whereas Motilal would have invited half of Allahabad, his son, always more austere, did not encourage ostentation. Indira did not want a public event, but Mahatma Gandhi insisted that it should be a celebration. Otherwise, he said, it would be thought that the Nehrus were ashamed of the whole affair and were bowing to pressure from those who were prejudiced against the marriage. That argument had convinced Indira. The guest list consisted of both families and their friends, local nationalist leaders and two foreigners: Sir Stafford Cripps, who was in India on a mission, and Eve Curie, the daughter of the

French scientist, Marie Curie. The ceremony passed off quietly, though an absent-minded Indira said to Sir Stafford during dinner: 'Do have some potato Cripps.' Interestingly enough, both Indira and Feroze had refused a ceremony which was totally non-religious. A set of semi-orthodox Vedic rites, supposely valid for mixed marriages, were used on this occasion. Indira's aunt, Krishna Hutheesing, left in her memoirs this sentimental description of her niece on the wedding day:

> Frail and almost ethereal, she laughed and talked to those around her, but sometimes her big black eyes would darken and hold a distant and sorrowful look. What dark cloud could mar the joy of this happy day? Was it due to a longing for the young mother who was no more, by whose absence a void had been created which even on this day remained unfulfilled? Or was it the thought of parting from the father, a father whose very life she had been. She was leaving him now to a life that would be lonelier for him than it had ever been before. Maybe it was the breaking of all the old ties and the starting of a new life which brought a passing look of sadness to the young bride's eyes, for who could foretell what the future held in store for her — happiness? sorrow? fulfilment? disillusionment?

Feroze and Indira left soon after the event for their honeymoon. The choice of Kashmir was hardly a surprise. Throughout her childhood Indira had heard of this magical valley from Swaruprani, Motilal, Kamala and her aunts. Her father had described it to her in words similar to those he wrote in the *Unity of India* in 1941:

> The loveliness of the land enthralled me and cast an enchantment all about me. I wandered about like one possessed and drunk with beauty, and the intoxication of it filled my mind. Like some supremely beautiful woman, whose beauty is almost impersonal and above human desire, such was Kashmir in all its feminine beauty of river and valley and lake and graceful trees. And then another aspect of this magic beauty would come to view, a masculine one, of hard mountains and precipices, and snow-capped peaks and glaciers, and cruel and fierce torrents rushing down to the valleys below.

Kashmir was extraordinarily beautiful at this time of the year. A carpet of daisies covered the valley, and cherry and almond blossom provided a guard of honour as the couple drove to Srinigar. Jawaharlal had abandoned Kamala during his honeymoon in Kashmir and fled to the mountains with a friend, but Feroze and Indira stayed together. They walked a lot, did some sightseeing and made love. They were a happy couple, but in the revivifying climate of Kashmir, Indira thought often of her father, trapped in the heat of the plains. They exchanged telegrams. Indira to Jawaharlal: WISH WE COULD SEND YOU SOME COOL BREEZE FROM HERE. 'Here' was the idyllic hill-resort of Gulmarg. Jawaharlal to Indira: THANKS. BUT YOU HAVE NO MANGOES. Indira's addiction to mangoes was well-known to all the Nehrus and she was always choosy as to which variety she ate. Alphonsos were her favourite. Some days later, Jawaharlal, obviously thinking of his daughter's happiness, sent another cable: DO NOT HURRY BACK. LIVE IN BEAUTY WHILE YOU MAY.

They could not, however, live in beauty indefinitely. The 'Quit India' movement was about to be launched. In London Feroze had become very close to Indian communists and worked with them against fascism and unemployment. Now in August 1942 he saw that the CPI, because of Hitler's attack on the USSR, had done a complete about-turn and declared the war to be a 'people's war'. They had virtually become recruiting sergeants for the British Indian Army. The defence of the Soviet Union had become more important than the freedom of India. Feroze and Indira agreed whole-heartedly with Nehru's analysis of the situation. Free India would fight against fascism alongside Britain and the USSR; unfree India would fight against the British. In this way, Feroze broke with his CPI friends and did not overcome his personal bitterness for a long time. He was not the only one. Similar breakups were taking place all over India.

By the end of November 1942, the British authorities had imprisoned over 100,000 nationalists. These included Indira, Feroze, Vijaylakshmi and, of course, Jawaharlal, who was kept in the safety of Chand Bibi's old fortress in Ahmadnagar. Indira did not find prison life easy. Conditions were not unbearable, but nor were they comfortable. She and her aunt were in the same room, which made life less stressful. This was the only time that Indira and Vijaylakshmi Pandit ever got on with each other. They giggled together at a plump wardress, Zainab, who always 'waddled like a duck'. They made friends with other prisoners. They became angry when told that a gift of mangoes from Jawaharlal to Indira had been consumed by the prison authorities.

Indira spent nine months in prison. She was released early because of her ill-health; Feroze was released after a year. They had bought a house of their own, but the pull of Anand Bhavan

Mother and Son: Jawaharlal and his mother, Swaruprani.

Early Years: Jawaharlal, Kamala and their daughter, Indira.

above right: Jawaharlal and grandson, Rajiv.

The man who came to dinner: Winston and Clementine Churchill with an old sparring partner.

The Brothers Gandhi: posing for posterity at a time when Sanjay was seen as the Crown Prince.

Odd Person Out: An opportunist election placard appropriates Mahatma Gandhi (no relation) for the dynasty.

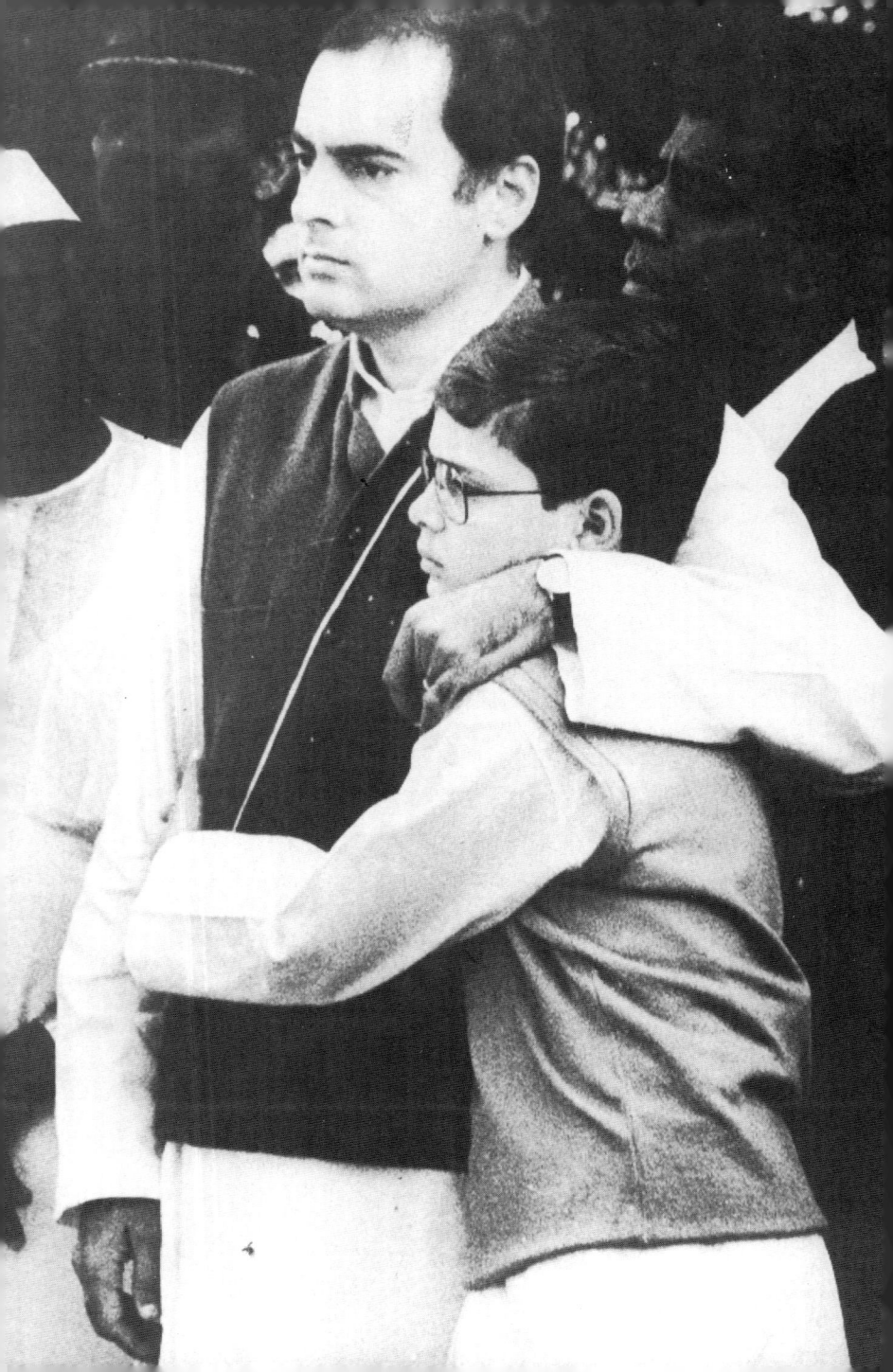

Days of Hope: Rajiv acknowledges the cheers of the crowd after his sensational electoral triumph in December 1984.

above right: Sonia voting in the 1991 General Elections while Rajiv looks on. A day later he was dead.

left: Father and Son: Rajiv and Rahul comfort each other, the day after Indira Gandhi's assassination.

Sonia, Rahul and Priyanka at Rajiv's funeral.

Indira's grand-daughter: Priyanka Gandhi.

was too great for Indira, and Feroze agreed that they should move there, especially as it was lying empty while Nehru was in prison. The aunts had married and the servants were the only other occupants. Feroze was a happy-go-lucky man. He did not bother about trivial matters such as living accommodation and if Indira was intent on Anand Bhavan he saw no reason to stand in her way. Later he would regret his failure to build their own life separately from Jawaharlal, but at the time the movement was everything. Personal matters took a secondary place. Both Indira and Feroze worried a great deal about Jawaharlal. Ever since Kamala had become involved in politics and 'come out', so to speak, she and Nehru had been close friends. Her companionship had become important. Without her he felt miserable in prison. He constantly thought of what prison life was doing to friendships and family life and wondered how they would all see each other when he was finally released. This was Nehru's last but longest spell in prison. He wrote to his sister Krishna:

> The private worlds each one of us lives in, worlds of fancy and feeling and imagination, have so long lain apart that they are apt to become strangers to each other, separate circles overlapping less than they used to. Partly that happens as we grow older, but the process is accelerated by the abnormal conditions we have been living in.

Jawaharlal was still in prison when he received the news that he now had a grandson, Rajiv, born in August 1944. 'To a woman, motherhood is the highest fulfillment,' Indira was to comment much later. 'To bring a new being into this world, to see its tiny perfection and to dream of its future greatness is the most moving of all experiences and fills one with wonder and exaltation.' Rajiv had been an easy delivery. His mother told a colleague when her son was a grown man that: 'I just felt hungry and I asked for a piece of toast. As I was eating, Rajiv came out. I was so sorry I couldn't finish my toast!'

Upon his release, Jawaharlal came home, held his grandson, embraced his daughter, appointed his son-in-law Managing Director of the *National Herald* in Lucknow and then, his domestic chores completed, went off to Delhi to head the new Interim Government and await the arrival of the last viceroy. Indira and Feroze Gandhi moved to Lucknow. The *National Herald* had suspended publication in August 1942 rather than submit to censorship. It was, after all, Jawaharlal's paper. In November 1946 it resumed publication. The following month Indira went to Delhi to help Jawaharlal, and while she was there she gave birth to another boy. They named him Sanjay (Victory). The daughter had now become a mother of two sons.

2
Daughter and father
1947–64

The first few years that Indira and Feroze spent in Lucknow were satisfying and free of tension. Both parents spent a lot of time with their sons. Indira recalled her own childhood and was determined that her children would not be left to the care of servants or nannies. She always remained proud of this fact and in an article, 'On Being a Mother', she wrote:

> When Rajiv and Sanjay were babies I did not like the idea of anyone else attending to their needs and tried to do as much for them as I could. Later when they began school, I took care to have my engagements during school hours so as to be free when the boys returned home. Once when Sanjay was quite small, a nursery-school friend of his came to our house with his mother. The mother, a society lady of means, commenting on my public work remarked that I could not be spending much time with my sons. This hurt Sanjay and before I could think of a reply he rushed to my rescue with the words – 'My mother does lots of important work yet she plays with me more than you do with your little boy.' It seemed his little friend had complained about his mother's bridge-playing!

Indira visited Delhi regularly to see her father and, occasionally, act as his official hostess. Soon she was virtually commuting from Lucknow to Delhi, a night's journey by train. Lucknow was an old stately city, built by the Nawab of Oudh on the shores of the river Gumti and adorned with colleges, mosques, houses for courtiers and a large palace. Before its occupation by the British (and for some time afterwards), it had a lazy, decadent atmosphere, still feudal in character. Its courtesans were amongst the most literate and cultured in all India. Mothers from respectable houses sent their daughters to these courtesans, well-chaperoned of course, to 'learn culture' and deportment and the art of conversation. The opulent houses of Lucknow's leading courtesans became the finishing schools for the daughters of the landed gentry. Poetry flourished as never before or since, although it was not always of a high quality – bad verse had, in fact, reached the proportions of an epidemic. The reputation of a poet was more often than not determined by the appreciation recorded at the private *soirées* which took place at different locations every night. All this had been harshly brought to an end by the British, though Warren Hastings, the first Governor-General, was subsequently impeached by the House of Commons for 'high crimes and misdemeanours', which included his venal persecution of the dowager-princesses of Oudh. He had almost starved them to death in order to ascertain the wherabouts of their fortune. Two old eunuchs employed by them as family retainers had been arrested and tortured. Edmund Burke, in his impeachment speech, had made great play of this episode. Some decades later, General Outram had deprived the Oudh royal family of its right to rule and the British had occupied Lucknow*. It was here that the British had resisted the 1857 rebellion, and the 'Siege of the Lucknow Residency' became part of English folklore at the time.

The old traditions were severely disturbed, but they could not be totally obliterated. Lucknow remained a city of culture, full of poets and literary critics, despite its dilapidated appearance. However, Indira was used to the hustle and bustle of Anand Bhavan. In contrast to the more exciting atmosphere of the Prime Minister's residence in Delhi, Lucknow was dull and nothing could relieve the monotony. Feroze was caring, but too much of an extrovert, and she felt that he could manage for himself far more easily than her father. Jawaharlal's sisters had occasionally helped their brother to entertain in the past, but they had now left Delhi. Indira felt responsible for him, but she also felt that in Delhi she was much closer to the centre of Indian politics. The thought of being a mother and a housewife in Lucknow indefinitely was something she found unacceptable. Ultimately the commuting got on her nerves. She decided to take the boys and move to Delhi.

Feroze was not particularly surprised, but he was obviously hurt. He did not try and stop her, but the fact that she was making this choice must have made him feel that the doubt he had expressed in London while wooing her had now become a certainty. She was a Nehru. The relationship of daughter and

---

* The Indian film-maker, Satyajit Ray, has evoked this atmosphere with great effect in *The Chess Players*, where a disintegrating landed aristocracy is depicted, oblivious to the pressures of time and imperialism.

father had always been very close, and since Kamala's death it had become even more emotional. For Indira, however, it was not simply a question of filial devotion. She respected her father's politics. She was not being a dutiful daughter; she was helping the country's foremost politician, who also happened to be the Prime Minister. The thought of him on his own in Delhi, dependent simply on civil servants and domestic servants, without any love or family life was unbearable to her. It was not, therefore, a case of putting her father above her husband. It was deciding who was a more crucial political figure. Here the answer was obvious. Nonetheless it could not have been a painless decision. She was, after all, taking her two sons away from their father. However much they loved their grandfather, he could never become a substitute for Feroze and nor did he try. The children saw Feroze regularly, but they must have been affected by the separation. Whatever doubts Indira may have had were settled for her after Gandhi's assassination. Now, she was convinced, her father needed her more than ever before.

She took Rajiv to see Mahatma Gandhi a day before his death. He was relaxing in the winter sun of Delhi, wearing a Bengali straw hat. On seeing Indira, her aunt Krishna and a female cousin enter, Gandhi teased the three women: 'Hullo! Have all these three princesses come to see *me*?' They did not talk about politics. Rajiv decorated the old man's feet with flower-chains. Indira complimented him on his hat. He laughed and said, 'An elegant Burmese hat is on its way. Shall I not look very handsome in that hat?' The next day he was assassinated. 'Little did we guess,' wrote Indira, 'that we would never see his wide toothless smile again, nor feel the glow of his protection.' Nor would her father.

Indira, Rajiv and Sanjay moved to Delhi. Nehru's residence had been the house of the British Commander-in-Chief in the days of the *raj*. It was designed in the Lutyens style and built in the golden and red sandstone which marked New Delhi. It had large cold rooms, which were full of giant oil paintings of the guardians of the *raj*, countless British Generals and heroes who stared down at one and whose presence Indira found objectionable. They were banished to the warehouse and Indira set about making this big mansion (it was much bigger than both Anand Bhavans in Allahabad) habitable. Teen Murti House (House of Three Statues) became a centre for visiting politicians, artists, heads of state, old friends and, of course, the leaders of the Congress Party. Nehru's life was undoubtedly transformed by the presence of his daughter and grandchildren: Teen Murti House now became a haven.

Indira regularly took the children to Lucknow so they could see their father, but Feroze soon realised that it would be easier for him to come and see them, which he did regularly. Jawaharlal always treated him correctly, but there was an unspoken tension between the two men, which was, in the case of Feroze, soon to reach the point of explosion. Feroze always felt an outsider at Teen Murti House and there was very little that his wife could do to make him feel at home. Even in the old days at Anand Bhavan it had been Kamala who was welcoming, whereas Jawaharlal's patrician reserve had always imparted a certain formality to their relationship. Before his marriage to Indira, Feroze and Jawaharlal did have a number of conversations alone, in which the older man had attempted to explain Indira and her habits to her future husband. These had been friendly occasions, but Feroze could never relax in the great man's presence. Now, on his visits to his family in Delhi, he felt a complete stranger. Jawaharlal's domestic style was very much coloured by Harrow and Cambridge. His table-manners were exquisite, he did not talk much during meals, his sense of humour was subtle, even dry, and he hated vulgarity in any shape or form. Feroze's eating habits were, by contrast, somewhat loud — he enjoyed his food and liked a lot of it, he had an enormous reserve of off-colour jokes. He found the atmosphere at Teen Murti House stifling and his visits decreased. He was more frequently offended and when angry he became coarse and even vicious. Indira was caught in the crossfire between the two men. Her father was, on occasion, extremely sharp with her, still treating her as a girl and sometimes telling her off in public; whereas Feroze vented all his resentment against her father on her. She became unhappy, but Jawaharlal, observing this, put all the blame on her husband rather than on the situation.

When Feroze decided to contest a parliamentary seat in Rae Bareilly, near Lucknow, Indira went to canvass support for him. Jawaharlal went too, though this did not prevent him from reprimanding Feroze for dragging his wife through the countryside in tiring conditions. Feroze swallowed his anger. He was elected, which gave him an opportunity to be in Delhi, where parliament was situated. A new problem arose. Where would Feroze decide to stay? Indira suggested that he move in with her and the boys, but Feroze refused to stay at the Prime Minister's house. Instead he accepted the small bungalow provided at a subsidised rate in Delhi to all members of parliament. Indira continued to stay with her father, thus putting the final seal on the separation.

Feroze had been called the 'nation's son-in-law' by some journalist soon after independence. Initially he laughed and made good-natured jokes at his own expense, but now he hated any mention of the joke and became angry when it was mentioned. He also defended his rights as an MP against his father-in-law. On one occasion he and another MP were refused admittance to some function because of a security bungle, and Feroze questioned Nehru about the incident in the Lok Sabha. The old man apologised, but he must have been furious. At another Congress gathering, Nehru, with Indira sitting next to him on the dais, rebuked the delegates who had brought along their entire families. Feroze, who was seated amongst the delegates, remarked in a very loud voice: '*I* did not bring *my* wife!' Nehru was not pleased.

Indira's role at Teen Murti House fell into three categories. She was responsible for the functioning of the entire household, which meant supervising every aspect: menus, servants' wages, feeding of the animals in the private zoo, guest-lists for dinner, tailors for her father and children, etc. On one occasion, when Jawaharlal gave a servant sixty rupees for an urgent journey to see a sick relative, he told him not to tell Indira or she might 'deduct it from your wage'. In an article for a Bombay magazine in 1957, Indira described her chores. She explained life with her father, travels abroad, the stifling nature of protocol, but above all she complained about 'the peculiar fads of our people. Apart from the main taboos of Hindus not eating beef and Muslims not eating pork, there are endless combinations and permutations! There are meat-eaters who are vegetarians on certain days of the week — there are vegetarians who eat eggs, others eat fish as well, and one distinguished guest who declared himself a vegetarian ended up by eating everything except chicken!' She also described Jawaharlal's habit of picking up new domestic styles from different countries: 'The first time he dined at Buckingham Palace he decided that at our house, too, milk and sugar should be poured before the coffee.' That Indira permitted this act of culinary philistinism to go through without a challenge indicates that Jawaharlal's bossiness extended to the domestic sphere. In an article for the *Ladies'*

Home Journal in May 1966 ('How Mrs Gandhi Shattered the Feminine Mystique'), Betty Friedan quoted an anonymous 'elder statesman' to the effect that 'in the early years Nehru used to bully Indira in an absolutely shocking way and shatter her self-confidence'.

Jawaharlal's temper was, of course, well-known to his intimates, but Indira was among the few who could get him back under control or even reproach him publicly. Then Nehru, whose anger was always short-lived, would laugh and tell the assembled company that if they had seen Motilal in a rage, they would never accuse him of being quick-tempered. He used to tell people of an occasion when he had just returned from Britain and was attending a dinner party at home. During the course of the evening, Motilal had recited a few couplets in Persian, then asked Jawaharlal to translate them for his guests. The young Nehru's Persian was not as fluent as his father's and, not wishing to expose his weakness, he declined. Motilal kept insisting and Jawaharlal finally mouthed a bad translation, whereupon Motilal chided him with not knowing the difference between two similar-sounding Persian words. By now very angry and humiliated, the younger man had remarked: 'At least I know the difference between dominion status and independence!' There was silence. The guests were aware of political differences between father and son. Motilal jumped to his feet in a blind rage and tipped the dining table's contents on to the floor. Nehru used to laugh when telling this story to his friends. Yet if Indira had been a communist and behaved in the same way to her father, the response might not have been so different. Motilal and Jawaharlal were alike in many respects. Indira was infinitely more controlled, though she harboured grudges for longer than either of the men.

The second role that she was called on to play was to travel abroad with him. In that sense she was the 'first lady' of India. She accompanied him to Britain, China, the United States, the USSR, Indonesia and many other places. She thus acquired a familiarity with foreign heads of state and government and received a unique education in the art of diplomacy as well as the intricacies of world politics. On the first occasion that she met Winston Churchill he remarked on the oddness of the occasion with two men, himself and Nehru, who had hated each other now sitting around the same table. Churchill was amazed that a man the British had locked up for so many years seemed to harbour no ill will. Indira remarked,

'We never hated you personally.' Churchill interrupted: 'But I did, I did!'

In some ways the role which was finally to bring her to power seemed the least demanding. In her capacity as the 'mistress of the household', Indira had to protect Nehru from the constant demand for interviews. His personal assistant, Mathai, did most of this, but Indira was in a superior position. On many occasions when persistent Congress leaders or MPs could not see Nehru, she used to talk to them, listen to their complaints and sort out some of the problems. In 1946, Pandit Govindvallabh Pant, a senior Congress leader, recognising her political capacities, suggested that she should stand for parliament, but she turned the offer down. At that time, pregnancy and the regular commuting between two households tired her and she did not want to take on a new role. Later she told everyone that she saw her main political task as ensuring an easy life for her father in his home. Nonetheless she was beginning to be asked to stand in for Jawaharlal at some meetings. It was at the first of these, she later admitted, that she realised she could make people listen to her. It was then that she knew definitively that she was going to be a politician. Further confirmation of her star appeal came in the Punjab, when she insisted on speaking at a village at dawn:

> It was a cold and misty January morning with a sharp breeze and at six a.m. still quite dark. Not a soul was in sight. All doors and windows seemed to be tightly secured. However there was a *takht* (wooden platform), a microphone and some *durries* (rough carpets), wet with the heavy dew. Hansraji (a Congress leader) felt that we had done our duty by coming and we could now drive on to the regular programme with a clear conscience. However, much to his embarassment, I insisted on giving a speech whether there was anybody to listen or not. Almost with my first word, windows started banging open and tousled heads appeared. Immediately afterwards the entire village poured out from the warmth of their houses, wrapped in blankets and *razais* (quilts stuffed with wool), some with *datun* sticks (sweet bark from a tree, used to clean teeth in India for centuries) and some with tumblers of steaming tea . . . Raizadaji remembered this as the most extraordinary meeting he had witnessed in his long life and spoke of it every time we met thereafter.

Experiences such as this gave Indira Gandhi's confidence an enormous boost. In 1955 she was approached by the Congress President, U.N. Dhebar, and another senior leader, Lal Bahadur Shastri, to accept nomination to the Congress Working Committee, the highest authority within the party. She accepted, was nominated and elected. She was also active within the Women's Department of the Congress Party, though here she never repeated Kamala Nehru's message of the 1930s which exhorted women to assert their equality and combat tradition. Indira was not a staunch supporter of women's emancipation, then or later. One reason for this could have been a desire to resist being typecast as from the Women's Department and thus becoming unable to assert herself in the party as a whole. All India's political parties had special sections for women, but these were in reality designed to hive women off and keep them busy elsewhere, while men ran the 'real thing'. This situation remains unaltered to this day.

Indira's rise to the top of the party was rapid. In 1957 she was elected to the party's Central Election Committee (getting more votes than Nehru himself), a body which discussed applications from prospective Congress parliamentary candidates. In the following year she was elected to the Congress Parliamentary Board, which decided on the nominations for parliament. In 1959 she was elected President of the Congress Party. Could the latter have happened without Jawaharlal's approval? There were two versions of how the Prime Minister's daughter had become the leader of the party. Indira's version was that 'I was terrified. I was really scared stiff, and I am sure my father didn't like it.' She was asked by Pandit Govindvallabh Pant, but replied that her father must be consulted before she decided. Pant said (according to Indira): 'It has nothing to do with your father. It is for you to decide.' Nehru made the same response, though she 'saw disapproval in his expression'. The press started a small campaign, arguing that the proposal should be rejected. She claimed that it was the press that made up her mind, for she refused to let them decide the issue.

The opposite view was largely put about by Morarji Desai, an old opponent of Nehru, a member of his Cabinet and a man who automatically assumed that he would be the next prime minister. Desai and his friends insisted that Nehru had pulled strings from behind the scenes. Whatever the truth, one thing is clear. Neither side was happy at the notion that a dynasty was being formed. In other words, even at this stage, the Congress was a somewhat different political party than it is today. During a press interview, Nehru explicitly stated: 'Normally speaking, it is not a good thing for my daughter to come in as Congress president when I am Prime Minister.' This seems to be a consistent approach. He had, after all, resisted many attempts by certain ministers and numerous sycophants to convince him that Indira should be a member of the government. 'Not while I am Prime Minister' had always been his retort to such suggestions.

However, there is no doubt that once she had decided, he was proud of her and paid a generous tribute to her talents at a meeting of the Congress Parliamentary Party after she became president:

> It is superfluous for me to say that Indira is my daughter and that I have love for her. I am proud of her good nature, proud of her energy and work, and proud of her integrity and truthfulness. What she has inherited from me I do not know. Maybe she has inherited these qualities from her mother!

Indira's presidential speech at the party's conference was short and straightforward. All she asked was to be treated as an ordinary party worker and amidst loud cheers and laughter she quoted from a popular Hindi film song of the time:

> We are the women of India,
> Don't imagine us as flower-maidens,
> We are the sparks in the fire.

The first to feel the effect of the sparks was the Communist government in Kerala. The CPI victory in India's southernmost province, as has already been indicated, was an important step in Indian politics. The Congress monopoly of power in India's states had been ended, and the CPI had shown the country that it could win elections. From the point of view of the Congress left, the result was or should have been welcome. It indicated that the real challenge came from people who wanted to move leftwards rather than towards right-wing communalism. In April 1959, Indira Gandhi visited Kerala as President of the Congress. The CPI leaders published an open letter to her which welcomed her visit; but after pointing out how the Kerala Congress was backing extreme right-wing agitation against the state's new progressive education and land policies, it asked whether 'the policy of isolating and annihilating the Communist Party was the aim of Congress throughout India?' The letter ended with the following appeal:

> We hope that you will seriously consider the repercussions such an agitation, challenging a law passed by the legislature, by a section of

the people affected by the law, will have throughout India. For it will mean that any sectional interest can challenge and try to defeat any progressive legislative measure by unlawful, threatening methods.

Indira ignored the plea. She was determined to show the Kerala Congress and units elsewhere that she was a tough and uncompromising leader. She sent a rude reply to the Kerala Government, challenging the credentials of the Communist Party by cold-war statements of the type that the CPI were, in effect, agents of China which was attempting to foment a war against India. She also defended the Kerala Congress alliance with communalist parties. Jawaharlal was unhappy about the role of the local Congress, but Indira told him that if Congress did not participate in the anti-communist agitation it was finished in the state. This was a classic case of pragmatism before principles. Once it is accepted that power is to be held at all costs, then it becomes impossible to defend any basic principle. Secularism remains a paper pledge and communalism walks in through a back door, deliberately left unlocked.

The Kerala episode is significant because it took place during Nehru's lifetime. He claimed, in private, that he was not in favour of getting rid of the communist government by an alliance with the right. In which case, why did he not move to prevent this from happening? There can be little doubt that a firm repudiation of Indira's manoeuvres by him would have ended the matter. All this recalled Subhas Chandra Bose's rueful remark to him in a private letter in the 1930s: 'When a crisis comes, you often do not succeed in making up your mind one way or the other – with the result that to the public you appear as if you are riding two horses.' In this case he was riding a tiger. He survived, but many Congress leaders ended up in the beast's stomach. The accommodation to communal politics in Kerala gave the green light to Congress units throughout the country. If Jawaharlal had lived longer he would have regretted the day that he had made this concession.

Indira's role in Kerala was an interesting, though dangerous, dress rehearsal for the future. The CPI had warned that such actions, unless stopped, would spread throughout the country. On this question, at least, history would vindicate their thesis. It is not that the communist government had not made mistakes. They had, but it was not for these that they were being attacked. It was their virtues that were under fire. The Congress High Command, with Jawaharlal reluctantly acquiescing, agreed to overthrow a legally elected provincial government, largely because it was *not* a Congress government. Backed by a press bitterly hostile to the CPI, a Socialist Party funded by the USA, and right-wing communalists of every variety, the President of India suspended the communist government in Kerala. New elections were organised. Here again the Congress, under Indira, decided that to defeat the CPI was crucial. If it meant a bloc with the 'holy war' politicians then it was unfortunate, but necessary. Congress joined forces with the Muslim League in Kerala to defeat the CPI. At a meeting of the Parliamentary Board on 2 August 1959, strong opposition to these unprincipled intrigues was voiced. It was the MP for Rae Bareilly, Feroze Gandhi, who denounced the leadership for getting involved with vested interests and right-wing forces in Kerala. In February 1960, the Congress-Muslim League united front won the elections in Kerala, but the results were interesting. The CPI vote had gone up from 35 per cent to 44 per cent, indicating increased popularity. The Congress vote declined from 37 per cent to 34 per cent. A 'first-past-the-post' electoral system, modelled on Britain, enabled Congress to head a coalition government.

Feroze Gandhi's politics had not changed since the glorious August days of 1942. He was a progressive Congressman, strongly committed to the state sector, and an able and effective member of parliament. In December 1957 he uncovered a corruption scandal involving private businessmen and a state-owned insurance corporation. There was a public judicial inquiry and the result was the resignation of the Finance Minister, T.T. Krishnamachari, who was a great favourite of Nehru. Feroze became extremely popular throughout the country. Those were days when corruption was beginning to grow and it still offended many Congress politicians, even though a majority of Congress leaders, especially at state level, had become part of the problem. Feroze was still on friendly terms with Indira and visited Teen Murti House regularly, but he could not have been too popular a visitor after he toppled the Finance Minister.

He suffered a slight heart attack in 1959, which scared Indira. A reconciliation was effected and they rushed off to Kashmir for a month. The trip was a big success. In September 1960, Feroze had a second attack. In terrible pain he drove himself to the hospital, where he fainted. Indira returned from Kerala at 11 p.m. and went straight to the hospital. She sat by him all night, holding his hand tightly. He died early in the morning of the next day. He was forty-eight years old. Indira was shattered. She had neglected Feroze in the belief that they had their lives ahead of them and that after Jawaharlal died, she and Feroze would be alone. The possibility of his death had never entered her mind. She was to recall that day with pain: 'I was actually physically ill. It upset my whole being for years, which is strange, because after all he was very, very ill and I should have expected that he would die. However, it was not just a mental shock, but it was as though somebody had cut me in two.' His funeral was attended by Indira, Jawaharlal and the Indian President as well as his many friends and numerous MPs. Thousands of people, however, had spontaneously lined the route and their grief was real. Nehru, surprised by the size of the crowd, remarked that he had never realised that Feroze had so many admirers among the people. The fact of the matter was that Feroze had never sunk to the level of an ordinary politician. That was the reason for his popularity.

Having lost her husband, Indira threw herself into politics again. She travelled a great deal, mainly on her own to talk and lecture about India abroad and to strengthen the Congress at home. The battle lines for the succession were beginning to be drawn. Nehru himself refused to nominate a successor. First, he argued, it was undemocratic. Why should he nominate anyone? Secondly, he pointed to the example of Britain in the 1950s when Churchill had appointed Eden as his 'crown prince' long before he retired. Eden, said Nehru, was one of the worst prime ministers Britain ever had in its long history. Thirdly, he stated that the new leader 'may well not emerge from within the parliamentary party and may be someone from outside'. This remark, whose meaning is clear, was later deliberately misinterpreted to prove that Nehru was grooming Indira for the job. This was false. If it had been otherwise the evidence would not have been lacking.

In reality Nehru was deeply concerned at the faction-fighting and corruption that began to characterise the Congress Party during the last few years of his life. He began to voice his concerns openly. He complained that there was no dynamism left in the party. Many leaders were totally obsessed with positions and power. A staleness and complacency had set in on every level and all this threatened Indian democracy. Kumaraswamy Kamaraj, the Congress President and also Chief Minister of Madras, backed Nehru and said that unless the situation changed mass disenchantment would increase a hundredfold, with drastic electoral consequences. Kamaraj now proposed that a number of senior cabinet ministers and chief ministers of states should resign from their posts and work full time to rebuild the party. Nehru was convinced by the Kamaraj Plan and it was implemented in 1963: six cabinet ministers and six chief ministers resigned. Among the ministers were Morarji Desai, Jagjivan Ram, Lal Bahadur Shastri and S.K. Patil. Kamaraj resigned as Chief Minister of Madras, Biju Patnaik as Chief Minister of Orissa. A year later Desai would allege that these resignations were designed to clear the decks for Indira Gandhi. Untrue. Within four months Nehru, now suffering from his illness, brought Lal Bahadur Shastri back to the Cabinet and made him *de facto* Deputy Prime Minister. He continued to resist, angrily, all attempts by her supporters to make Indira the Foreign Minister.

At the same time Kamaraj organised a secret caucus of five regional bosses of the Congress Party, whose aim was to determine Nehru's successor. This caucus became known as the Syndicate. Its members were Kamaraj (Madras), Atulya Ghosh (West Bengal), S.K. Patil (Bombay city), Sanjiva Reddy (Chief Minister of Andhra Pradesh), and S. Nijalingappa (Chief Minister of Mysore). Nehru knew perfectly well what was going on. He knew that the Syndicate was looking for a successor and that it was a powerful combination of regional power-brokers. Nonetheless he treated these men with utter contempt: Syndicate was too polite a name as far as he was concerned. Would a man hell-bent on obtaining the succession for his daughter, as his enemies alleged, have treated the kingmakers of the future in such a cavalier fashion?

After her father's death, Indira was temporarily inconsolable. She seriously considered a long stay abroad and she told friends that on her return she would like to settle down in a small cottage in the Himalayan foothills. She was dazed with grief. With Feroze and Jawaharlal both gone, Indira had lost a Nehru and a Gandhi. She was alone now except for her two sons. In the world of politics it was widely rumoured that her time was up, and that without her father she could not survive — but the people who said this seriously underestimated the position she had carved out for herself during the last ten years. As she accompanied her father's ashes from Delhi to Allahabad for the immersion in the sacred river Ganges, the crowds that gathered at small railway stations on the route of the five-hundred-mile journey were exceptionally large. Indira, attired in a white sari (white being the colour of mourning in India), did not appear to notice them. They would not have come if the ashes had been transported by anyone else. Large numbers of them had come mainly to get a glimpse of Indira.

3
Indira independent
1964–74

No sooner had Jawaharlal Nehru been cremated than the Syndicate cut down the short-list of contenders for his successor to two men: Morarji Desai and Lal Bahadur Shastri. It was clear to all, including Nehru's most vociferous opponents, that with his death India had lost a giant. He had successfully transformed the country into a capitalist democracy, albeit one with special features. G. D. Birla's astute warning to his fellow industrialists, as long ago as the 1930s, not to antagonise Jawaharlal, since he would be the best possible leader for India that they could want, had turned out to be correct. If one were to make a comparative survey of the politics of our century and the leaders that have played a formative role both in preserving a certain continuity and even reinforcing it according to the specific conditions of their country, then the following names come immediately to the fore: Franklin Delano Roosevelt (USA), Winston Churchill (Britain), Charles de Gaulle (France) and Jawaharlal Nehru (India). None of them were ordinary politicians. All of them helped to preserve the social and economic status quo at difficult times: depression, war, anti-fascist resistance and struggle against imperialism. All four could be described, in a way, as the Lenins of the other side. None of them had memorable successors. The only reason that Eden, Truman and Pompidou are remembered is because they followed their predecessors and in the case of two of them for disasters (invasion of Suez and Hiroshima). The same is true of Lal Bahadur Shastri in India.

Nehru's old friend and cabinet colleague, Krishna Menon, described the scene in the room where Nehru's body was lying ready to be taken away for cremation:

> The moment his last breath was drawn, the issue arose. None of these people who professed loyalty to him, who came from his state, in whose interests he has sometimes disregarded people like me just to

keep the peace, none of them had the decency to keep their mouths shut until he was cremated. Around his body . . . were these people, sitting around discussing this matter [the succession], not discussing seriously — I am using the word 'discussing' as a euphemism.

The President, Radhakrishnan, appointed the most senior cabinet minister, G. Nanda, as acting Prime Minister. The recommendation was made by the Emergency Committee of the Cabinet. Krishna Menon, a veteran of constitutional practice, denounced the decision:

> It was unconstitutional. That is the worst thing that could have been done. Even for the President to exercise his emergency powers would have been more constitutional, in my opinion. Or they should have called an emergency meeting of the Parliamentary Party or the Party Executive and there would have been no objection.

Menon was establishing a point of fact: the Constitution did not permit a handful of senior Cabinet ministers to decide who would be acting Prime Minister. As it happened, the Congress Party did not confirm the choice a few days later.

The Syndicate was determined to prevent Morarji Desai succeeding Nehru. So, for other reasons, were plenty of other people. Desai was an oddball even in the fad-ridden world of Hinduism. The reason he was not selected, however, had nothing to do with an old habit of drinking a glass of his own urine every morning. This caused merriment and consternation, but India was a democracy and it was Morarji's right to drink what he wanted in the morning. Most of his colleagues drank water or tea. Some, like Jawaharlal, preferred fresh fruit juice. If Morarji was happier with his own water it was entirely up to him. What the old Congress left (Nehru's followers) did not like was Desai's friendship with Washington and his hostility to public sector projects. The Syndicate objected most strongly to his individualism. He could not work as part of a team. In other words he would not accept their control. Many others found Desai's moral, holier-than-thou attitudes extremely hypocritical, given that he had spent most of his years in the Cabinet sniping away against his leader behind his back. Nehru had been aware of the fact, but had preferred to keep Desai under his control and hence in the government.

The machinations that went on behind the scenes to secure the succession were truly byzantine. The Congress Working Committee decided that democracy would not be helped by an open contest. 'A strange way to describe democracy,' Krishna Menon, who had been present, remarked acidly. The Congress High Command wanted a consensus and no unseemly wrangling. Kamaraj was selected to ascertain the views of the Congress Parliamentary Party, and he reported that a majority wanted Shastri. Desai could still have pressed his claims, but he accepted Working Committee discipline and withdrew his nomination. On 2 June 1964, Nanda, the acting Prime Minister, proposed Lal Bahadur Shastri as party leader. Morarji seconded the motion. Shastri was elected by acclamation. Kamaraj then spoke to the parliamentary party and made it clear that since no one present could fill Nehru's shoes, the only basis on which Congress could function was one of 'collective responsibility, collective leadership, and collective approach'. Shastri was asked by the President to form a new government. There was only one new addition to his list: Indira Gandhi. She could have asked for the Foreign Ministry and might even have obtained the post, but she said she wanted the Ministry of Information and Broadcasting. Shastri obliged. Indira was now a member of the government, ranking fourth in the hierarchy, and a member of the elite Emergency Committee of the Cabinet. She was approaching her forty-seventh year. At her age, Jawaharlal had been in prison. When he was fifty-three (seven years older than she was at this time) he had written her a letter from prison. It was one of many, but she often recalled this particular epistle, possibly because of its theme:

> Being your father, my mind inevitably goes back to a similar period of my own growth. I took a mighty long time in growing — perhaps I am not quite grown-up yet? Or, more correctly, I am grown-up in part only, the rest of me is still struggling to find out and understand. I was amazingly ungrown-up even in my middle twenties and even afterwards the process was slow. Possibly that is why I am still younger in mind and body than almost all my contemporaries. I imagine you are more grown-up now [Indira was then 25] than I was when I was your age. That is easily understandable for you have lived through a far more turbulent period of history than I had done then. My life till then had been quiet and peaceful and almost uneventful — the events were piling up for later days.
>
> It was about the time of your birth, or soon after, that these events started on their mad career. Almost you were a child of a turbulent world. I do not know what memories of these early days you carry about you. But whether you remember them or not, they must have influenced you and subconsciously they must cling to you. You wrote to me once about the old days at Anand Bhavan. But you have no real experience of those old days, for the great change came in our lives

when you were a babe in arms. It is difficult for the younger generation to picture to themselves the world which vanished, it seems now, so long ago. They have lived all their young lives transitionally, and we have all become wayfarers and travellers marching on and on, sometimes footsore and weary, but without resting place or haven. Yet, for those who can adapt themselves to this continuous journeying, there is no regret and they would not have it otherwise. A return to the dull uneventful past is unthinkable.

The last sentence summed up Indira's attitude to life. She had been stunned by the fact that she was now all alone and had, briefly, considered retirement, but had soon rejected the option. Her life had been too dominated by politics of one sort or another to permit a retreat at this stage.

She took to her new job with characteristic zeal, but not much enthusiasm. She was efficient, hardworking, but did not have many new ideas. What actually happened was that Indira Gandhi, as a cabinet minister, came increasingly to be seen as a cut above the average member of the Cabinet. She had vacated the palatial Teen Murti House and moved to 1 Safdarjung Road, a typical old-fashioned, white-washed colonial bungalow, with spacious rooms. The new Prime Minister, Shastri, was a man of modest tastes. He was short, and hence the butt of many a cartoonist; he came from a low-caste background and had been born into a poor family. Shastri told his colleagues that he had no desire to live in such a splendid mansion as Teen Murti House. He would feel awkward and out of place. Before he had finally decided, however, he received an arrogant, rude and, one might say, snobbish letter from the dead Prime Minister's younger sister, Krishna Hutheesing, asking him how he dared even think of living in a house that had been graced by a Nehru for seventeen years! This was intolerable behaviour, to put it generously, but Shastri merely hurried his decision. He would live elsewhere, and Teen Murti became the Nehru Museum. The family honour had been maintained.

It had been Nehru's habit to receive visitors, regardless of their position and social standing, between eight and nine in the morning. It was like the *durbar* (public audience) of the old Mogul kings, but it was well-intentioned. Nehru felt that any citizen should have the right to see the prime minister. In practice, of course, his private staff kept the numbers to a minimum, but nonetheless he did meet people from different walks of life. When

Indira moved to 1 Safdarjung Road, the morning *durbar* moved with her. She made it clear that her new house would remain open to all comers during the same hour, and people came in large numbers. This was the first real indication that the Nehru mystique had not evaporated.

Shastri had given the foreign affairs portfolio to Swaran Singh. This meant that an important area was under the control of inexperienced men, for neither Shastri nor Singh had a particularly astute grasp of world politics. The new Prime Minister called on Nehru's daughter to represent India at the Commonwealth Prime Minister's Conference in 1964, and she subsequently visited France, USA, Yugoslavia, Canada, Mongolia and Burma. She was the first foreign politician to meet the men in Moscow who had deposed the ebullient Nikita Khruschev. They reassured her that USSR policy towards India would not change one iota. In February 1965 she went to Moscow again on behalf of Shastri. This time it was her turn to reassure Moscow that Shastri's indecision should not be seen as a movement away from non-alignment. These trips did not go unnoticed in India, where they enhanced her prestige both inside Congress and in the country as a whole.

In August 1965 she decided to take a rest. The choice of the holiday resort was, inevitably, Kashmir. She had barely landed at Srinigar, the provincial capital, when news began to come through that Pakistani troops, disguised as 'civilian volunteers', had raided Kashmir. The Pakistani aim was to surprise India, capture Srinigar airport and foment a massive pro-Pakistani uprising in the valley, which was predominantly Muslim in religious composition. The Pakistani infiltrators had come within a few miles of Srinigar Airport. Indira was advised to take the next flight back to Delhi, but she refused pointblank. Instead she went to the city and helped the local chief minister, Ghulam Sadiq, to organise the defence of the province. The Pakistan Army Intelligence had correctly estimated India's unpreparedness, but they had overestimated support for Pakistan in the region. There was no mass uprising. Instead, there was a full-scale war between India and Pakistan. The diminutive Shastri (he was known in Pakistan as a 'bird wrestler') soon took charge of the situation, and the Pakistan Army was defeated and driven back, after which a ceasefire was imposed by India. This defeat weakened the Ayub military regime in Pakistan beyond repair; within two years it was overthrown by a gigantic popular upsurge. The attempt to foment an insurrection in

Kashmir had, in the end, led to the fall of an unpopular dictatorship.

The Soviet Union had played a certain role in the ceasefire and they asked both leaders to sign the peace agreement in Tashkent, an old city in Soviet Central Asia. Field-Marshal Ayub, a tall, big man from the northernmost tip of the Punjab, was in sharp contrast to the tiny Indian leader, but it was the latter who had won. Shastri left for Tashkent on 31 December 1966 from Delhi. He had suddenly become extremely popular in the country. His low-profile leadership could not have been in greater contrast to the regal Nehru, and initially Shastri's appearance on newsreels in the popular cinemas, packed with millions every night throughout India, had been greeted with ribald comments and jokes and laughter. Now his images on the screen were greeted with applause. Two weeks before he left for Tashkent, he spoke at a public meeting in Bombay: a million people turned up to hear him. Even Jawaharlal had not seen such a big audience during the last five years of his reign. Shastri's efficient handling of the war and his new-found popularity gave him new confidence. He appeared far more decisive and all the signs were that on his return from Tashkent he intended to reshuffle the Cabinet and choose his own ministers. Kamaraj and the Syndicate were not too pleased by this turn, but in the face of Shastri's determination they were powerless. On the political level, the transition of power from Nehru to Shastri had now been completed: the war had finally enabled the new Prime Minister to exorcise his predecessor's shadow, and the Congress leaders awaited his return from Tashkent with a mixture of anticipation and fear. He never returned alive. On 10 January 1966, Lal Bahadur Shastri had a massive heart attack and died soon afterwards.

The country was numbed by the shock. In Nehru's case there had been grief, but not surprise. Everyone knew that the old giant had reached his last days, but Shastri's death took everyone by surprise. The Syndicate were unprepared. Morarji Desai was caught off balance. The whole network of factional hierarchies could not possibly have been alerted. To be fair, it did not take them long to recover. Within forty-eight hours Morarji Desai had let it be known that he now expected the job. He had tolerated Nehru's arrogance, he had acknowledged Kamaraj's manipulative skills and accepted Shastri, but now he wanted his just reward. There could not be any question of a consensus, he told the messengers of the Syndicate. Once bitten, twice shy. The Syndicate were in a real quandary. Desai had to be stopped. Who could they find as an alternative?

They searched for five long days. Some of the Syndicate toyed with the idea of Kamaraj himself, but this was rejected by the nominee. The big, fat man knew his own limitations. There were others who didn't and Kamaraj slowly began to exclude names from his short-list. The party bosses needed someone pliable, weak and susceptible to their control — a lump of clay they could mould and remould according to need. They finally settled on one name to confront Desai: Indira Gandhi, the Minister for Information and Broadcasting. They had, without being aware of it, signed their own death warrants as politicians.

Indira Gandhi told her friends, who had gathered at 1 Safdarjung Road in the early hours after hearing of Shastri's death, that under no circumstances should they let it be known that she was putting herself forward as a candidate. She told them how Desai had ruined his chances after her father's death by behaving at the funeral as though he were the successor. None of her followers were to go in search of the Syndicate. Let Kamaraj or one of his men come to her. Indira was not lacking in guile during Shastri's lifetime. Although she had made a number of public attacks on Shastri's stewardship, she had never, unlike her father, criticised Kamaraj. In fact she had gone out of her way to pay tribute to his organisational talents and his spirit of self-sacrifice at a public occasion in his hometown of Madras.

After five days the Syndicate came to Safdarjung Road and Indira agreed to contest the election for the Congress leadership. The other candidates were Desai and Nanda. Kamaraj lined up ten chief ministers from the provinces to declare publicly in favour of Indira Gandhi. They did so without hesitation, and the gesture served its purpose. A demoralised Nanda dropped out of the race. Desai did not exactly panic, but he issued a public statement denouncing Kamaraj's manoeuvres. The big man from the south was unbothered. He responded by making a shameless appeal to Desai to withdraw from the contest in the interests of party unity. Desai treated his request as an open provocation, which it was, but instead of maintaining his dignity, he launched a new attack on the Syndicate and their favoured candidate, describing her as a *chokri* (a young girl beneath contempt). Throughout this period Indira Gandhi demonstrated her coolness. She did not make a single public attack on Desai and appeared almost as if she was above the more unseemly aspects of the party dispute. When a foreign correspondent asked Mrs Gandhi what it felt like to be on the verge of becoming India's first woman prime minister, she replied: 'I am not a feminist at all. I am simply doing a particular job and would do it wherever I was placed.'

The Parliamentary Congress Party met on 19 January, 1966. In the streets outside there was tension and excitement. In the corridors the journalists paced up and down. Kamaraj was lining up votes until the last minute. Jagjivan Ram commanded the support of the 'untouchable' (low-caste Hindus) MPs. The man from the Syndicate promised him a senior cabinet post. Morarji, to his credit, had refused to indulge in horse-trading in this fashion. Ram switched sides. Nehru's sister, Vijayalakshmi, who was an MP from the largest Indian state, the United Provinces, initially supported Morarji, but after a meeting with her niece, she changed her mind and said: 'It is a certainty that Mrs Indira Gandhi will be India's next prime minister. We Nehrus are very proud of our family. When a Nehru is chosen as prime minister, the people will rejoice.' Then with a big smile on her small face, she lived up to her reputation with the following stinging comment: 'Mrs Gandhi has the qualities. Now she needs experience. With a little experience she will make as fine a prime minister as we could wish for . . . She is in very frail health indeed. But with the help of her colleagues, she will manage.'

Indira herself made a symbolic visit early in the morning to the cremation sites of Nehru and Mahatama Gandhi, then to Teen Murti House and finally to the meeting of the Parliamentary Party. She was greeted by large crowds which had assembled outside Parliament to await the verdict. As they saw her alight from her car, they noticed that on her simple white sari was pinned a red rose, in the style of Jawaharlal. The message was obvious. The crowds began to chant *Lal ghulab zindabad* ('Long live the red rose'). Five hundred and twenty-six Congress MPs had gathered to determine the succession. What would it be? Monarchy or puritanism? Outside the journalists were becoming irritable, though the assembled masses were in good heart. When a government minister appeared on the balcony to announce the result, a wit shouted: 'A boy or a girl?' The minister replied: 'A girl'. The crowd, sensing something important, burst into a rhythmic chant: *'Jawaharlal Nehru zindabad!'* ('Long live Jawaharlal Nehru!') This was the noise that greeted India's new Prime Minister as she came out of the meeting. She smiled. In a letter she wrote to Rajiv after the event she confided that a line from a poem of Robert Frost had been repeating itself in her head that day: 'How hard it is to keep from being king, when it's in you and in the situation.' She had won by 355 votes to Desai's 169.

A woman prime minister

The new Prime Minister's first address to the nation was a familiar mixture of banalities and repetitions of old promises. She could not have been in too spirited a mood when she made the broadcast. Her attempts to remove Gulzarlal Nanda from the Cabinet and to avoid giving Jagjivan Ram a place in the new government had been defeated by the Syndicate. Indira Gandhi realised then that she had to establish her grip on the party machine. Jawaharlal had not needed to dirty his hands in the everyday mess of politics, because his popularity in the country was such that he could easily override any manoeuvres of which he disapproved. Furthermore, after the death of Patel, he had ensured that Nehru loyalists were running the party, though his definition of 'loyalist' remained very broad. Indira had not yet reached that stage. She lacked Shastri's long years of experience as a cabinet minister and as a party politician. The Syndicate believed that she was weak and they would be able to manipulate her with far greater ease than Shastri. One important reason for this miscalculation was her gender. Her opponents believed that because she was a woman, the Indian people of every caste and creed would not readily accept her as Prime Minister for a long period.

In the whole of its history India had only known one woman ruler. That was in 1236, when the founder of the Muslim Slave Dynasty, Shamsuddin Iltutmish (a former slave) had chosen his daughter Razia as his successor, remarking that he considered her a 'better man' than his sons. Razia had turned out to be an intelligent and courageous monarch, who organised her court and transacted the business of the realm in an efficient manner. Her romance with one of her commanders, an Abyssinian Master of the Horse, excited jealousies amongst her nobles. After a three and a half year reign, she was overthrown by a palace coup and put to death by her former armed protectors. It was probably with all this in mind that Bombay's *Economic and Political Weekly*, the most serious and sophisticated journal in the country, commented soon after Indira's victory:

> A woman ruler is under a social handicap until she has been able to consolidate her position. In the beginning every group leader wants to advise and control her and so faction fights start among them. Either the ruler is able to satisfy everyone that she is not too close to anyone in particular, as Queen Elizabeth I did, and enjoy a long tenure of office, or fails to survive the initial period of uncertainty, as was Sultana Razia's sad fate.

Indira Gandhi had already subconsciously chosen the model of Queen Elizabeth I, lightly influenced by Joan of Arc. Her sponsors in the Syndicate would soon understand that fact and then would act accordingly, but the most pressing engagement that lay ahead was the general election of 1967. In fact that had been an important factor in helping Congress MPs choose Mrs Gandhi in the leadership contest. They felt that a bit of the Nehru magic was badly needed. The social polarisations had not halted since independence, and despite the egalitarian rhetoric of the two Five-Year Plans, the gap between the privileged and the dispossessed was growing rapidly. In some parts of the country, particularly Andhra Pradesh and West Bengal, there were indications of an embryonic peasant insurgency. The 1964 split in the Communist Party resulted in two, soon three, warring factions. This helped the Congress electorally, but not at the grassroots level, where alienation was increasing. A large section of the base of the breakaway Communist Party (Marxist) — CPM — consisted of a new breed of activists. Many of them had seen Congress only in office and had become totally disillusioned with the social and political order. Their inspiration was not Moscow, but Peking. Their slogan was simplistic: 'China's Chairman is *our* Chairman'. Their way of thinking owed more to religious habits than to the rationalism of Marx. But they were angry people and there was reason for the anger. It was the remedies that proved to be disastrously wrong.

All these elements were so far straws in the wind, but they indicated that the people would no longer simply vote for the Congress on trust. Their trust, and many began to say as much, had been badly betrayed. Indira Gandhi was aware of these realities. Her political instincts were fairly sharp and she told close colleagues that the 1967 elections would be a far tougher contest than either the Syndicate or the other aspirants to the throne had realised.

There was also an important political question that needed to be settled. The linguistic provincial borders had not dealt with the Punjabi language. The Sikhs in the north were pressing for a Punjabi province and Sant Fateh Singh, the leader of the Akali Dal, the party of Sikh nationalism, was threatening a fast until death. On this question Mrs Gandhi moved rapidly. With Kamaraj's support, she pushed through a Punjabi state with Punjabi as the official language. Hindu communalists who claimed that their first language was Hindi were given a portion of the old Punjab which was named Haryana. This made Indira extremely popular with the Sikhs, though the Haryana concession would, in retrospect, appear misguided. It had been conceded as a result of communal riots in Delhi instigated by the Jan Sangh. Three Congressmen had been burnt alive and the Indian Prime Minister, speaking at a public rally welcoming the Yugoslav Prime Minister, had angrily shouted at the assembled gathering:

> There are no tears in my eyes. There is anger in my heart . . . Is it for all this that so many freedom fighters and martyrs have sacrificed their lives? How would I hold my head high and say India is a great country and meet foreign dignitaries when violence and discord have fouled the atmosphere? . . . The political parties who are instigating this violence are doing India great harm. They are not true Indians.

The speech was an indication that, when aroused, she could be forceful. This was not the impression given by her monotonous deliveries in the Lok Sabha, where she was mercilessly mocked and attacked by the opposition. Ram Manohar Lohia, a veteran social democrat, was a particularly irksome thorn in her flesh, because of his sexist refusal to take her seriously.* He hoped that Congress would soon be despatched by the electors so that 'this pretty woman does not have to suffer pain and trouble beyond her endurance . . . We will have a pretty face for a time and she will be burdened with the weight of her father's and Mr Shastri's misdeeds. To that we can safely add the burden of her own misdeeds.' Indira Gandhi's response was to justify and defend pragmatism as an essential corollary of 'idealism'. In order to

---

* Lohia's attitude was, in fact, very similar to that of the British Prime Minister, James Callaghan, when the Conservative Party had elected Margaret Thatcher as its leader. Both would learn the truth the hard way.

prove this point she told a Western journalist that the three non-Indians she admired the most were Roosevelt, Kennedy and Einstein!

This reference to two American presidents was not a slip of the tongue. Indira was well aware of the economic effects of the terrible drought that year. There was a very real danger of famine in at least three large provinces. India needed foreign aid, foreign investments and, hence, goodwill on the part of Washington. Shastri's intended visit to Washington had been abruptly cancelled by the State Department after the Indian Prime Minister had denounced the US bombing of North Vietnam.

The new Prime Minister visited Washington and received a grand welcome from President Lyndon Johnson. She was impressed. Johnson, not a great stickler for protocol (his loud scream to test the echo in the Taj Mahal while on a Vice-Presidential trip to India was still remembered by Indian diplomats) decided on one occasion to extend his visit to the Indian Embassy, and after a cocktail party he said he would like to stay for dinner. Arrangements were hurriedly made and a senior adviser to Mrs Gandhi, P. N. Haksar, known for his leftist views, was deprived of his place at the top table that night. At a subsequent White House banquet, where the atmosphere was extremely friendly, Lyndon Johnson approached Indira Gandhi for a dance. She declined and explained to the bewildered President that: 'My countrymen would not approve if they heard I had been dancing.' She could not be seen dancing with the Texan while Vietnam burned. She probably visualised the photographs in the Indian press, the use her opponents would make of them and the delight of the cartoonists. A more serious reason probably was that she had been compelled to make some concessions. Throughout her trip she made no critical reference to US policy on Vietnam, which shocked the two remaining veterans of the non-aligned camp, Nasser and Tito. She promised American investors 'equal terms' to those enjoyed by Indian capitalists and she made another concession, which had been angrily rejected in the past by both Nehru and Shastri. She accepted the US offer to set up in India an Indo-American Education Foundation, which would be endowed with 300 million dollars and would operate in much the same way as the Ford Foundation. Nehru had stated that this would give the United States too much influence in the realm of research and higher education in India and threaten the country's cultural independence. Shastri had repeated these arguments. Indira also agreed to 'tone down' Indian criticisms of US policies in Indo-China, a compromise that would have enraged her father more than the other concessions. What did she get in return? A promise that 3.5 million tons of food-grains would be despatched rapidly, followed by 900 million dollars worth of non-project aid. Pleased with herself, she left Washington for Delhi, with one stopover: Moscow.

In the Soviet capital she met the Prime Minister, Alexei Kosygin, for a brief talk. After the usual pleasantries, Indira and Kosygin discussed the war in Vietnam. Indira Gandhi put a question to the Russian: 'How can you expect the Americans to pull out of Vietnam until they can find a way to save face?' The reply was angry: 'And how many Asian lives will be lost while the Americans are thinking up a way to save face?' She could not reply. It may not have occurred to her at the time, but it was exactly the sort of question which Jawaharlal would have posed to a Western apologist for US policies.

Her troubles were just beginning. The trip to Washington and her performance there had antagonised important sections of the Congress Party. The left saw it as a break with India's non-aligned status; the Communist Parties made use of the whole affair to improve their standing with the electorate; even the Congress right made critical noises. She responded angrily to these criticisms, and broadcast a special radio message to the nation: 'Is there a country today which needs nothing from others? The fear that we have "sold out" under Western pressure or that we are going to be dominated by foreign capital is absurd . . . '

The critics were not satisfied. In Parliament, Nehru's old colleague, Krishna Menon, led a savage attack on Indira's foreign policy. He demanded an explanation for the government's silence on Vietnam, calling it a 'shameful' and 'disgraceful' breach in the country's anti-imperialist policies. He denounced the agreement on the Indo-American Foundation as 'an intrusion into the cultural and intellectual life of the Indian people'. Where was she taking this country? Menon thundered. Did she want India to become another Brazil? Indira was shaken by the assault. Her reply was not convincing: 'History is replete with instances of less developed countries having accepted aid from developed ones. Lenin took American aid after the Russian Revolution.' The point that was being made, however, was not the acceptance of aid so much as the conditions attached to it which, it was felt, threatened India's independence. Within the Congress, Indira was punished by a left-right bloc in the parliamentary party, which elected a new executive, removing in the process all those regarded as her men. Kamaraj, the Congress President, flew off to the Soviet Union to reassure them that the Congress Party was still committed to non-alignment. He was hailed in *Pravda* as a 'man of the people . . . and a real representative of the Indian masses'. If an election had not been on the horizon, it is likely that an attempt would have been made to topple Indira and elect a new leader. Her controversial decision to devalue the Indian rupee, part of the deal agreed in Washington, was attacked by every conceivable faction in the Congress. Morarji Desai was waiting patiently in the wings. He felt that his time had come and he would soon be prime minister.

On 1 July 1966, the Indian Prime Minister, under strong pressure from Krishna Menon, broke her long silence on Vietnam. She criticised the American decision to bomb the Vietnamese capital Hanoi and the largest port, Haiphong. She also withdrew support from the Indo-American Foundations Project. Lyndon Johnson was not pleased. Indira then left for an official visit to the Soviet Union with stopovers in Cairo and Belgrade. Nasser and Tito insisted that the US bombing must be halted unilaterally before there could be any talks. Indira's position on Washington was much softer than that of Nasser. In Moscow, however, she went further and signed a joint communiqué with Kosygin which labelled American action as 'imperialist aggression', demanded an unconditional end to the bombing and stressed that the only solution lay within the framework of the Geneva Conference decisions of 1954.

The consequences were a souring of relations with Washington. Against the advice of Ambassador Chester Bowles, Johnson ordered a sharp reduction in the flow of aid, thus confirming what every US critic in Delhi had argued for months — the US only provided aid with strings. The US Ambassador to India was annoyed by this and appealed to Washington for a more subtle approach. He was instructed to tell the Indian Minister for Food to revamp the rural development schemes. When Bowles gently chided a White House official with the remark that Indira Gandhi's views on the US bombing only repeated what the Pope and UN Secretary-General U Thant had already stated, he was told sharply that 'the Pope and U Thant do not need our wheat'. The American tactics were characteristically counter-productive. Indira's attacks of US foreign policy became more pronounced and she despatched a warm greetings message to Ho Chi Minh on his seventy-seventh birthday. She was beginning to find her feet, but the situation inside the Congress did not help her self-confidence.

The Syndicate was largely in control of the Congress Party machine. In the crucial task of deciding a list of candidates for the next elections, she found that she had very little say in the matter — she could not even overturn the Syndicate's decision not to reselect the veteran leftist, Krishna Menon, in his Bombay constituency. Since her return to non-alignment, Menon had become a close adviser and she valued his judgement on many questions. She had known him for a long time. They had met when she first went to England. He had been a founder of the anti-colonial India League and had influenced many English people against colonialism, among them, Edwina Mountbatten. Her father and Menon had been close friends. Even after he had been sacrificed as Defence Minister in the wake of the Sino-Indian war disaster, Nehru and he had retained a close personal friendship. Menon had been virtually hero-worshipped by Indira's late husband, Feroze Gandhi. The most impressive feature of this South Indian politician was his intellect, his outspokenness and his unshakeable honesty. Menon always kept aloof from petty squabbles, inner-party intrigues and the power-struggles of the local and national party machines. He despised that side of politics. Nor did he suffer from an overpowering personal ambition, as the pro-American lobby in India constantly asserted in the press and in Parliament. If he had so desired, he could have played the part of Brutus to Jawaharlal's Caesar. There were people who would happily have handed him the knife, but he rudely rebuffed any such suggestions. He was, above all, a man of principle, and this was already becoming an extremely rare quality in Congress circles. The Syndicate removed him to punish Indira, but also to teach him a lesson. We control the apparatus, they appeared to be saying, and if you want to stay in Parliament you deal with *us*. Menon's response was typical of the man. He severed his connections with Congress and decided to contest the elections as an independent! He lost, but by a narrow margin.

Within the party it appeared that certain leaders were more

interested in the election for the leadership of their party after the removal of Indira, than the impending general elections. Menon had warned them in so many words: 'The choice of a prime minister is never a vocal issue at election time in a parliamentary democracy.' They paid no attention to him, but kept manoeuvring and lining up their forces. Morarji Desai was busy organising his supporters. Kamaraj and the Bombay politician, Y. B. Chavan, were also in the running and it was not the best possible atmosphere for Mrs Gandhi to go to the country. She decided, wisely as it turned out, that the only way she could disarm the men who were waiting, knives sharpened and glistening, to stab her in the back, was by improving her standing in the country as a whole. She made no secret of her plan. On Christmas Day 1966 she told the *Times of India*: 'There is a question of whom the party wants and whom the people want. My position among the people is uncontested.' She was publicly warning the Syndicate that if they waged war she would overwhelm and outflank them from below. They chose to disregard this warning.

Throughout January and February she campaigned with a passion that was intended to, and did, revive memories of her late father. She travelled 15,000 miles and spoke at 160 public meetings. More important than this statistic was the fact that the people came to listen, and in large numbers. Local Congress candidates did not fail to take note of this lesson. The party had no other leader capable of drawing consistently large crowds throughout the country. The regional bosses could get an audience in their own backyards, but nowhere else. This was her strength and she demonstrated it time and time again. She was often heckled, as in Jaipur City, a stronghold of the Swatantra Party, a right-wing amalgam of malcontents, but she did not retreat. The Maharani of Jaipur had instructed her supporters to break up the meeting, but Indira Gandhi shouted angrily at them:

> Go and ask the Maharajas how many wells they dug for the people in their states when they ruled them, how many roads they constructed, what they did to fight the slavery of the British? If you look for an account of their achievements before we became independent all you will find is a great big zero!

She was loudly applauded by the audience. In Orrissa, a Swatantra Party supporter hurled a stone at her. She was badly hurt and bleeding, but insisted on continuing the meeting.

Her popularity throughout the country increased. She was not a powerful orator, yet she gradually developed a style which went down well with her largely peasant audiences. She spoke simply, using metaphors which they could easily comprehend, but she never attempted to educate them politically in the Nehru fashion. Jawaharlal had occasionally rambled, but his habit of talking to people about serious problems was appreciated by his audiences. They never felt that he was talking down to them, and he never did. He had attempted instead to lift them up, make them more critical and more aware. In the early days it had worked, but later on, as they saw that Congress could not deliver what it promised, they listened to him in silence. Indira's message was spiced with common-sense virtues of which they were already aware. She also developed the knack of using her maternal knowledge to good effect. It was during this campaign that 'Mother Indira' was born. In a speech at her own constituency (once that of her husband Feroze) in Rai Bareilly in the country's largest province, Uttar Pradesh, she explained:

> My family is not confined to a few individuals. It consists of scores of people. Your burdens are comparatively light, because your families are limited and viable. But my burden is manifold, because scores of my family members are poverty-stricken and I have to look after them. Since they belong to different castes and creeds, they sometimes fight among themselves, and I have to intervene, especially to look after the weaker members of my family, so that the stronger ones do not take advantage of them.

The merit of this approach was twofold. It avoided explaining why the country was in such a mess and why poverty was increasing, and it simultaneously projected her as a leader above parties. They were *her* family, *her* responsibilities. The Congress was not mentioned very often.

The 1967 election results were the clearest indication of the fact that the long love affair between the Congress and the Indian electorate was coming to an end. They represented a severe setback for the party. The Congress was still the largest party in the Lok Sabha, but its strength was reduced from 361 to 283 out of a total of 520 seats. The remaining results reflected the polarisation that was taking place in the country. The two Communist Parties did remarkably well: the CPI won 23 seats and the CPM 19. Their combined total was 42, as compared to 29 in the old parliament. The extreme right also increased its strength. The Jan

Sangh increased its representation from 14 to 35 and the Swatantra Party from 18 to 44.

The situation in the states provided a more accurate reflection of the Congress debacle. It lost a total of 8 states. In West Bengal, the CPM was the largest single party and its leader, Jyoti Basu, formed a coalition government. In Kerala the two CPs also headed a coalition. Gujarat was lost to the Congress. Tamil Nad saw the rise of a regional party, which had campaigned strongly against Hindi as a national language and defended the cultural and political heritage of the south. The Dravida Munnetra Kazahgam (DMK) had swept the Congress aside. The king-maker, Kamaraj, had lost in both the constituencies which he had contested. Two other Syndicate big boys had been defeated personally: Atulya Ghosh in West Bengal and S. K. Patil in Bombay city. Its leadership strength in the new Parliament was reduced to Sanjiva Reddy and Nijalingappa. Desai had won his seat, but another rival of Mrs Gandhi, C. B. Gupta, had been defeated in Uttar Pradesh. The Uttar Pradesh results had pleased her more than anything else. Indira Gandhi's supporters had been elected to the Lok Sabha, but many of Gupta's hand-picked candidates to the state legislature had been defeated. Overall it was a bad result for the Congress, but a good one for Indira Gandhi.

The fact that the Congress was weaker did not lead to party unity. Congress MPs realised that in Indira they had an effective vote-winner and that, without her, the results would have been much worse. Nonetheless Morarji Desai let it be known that he was preparing a challenge to her leadership. This turned out to be an elaborate piece of horse-trading. He agreed not to stand provided she accepted a *de facto* 'dual leadership', with himself as deputy prime minister. Desai demanded, in addition, the Home Ministry and authority over other ministers. She refused. When Kamaraj pleaded on Desai's behalf she repeated her refusal with the remark that 'there cannot be two captains of the team'. Desai had, as usual, publicly attacked her leadership, declared that she was an inexperienced, incompetent amateur and that he would only serve under her if he was effectively in control. She had, as usual, remained silent. Her only statement to the public was that she had offered the deputy prime ministership to Desai in order to preserve party unity. It was the supposedly pristine Desai who had to explain why he had joined a Cabinet in which he had very little power. His explanation: 'My friends wanted me to do so'. With enemies like this she did not need to rely on too many friends. She was elected party leader by a unanimous vote. Desai quipped that 'We are placing on her head a crown of thorns'. Her new Cabinet reflected this strength. She rewarded her supporters, dropped Sanjiva Reddy, a staunch supporter of the Syndicate, and isolated Desai completely by not permitting him even a single supporter at Cabinet level.

She now began to enjoy the exercise of power. The earlier hesitations and doubts which were revealed in her own unstable political behaviour started to disappear. A friend had recommended that she see the film *Becket* and a special showing was organised at 1 Safdarjung Road. Indira enjoyed the film enormously; whether the cinema in Delhi where it was showing at the time was ever visited by Desai or the Syndicate has never been revealed. The opposition jibes in the Lok Sabha did not stop, but she developed a certain immunity to them so that they no longer hurt as they had done when she first became prime minister. The re-election, albeit with a reduced majority, had worked wonders for her self-confidence. She also told Arnold Michaelis of *McCalls* in an interview in 1966 that she was beginning to develop the capacity to detach herself from her physical surroundings and become an observer of her own actions: 'I do remove myself from a place if I need to or if I am tired. I do have the feeling sometimes if I am addressing a meeting that I am watching the whole procedure from the outside. And I sort of say: "Now I wonder what she is going to say or what she is going to do".'

The big fight was yet to come, for the Syndicate politicians were not prepared to give up their hegemony within the Congress without a battle. They now realised that she had been the wrong choice in the first place. It was too late to do anything about that, but the future had to be safeguarded. At the same time as the Congress Old Guard were planning their coup, a younger group of Congress members had become increasingly concerned at the growth of the two Communist Parties and the right-wing groupings. They felt that a new radical thrust by the party was necessary in order to win back the millions of lost votes. This group, which became known as the 'Young Turks', favoured a collaboration with the CPI, CPM and the left. The Old Guard preferred a deal with the Swatantra and the Jan Sangh. The Young Turks were led by a man named Chandrashekhar. The Old Guard had plenty of leaders, but also one potential prime minister: Morarji Desai. The polarisation revealed by the last elections was now reflected inside the Congress Parliamentary Party itself. Indira Gandhi did not initially back either side. She attempted to keep the party united, for the opposition was anxious to split the Congress and break its political monopoly at the centre as it had done in the states, but pressures began to build up and it became increasingly difficult for her to stand aside.

The battlelines were drawn for Indira Gandhi around the nominations for the post of president and vice-president of India. Normally the presidency was given to a widely respected figure, who was not so much apolitical as 'above party politics'. The electoral college for these two posts was the Lok Sabha *and* all the state legislatures. The Congress majority in the combined national and state parliaments was two per cent, so it needed only a slight shift by Congress parliamentarians for a major upset to take place. Sensing this, the opposition persuaded a judge of the Supreme Court, K. Subha Rao, to be their candidate. The sitting President Radhakrishnan was popular throughout the Congress and widely respected as the foremost expert on Indian philosophy. The problem was that he had already served two terms, but more importantly, he was going blind. Mrs Gandhi insisted that the Vice-President Zakir Hussein, a Muslim, should be the Congress candidate. Kamaraj insisted that because of the opposition from Subha Rao, they should continue to support the candidature of Radhakrishnan. Zakir Hussein, he argued, might not obtain all the Congress votes because he was not a Hindu. Hussein was a well-known scholar and academic and Mrs Gandhi felt that India's secularism would be emphasised to Indian Muslims and the rest of the world. She was firm in her choice and refused to change her mind, though Kamaraj was not wrong in pointing out the risks involved. At one stage Mrs Gandhi asked the opposition to nominate Rao as vice-president so the slate could be voted unanimously. They were not unresponsive, but Kamaraj stepped in and said that there could be no question of any deal with the opposition. The Congress Parliamentary Board met and decided to nominate Hussein for president and V. V. Giri, a South Indian trade union leader, as vice-president. What Kamaraj had not foreseen was that in the event of the right making the fight a communal issue, the votes of the communists and independent left would come to Hussein. That is what happened and he won by a clear margin of seven per cent, both strengthening his chief sponsor's position and terminating the unity of the opposition parties.

This was Indira's first organisational victory against her opponents inside the party. She could not, however, make progress on other fronts immediately. In the elections for the party presidency, she opposed Kamaraj standing again, but none of her candidates were accepted and it was a Syndicate person, Nijalingappa, who got the post. The struggle was beginning to escalate. In Parliament, the 'Young Turk' Chandrashekhar accused the Finance Minister, Morarji Desai, of conniving in the corruption of his son, Kantibhai, who was on the payroll of various businessmen. There was uproar, but Mrs Gandhi did not come to the defence of her Deputy Prime Minister. When the Congress Working Committee later instructed her to administer a sharp rebuke to Chandrashekhar, she did not carry out the injunction —Desai had annoyed her a great deal by making pro-Western remarks, which were not official government policy, on his trips to Washington and Tokyo.

It was obvious that both sides were preparing for a final showdown. Ironically enough, the cause was once again the presidency of India. On 12 March 1969, the Congress President noted in his diary: 'I am not sure if she deserves to continue as Prime Minister.' On 3 May, Zakir Hussein died after a heart attack. The Syndicate decided to teach Indira a lesson which she would not forget — they began to prepare for her removal. The Vice-President V. V. Giri took Hussein's place while the election was prepared. The Syndicate wanted to nominate one of their own men, Sanjiva Reddy, and the Congress Working Committee approved their choice against Indira's wishes. She argued for Giri. Too old, came the reply. She proposed Jagjivan Ram. Too close to the Prime Minister, they said to one another. Reddy was the one, but for whom?

The Bangalore session of the All India Congress Committee was taking place in July. She decided to raise the stakes by preparing a radical economic plan which included nationalisation of the country's banks. Her aim was now to rally the Young Turks behind her and split the Kamaraj-Desai axis, but the parties involved did not allow themselves to be provoked. A compromise was drafted by the Maharashtra boss, Chavan, and passed unanimously by the Working Committee. The Syndicate was determined that Reddy should become president of India and they did not want to extend the battle to other fronts. The Congress Parliamentary Board confirmed their choice, and Indira was outraged. She now threw caution to the winds and took them by surprise in a series of well-executed moves.

First she dismissed Morarji Desai as Finance Minister, but requested him to continue as Deputy Prime Minister: an impossible request, as she knew. Desai resigned. Three days later, as her own Finance Minister, she pushed through a presidential ordnance nationalising fourteen banks. It was a political move designed to isolate, outflank and defeat her inner-party opponents, and she was also aware that this measure would be seen by the populace as something in their favour. The Young Turks made it clear that it was a sharp blow against 'monopoly capitalism' and would aid the state sector considerably. At the same time farmers, traders and others were assured that credits would become easier for small businessmen. Large crowds gathered outside 1 Safdarjung Road to congratulate her for the nationalisations. The third blow against her opposition was to prove decisive. V. V. Giri stated that he was opposing Sanjiva Reddy, the official Congress nominee, and he was backed by the left parties in Parliament. Indira now took two crucial decisions. She refused to call on Congress representatives to vote for Reddy and simultaneously made the whole question of party discipline irrelevant by calling for a 'free vote' determined by the conscience of individual MPs. The Syndicate now approached the Jan Sangh and Swatantra to support Reddy against the candidate backed by the two Communist Parties. She now realised that the central issue was her political survival. She denounced the Congress leaders who had approached the right, arguing that this had breached an important principle of the Congress – secularism – and added, 'I do not think therefore that in these circumstances and for constitutional reasons, it would be right for me to have a whip issued.' The 'free vote' was a superb tactical manoeuvre. It avoided openly opposing Reddy, but it totally undermined his support inside Congress. On the day before the election, she made her position clear in public: 'Vote according to conscience'. Behind the scenes she built support for Giri and on 20 August her strategy paid off; Giri was elected President of India.

Sixty Congress MPs demanded that Indira Gandhi be disciplined by the party for having organised the defeat of its presidential candidate. The Young Turks responded by demanding that the Congress President be charged with breaching party rules by his secret talks with the Jan Sangh and Swatantra. The split was beginning to develop. On 22 August both Communist Parties declared that they would be prepared to vote for a 'progressive government' headed by Indira Gandhi. That meant 42 votes for her. 22 independent MPs backed the CP's decision, which brought the total to 64, already a majority over the dissident Congress MPs. Then Congress MPs by a large majority also backed her up. Chavan had seen which way the wind was blowing and left the Syndicate/Desai boat. No grouping now had a majority on the Congress Working Committee. A truce was hurriedly organised and the Syndicate leaders dropped their proposed disciplinary charges against the Prime Minister. She was now determined to defeat them permanently. Her supporters began to collect signatures for an emergency meeting of the All India Congress Committee (AICC) to elect a new Working Committee. Trust between the two sides broke down and Desai commented sourly: 'We have been hoodwinked by this lady before. Never again.' Indira claimed she was fighting for democratic socialism against reaction. Her opponents argued that they were fighting for democracy against a communist dictatorship. Both claims were utterly spurious, but by invoking the bogey of communism, the Syndicate, in reality, gave credibility to the version of the left-right split. They played into her hands. Both sides prepared for the denouncement and issued their last statements. Indira Gandhi's open letter to Congress members was published on 8 November 1969. Its essence was as follows:

> It is a conflict between two outlooks and attitudes in regard to the objectives of Congress and the methods in which the Congress itself should function. It is a conflict between those who are for socialism, for change and for the fullest internal democracy and debate in the organisation . . . and those who are for the status quo, for conformism and for less than full discussion inside Congress . . . People of this group paid only lip-service to these ideals (democracy, socialism, secularism and non-alignment) . . . I know that this group constantly tried to check and frustrate my father's attempts to bring about far-reaching economic and social changes.

On 11 November 1969, Nijalingappa sent her a public reply:

> The persistence with which you are attempting to paint your bid for one-man rule [sic] in the organisation and the government as a conflict between the so-called progressive and radical section of the Congress and the so-called reactionary section . . . cannot mislead anyone

except the stormtroopers. No aspirants for dictatorial powers in the 20th century have omitted to put on the garb of socialism . . . You have referred to bogus membership and bossism in the organisation . . . But I am not aware of any action you initiated when you were President of the Congress . . . to deal with these problems . . .

The following day the Syndicate expelled Indira Gandhi from the Indian Congress and called on the parliamentary party to elect a new leader. She was backed by 310 of the 429 Congress MPs the next day. Some were absent. A handful of Syndicate MPs crossed over to the opposition, but the communists, socialists and the DMK together with the independents made her position fairly secure. The crowds supported her wholeheartedly. She had convinced them that the split had happened because she was fighting for the interests of common people. When the emergency session of the AICC took place, 446 out of 705 delegates voted for Indira Gandhi. The Congress had split. Long live the Congress.

Indira had done what Jawaharlal was never able to achieve. True, the choices in his time had been more difficult, but the issues, too, had been far more real. In the 1930s the Congress was divided between radical socialists and the upholders of the social status quo: a split at that time might well have transformed Indian history. The present breach was not exclusively about power. The people saw it in ideological terms and the next election would be fought on a radical-populist basis, but the reality would be different. What the 1969 split had done was to cement Indira Gandhi's hold over the Congress Party. She had revealed certain features in this fight that had not been seen before and this determined ruthlessness would soon come in handy in dealing with some of the problems developing in India's neighbouring countries.

The split in the Congress Party provided Indira Gandhi with a real opportunity to start afresh. She had defeated the Syndicate, which, apart from Kamaraj and Nijalingappa, was generally acknowledged to be riddled with corruption, and she had dispensed with Morarji Desai and his conservatives. She was still Prime Minister of India because the parties of the left and the Tamil and Sikh regionalists were backing her rather than her opponents, but she knew that, sooner rather than later, she would need a fresh mandate from the electorate. Here was a chance to construct a new political party along more principled lines and with a firm political basis — a party whose members were in agreement with its programme. Such a step would indeed have been possible, *if* there had been a solid ideological reason for the division. One of Mrs Gandhi's more intelligent biographers, Zareer Masani, shrewdly observed that:

> Had the Syndicate not challenged her leadership, there is little doubt that Mrs Gandhi, like her father, would have placed Congress unity before socialism. Though she had emerged from the split as the leader of the Indian left, Indira Gandhi was neither a Lenin nor a Mao Zedong, but a cautious and pragmatic Congresswoman. She had shown a capacity to take risks when the immediate situation demanded it; but this did not mean that she would stake her political future on a comprehensive and sweeping programme of social change . . . Though more sensitive than other Congress leaders to popular aspirations, Mrs Gandhi in the last analysis remained a product of the traditional Congress mould . . .

This assessment would soon be vindicated by history, but until then Mrs Gandhi's populism undoubtedly excited a mass response that had been absent in India since independence. The nationalisation of the banks was followed by abolishing the 'privy purses' of the royal houses of India's nobility. The rulers had been guaranteed a large pension from the state and various other privileges by the new constitution. She introduced a bill to amend that particular clause in the constitution, and although the Maharajahs and Maharanis squealed with anger, the measure was extremely popular with the common people. The rival Congress had linked up with Swatantra and the Jan Sangh to oppose the measure. Mrs Gandhi also warned India's capitalists that, although she would support them, they must permit reforms or else everything could be swept aside. In an address to the Associated Chambers of Commerce and Industry (ACCI) in December 1970 she was to spell her message out very clearly:

> You have spoken, as many business people speak, about not bringing politics into economics. But you have no hesitation in trying to influence politics in every way you can to serve your own interests . . . In other countries whole classes have been wiped out. We are trying to prevent it. We are trying to have a kind of change which will prevent it, which will be peaceful, which will give a place to all in our country without thinking of wiping them out. It is for the business community to decide whether they will agree to have this sort of change or they will, by not agreeing at this stage, invite something which will be far more drastic, and certainly for which people like us will not be responsible.

This display of pragmatic populism coupled with a radical rhetoric at mass meetings was necessary, in her opinion, to prevent the communists from gaining too much ground. She was beginning to think of an early election to end the anomalous position in Parliament, where she did not have an absolute majority. Within the government and her Congress Party, she had established control in a decisive fashion, wielding far greater power over both party and government than had been enjoyed by Jawaharlal Nehru. On 27 December 1970, she dissolved Parliament and told the nation in a broadcast that a new election was necessary, a year ahead of schedule, because 'we are concerned not merely with remaining in power, but with using that power to ensure a better life for the vast majority of our people and to satisfy their aspirations for a just social order. In the present situation, we feel we cannot go ahead with our proclaimed programme and keep our pledges to our people . . . Time will not wait for us. The millions who demand food, shelter and jobs are pressing for action. Power in a democracy resides with the people. That is why we have decided to go to our people and to seek a fresh mandate from them.'

This gave a very clear indication of the tenor of the campaign which lay ahead. She would fight as the champion of the underprivileged against their oppressors. The major right-wing opposition parties formed a 'Grand Alliance' to confront her challenge, but they once again proved themselves tactically inept. They stated that their slogan was '*Indira Hatao*' ('Remove Indira'). She responded that her assault was not on any particular individual, but against the status quo. She then unfurled her banner, on which there was inscribed a giant slogan, *Gharibi Hatao* ('Remove Poverty'), which became her battlecry throughout the campaign. She toured the country tirelessly and relentlessly, being greeted by even larger crowds than before. She was no longer seen simply as the frail daughter of the much-loved Nehru, but as a politician in her own right, with her own methods and her own party. From January to March 1971 she covered 30,000 miles by air, 3,000 by road and rail and addressed a total of 410 meetings; 20 million people were estimated to have attended her election rallies. Like her father, she worked a long day, starting at 7 a.m. and continuing till 1 a.m. the next morning. This was an unprecedented election performance. There was not a day lost through illness or fatigue. Her electoral message promised stability to the propertied classes and radical social reforms to the poor. She herself provided a surprisingly accurate estimate of the campaign in a letter to a friendly journalist in London. 'What has been extraordinary and exhilarating is that the elections became a sort of movement — a people's movement . . . The peasant, the worker and, above all, the youth, cut across all caste, religious and other barriers to make this their own campaign with tremendous enthusiasm . . . ' The 1971 elections undoubtedly aroused the masses. This was evident not simply by the size of her meetings, but by the slogans that were chanted during her speeches. Her version of the split in the Congress had been only too acceptable to the people. The campaign had aroused their expectations and raised their political awareness, and they gave her a gigantic majority.

Indira Gandhi's Congress Party won 352 seats out of a total of 518. The rival Congress slumped to 16 members in the new Parliament. The communist vote also increased, but it was the Communist Party (Marxist) that made the gains, increasing its representation from 19 to 25. The right-wing Swatantra Party, which had won 44 seats in 1967, now had eight and the other right-wing group, the Jan Sangh, declined from 35 to 22. It was a crushing defeat for the right. The electorate had undoubtedly moved to the left and would soon begin to ask when poverty was going to be removed. However, the domestic situation was virtually frozen by the dramatic events that were taking place on the country's border at that time.

In neighbouring Pakistan, Field-Marshal Ayub's adventure in Kashmir had exploded in his face. The Tashkent Peace Treaty was viewed as a humiliation and the military regime had begun to weaken. In November 1968, a series of student demonstrations in West Pakistan had snowballed into a movement for democracy and social change. Within two months, every major city in West and East Pakistan was paralysed by an unparalleled insurgency. Students in Dhaka and Chittagong marched along with their counterparts in Rawalpindi, Peshawar, Karachi and Lahore. This was the only real unity that the state created by Jinnah was ever to realise, and even this was short-lived. In March 1969, Ayub was toppled. His replacement, General Yahya Khan, was better known for his addiction to alcohol than his grasp of political strategy. Nonetheless, he promised that general elections would be held in December 1970, the first free plebiscite in the country's history.

The divisions soon became clear. In the western part of the country there resided the ruling class, the Army (80 per cent of which was recruited from West Pakistan, which had 40 per cent of the total population) and the landlords, who held substantial power over the population. The east contained the majority of Pakistan's population as well as a large dispossessed middle-class, which was denied its fair share of the jobs and capital distributed by the State. In the elections of 1970, a populist Pakistan People's Party (PPP) won in the West on a platform extremely similar to that of Indira Gandhi. She said, 'Remove poverty'; the PPP leader, Zulfiqar Ali Bhutto, shouted, 'Food, clothing and shelter'. She promised to spread wealth more evenly; Bhutto pledged to end the rule of the 'twenty-two families' who controlled the bulk of the country's resources. In East Pakistan, however, Bengali nationalists in the revitalised Awami League fought the campaign on the basis of its Six-Point Charter, which demanded a confederation between the two segments of Pakistan and an equal share of the cake — including, said Mujibur Rehman, the Awami League leader, an equal number of Bengalis in the Army. Even though East Pakistan contained 60 per cent of the country's population, an overwhelming bulk of the Army and Civil Service was recruited from West Pakistan.

The Pakistan elections gave Mujibur Rehman's Awami League an overall majority in the country as a whole. He won every single seat in East Bengal. Bhutto triumphed in the West, but refused to accept Mujib as prime minister because of the Charter. In East Pakistan, the people took to the streets and a strange form of dual power came into existence. The Pakistan Army poured troops into the eastern half of the country, ready for any emergency. In March 1971, Mujib was arrested and taken to West Pakistan.

Mrs Gandhi's phenomenal election victory was announced on 10 March 1971. Exactly fifteen days later, the Pakistan Army began a murderous assault on the Bengali citizens of Pakistan. Many young officers had boasted that they were going to Bengal to improve the genes of Bengali children. Rape was commonplace. Massacres took place for the first few weeks, until gradually a Bengali armed resistance began to emerge. It then became clear that General Yahya had embarked on a civil war, thus signing the death-warrant of Jinnah's Pakistan.

Sympathies in India, with the exception of some Maoist groups, were universally with Bengali East Pakistan though for different reasons. India was involved from the beginning since refugees from the war-zones began to pour into West Bengal. The Awami League set up a government-in-exile in Calcutta, the capital of West Bengal. Inside East Pakistan a differentiation was beginning to take place within the resistance. A radical group suggested that the Awami League, a party not dissimilar to the Indian Congress, was partially responsible for the deaths by having failed to prepare and arm the population. Delhi was confronted with a dilemma. If they did not intervene, there was a danger that East Pakistan might go communist, thus posing the question of a united communist Bengal and threatening the Indian federation. This would have meant that the Awami League would be bypassed. If they did intervene, it would mean another war with Pakistan. This could provoke the United States, which was 'tilting towards Yahya's dictatorship' and China, which was supplying weaponry and other aid to the Islamabad war machine.

In India there was strong pressure for intervention, but Indira Gandhi resisted it for several months. Meanwhile she travelled abroad — to the West, where she disassociated herself from Yahya and compared his intervention in Bengal to Nazi conquests in Europe, and to the USSR, where in August 1971 she visited Moscow and signed a Treaty of Peace and Friendship. The Indo-Soviet Treaty shocked the West, but she was mainly guarding her northern flank against the Chinese. The treaty was intended as a warning to Peking. Kissinger rushed to Delhi. She tartly told him to get Mujibur Rehman released from prison and push for a political settlement. She continued to argue that the best solution would be a unilateral retreat by the Pakistan Army, the unconditional release of Mujib and the right of the Bengali people to determine their relations with Pakistan. This was an unlikely prospect and the Indian High Command was told to prepare an offensive in strict secrecy.

On 3 December 1971, the Pakistan Air Force launched a pre-emptive strike against eight Indian airfields. Mrs Gandhi was in Calcutta, addressing a public meeting, when the news was conveyed to her. She ended her speech and was flown back to Delhi in an Air Force plane, protected by Indian jet fighters all the way. In Delhi, the Cabinet was ready for its emergency meeting. It agreed to declare war. The opposition leaders backed the Cabinet. The

President declared an emergency and the Indian Army entered East Pakistan, known to its own people now as Bangladesh (the Bengali nation). Pakistan sent its troops across the western frontiers in an attempt to achieve a breakthrough in Kashmir. They were held back by an effective defence, while the Indian Army, supported and helped by the Bengali guerrilla fighters, marched towards the capital, Dacca. The United States cut off all economic and military aid to India, while maintaining supplies to the military regime in Pakistan. On 9 December, the United States sent the US Seventh Fleet to the Bay of Bengal, with the aim of delaying the Indian advance to Dacca. An emergency meeting presided over by Indira Gandhi and including all the Service Chiefs was held at midnight, at which Mrs Gandhi decided to ignore the Seventh Fleet and press on towards the Bengali capital. A special messenger, however, was sent to Moscow. The Soviet Union despatched its fleet from Vladivostok to the Bay of Bengal and a senior Soviet minister arrived in Delhi on 12 December to monitor the war. The USSR assured India that if the Chinese or Americans intervened, they would be punished.

Throughout the war Mrs Gandhi was informed of every single initiative on the battlefield. On 13 December, General Maneckshaw, in command of the Indian operations, sent an ultimatum to his Pakistani counterpart. They were surrounded and had three days to surrender. On 16 December 1971, the Pakistani Army surrendered to Indian troops. The captured troops and officers, in their tens of thousands, were soon to be transported to India. The genocidal war against Bangladesh had come to an end, and the new state was accorded recognition by a number of countries. In Pakistan, Yahya faced the prospect of a mutiny. He was forced to resign and the Army, totally discredited, and at the end of its tether, sent for Zulfiqar Ali Bhutto to take over what was left of Pakistan.

The formation of Bangladesh had a dramatic impact on India's Muslim minority. For the first time since 1947, there was virtually no sympathy for Pakistan. Even in Kashmir the Pakistani treatment of Bengali Muslims had disgusted former supporters of Jinnah. Elsewhere there was anger and outrage. This was the clearest sign yet that the partition of 1947 had marked a major tragedy for the whole sub-continent.

On the domestic front, Indira's position was now unassailable. She was the 'liberator of Bangladesh'; she had destroyed the

Pakistani military machine and brought down Yahya Khan. Even the most determined opposition leaders felt that they were destined to spend a long time in the wilderness, for her handling of the war had shown her at her best. But how would she confront the peace? There was enormous pressure to continue the conflict and humiliate Yahya Khan and his cohorts in their lair. The Indian Army could have taken Lahore easily, but they had resisted the temptation. In a conversation with the author in January 1984, Mrs Gandhi described an interesting feature of Indian politics: the civilian control of the Army, which had come into prominence during the Bangladesh war:

> I was being interviewed by Swedish TV (on 16 December 1971), when the phone rang. It was General Maneckshaw. 'Madame,' he said, 'we have defeated them. They have surrendered. Dacca has fallen.' I thanked him, fixed a meeting for the next day and finished my television interview. After informing Parliament, I called an emergency Cabinet meeting. Many of the present opposition leaders who are now attacking me for being too hard on General Zia, were then in my Cabinet. They entered the room jubilant — 'we have won, we have won' — and insisted that the war be fought to a finish. 'Let's crush the enemy permanently' was a common theme.
>
> Let me tell you that when the meeting started I was alone in demanding a unilateral ceasefire on our part. By the end of the Cabinet session I had got my way. You know I am a very determined person when I'm convinced I'm right. The Cabinet then passed a resolution calling for an implementation of the ceasefire.
>
> Later that day I met the High Command. Naturally, as generals who had won a decisive battle, they wanted to finish the war in their way. I lectured them on my position, which was based on a political appreciation of the overall situation. They choked and spluttered, but I informed them that I was speaking with the authority of a unanimous Cabinet. Well, they saluted and said they would carry out our instructions. Now this could not have happened in many countries and I don't just mean the Third World.

As a result of the momentous events of 1971, the year that followed was unique in the post-independence history of the sub-continent. A new state had been created, but more importantly, each of the four governments within the sub-continent was in power as the result of a popular mandate. The problems that confronted Indira Gandhi in India, Bhutto in Pakistan, Mujibur Rehman in Bangladesh and Srimavo Bandaranaike in Sri Lanka were remarkably similar. So were their responses. Concealed beneath the populism was an authoritarian streak. For Indira, the first few months of 1972, proved to be a relatively calm period. The storms on the horizon were visible, but she could afford to bask for a while in the atmosphere generated by her undeniable popularity.

The Republic Day celebrations in New Delhi on 26 January 1972, threw austerity aside in a remarkable display of pageantry and colour. It was a reflection of the prevailing euphoria and Indira Gandhi was cheered wildly as she took the salute at the marchpast. In the sphere of external relations 1972 proved to be a grand year. The Bangladesh leader, Sheikh Mujibur Rehman, was given a gigantic welcome in Delhi and Mrs Gandhi received a heroine's reception in Dacca. Pakistan's leader, Zulfiqar Ali Bhutto, was forced to visit India in order to secure the release of Pakistani POWs. The Simla Summit between Bhutto and Mrs Gandhi was a success, despite some hiccups, and resulted in the Pakistani recognition of Bangladesh some months later. Like her father, Indira Gandhi had developed a real passion for world politics, and there were times when it appeared that she preferred the larger stage of international affairs to the makeshift wooden platform that was India. It was always on the latter that the problems erupted. On the larger, more solid platform she appeared to her people as a latter-day Durga, the ancient Indian goddess of war. At the national level, however, the Durga image evaporated quickly and she appeared as the leader of a political party which promised a lot, but delivered very little.

1972 was a year of triumph, but also of crisis. There was a terrible drought in most parts of the country, affecting 180 million people. In some areas drinking water became a luxury, reducing the poor to destitution. At the same time as the economic crisis was worsening, a number of scandals erupted — involving Cabinet ministers and, in one case, Indira Gandhi herself. The ministers were accused of accepting donations on behalf of the Congress from smugglers and Mafia bosses in return for unspecified favours. Indian politics in this period and subsequently came to resemble the United States in the 1920s and 1930s, prior to the New Deal. In a number of towns politics became business, business became politics and gangsterism overwhelmed both big business and big politics. Political, business and criminal mafias began to amalgamate. A commission of inquiry found a senior Congress politician, Harekrishna Mahatab, ex-Chief Minister of Orissa, guilty of accepting large bribes from industrialists. He remained unscathed. Indira herself was accused of favouring a spurious project presented by her younger son, Sanjay, to develop a new car for India, called Maruti (the Son of the Wind God). The charge was denied, but discontent began to spread.

In 1972–3 prices rose by 22 per cent, under a government that had pledged to remove poverty. A wave of strikes began to spread in different parts of the country. There were a total of 12,089 strikes and sit-in protests in Bombay alone, the industrial capital of India, in 1972–3. In April 1973, fed up with the taunts from hecklers who reminded her about removing poverty, she told *Blitz*, a Bombay weekly: 'If anybody tries to say that poverty can go in my lifetime or during my tenure as Prime Minister, it just cannot. It has very deep roots.' At virtually the same time Bhutto was telling hecklers at a public meeting in Karachi: 'When I promised food, clothing and shelter in our manifesto, I did not mean *for everyone*.' In Dacca, Mujibur Rehman was discovering that his paternalistic style and his constant refrain: 'I love my people. My people love me,' was not being accepted as sufficient any longer. In Sri Lanka, Mrs Bandaranaike had just presided over the butchery of a massive youth rebellion which had taken the island by surprise in 1971. Indira, Bhutto and Mujib claimed to be socialists. Mrs Bandaranaike was a Buddhist. None of the four leaders was fully aware of the fact that they were planting the seeds of self-destruction.

4
Empress of India
1974–79

Democracy was preparing to confront its most critical period. Hard times were on the way. Famine, death, destruction, slaughter, beggary, infamy, despair and servitude were the ingredients and the gigantic flagon which contained them would soon be poured, all at once, over the head of Mother India. The same Mother India which Jawaharlal had defined so movingly in the 1930s: the faceless millions who toiled endlessly to produce the country's wealth. What was needed was a liberating deluge which could sweep aside the oppressions of caste and class, obliterate the landmarks of poverty and hunger and create new living conditions. Many had thought that the 'Remove Poverty' campaign would begin to do just that and, perhaps, a little more — but it did nothing of the kind, and the eternal despair of the peasant and the worker gave way, once again, to anger and even hatred. Indira Gandhi was not unaware of this shift in mass perception. The evidence was to be found all over the country.

In 1967, in Naxalbari, a small village in Northern Bengal, the District Committee of the CP(M) unleashed a peasant insurgency, which spread slowly to other parts of the country. It had the biggest impact on the post-1947 products of Indian universities. In 1951 there were 65,000 engineers; in 1963 the figure had risen to 330,000. The number of doctors rose from 62,000 to 103,000 in the same period. There were 150,000 teachers in higher education, 65,000 research scientists, several thousand journalists, 50,000 lawyers and hundreds of thousands of graduates from other fields. A large proportion of them could not find employment. The situation in West Bengal was particularly bad (it was intelligently depicted by Satyajit Ray in *The Middleman*, a cinematic essay on urban unemployment) and the advocates of violent revolution in Naxalbari found hundreds of recruits amongst the educated middle-class youths in the cities. The CP(M) disavowed the

Naxalite movement and expelled its leaders, who immediately set up another Communist Party, with the appellation Marxist-Leninist. On the walls of Calcutta, and in various villages, the new initials made a dramatic appearance: CPI(M-L).

This new wave was part, in many ways, of a larger radicalisation that had swept the advanced countries of Japan, Western Europe and North America in 1968–75. In India it partially defeated itself and would have petered out on its own, but was subjected to brutal and degrading repression. By 1974–5, the Maoist movement was on the retreat and what Delhi could not accomplish was completed by the old men in Peking. The Sino-American alliance, the death of Lin Piao, the rise and subsequent defeat of the 'Gang of Four', the new-style softer approach of Deng Xiaoping was too much for even the most slavish supporters of Peking.

The Indian Maoists had tried to defeat the Moscow-is-Mecca parties with the slogan of Peking-is-Mecca. When they discovered that there was, in fact, no Mecca at all, they collapsed. Even at the peak of their strength it could hardly be said that they posed a serious threat to the Indian State.

A more serious situation was developing within the urban workforce, for whom the economic situation was more of a catastrophe than an ordinary crisis. Famines and floods had been accompanied by an increase in the world price of oil. In 1974 the balance of payments deficit stood at 2,000 million dollars, more than the net amount of aid received from abroad. This was compounded by an already enormous foreign debt, which had claimed 25 per cent of the country's annual export. Thus the regime had to restrict the import of raw materials. This meant that in addition to the food shortage, there was a scarcity of cooking oil, fuel oil, matches, wood and even paper. The *Times of India*, printed on paper so yellow that it was virtually illegible, wrote an editorial which sympathised with the shopping problems of the middle-class housewife who was now compelled to 'live dangerously', since 'going shopping has become a daily adventure that involves new surprises every day'. It did not remind its readers of the 'daily adventures' of the pavement-dwellers of Bombay, forced to live on one meal a day and spend a lot of time scavenging in the dustbins of the big hotels to find food. In 1974, an average meal in the Taj Mahal hotel in Bombay cost between 17 and 35 dollars a head. In 1974, 40 per cent of the population lived on less than half a rupee (12 US cents) a day.

If these conditions had developed ten years earlier, the Communist Parties would have experienced a massive growth of support. The situation had now altered. The CPI, under the leadership of a veteran communist, Dange, had aligned itself with Indira's Congress and suffered as a result from the discredit accumulated by the ruling party. Its rival CP(M) was in slightly better shape, but had been weakened by its lacklustre performance in the coalition governments it headed in Kerala and West Bengal. Its use of open violence against the Naxalites had caused further demoralisation amongst its own supporters. In a country afflicted with many cancers, of which corruption seemed to be the most deeply rooted, there were two 'cancer wards': Kerala and West Bengal. When, at the end of the treatment, it became obvious that the doctors had also succumbed to the disease, the left-wing alternative to Indira Gandhi, in the eyes of the masses, gradually disappeared from sight.

In desperation the workers had to fight on their own. In the late 1960s and 1970s a new tactic emerged in Bengal and spread throughout the sub-continent. The workers called it '*gherao*' (encircle and beseige) and its aim was to keep the managers and proprietors in their factories and offices until they agreed to the workers' demands in writing. The *gheraos* became popular because many of them were successful and appeared far more dynamic than a passive withdrawal of labour or even a factory occupation. The factory owners and investors became angry, which was hardly surprising — they began to call for firm action. Tata and Birla spoke openly about anarchy and chaos enveloping the country. They did not speak so openly about the grim living conditions of the majority of Indians. Nonetheless the government was aware of India's status. It was a capitalist democracy, and if the capitalists were angry, then they had to be appeased and their minds and pockets set at rest. New paramilitary units were set up to deal with the industrial rebels: repression became routine. The police and private goon-squads collaborated to intimidate and assault trades unionists. Working class activists were tortured in prison. The *gherao* phase came to a rapid end. A poet, Habib Jalib, wrote from his city in Pakistan (*gheraos* did not respect frontiers):

We were *gherao*ed by every Age,
No one ever came to our rescue!
Then, one day, *we gherao*ed *them*,

And every tyrant shouted his rage.
No reason to worry:
We shall rise soon despite the pain.
And every city which is now dark
Will see the light once again.

The *gheraos* had ended, but the wave of 'normal' strikes continued to paralyse industry. From March 1974, the government was aware of the demands of the railway unions. India had 64,000 kilometres of railways, one of the more solid achievements of the *raj*. In a country where the trade union movement was divided along political lines, there was no possibility of a single union spanning the entire industry; the workforce of the railways belonged, in fact, to one hundred unions, big and small. The only previous attempt at an all-India rail strike had been defeated in 1948. The government said that what they had been given did not constitute 'a formal strike notice'. That was served on 23 April 1974, but Indira Gandhi said that any strike would be declared illegal. Emergency Defence of India Regulations were invoked as a precautionary measure. On 27 April, the government, instead of resuming negotiations, announced the cancellation of a number of passenger trains. The 'Political Affairs Committee' of the Cabinet was determined to teach the workers a lesson. As a result the union demands, which were purely economic, were dismissed out of hand.

The government decided to make the strike a test of strength and treat it as a political challenge to the state. In addition to cancelling trains on 27 April, the government ordered the armed forces and paramilitary organisations to go on 'full alert'. On 1 May, a railway worker's leader, George Fernandes, was arrested and this was followed by a round-up of all local officials of the National Co-Ordinating Committee for Railwaymen's Struggle (NCCRS), as whose convenor Fernandes had been elected. On 7 May the strike began, with all unions involved except those affiliated to INTUC, the Congress federation.

A million workers were on strike. Within the first few days 60,000 workers were arrested and many activists and union leaders went underground to avoid arrest. The campaign against the strikers was personally conducted by Indira Gandhi, who was reported as telling a Cabinet colleague in favour of mediation that once this strike had been crushed, there would not be another for fifty years. The whole operation was, in fact, conducted like a war.

The Secretary of the National Railway Workers Union, C. Radhakrishnan, told an interviewer from the British magazine *Race Today* in April 1975:

> The government tried everything. We were hunted like criminals and they literally tried to starve us into submission. During the strike, short of using the Air Force to bomb the railway colonies, they used every method to terrorise us and break the strike. The Army and Navy were both called out. They were used to guard all railway installations against sabotage, to operate signals and telecommunications, to run trains under the protection of armed guards and generally to keep order. Almost overnight, the Central and State Reserve Police turned the railway colonies into armed camps. It was like an occupation. Early every morning police and troops would go into every house and ask workers if they were reporting on duty. Those who refused to go were arrested. Under these conditions people started returning to work . . . Our family members were also terrorised. There were cases where the police, failing to find a particular worker, picked up his kids and took them to the police station. From there they sent notices saying, 'If you want your child back alive, come and get him from the police station and then go back to work.' Old women, mothers of workers, were taken in this way to the police station and told, 'If your son doesn't put in an appearance by such and such a time, you will be arrested. Tell him that.'
>
> These are not exaggerations. They are things we have seen and heard with our own eyes and ears . . .

Many similar incidents were reported in the Indian press and at some of the giant meetings which took place outside railway stations. There was one instance of railway workers' huts being set on fire, leaving their families homeless. These were incidents from a civil war: even those who were not sympathetic to the strike were shocked by the brutality. The strike lasted for twenty-two days. It was defeated by an unprecedented use of force. The railway workers were used as a scapegoat by Mrs Gandhi, who displayed an iron fist in order to restore the confidence of the chambers of commerce. Many workers were sacked, but it is not easy for any government to replace a million workers. The dismissals were selective: the more articulate workers were sacked without recourse to appeal; the rest were forced to sign a pledge of loyalty to the railways. Some workers refused to sign the 'loyalty certificates' and were instantly dismissed.

The railway strike ended in a major victory for Indira Gandhi. The Railway Minister, L. N. Mishra, was one important government casualty. He was killed in a bomb explosion. The killers were never uncovered. Mishra had been an important collector of money for the Congress from the criminal classes. Mrs Gandhi had now demonstrated her skills as a ruthless and hardened war-leader. Whereas Bangladesh had enhanced her status, the defeat of the railway workers left an unpleasant aftertaste. The flavour of fear was far too strong. The chambers of commerce were pleased, of course, but they did not command many votes in the elections. Even political observers sympathetic to Mrs Gandhi were compelled to admit that she was now deeply unpopular. The elections were scheduled for 1976 and a Congress defeat was a real possibility. It appeared to many that she was not so much trying to remove poverty as get rid of the poor. A South Indian poet captured the atmosphere of the time:

. . . The audience started to leave.
The accursed gang, sensing this,
Shouted 'Socialism!'
Postered the walls, 'Socialism!' . . . 'Socialism!'
All over the land, the slogans rebounded.
But amidst the infernal din,
The looting of the people went on . . .

By-elections and state elections in the country reflected this mood. The Congress began to lose seats with a rapidity that indicated the volatility of the electorate. In a number of places, including Congress strongholds such as Gujarat, Indira was now greeted with stones, abuse and the black flags that were a sign of opposition. Mrs Gandhi lost the state elections in Gujarat. Who would harness this mass opposition and give it a political direction? This was the question being asked by the press, political parties and the Cabinet. The answer, when it came, was peculiarly Indian.

In the early months of 1974 an old friend and onetime ally of Jawaharlal Nehru decided to make a major intervention in Indian politics. His name was Jayaprakash Narayan. He had resigned from the Congress after the Lucknow Session in 1936 because he had felt that Gandhi's victory against Nehru marked a turning-point in the course of the struggle for independence. Subsequently JP (as he became known) had become a founder-member of the Socialist Party, a member of parliament and later an independent. In the latter capacity he had visited Pakistan in 1962 and been charmed by the military dictator at the time, General Ayub Khan.

The dictatorship had discovered a method of indirect elections, which it had named 'basic democracy'. The entire operation was bogus, but JP was impressed and had made statements suggesting that India needed a similar system. He was not taken very seriously by anyone.

Now JP, taking advantage of the failures of the left, called for a mass campaign in favour of lower prices and the rooting out of corruption. Narayan had now become a Gandhian and believed that only a return to the village as the central unit of political and economic life would take India forward. His programme was simple. He wanted a voluntary federation of village republics based on *sarvodaya* (welfare of the community). The means to be used to gain this end would be non-violent mass resistance as popularised by Gandhi. In normal circumstances this attempt to parody history would have ended in farce, but the particular circumstances in India at the time were such that people were waiting for a lead. Narayan's programme was not properly understood, but his own description of it as 'total revolution' was popular and everyone below a certain income level favoured price reductions and hated corruption. In Bihar and Gujerat a mass movement erupted on the basis of JP's demands. The press began to refer to it as the JP Movement and given Indira's electoral defeat in Gujerat, she began to show signs of nervousness. The Gandhian former socialist began to develop Bonapartist airs. He agreed to an alliance with the Jan Sangh, knowing full well that with his appeal and the Sangh's well-oiled party machine, they could produce a large number of electoral surprises in the 1976 elections. The urban upheavals were repressed, but their scale made it difficult to end them altogether.

In the middle of this crisis the Allahabad High Court stunned the country by its judgement of 12 June 1975 on the case brought by a maverick named Raj Narain, whom Mrs Gandhi had defeated by 100,000 votes. It found Mrs Gandhi guilty of electoral malpractice, and instructed her to stop voting in Parliament, while continuing as Prime Minister. Most importantly, this ruling disqualified her from holding public office for a period of six years. The Congress Party was shaken by this decision. The opposition was jubilant. Indira's offence had been minor. It had involved the use of government transport and personnel during her last election campaign. In private, everyone, including her opponents, agreed that the charges against her were trivial and that the judge had exceeded his brief. If this had happened at the end of the Bangladesh War or just after the 'Remove Poverty' campaign, there can be little doubt that there would have been a wave of massive demonstrations on her behalf. It is unlikely that any judge would have made such a decision, for the judiciary in India, as in Britain, is susceptible to public opinion. In 1975, however, the people celebrated. JP now escalated his verbal onslaughts and called on police and army officers not to obey 'unlawful' orders. He followed this up by challenging Congress on every issue: smuggling, black-marketing, corruption, poverty, wealth, price rises, election misdeeds, repression and so on. On 25 June 1975, JP announced that he was organising a week-long protest outside the Prime Minister's residence from 29 June to 5 July 1975. This would be part of a series of actions designed to reawaken the people of India.

On the same day, Indira Gandhi paid a surprise call on the President of India, Fakhrudin Ali Ahmed, to inform him in strictest confidence that his services would soon be needed and he should stay on call. At 11 p.m. the same night she paid another visit to the President with a document, which he had agreed to sign. It was the proclamation of an emergency. Even before the paper had been signed the Indian intelligence services were warning prison governors throughout the country to be prepared for a mass influx in the very near future. On 26 June 1975, the following statement was made: 'In exercise of the powers conferred by clause 1, article 352 of the constitution, I, Fakhrudin Ali Ahmed, President of India, by this proclamation declare that a grave emergency exists, whereby the security of India is threatened by internal disturbances.' Shortly afterwards, Indira Gandhi explained the action in a special broadcast. Her opening remark was a masterpiece of understatement: 'The President has proclaimed an emergency. There is nothing to panic about.'

What followed was the mass arrest of opposition leaders (Narayan, Desai and leading Jan Sangh and RSS activists were all imprisoned); a draconian press censorship; a ban on demonstrations and strikes, coupled with a wage freeze. The censorship was, at one stage, so severe that even the writings of Mahatma Gandhi and Jawaharlal Nehru concerning the struggle for democratic rights and press freedom under the British were banned. Indira had been worried that she might not get her own Cabinet to support such measures. As a result, the decision to go to the

President was not taken by a unanimous Cabinet, but by a tiny clique consisting of the Prime Minister's closest advisers, many of whom were not elected in any capacity. The Shah Commission Report on the Emergency, published six years later, was a sober and carefully documented account, avoiding hyperbole and the settling of scores. It stated that there was no evidence of any serious threat to the constitution or to law and order:

> There is no evidence of any breakdown of law and order in any part of the country — nor of any apprehension in that behalf; the economic condition was well under control and had in no way deteriorated. There is not even a report of an apprehension of any serious breakdown of the law and order situation or deterioration of the economic condition from any public functionary. The public records of the times, secret, confidential or public and publications in newspapers, speak with unanimity that there was no unusual event or even a tendency in that direction to justify the imposition of emergency. There was no threat to the well-being of the nation from sources external or internal. The conclusion appears in the absence of any evidence given by Indira Gandhi or anyone else, that the one and the only motivating force for tendering the extraordinary advice to the President to declare an 'internal emergency' was the intense political activity generated in the ruling party and the opposition, by the decision of the Allahabad High Court declaring the election of the Prime Minister of the day invalid on the grounds of corrupt election practices. There is no reason to think that if the democratic conventions were followed, the whole political upsurge would in the normal course have not subsided. But Madame Gandhi in her anxiety to continue in power, brought about instead a situation which directly contributed to her continuance in power and also generated forces which sacrificed the interests of many to serve the ambitions of a few. Thousands were detained and a series of totally illegal and unwarranted actions followed involving untold human misery and suffering.

The official propaganda painted the emergency as a blow against 'fascism' and attempts by right-wing parties to overturn the constitution and make India another Chile. The CPI, which backed the emergency (and won for itself the soubriquet of Communist Party of Indira) stated that a 'blow had been struck against counter-revolution' and 'neo-colonialist, reactionary, communal and fascist forces'. Words of this sort had a hollow ring even at the time, but in retrospect they appear utterly ridiculous. If Mrs Gandhi had attempted to implement a radical programme of social reforms *à la* Salvador Allende in Chile, she would have found massive support in her favour. India in 1975 was not Chile. If Indira Gandhi had thought she could win the 1976 elections there would not have been an emergency. Its purpose was basically two-fold: to safeguard the Congress Party and her own political position while forcibly bringing to an end rural and urban unrest in many parts of the country.

As part of the emergency Mrs Gandhi introduced a twenty-point economic programme, which was parroted repeatedly on the radio and in the press, and was the familiar mixture of old Congress promises. It pledged radical agrarian reforms and a relaxation of curbs on private enterprise. Only one of the agrarian reforms was to be implemented: there was increased credit for the land-owning peasants. In fact the emergency was welcomed both at home and abroad by the owners and investors of capital, who saw in it a discipline much-needed at the time. J. R. D. Tata, the richest man in India, confided to a journalist: 'Things had gone too far. You can't imagine what we have been through here — strikes, boycotts, demonstrations. Why, there were days I couldn't walk out of my office on to the street. The parliamentary system is not suited to our needs.'

The emergency had seemed, initially, to hit the states in Northern India. In Tamil Nadu in the south, the DMK Chief Minister M. Karunanidhi, called a protest rally the same evening. At least a quarter of a million people responded, though some reports claimed that the figure was nearer a million. As the sun set on the Coromandel coast, Karunanidhi asked the people present to take an oath and repeat after him:

> We solemnly affirm that we would not hesitate in any manner to safeguard India's democracy, whatever be the odds against us and whatever be the crisis that confronts us. This vast assemblage of the people of Tamil Nadu requests the Prime Minister of India to fulfil its demands that the national leaders now in detention be set at liberty and the legitimate rights of the press restored. Long live democracy.

The state government would soon be dismissed, but the act of defiance by such a gigantic gathering partially helped to protect the south of the country against the excesses which became common in the north.

A total of 34,630 people were detained without trial throughout the emergency years under the provisions of the Maintenance of Internal Security Act (MISA); 72,000 were arrested under the Defence of India Regulations (DIR). The arrests were by no means confined to right-wingers. Large numbers of CP(M) supporters and members, left-wing students and trade unionists, radical or even slightly critical professors found themselves in prison. Here they met many Maoists, who had been imprisoned some years ago.

What soon became very clear was that the emergency was not an extra-parliamentary phenomenon. It was a constitutional *coup d'état*, carried out with the support of the large Congress majority in Parliament. Without this support, Indira Gandhi could not have imposed an emergency of this magnitude. Since patronage was now insufficient to maintain the dominant position of the Congress party, fear was used instead. However, any party in a capitalist democracy that rules indefinitely after suspending the constitution must ask itself how far it can go without the support of the Army. None of the powerful social forces in the country were anxious to see any form of military dictatorship: apart from anything else, it would have posed a very serious threat to the unity of the Indian Federation.

The years of the rising son

Sanjay Gandhi's reaction to the radio announcement that his mother had been de-seated by a High Court decision was one of anger. Yet fear was also present, since the Maruti affair could have led to prosecutions had she not been the Prime Minister. He needed another year to clean up the mess.

> I was in the factory when I heard the news. I immediately came here (1 Safdarjung Road). Hundreds of people were already here. I did not hear anything about resignation from my mother, but such things were being said. My own spontaneous reaction was that she must stay on since the Allahabad High Court had granted her an absolute stay of its order.

Indira herself had been taken totally by surprise. She was stunned by the judgement. A number of her Congress colleagues had begun to informally discuss who would replace her and the name of the Maharashtra leader, Chavan, was being mentioned in this context. Sanjay's 'spontaneous reaction' was no doubt warmly received by his mother, but accounts which suggested that she was seriously considering resignation were grossly exaggerated. Her first reaction on suffering a personal or political setback was to retreat into herself. This was always a temporary phase and she had hitherto always returned to the fray. It is therefore extremely unlikely that Sanjay's support was decisive at this stage. She was delighted to get his active support, but more for personal and psychological reasons than anything else.

It was during the years of the emergency that Sanjay became a regular fixture at the political discussions that took place at 1 Safdarjung Road. His new interest in politics was a boon to the toadies and hangers-on who were never too far from the centres of power. Sanjay had, during the Maruti years, acquired a set of *chamchas*. The word literally means 'spoons', but was a synonym for sycophants without any shame or scruples. It was during the first years of British rule that the word *chamcha* acquired a new currency. Prior to that time everyone in India, despite differences of class and caste, ate with their fingers. When the landed gentry in the north began to invite the new conquerors to their homes and entertain them in a lavish style, they needed cutlery. As time passed they began to ape the new rulers and were described by a wit (who remains, alas, anonymous) as *chamchas* of the English.

Sanjay's gang included his old Doon School friends. His *chamchas* included the Chief Minister of Haryana, Bansi Lall, who had authorised the sale of land (and the eviction of peasants) in order to provide Maruti Inc. with a good start. Vidya Charan Shukla had also been described as a *chamcha*, but he was a characteristically opportunist Congress politician, making sure that his career was not jeopardised. As Minister for Information he had become responsible for ensuring that the censored press did not exceed the agreed limits. Nikhil Chakravarty of *Mainstream*, a magazine, which acted as the critical conscience of the Congress, had tried to make a point by printing a poem by Tagore in his Editor's Notebook under the caption, *Tagore for Today*:

Freedom from fear is the freedom I claim for you, My motherland! — fear, the phantom demon, shaped by your own distorted dreams;
Freedom from the burden of ages, bending your head, breaking your back, blinding your eyes to the beckoning call of the future;
Freedom from shackles of slumber wherewith you fasten yourself to night's stillness, mistrusting the star that speaks of truth's adventurous path;
Freedom from the anarchy of a destiny, whose sails are weakly yielded to blind uncertain winds, and the helm to a hand ever rigid and cold as Death;

Freedom from the insult of the dwelling in a puppet's world, where movements are started through brainless wires, repeated through mindless habits; where figures wait with patient obedience for a master of show to be stirred into a moment's mimicry of life.

Other newspapers had adopted an equally defiant stance by publishing Jawaharlal Nehru and Mahatama Gandhi on the importance of democracy and press freedom. V. C. Shukla, a deeply cultured man, summoned them all and told them in blunt down-to-earth language that the game was over. Tagore, Nehru and Gandhi were not immune to censorship. Then, as if reading the thoughts of the assembled editors, Shukla had stated: 'This is not the British colonial regime. This is a national emergency.'

Shukla was not acting on his own authority. He was speaking with the voices of Indira and Sanjay. The increase in the authority of the latter was one of the more alarming sides of the emergency. It was the first real glimpse that India got of both a dynasty in the making and the concentration of power in the hands of an extra-constitutional figure. Sanjay's authority derived from one fact and one fact alone: he was the son of the Prime Minister of India. The government-controlled media had, during the emergency, boosted his personality cult quite shamelessly. When he arrived at a provincial capital, he was greeted by the chief minister of the state in question. He held no official position in the Congress High Command or the government. He was not a member of any elected body. He was simply his mother's son. And, of course, there was the emergency.

This attempt to project Sanjay Gandhi as her successor created a generalised feeling of disgust in a country with a real democratic tradition, however weak and frayed at the edges it might have become. The two measures which roused the cumulative anger of the people to the point of active resistance were both initiated by Sanjay Gandhi: a forced sterilisation campaign and the brutal uprooting of slum-dwellers from the major cities of India. This surgical intervention into Indian politics played a major role in splitting the Congress parliamentary party and alienating the traditional supporters of the Congress. Amongst this were members of the Muslim minority, which had constituted a sizeable bloc of votes for the Congress since 1947.

In theory, of course, every enlightened person could agree with the need for birth-control, new housing projects and other reforms. It was in their implementation that Sanjay, described in the press as a sun, a moon, a Messiah, and the 'voice of youth and reason' went badly astray. He succeeded in totally discrediting the emergency. Friends of Mrs Gandhi who had warned her of what was going on were socially and politically ostracised. Two of India's most intelligent senior civil servants, P. N. Haksar and T. N. Kaul, had both warned her that Sanjay's business methods and political style were reflecting badly on her prestige in the country. Haksar had fallen out of favour as a result. Kaul had been ignored. At one stage she had got so fed up with the constant attacks on Sanjay that she had shouted: 'Those who attack Sanjay attack me.' It was a fair comment.

Shukla ensured that Sanjay Gandhi, the young genius, was seen every day on television, heard regularly on radio and had his photograph published repeatedly in the national press. Armed in this fashion, Sanjay embarked on the forced sterilisation campaign. Villagers were kidnapped, sterilised and then returned. When angry peasants stoned the vans carrying the sterilisation teams, the police were used to repress their rebellion. There were numerous incidents in Northern India of terror being applied to fulfil the Young Master's orders. Every man forcibly sterilised became a statistic in Sanjay Gandhi's office, which would be added up and then utilised to demonstrate the success of the campaign. The demolition of Muslim houses in the areas around the old Jama Masjid (mosque) in order to 'clean up' Delhi for the property-speculators sealed the fate of the emergency. The President of India, a Muslim, personally pleaded with Sanjay to go slow. He was ignored. Sheikh Abdullah, the veteran Kashmiri Muslim leader, came to Delhi, pleaded with Mrs Gandhi to intervene on behalf of Delhi's Muslims and prevent this humiliation. He was effectively ignored.

The inhabitants around Turkman Gate did not live in makeshift or unauthorized dwellings. They and their families before them had resided in this area for centuries. Many deputations came to authority and wept. Jag Mohan, the vice-chairman of the Delhi Development Authority, a *chamcha*, a rogue and a communalist sneered at one deputation: 'So you want to create a mini-Pakistan here in the heart of Delhi?' These Muslims had decided not to go to Pakistan in 1947. Abul Kalam Azad and Jawaharlal Nehru had convinced them that Delhi was their home. Many of their relations had died during the riots of 1947. Now Nehru's grandson, watched by Nehru's daughter, was preparing to render them homeless, and to break up their community. Jag Mohan was virtually accusing them of treason. Secularism, even of the weak Congress variety, suffered a mortal blow during the emergency. Every gutter-instinct was encouraged and every reactionary reflex given support in the name of the emergency. This having been promulgated because there was the danger of a right-wing coup as in Chile!

On 18 April 1976, the Muslim population of Turkman Gate had resisted the attempt to deprive them of their homes. The police had opened fire. Twelve people had been killed, many wounded and large numbers had been beaten up by the police. A non-Muslim social worker in the area, Inder Mohan, had gone to Sanjay Gandhi and complained bitterly on behalf of the shop-keepers whose shops had been bulldozed into the ground. Mohan was arrested two days later, badly beaten up by the police and locked up without trial. He remained there till the end of the emergency. The sycophants and *chamchas* continued to reassure mother and son that all was well. The doctors in the sterilisation vans knew different. Wherever they went they were greeted by the chant: *Nasabandi ke teen dalal. Indira, Sanjay, Bansi Lall* ('Sterilisation has three big pimps: Indira, Sanjay and Bansi Lall').

Sanjay's main purpose was to clear the ground for an uninhibited display of free enterprise in town and countryside. The men he was gathering behind him in the Youth Congress were people who agreed that traditional caste and class prejudices should not be permitted to stand in the way of constructing a unified group of property-owners which spanned both village and city. In the countryside he felt that it was the middle castes who were obstructed by the upper castes and prevented from exercising all their entrepreneurial talents. The problem was that the upper castes were well represented in the Congress at every level. In order to break their economic stranglehold, Sanjay felt that it was first necessary to break their grip on political power in the provinces and the centre. That was his real programme. First break the power of the old classes, then consolidate the middle-ranking bourgeoisie in countryside and town while simultaneously developing a strong state apparatus to keep the poor under control. The latter plank was crucial because what was being planned would have enhanced class polarisations five hundred times over. It was a process already in motion, but slowly, like many other things in the country. Sanjay had wanted to speed up the film. In this fashion he antagonized many of those whose

Early years: A late-Victorian Indian family in Allahabad: Motilal Nehru, his wife, Swaruprani and the boy Jawaharlal.

Left Portrait of a young Indian at an English public school: Jawaharlal Nehru at Harrow, 1906. *bottom left* A marriage of convenience: Jawaharlal Nehru and Kamala Kaul on their wedding day, 1916. *bottom right* ... And fifteen years later in 1931. *and below* Father and daughter: Jawaharlal and Indira.

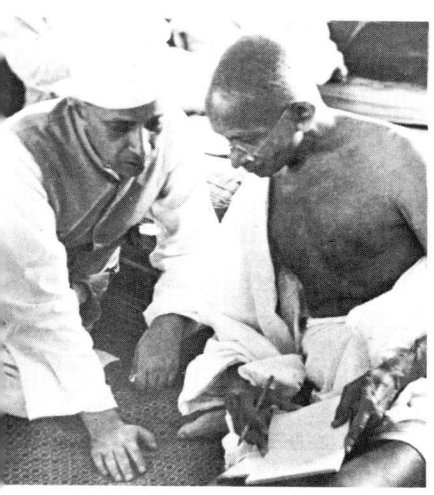

Nehru and Gandhi in dispute.

Gandhi and Nehru in agreement.

Prime Minister and family: Indira, Rajiv (on lap) and Sanjay.

Jawaharlal, Indira and Rajiv. The Prime Minister is dressed in his office uniform, complete with red rose in buttonhole, a Nehru hallmark.

WORLD STATESMAN:

Left Welcoming China's Prime Minister, Chou-en-Lai, to Delhi in 1954. The crowds chanted, *Chini-Hindi bhai bhai* (Chinese and Indians are brothers). *below* Welcoming Russia's Nikita Khrushchev and Nikolai Bulganin to India. *bottom left* A bouncy Jawaharlal arrives in London to attend the coronation of Elizabeth II and meet Edwina Mountbatten. *and bottom right* Renewing acquaintances: Jawaharlal Nehru had first met Ho Chi Minh at Brussels in 1926. Here they met as heads of their respective governments. Delhi 1954.

Indira Gandhi, Prime Minister of India, welcomes Sheikh Mujibur Rehman, the first Prime Minister of Bangladesh (formerly, East Pakistan). Mujib was assassinated by young army officers in a successful *coup d'etat*.

Indira and Pakistan's last elected Prime Minister, Zulfiqar Ali Bhutto, in Simla, an old hill-resort of the *raj*, for their summit in 1972. Bhutto was hanged on the orders of Pakistan's military dictator, General Zia-ul-Haq.

Mother and son. Indira and Sanjay, who died in a plane crash on 23 June 1980.

Sanjay engrossed in discussion with Ambika Soni, President of the Congress Youth, during the years of the Emergency. In the centre is V. C. Shukla, the Minister of Information.

Above left Indira Nehru at a People's Convention in London in 1941 just before she returned to India. She is at a leftwing bookstall selling copies of her father's book. *above right* A portrait of Indira by the Canadian photographer Karsh. *left* The world's first women premiers: Indira with Mrs. Sirimavo Bandaranaike of Ceylon. *bottom left* Indira Gandhi and Margaret Thatcher at the opening of the Festival of India Year in Britain, 1982. *and bottom right* Indira meets Youth Congress leaders, among them Sanjay (right).

Jawaharlal Nehru with Soviet leaders Khrushchev and Bulganin in an open car on their way back from a giant public rally in Calcutta, 1955.

The Big Three of the non-aligned world: Tito (Yugoslavia), Nehru (India) and Nasser (Egypt) at a summit in Cairo, 1961.

Mother and sons: Indira, Rajiv (right) and Sanjay, 1971.

Rajiv and Sonia on their wedding day, 25 February 1968.

Rajiv Gandhi: the last dynast?

Prime Minister Rajiv Gandhi watches as his assassinated mother is cremated.

position as brokers of power and votes was crucial for Congress to stay in power. This is not to imply that without Sanjay the emergency would have been popular. It is simply that with his obsession for speed, he accelerated its unpopularity at home.

The emergency had been denounced in virtually every Western capital, but here Indira had felt on strong ground. She did not take American criticisms too seriously. She often mocked Washington's hypocritical stance towards India, which had become so blatant during the Nixon-Kissinger years. Now she observed that the same governments in Western Europe and North America who criticised the emergency were happily supporting and sustaining brutal military dictatorships throughout the world. When President Ford cancelled his visit to India because of the emergency, the initial anger in Delhi gave way to cynical amusement as the White House announced the President's forthcoming trip to Peking. (It has since become public knowledge that hundreds of thousands of Chinese people died during the so-called 'Great Proletarian Cultural Revolution'.) But when her own party began to fragment, with the defection of the important Jagjivan Ram and his decision to form the Congress for Democracy (CFD), she decided on an election to decide the issues.

It is possible too, that events in Bangladesh, where the founding-father of the state, Mujibur Rehman and almost his entire family were brutally murdered, made Indira anxious for a rapid return to normality. Mujib had created a one-party state and his relatives were openly engaged in corrupt practices on a gigantic scale — the young army officers who shot him dead claimed that they were doing so to free the country from tyranny. Very few people had come out in Dacca to protest at his murder. Mrs Gandhi was shattered by the news. She recalled to friends how she had often told Mujib that the security arrangements at his residence in Dacca were insufficient, but he had always laughed and replied: 'Who will kill me? I am popular with my people.' The combination of these events at home and abroad helped her to make up her mind. An election was announced for 21 March 1977; the emergency was relaxed. Political leaders were released and all those who had talked of a permanent dictatorship in India began to look rather foolish.

The outcome of the 1977 general election represented a watershed in modern Indian politics. For four whole days the Indian electors — almost 200 million women and men — flocked to the polling booths in the towns and the countryside. Deprived by the emergency of virtually all forms of extra-parliamentary dissent such as strikes, street demonstrations or distribution of literature opposing the government, the Indian masses used the ballot-box to express their deep discontent. The result was a political earthquake which shook India and whose tremors were felt in neighbouring Pakistan and Sri Lanka. The Empress had fallen. The impact in other parts of the world was considerable: it produced gloom and despondency in Moscow; ill-suppressed, albeit short-sighted, jubilation in Washington; in Peking it was greeted as a blow 'against Soviet social-imperialism'.

The choice which confronted the Indian people was not a complex one. The election was about the emergency, and as such it was more of a referendum than an election. The emergency was identified with Congress rule, and portraits and photographs of Indira Gandhi — rather than local Congress candidates — hung in every local polling-station, so the people decided to reject the Congress. It was not a choice between bread and freedom. If anything, it was an opportunity to select the conditions under which it would be more favourable to agitate for bread. The urban and rural poor demonstrated in a very concrete and striking fashion that questions of basic civil rights were not merely the preoccupations of the urban middle classes.

The total number entitled to vote was 320 million, which made this the largest democratic election in the world. The percentage that voted was 60.54 per cent, much higher than the famous 'Indira wave' of 1971. In absolute terms, it was the highest recorded vote in Indian history. The Congress was displaced as the major ruling party, and the political tradition established in 1937 crumbled in 1977. The northern and central strongholds of Congress were gained by an opposition coalition, the Janata Party. Of 49 ministers contesting the election, only 15 were successful; in the largest state, Uttar Pradesh, the Congress were unable to win a single seat! Indira Gandhi herself was defeated by a comic figure from the opposition, Raj Narain, the man who had been partly responsible for provoking the emergency by challenging her previous election in the Allahabad High Court. This is the only occasion in the annals of representative democracy when a sitting prime minister has been humiliated in such a fashion. It constitutes a remarkable tribute to the resilience of Indian political institutions. Indira's personal defeat (together with that of her son

Sanjay in a neighbouring constituency) marked the lowest point in the history of the Nehru dynasty. Her father Jawaharlal and grandfather Motilal had always remained popular in Allahabad.

The other main loser was the CPI, the shame-faced ally of the Congress. It slumped ignominiously to seven seats, confined to the southern states of Kerala and Tamil Nadu. The CP(M) (which had suffered under the emergency) retained its strength, though all but six of its seats were won in West Bengal. The total Congress vote was 35.54 per cent, and but for its gains in the south the defeat would have been complete. There were special reasons for Congress gains in the southern states of Andhra Pradesh, Kerala, Tamil Nadu and Karnataka. There was a fear that the Janata coalition, a right-wing cartel, might attempt to re-impose Hindi as the national language and ride roughshod over the linguistic and cultural heritage of the south. Secondly, the excesses of the emergency had not been felt in the south and thirdly the Congress-CPI coalition in Kerala had been less corrupt than other state governments. The Kerala Congress leaders, for example, had firmly refused to allow Sanjay Gandhi to visit their state during the emergency. This shrewd move on their part paid handsome electoral dividends.

The Congress defeat was greeted by widespread celebrations. Delhi's historic mosque, Juma Masjid, was illuminated to celebrate Sanjay Gandhi's downfall. The euphoric atmosphere dissolved old tensions within the opposition, but once the rejoicing was over, people began to ask a new question. Indira had been defeated, but who had won? The victorious Janata Party was a heterogeneous combination dominated by right-wing political parties. At its head was J. P. Narayan, who had symbolised opposition to the emergency, but the policy statements of the Janata Party had been vague throughout the election campaign. Their central focus had been a ferocious personal attack on Mrs Gandhi, her son Sanjay and the two most sycophantic members of her entourage, Cabinet Ministers Bansi Lal (Defence) and V. C. Shukla (Information). They had been referred to as the 'Gang of Four': the Indian equivalents of the more dramatic Chiang Ching (Mao's widow) and her three associates who were losing power at the same time in China. The demand for unrestricted civil liberties and denunciations of the forced sterilisation campaign made up the entire substance of the Janata's campaign, but it was a startling success. Janata captured 270 seats out of a total of 493 which it contested, and gained 43.17 per cent of the popular vote. This gave it half the seats in the new Parliament, and together with the seats won by the Congress for Democracy (Jagjivan Ram's grouping) and the CP(M), the new government was assured of a comfortable majority. In real terms, however, the major victor was the communalist Jan Sangh party. Its organisational dominance of the Janata coalition paid off in terms of placing their members in Parliament. The Sangh had a hard core of at least 90 members in the new Parliament, in contrast to 22 in the outgoing legislature, which gave it a commanding position within the alliance itself.

Communalism in India had been mothered politically by the Hindu Mahasabha, which held its first session in 1923, a gathering which was graced by well-known Congress leaders. For ten years the Mahasabha existed both within and outside the Congress, but the latter's secular ideology and recognition of certain democratic rights demanded by Muslims angered the communalists. In 1933 they split from the Congress, denouncing it for 'appeasing the Muslims'. The Hindu Mahasabha was so carried away by its own brand of communalism that they were quite prepared to do a deal with the colonial authorities, provided they were given certain guarantees. At their convention in Ajmer in 1933, a Mahasabha leader declared: 'I feel an impulse in me that Hindus will willingly cooperate with Great Britain if their status and responsible position as the premier community in India is recognised in the political institutions of new India.'

In 1925, the Mahasabha had initiated the formation of the Rashtriya Swayamsevak Sangh (RSS) — National Volunteer Corps — an organisation designed to provide Hindu communalism with its own shock-troops. The RSS organised systematic attacks on Muslims and carried out acts of arson and sabotage aimed at demoralising the minority religious community. Jawaharlal had denounced them in no uncertain terms: 'Hindu communalism is the Indian version of fascism.' A more precise analogy, however, would be with the Protestant Orange Lodges and loyalist communalism in the six northern counties of Ireland. The RSS was conceived of as a corps which would defend 'Hindu interests as a whole' regardless of party. There was an intensive training involving ideological discussions, military training, Sangh rituals, calisthenics and drill. The assassins of Mahatama Gandhi had been educated in such a school.

The RSS was structured hierarchically, with the leader having absolute control of the organisation. The leader himself was chosen by his predecessor, after consultations with an inner circle. The RSS's political ideas were supplied by the Hindu Mahasabha, whose best-known and most influential leader was V. D. Savarkar. He presided over the organisation during the decisive years of 1937–42. It was Savarkar who gave his movement the definition of a true believer: 'A Hindu means a person who regards this land of Bharat Varsha, from the Indus to the seas, as his fatherland as well as his Holy Land, that is the cradle land of his religion.' For Savarkar's supporters and the RSS faithful, the country which served as a model was the backward-looking, rite-laden monarchy of Nepal. Its king was regarded as a cult figure. The votaries of Hindu confessionalism no doubt believed that their leader would, one day, occupy a similar position in India. The main problem for Savarkar was the substantial size of the Muslim minority and, of course, the Congress supporters who pandered and appeased it. Thus the Muslims had to be taught their real place in Indian society. To achieve this, communal riots and killings were encouraged. Every Congress politician who opposed the RSS was denounced as a traitor. Nehru was a prime target for their hatred, but it was Gandhi himself whose influence was regarded as intolerable. Gandhi had no time for the RSS or the Mahasabha's brand of religious politics. His effect on rural India, however, was such that the RSS decided to eliminate him permanently. Hence the assassination in 1948. The RSS was banned for two years, but it was never really dissolved.

It was against this backdrop that the Jan Sangh (People's Organisation) was formed by S. P. Mookerji in the early 1950s. Mookerji had been President of the Hindu Mahasabha in 1943. He had also, more surprisingly, served as a non-Congress independent in the first Nehru cabinet for three years (1947–50), but had resigned in protest against Nehru's secular politics. Mookerji's mentors had been Savarkar and Hedgewar (the founder of the RSS), but he regarded their approach as too crude and had left the Mahasabha because of its refusal to permit non-Hindus to join its ranks. The Jan Sangh represented a sophisticated attempt to remodel right-wing politics in India and draw behind it serious rightist forces who were repelled by the crude communalism of the RSS. The Jan Sangh was formally non-communal, but this was basically a tactical re-orientation. Nehru had immediately denounced its formation in characteristic fashion: 'It is the illegitimate child of the RSS.' The Sangh had replied by branding him a 'Muslim appeaser'. The four pillars of Jan Sangh ideology were clear cut. In a country containing dozens of different nationalities, over twenty important languages and substantial religious minorities, the Jan Sangh stated that it stood for: 'One country, one nation, one culture and the rule of law.' And so as not to leave any room for ambiguity, they argued for 'Nationalising all non-Hindus by inculcating in them the idea of Bharitya culture.' Small wonder, then, that this party has remained deeply unpopular in India's southern states.

As disillusion with the Congress began to set in, so a section of its base, especially in the northern Hindi-speaking belt, began to abandon it electorally. In 1952 the Hindu Mahasabha obtained four MPs and the Jan Sangh (JS) three; in 1957 the JS won four and the Mahasabha dropped to two; in 1962 the JS increased its representation to 14 MPs and 115 seats in state assemblies (becoming the second party in Uttar Pradesh and Madhya Pradesh); in 1967 the Sangh won 35 seats; in 1971 it declined as a result of the Indira 'wave' to 22. Its 1977 results represented a qualitative leap forward.

The Jan Sangh party had a powerful appeal in both town and countryside. In its election manifestoes of 1967 and 1971 it openly defended the interests of the rich farmers, attacked land reforms and all peasant cooperatives. Its general secretary, S. S. Bhandari, declared in 1971: 'The move to lower the maximum size of land holdings might create uncertainty in rural areas.' It changed course slightly in 1972, embarking on a social demagogy familiar throughout the sub-continent. In the cities it had a substantial following in the bazaars amongst the massive group of shopkeepers big and small, traders and moneylenders, as well as within the ranks of the city unemployed.

Its membership jumped, according to its own statistics, from 275,000 in 1960–61 to two million in 1973. Even if that figure were divided by two, it remained a substantial organisation, with far greater discipline and political cohesiveness than most of its rivals, including those on the left. It is, therefore, not too difficult to grasp how it became the organisational mainstay of the JP movement which preceded the emergency and the principal generator of the 1977 election campaign. Its central leader, Atal Behari Vajpayee, who became the Janata's Foreign Minister, was an experienced and sophisticated political leader. An effective orator, he served many years of political apprenticeship as Mookerji's private secretary.

The other political parties within the Janata were, in organisational terms, relatively weak. Desai's Congress was on its last legs and certainly not as healthy as its leader. The railway workers' leader, George Fernandes, had been elected by a 340,000 vote majority from Bihar, but this was more of a personal tribute than a reflection of the Socialist Party's strength. One of Fernandes' first acts was the reinstatement, in his capacity as Minister for Communications, of all the railway workers who had been dismissed after the strike of 1974. It was also, in some ways, his last effective statement as a leader of the left. The Bharatiya Lok Dal (Indian People's Organisation) was formed by a fusion of half a dozen right-wing parties in 1974, the most prominent of which was the Swatantra Party. Its leader was a rich farmer, Charan Singh, who made no secret of his antipathy to any kind of land reform. A late entrant to the opposition ranks was Jagjivan Ram, the leader of the 'untouchables'. It was his defection from Indira's Congress that had helped to shift the balance of power towards the opposition, for it had encouraged people to believe that it was possible to get rid of Indira Gandhi and the emergency.

The most crucial question which the new coalition needed to resolve, however, was the choice of prime minister. Three candidates emerged. Top of the list was 81-year-old Morarji Desai. In his favour was his substantial experience and the fact that he had been trying for the job since Nehru's demise in 1964. Then there was the down-to-earth 74-year-old farmer Charan Singh, who claimed to speak for the real India — the countryside. There was a problem here, since poor peasants outnumbered Charan Singh's rich farmers and their animals put together. The third candidate was Jagjivan Ram, a sprightly 64, though his opponents swore that he was in fact 70 years old and was trying to cheat the laws of biology. Given that the Janata had been campaigning for an end to all undemocratic practices of the past, it was widely assumed that the Janata parliamentary party would elect its leader and prime minister. The bickering was getting so noisy that the three old men agreed amongst themselves to let JP decide. Hardly were they in power than they were ignoring Parliament and deferring to the judgement of Jayaprakash. The veteran mystagogue took a look at the three candidates and chose

Moraji Desai. At long last he had become Prime Minister of India. In what turned out to be an extremely astute appraisal, Inder Malhotra wrote in the *Illustrated Weekly of India* on 14 April 1977:

> Those who took so much time to finalise the composition of the Cabinet or allocation of portfolios, showing themselves terribly touchy over minor matters of personal pride and prejudice, may well turn out to be even more quarrelsome when differences over high policy, affecting various classes having conflicting interests, are concerned. The problem used to be acute even when the Congress was in power. It cannot but be worse at a time when the four constituents of the Janata Party have different social moorings and political predilections.

Within two years the Janata split into warring factions, lost its majority and early elections were announced for 1980.

After the defeat of the Congress in 1977, its remaining Members of Parliament were compelled to elect a new leader, since Indira Gandhi had not been returned by her constituency. Their choice was Y. B. Chavan, a former Cabinet Minister from Maharashtra state, a man of fairly conventional right-wing views. He was not the most dynamic of men. Few believed that he could rally a dispirited and demoralised group and transform it into a fighting organisation, but the party was too shell-shocked to think about the future. At the first meeting of the Working Committee after the defeat there was pandemonium, though nobody attacked Mrs Gandhi. She herself took the initiative, and sent the Congress President and the committee a letter accepting full responsibility for the defeat and stating that: 'I am not interested in finding alibis or excuses for myself, nor am I interested in shielding anyone.' She pleaded that instead of searching for scapegoats the Congress should prepare for the battles that lay ahead. Her colleagues were not convinced. Bansi Lal, the notorious Minister for Defence and close crony of Sanjay Gandhi, was loathed by most members of the Working Committee. In Mrs Gandhi's absence, Bansi Lal was expelled from the Congress for 'undemocratic, autocratic and undignified activities'. All three adjectives were, in fact, euphemisms. At an earlier meeting when Lal had been attacked, Indira had challenged them to expel her since she was responsible for everything. Her logic was, as usual, impeccable, and she was aware that without her they would have become political orphans. V. C. Shukla, the ex-Information Minister, was let off with a reprimand. He subsequently denied that he and Sanjay had been close friends. He also had this to say about his disgraced former colleague: 'Of course I know Bansi Lal, but he is an oaf, he has no eye for painting, no ear for music. He is the kind of man who, if he saw a beautiful sunset behind a field of wheat, would be preoccupied calculating how much the wheat was worth.' Sanjay Gandhi was not censured. The main discussion that took place within the Working Committee centred on organisational questions. How and when should or could a collective leadership be instituted? Should the Working Committee resign *en masse* as a moral gesture? What was totally lacking was the will and the capacity to draw up a political balance sheet. This would have necessitated a sharp critique of the emergency and a public apology to those who had been its victims. The Congress leaders were not yet aware that there would be no need to do any of this — the failings of the Janata Government itself were to become Indira Gandhi's not-so-secret weapon.

Soon after her reversal, Indira Gandhi had to vacate 1 Safdarjung Road. Anand Bhavan in Allahabad had been donated to the nation and she found herself without a house for the first time in her life. An old family friend, Mohammed Yunus, a veteran Pathan Congressman from the Frontier province now in Pakistan, immediately vacated his house in Willingdon Crescent in New Delhi. Yunus was one of the few Muslims (if not the only one) who had actually forsaken his home and moved to India as a protest against the partition of the sub-continent in 1947. He had remained close to Nehru and Indira since the 1930s and was generally acknowledged to be a close family friend. There is little doubt that she was now in need of friends. She was more isolated than ever before. Although she may have expected the Congress to be defeated it had not seriously occurred to her that her own seat was at stake. Her opponent was a well-known buffoon, who was an embarrassment to his own side. Nonetheless her unpopularity had reached such a level that if the Janata Party had put up a parrot, it would have won.

Although she was not in the least bit remorseful, during the first few days after the defeat she considered retirement. It was her first reaction to the shock. She had felt the same after her father's death. Now she told friends and journalists that she was relieved to be without the burden of responsibility, and this was not a complete fabrication. She was approaching her sixtieth year, was extremely attached to her grandchildren and had grown close to her Italian daughter-in-law, Sonia, who had married Rajiv.

Undoubtedly there was one part of her which considered the easy solution to the problems that were posed. There was another side to her character, however, which had always proved the stronger on previous occasions: she did not like to accept defeats or compromises passively. In this, it should be said, she was somewhat different from Jawaharlal. The combination of his early politics and her strength of character would have produced an amazing personality.

Too much has been made, by some, of her childhood infatuation with Joan of Arc. She neither desired nor enjoyed martyrdom. Her primary interest lay in the exercise of political power. If, during the days and months of her Willingdon Crescent exile, she had felt that she had been deserted by those who determined the results of elections, she might well have retired. Within weeks, however, her new home saw the arrival of the poor. They knew she had nothing to give in terms of material benefits; they came only to speak of their bitterness about life in general. What started as a slow trickle became, after the first six months, a flood. It had taken the Janata government about six months to demonstrate to the electorate that it was not able to do anything to alleviate the general misery. When a friend took a visiting American couple to meet Mrs Gandhi, the foreigners were amazed at the number of poverty-stricken supplicants waiting to see her. One American remarked that she must have done a lot for them if they still came back to her. Indira was remarkably frank on this occasion: 'No. Those for whom something was done are nowhere to be seen!'

It was an odd coincidence, but her defeat in the elections was to have an impact on the fortunes of another populist leader: Pakistan's Zulfiqar Ali Bhutto. In Pakistan, too, there had been elections in early 1977. Bhutto would have won in any event, but over-zealous party loyalists and civil servants carried out election-rigging on a gigantic scale, virtually eliminating the opposition. Indira's graceful exit provided too recent a contrast and the Pakistani opposition, also gathered under a Janata-style umbrella, began a campaign of civil disobedience, which ultimately paved the way for the military *coup* carried out by General Zia in July 1977. When Bhutto was released from house-arrest, he organised a national campaign. On his arrival at Lahore he was greeted by hundreds of thousands of people, a reception that moved him so deeply that he wept. Later that evening he said to a friend: 'They came out for me despite everything I've done to them!' Indira's situation was not dissimilar. When discussing this remark of Bhutto's with the author in January 1984 she smiled knowingly and said: 'I thought of him often during that period. When he was sentenced to death by the Army, I was in prison myself. I remember writing letters to various Heads of State pleading that they intervene to save his life. The Janata people who were in power at the time did not lift a finger to save him. We would have reacted differently.'

Once she knew that she could win back her popular base, she decided to fight. Wars, political or military, brought her out of herself and everything else was subordinated to the one overriding aim of victory. The incessant noise of squabbling politicians that emanated from the Janata Government's first year in office paved the way for a renewed triumph for Indira.

The Janata leaders, who had even less substantial a programme than Congress, thought that they could stay in power by reminding people constantly of the emergency and its perpetrators. Here they made a serious miscalculation. They made Indira Gandhi a martyr, and public opinion began to turn away from them. The attempt to personalise everything into an attack on her made her appear more powerful than she actually was and the sight of a whole government pursuing a lone woman did not appeal to Mother India. It was an effective admission of total impotence on the part of the new government. If they had been pushing through plans to improve living conditions even gradually, though visibly, they would not have needed to remain obsessed with a politician whom they had decisively defeated at the polls only a few months ago.

Scandals soon began to buffet the Janata Government. It became public knowledge that Morarji's son was engaged in some crooked deals with businessmen. Defence Minister Jagjivan Ram's son, was photographed copulating out of doors with a lady who was not his wife, and the photographs, suitably shaded, appeared in sections of the press. Ram junior said that he and the girl had been drugged, stripped and photographed in order to embarass the government. The pictures painted a different story, though it should be said that they were published in *Surya*, a magazine edited by Maneka Gandhi, Sanjay's wife.

As if this were not enough, Raj Narain, the joker in the Janata pack, embarked on a number of absurd statements which mocked his own leaders. He was Minister for Health in the new government and his regular attacks on modern medicine were beginning to alienate the medical profession and make the government look utterly ridiculous. He appeared to have modelled himself on the Ugandan dictator, Idi Amin. Narain's continual intrigues against Desai drove the latter to distraction. On one occasion, when Desai was returning from an official trip abroad, Raj Narain arrived at the airport unannounced to greet his leader. As Desai stepped off the plane, Narain sprinkled him with *attar* (an Indian scent) and welcomed him back to India. Desai was furious as he observed the smiles on the faces of the journalists and lost control of himself. 'You wretch,' he shouted at his Health Minister, 'now you douse me with *attar*. While I am away you emit a foul stench!' Narain laughed heartily at this repartee and departed. The episode received wide publicity the following day. This was followed by a public letter from Cabinet Minister Charan Singh to Prime Minister Morarji Desai asking that the latter's son be called to order for his corrupt dealings and an investigation be instigated without further delay. Desai replied, again in public, stating among other facts that: 'I have had a number of letters making allegations about you, your sons-in-law and, painful to state, even your wife . . . ' The comic duel continued for a few more weeks with more exchanges of letters.

Charan Singh soon turned his attention to other matters. He made a wild accusation in Parliament stating that Mrs Gandhi had planned to kill all the opposition leaders in jail during the emergency. She was not back in Parliament as yet, but this absurd charge backfired. The public statement she made marked her re-entry into the politics of the country and was widely seen as an effective rebuttal of Charan Singh:

> Since the last elections, when in all humility I accepted the full responsibility for the heavy reverses suffered by my party, the Congress, in the northern states, I deliberately decided to keep away from politics and from personal and press publicity.
>
> The institution of various commissions, covering a wide range of activities connected with my period in office, had led to the expectation that the law would be allowed to take its course.
>
> However, I find that some leaders of the Janata Party Government are determined to pursue their smear campaign of character assassination inside and outside Parliament so as to denigrate not only me but the Congress Party as a whole. The Home Minister's recent statement about an alleged plan (or 'thinking') in my government to shoot down leaders of the opposition in jail is shocking and preposterous and has

no basis whatsoever . . . In fact, Mr J. P. Narayan, Mr Vajpayee, Mr Charan Singh himself and other prominent leaders were allowed out on parole on information of ill-health.

That we believe in democracy is borne out by the fact that we took the major decision of holding elections which gave our people the opportunity of expressing their views and having a government of their choice . . .

I hope that the leaders of the Janata Party will at least now address themselves to the more serious and mounting problems affecting different sections of the people, especially industrial labour, farmers, the rural and urban poor, the minorities, the weaker sections and the middle classes. Immediate attention has to be given to the atrocities against untouchables, increasing lawlessness and spiralling prices.

The last paragraph was a clear indication of the shape that Indira Gandhi's campaign would take in the next elections. In the meantime she busied herself by preparing to re-enter Parliament and overhauling her party, the instrument she would need to defeat Janata. The men who had supported the emergency slavishly, coined servile slogans such as 'Indira is India' and flattered Sanjay Gandhi endlessly, now decided to break with her, not because they had learnt the errors of their ways, but because they thought she was finished. It would be rash to ascribe to the decisions of men like Chavan, Reddy and Borooah anything remotely resembling political principles.

In May 1977 the Congress was split again and Mrs Gandhi's band of loyalists became known as Congress(I). The I was for Indira, not India. In November 1978 she contested a by-election in Karanataka. The Janata Cabinet panicked and sent its top ministers to campaign against her and from his sickbed old JP appealed to the voters not to let her back again.

The southern voters were not swayed and returned her to Parliament by a large majority. More panic on the government front-bench. At first they arrested her and imprisoned her for a week, but then released her. Proceedings then began to deprive her of her newly won parliamentary seat. This decision was taken by a Privileges Committee which found irregularities, but the measure discredited Janata throughout the country. They had been elected to preserve democracy, if nothing else, and now they were tampering with the electoral process. This constant fear of Indira Gandhi had become a hallmark of the Janata years. It was the threat of Mrs Gandhi's return that had kept the motley collection together.

When Devraj Urs, the leader of Congress in Karanataka withdrew support from Mrs Gandhi after her by-election triumph and subsequent de-seating because he could not tolerate Sanjay Gandhi's growing influence, the Janata leaders thought that without him she would be completely finished. They stopped concentrating on her and turned on each other.

Two members of Desai's Cabinet who had been at each other's throats, Charan Singh and H. N. Bahuguna, decided to link arms and remove the octogenarian Desai. Not so long ago Singh had said that Bahuguna was a KGB agent, and Bahuguna had referred to Singh as a 'mentally deranged person', but now the two ministers issued a joint statement stating that they could not remain in a government headed by a prime minister under the influence of the Jan Sangh and the RSS. In various regions in the north, there had been a spate of killings. The victims were untouchables and the oppressors and killers were upper-caste Hindu communalists. There had also been a sharp increase in Hindu-Muslim riots and the RSS involvement had been obvious. So Bahuguna and Charan Singh now stated 'that there is a compelling need to forge a common front to fight the fascist forces, represented by those who believe in the Hitlerian theory of ethnic purism, religious supremacy and bigotry'. They appealed for secularism, justice and a defence of untouchables and tribals *(adivasis)*. It was on 12 July 1979 that these ministers started their campaign to dethrone Desai. On 15 July, George Fernandes resigned from the Cabinet. A game of musical chairs now began. The most significant piper was Indira Gandhi. She was not even in Parliament, but was represented by a rump of 71 MPs, whose votes now become critically important. On 27 July, Desai resigned in disgust, with a virulent attack on Charan Singh, who had now abandoned his plans to try Mrs Gandhi in a special court, and was instead courting her MPs.

On 28 July Charan Singh was asked by the President to form a new government. Six of his list of ministers were members of the Congress(O) (official) which had split from Mrs Gandhi. Five had been ministers of the emergency government. Chavan was named Deputy Prime Minister. Mrs Gandhi now withdrew her support from Charan Singh. It was clear that he would not get a majority, and the President gave him a three-week period in which to do so. He pleaded with Mrs Gandhi for her support. She kept him guessing for a few days, then on 20 August she stated that her

Congress could not support his ministry. The Janata leader who had replaced Desai was Jagjivan Ram. As the head of the largest single party he wanted to be given the chance to form a government. How he would do so remained a mystery. In response to a journalist's question concerning the composition of his government — as to whether it would be a single-party government or a coalition — Jagjivan Ram thought carefully and then came up with an incisive reply: 'Both.'

On 22 August 1979, the President of India dissolved Parliament. Till the next election Charan Singh continued as caretaker Prime Minister. The Janata leaders gave a display of bad temper. With the Janata's professed concern for democracy the public had expected at least a token display of pleasure at the fact that the choice was, once again, with the people of India. Instead Jagjivan Ram and Chandrashekhar (once an Indira Young Turk, then imprisoned by her during the emergency and now a stalwart of Janata) charged that India was on the road to a Presidential dictatorship.

Janata had come to power because of a reaction against the emergency. It had promised a return to decent political norms, a strengthening of democracy, an end to arbitrary terror and the perennial promise of better conditions for the poor. Within two years the economic and political situation had deteriorated. In addition to the caste and communal violence associated with an important component of the Janata, the RSS/Jan Sangh, there was the intolerable puritanism of Morarji Desai, the intemperance of Charan Singh, the political promiscuity of Jagjivan Ram, the unforgivable impotence of George Fernandes, the uncontrollable avarice of countless hangers-on, the endless intrigue and manoeuvres and scandals; all this had made Janata not so much an object of hatred, but of contempt and indifference.

The choice at the 1980 elections was simple: government or no government? As the campaign progressed it became clear yet again that only one leader had a national appeal — Indira Gandhi. She travelled 40,000 miles, spoke at 22 public meetings a day and addressed a total of one hundred million people. Occasionally she would apologise for some of the excesses of the emergency, but she would then tell them that they had punished her effectively and ask if they were pleased with what had replaced her. She would talk of the price of kerosene and essential commodities and how high the level of inflation was in contrast to when Congress had been in power. She lifted her outstretched palm and told them that this was the new symbol of the party. That is where they must make the mark if they wanted her back. As the effectiveness of her campaign increased so did the number of Congress defectors who now rushed back to the fold. Bahuguna returned. She made him the Secretary-General of the Party. He was widely respected by Muslims throughout the north. Because of the scale of defections from her ranks, she permitted young Sanjay to get the youth into the Congress, and he had well over a hundred carefully hand-picked candidates ready to contest the 1980 elections. She returned to Rae Bareilly; Sanjay was contesting the elections from a neighbouring constituency, Amethi. Neither was very far from Allahabad, the old starting-point of the Nehru family.

The opposition disintegrated at a remarkable speed. Apart from the two Communist Parties on the left and the Jan Sangh/RSS lobby on the right there was little else. Some of the old guard made sure that the comic side of the Janata years should not be forgotten. At the height of the campaign, Charan Singh said that Jagjivan Ram was a CIA agent. Seymour Hersh, the American writer-journalist, later corrected this assertion in his book on Kissinger and alleged that the CIA mole in the Indian government during 1971 was, in fact, Morarji Desai!

On 3 January 1980, Indians went to the polls again. There had been widespread fears of trouble and violence, but none of this materialised. It was one of the calmest elections in recent Indian history. In contrast to previous polls the turnout was low, reflecting the cynicism, despair and indifference towards the whole process. The verdict was hardly a surprise: Indira Gandhi became Prime Minister of India for the third time; both Janata and the emergency were consigned to history. The combined vote of the two Communist Parties reflected the strongest opposition in this election. Indira Gandhi's own comment on this phase of Indian politics was brief and to the point. She told the author: 'They had their chance and what did they do? They made a big mess. The people voted us back into power with a big majority.' As a statement of fact this was indisputable.

5.
The last years 1980-84

She was sworn in for the fourth time as Prime Minister of India. The size of the majority pleased her enormously. Her Congress won 351 out of the total of 542 seats in the Lok Sabha, although the opposition pointed out, accurately enough, that half the electorate had abstained – only 196 million people had registered their votes. This is considerably higher than the average proportion of voters in US Presidential elections, but for India it was, undoubtedly, a low turn-out, in fact the lowest in any election.

Who were the 351 new Congress representatives in Parliament? Some were old, familiar Congress faces from the past. Others were men from the emergency period who had stuck by her and were now back: Bansi Lall, V.C. Shukla and Sanjay Gandhi had all been elected. There was, however, a majority of new young men. There were 234 Congress MPs for whom not only Parliament, but politics itself was a novelty. Of these between 100 and 150 were widely regarded as Sanjay's boys. He was their supreme leader, and his word was law. They had little knowledge or understanding of traditional Congress politics; for them politics was about power, and power was necessary to make money. The new intake did not regard idealism or principle as a virtue. They were prepared to be even more 'pragmatic' than Indira Gandhi.

The election campaign itself had been a lacklustre affair. There was none of the magic or sparkle of the old 'Remove poverty' days. This time it was the Janata's manifest failures that formed the *leitmotiv* of Mrs Gandhi's speeches. That and, of course, rising prices – in particular the scandalous increase in the price of onions. She pledged that the Congress would keep the prices of onions stabilised. She won, however, not because of onions, but because the Janata had discredited itself beyond repair. It was an interesting reversal. In 1977 she had lost because of the emergency, so her rivals had won the vote for largely negative reasons: the same could be said of the Congress victory of 1980. For that reason, she was not permitted a breathing space. The problems that continued to plague her from the first month after returning to 1 Safdarjung Road stayed with her right till the end.

The Soviet Union invaded Afghanistan in the middle of the Indian election campaign. Tens of thousands of Soviet combat troops crossed the Oxus river that forms the frontier between the USSR and Afghanistan on 27 December 1979. Her initial reaction after becoming Prime Minister was to adopt an 'understanding attitude' towards Moscow, but this was altered to a strong demand for troop withdrawal by the USSR. What she refused to countenance was Indian alignment with the West or with neighbouring Pakistan on this issue. In her view the Pentagon was not at all anxious for a rapid Soviet withdrawal for reasons of its own, and she wanted to create conditions which would facilitate a Soviet exit from Afghanistan. Apart from the issues involved in that country itself – the central question being the right of the Afghan people to self-determination – there was a related problem which affected India's strategic interests in a direct sense. The Soviet entry into Kabul had transformed the sordid military regime of General Zia in Pakistan into a 'frontier of the free world', which meant that US economic and military aid would soon start pouring into the country. The Pakistan Army had, in the past, used US weaponry against two targets: its own population and that of India. Delhi now feared that the West would provide Pakistan with the most up-to-date weaponry and turn a blind eye to its plans to test a nuclear device. Hence Indian leaders were anxious for a political settlement in Afghanistan.

The biggest problems Indira Gandhi was to confront, however, lay at home. There was the economy, which was the subject of permanent debate by economists and politicians; there was the question of political management of the country, which was highlighted by the fact that at the beginning of 1980 most of the states were under the control of opposition governments and, last but not least, Mrs Gandhi could not fail to see that communalism was once again on the increase.

The Congress Party, in terms of social composition, was an alliance of the rural rich and the urban capitalists, but it also possessed its own trade union, the Indian Trades Union Congress (INTUC), which dated from the 1930s and was seen largely as a company union in most plants. This alliance was reflected in the Congress at every level, but the splits, defections and, finally, the total hegemony of Indira Gandhi had meant that the men who held economic power were somewhat uneasy. Their experience of the Janata, however, sent them rushing back to the prime minister they knew. By this time it was obvious that major structural changes were needed in the countryside in order to increase the purchasing power of the peasants and thus increase the country's industrial growth. The comparisons made by economists were usually with South Korea and Mexico, both of which were middle-income countries. India was still classified as a low-income country (LIC). The reason for this disparity could not be the so-called drain of investment towards the public sector in India, for South Korea, contrary to general opinion, also possessed a sizeable state-owned sector and, like India, it also had a strategy of import-substitution. The difference, of course, was on the political level. South Korea was a dictatorship and could thus provide a quiescent workforce, without strikes and militant trades unions, under the strict control of the army, which ran the country. Inevitably, there were some who were beginning to argue that India needed the same sort of discipline. The emergency had been an attempt along these lines, but it had been badly handled. The main spokesman for this view of Indian politics was Sanjay Gandhi, already regarded as the crown prince.

Other statistics were also available, but these tended to be ignored. For instance, the only country of a comparable size and population within the LIC category, was China. The growth rate of the two Asian giants was not dissimilar, but in the distribution of wealth the contrast was noticeable. China's literacy rate was 76 per cent; India's was 36 per cent. Infant mortality in China was 81 per 1000 and life expectancy at birth was 67. In India the two were 121 and 52 respectively. It was in this sphere that changes needed to be made in order to make use of the economic growth since 1947, but this was virtually impossible without a social transformation of the Chinese magnitude.

The Congress, in any case, was not the instrument for such a change. Nor, it should be added, were any of the Communist Parties particularly well-suited for this task. Their strength lay in specific states and since the split in 1964 they had ceased to appear as a national force in Indian politics. The CPI had damaged its standing by being associated with the emergency. The CP(M) had opposed the emergency. Many of its trade union militants and student supporters had been imprisoned and tortured. This had enabled it to overtake the CPI in electoral terms. It got over 8 million votes in 1977 and retained its support in 1980. It had swept to victory in West Bengal and Tripura in the state elections of 1977. Now with Indira back in her South Block office, the CP(M) leaders wondered whether she would get rid of them again as she had done in the late 1960s.

The division between centre and states was a relatively new phenomenom. In Nehru's time the idea of non-Congress administrations was a novelty and when the CPI won Kerala, Indira, as we have seen, rushed there to ensure that it remained a short-term novelty.

In the late 1960s she had toppled the elected CP(M) government in West Bengal and imposed President's Rule. Indira's new government decided to end the situation whereby opposition coalitions ran the provinces. These provincial governments were dissolved and new elections ordered. A precedent had been established by Janata after its 1977 victory. Morarji Desai had dissolved all the state assemblies and ordered new elections on the grounds that the country wanted a change. This precedent was now used by Indira. The argument was that it was difficult for the centre to function effectively while not in control of at least a majority of the provinces. It was an unconstitutional argument which only increased regional fears and encouraged an unnecessary tension between the states and the central authority.

In accordance with the new decisions, nine state governments were immediately dissolved, and new elections were announced. Interestingly enough, the CP(M) governments in West Bengal and Tripura were left untouched. In the provincial polls, Congress won eight out of the nine states. The odd one out was Tamil Nadu, where Congress was defeated by a combination of regional organisations and the two Communist Parties. The results seemed to be a confirmation that the Congress was once again in command of national politics. Yet, within the next four months, the mood of the public began to change again. One major reason was the failure to bring prices down, but an important factor must have been the charades that were taking place in the newly-won Congress states and at the centre. Indira Gandhi took a whole year to determine the composition of her new Cabinet, and while she was meditating on the subject a vicious round of factional struggles and in-fighting broke out in the state units of the Congress. In the three largest states of Uttar Pradesh, Maharashtra and Andhra Pradesh, Congress chief ministers rose and fell at a speed which began to make their predecessors appear paragons of stability.

All this kept Mrs Gandhi busy for a long time. She heard the views of contending factions, discussed with her son Sanjay the balance of power in the state concerned; both mother and son sized up the interests represented by the competitors and then the final decision was made. She had the power of political life and death in the civil war which appeared permanently to afflict the new model Congress Party. It was part of the wargame that the vanquished faction, those regarded as dead by the victors, never gave up hope. This could have been a result of the old in-grained belief in reincarnation, but there was a simpler explanation. They were fully aware that the selected favourites would, sooner or later, run out of steam. When they did, the disgraced ones would cleanse themselves, dress in the white uniform of the Congress, emerge from behind the curtains and await the summons to Delhi.

How this game would have ended is anyone's guess. There was much talk that Sanjay was working towards a clean sweep of the old guard. His men did not have a majority in the Congress parliamentary party, but they were beginning to behave as though they did and this worried some of the veterans. Not Indira. She was not particularly concerned, because she valued Sanjay's advice. He had been a pillar of strength in the period leading up to the emergency, during those years and, most importantly, when she had been consigned by India's voters to the wilderness.

Then, when her dependence on him had reached a peak, he died in a flying accident, on 23 June 1980. He was 33 years old. Indira was stunned beyond belief. Friends who were with her in those days are certain that the shock of his death did something to her. A part of her died. In the preceding year, the Indian writer and poet Dom Moraes had asked her whose death had hurt her the most. There had, till then, been three key men in her life: Motilal, Jawaharlal and Feroze. She replied that Motilal and Jawaharlal's deaths had grieved her, but they had not come as a surprise. Both were old men; both had shown grave signs of fatigue and illness. 'The most important death in my life was my husband's... My whole mental and physical life changed suddenly, my bodily functions changed... Whatever happened between us, Feroze never made a fuss.' Even in the case of Feroze there had been some warning, as he had suffered a mild heart attack many months before the fatal one which killed him. But Sanjay's death was a sudden and cruel blow. Even her staunchest opponents felt for her and expressed their condolences. It was undoubtedly a personal tragedy, but those who recommended a posthumous personality cult of Sanjay and an expensive state funeral could not have been amongst her more loyal supporters. If she took the decision herself, it was surely a sign that she was in a state of distress and should have been advised to the contrary. Rajiv was the only person to recommend a private funeral, but he was overruled. The turn-out at Feroze Gandhi's cremation had been a spontaneous demonstration of the affection in which he was held by thousands. In his son's case we will never know the truth, because sycophancy tended to drown any genuine emotions.

The ephemeral and slightly bizarre character of the funeral, the orchestrated display of grief, the plans to build Sanjay statues, Sanjay hospitals, and to rename streets after the young god, have all disappeared. They were, and it is far from cruel to say so, a crude and cynical attempt by the MPs who were personally beholden to him for their careers, to make doubly sure that their privileges would not come to an end. These were not parliamentary privileges: these were the privileges necessary to get into Parliament in the first place.

Indira did not fully recover from the blow. She visited the site of the crash twice on that fatal day – on one occasion she inspected the plane, on the other she inquired about Sanjay's keys and his watch. The Delhi rumour factory suggested that the keys held the clue to a large private fortune and other stories, equally improbable and malicious, were told and retold in those days. It was, probably, the act of a mother numbed with grief, searching for mementoes, looking again and again in disbelief at the machine that had killed her child. She must have inwardly cursed the obsession with flying displayed by her father and two sons.

Indira did not have the time to weep for long. Sorrow had to be fought as the needs of the state became paramount. The exercise of power is a great devourer of time. In Indira Gandhi's situation, where the bulk of her Cabinet consisted of opportunists and placemen (sitting there on her own choosing), she could never fully rely on her team. Apart from Narasimha Rao, the Foreign Minister, an intelligent and capable administrator from Andhra Pradesh, there was no one she could fully trust. That is why Sanjay had been so important to her; that is why his elder brother, Rajiv Gandhi, an airline pilot, was to receive a maternal summons. It could have been that she did not want him to fly any more, that she hated the very sight of planes. Much better to fly in one's dreams without these horrible appliances. Although that could have been the reason, it was not. Rajiv was needed for strictly dynastic purposes. She felt that she needed a Nehru-Gandhi by her side.

This was a result of too much concentration on means with no ends in sight. In a context where a political party has no principles left except the retention of power and the preservation of the status quo, then, provided that the state has a solid infrastructure, the quality of a party is not such a decisive issue.

However what even a stable state needs is a powerful leader and the rudiments of a national political party. Jawaharlal Nehru, Shastri and Indira Gandhi all supplied, in their very different ways, the first requirement. It was the political party which was beginning to fray at the edges. This was largely Mrs Gandhi's doing. Gangsterism and corruption were becoming very pronounced. The basis for recruitment to the Congress was no longer politics in the shape of a programme, but the lure of office, the hope of patronage and the licences to print money in the shape of lucrative agri-business deals and the like. It sometimes appeared that running the Congress machine was a far more arduous task than governing India.

Sanjay's fiery widow, Maneka Gandhi, was not happy when Rajiv was chosen to take Sanjay's place at his mother's side. She felt she could manipulate her late husband's gang in Parliament and elsewhere just as well as he had done, but she was proved wrong. It was a costly mistake. She left 1 Safdarjung Road with her infant son, Feroze, and declared war on her mother-in-law and the usurper Rajiv, who was stealing her beloved Sanjay's mantle. She proved to be a clever politician and, more to the point, one with a killer instinct. In this way she resembled her mother-in-law. Her politics are right-wing, even sinister, but she has the Gandhi name and a Gandhi son to prove her credentials. And so India might learn that popularising dynasties could be an expensive mistake.

Family quarrels could not, however, distract attention for too long from the precarious state of the economy. The GNP had registered a small decrease in 1980; the number of unemployed had grown rapidly in the countryside and slowly in the towns and trouble of a nasty sort was brewing in the north-eastern state of Assam, where an organisation calling itself the All-Assam Students Union (AASU) had begun a campaign against immigrant labour, which would in a few years become extremely unpleasant. The political climate was becoming unpredictable. A special sort of despair began to spread. In the past people had felt that there were some alternatives to the miseries of everyday existence. They had moved leftwards and tried the Communist Party. That had not been a totally negative experience, but it had been restricted to two states. Then they had tried the Janata, which was a disaster. Politics had become discredited. The right turned shamelessly to exploit religion once again, and the RSS started making preparations for an organised religious march through India. This caravan of reactionary religious revivalism was supposed to be apolitical, but it was in fact a thinly disguised provocation of the religious minorities in India.

Two other episodes typified Indian realities at this time. In the Bhagalpur district of Bihar, a state with one of the highest levels of rural unemployment in India, it had come to light in late 1979 that the local police had devised a new method for dealing with criminals in their custody – acid was poured into their eyes, blinding them for life. An Indian newspaper uncovered the scandal, interviewed the blind people and exposed the police. This was made possible because an official in the prison had been horrified by what had taken place and refused to keep silent. There was a national outcry. A few cosmetic changes were carried out, but the virtual autonomy of the police and para-military forces in parts of the country continued unchanged.

The second incident concerned a legendary woman bandit, Phoolan Devi (Flower Goddess), who became a heroine in many parts of the countryside. This 24-year-old illiterate peasant woman was one of the most sought-after 'criminals' in India in 1980-81, after her escape from prison. She was imprisoned on the basis of false evidence, like thousands of others, but Phoolan Devi refused to be shackled. She broke loose and escaped from prison. Her first act once outside, was to discard her husband and take a lover, a young man called Vikram. This angered the local Thakurs (upper-caste Hindus) in her area and they decided to teach her a lesson. They killed Vikram, kidnapped Phoolan Devi and took her to the village of Behmai. Here she was confined to a tiny room and gang-raped for twenty days: caste, class and sexual oppression was combined in a prolonged criminal assault. Many a woman would have been driven mad or succumbed to a fatalistic passivity; this woman, however, was different. She finally eluded her tormentors and linked up with a gang of dacoits. Within weeks she had become their recognised leader. Social banditry has a long history in the countryside, but it is unusual for veteran bandits to accept a woman as their leader – especially a woman who flaunts her independence.

It was in these bandit hideouts that Phoolan found the first real freedom she had tasted in her life: economic and sexual. It was *she* who determined her lovers and it was *she* who worked out the strategy of the group. For two whole years her gang carried out armed raids on the rural rich, but it was one act in particular which won her the respect of women throughout the country. She returned to the village of Behmai, the scene of her humiliation, where she gave the following terse instruction to her followers: 'Today we have to take revenge on the Thakurs.' Twenty Thakurs were captured. In front of the villagers, many of whom were from a low caste like Phoolan herself, they were lined up against a wall and shot. This was the first time in the history of the region that upper-caste Hindus had been despatched in this fashion. On this episode she remained unrepentant. When a sympathetic woman journalist asked her about the future, she remained remarkably cool. Did she not want a normal life? 'If anyone,' she replied, 'were to go through my experience, then she, too, would never think of a normal life. Often when I have thought of this, I have felt that I would prefer death to surrender.' She was soon faced with a choice: to remain an outlaw and be hunted down by the Thakurs and their agents or to surrender to the authorities. Anything was better than falling into the hands of the

Thakurs again, for she had no illusions as to how they would have killed her. So she gave herself up to the authorities, watched in helpless anger by the Thakurs. She is, at the time of writing, in prison. A number of films about her life, however, are already in preparation.

Indira Gandhi and Phoolan Devi. Two women: one at the top of the pyramid of power, the other buried underneath. There could not be a greater contrast than between these two, but both of them symbolised contemporary India. Did the photographs of Phoolan Devi, which were flashed around the world, leave an impression on the Prime Minister? Indira's father would have been moved by the sight of that defiant, determined face which stared angrily at dozens of cameras. This shortish woman with a white headband, carrying a rifle bigger than herself would, undoubtedly, have made a mark on the old romantic. He would have talked about the episode, found historical parallels, mentioned it in a speech or two and used it to rap Congressmen on their collective knuckles. That would have been all, but the event would have been registered. Indira never referred to Phoolan Devi in public. She had to contend with other, more serious, problems. India in the 1980s was different from in the 1950s. There was little time now for sentimentality.

The Soviet leader, Brezhnev, visited India in 1980. On his previous visit in 1973 he had annoyed the opposition (including the CPs) by expressing his doubts as to the rôle of an opposition. With Indira in command, he did not see any need of one. This time he was more circumspect, but gave Congress the green light of his approval. He signed a number of economic agreements to accelerate industrialisation and cement the previous close links with Indira. The Janata leaders had tilted towards the United States, but without breaking from India's non-aligned status, an important indication of the material basis of neutrality.

The CPI, usually silent after visits by Soviet dignitaries, had on this occasion expressed certain misgivings. The CPI Congress in Varanasi (Benares) in March 1982 did not criticise Brezhnev directly, but unleashed a blistering attack on the regime, accusing it of strengthening anti-democratic security legislation in order to imprison workers and peasants without trial and to keep down mass discontent. This was not a false estimate. What surprised observers, though, was that the CPI seemed intent to make its breach with Indira complete, by washing its hands to get rid of the filth of the emergency period. Hence the Varanasi convention of the CPI declared:

> Indira Gandhi is not only fostering her own cult, but also the cult of the family so that dynastic rule is perpetuated. Her word is law inside the Congress(I). Nobody can raise even a little finger against her policies. All sorts of yes-men,

blackmarketeers, antisocial and criminal elements have entered the Congress(I). Corruption has become the order of the day even in higher echelons of Congress(I) governments. The class character of the Congress(I) has not changed basically. But it must be stated that the Congress(I) is not the same old Congress with its democratic traditions.

This was a widespread view. What was novel was that the CPI leaders were joining in the chorus. It annoyed Indira Gandhi a great deal. It was almost as if she realised that a supportive CPI could put her case to the people at grassroots level better than the Congress Party membership. She told the author: 'I hear you've met Rajeshwar Rao on this visit. You know they attack me a lot these days, but look at their new allies! They're linking up with the communalists and people who have traditionally been their enemies like Charan Singh. So I don't take their criticisms too seriously. I think they're being very unprincipled.' Yet, I asked, was it not the case that the Congress itself was fraying at the edges? Could dynastic rule become a substitute for a proper political party? Wasn't there a gigantic difference, in terms of political consciousness, between the present Congress and the old party of Nehru and the other Gandhi? She smiled: 'But standards are going down everywhere, are they not? Is the Conservative Party in Britain today the same as it was under Churchill, or Labour when Mr Bevan was alive?' There was no serious attempt on her part to deny the fundamental decline in the Congress Party. Even to suggest that it could do something socially useful was treated as a joke.

Something had to be done. In ancient Rome, the tribunes seeking re-election used to organise the distribution of free bread and circuses in order to win votes. But this is the age of television and satellites. So a few grandiose plans were prepared – an Asiad in Delhi, followed by a meeting of the Commonwealth Heads of State in Goa, and of course the Non-Aligned Summit. These three big events could be staged in real splendour, regardless of the cost. They were. Perhaps they would distract a nation from its problems, and give the impression that all was well with the world, a government was governing, and a leader leading.

The transformation of Delhi as a result of the Asian Games had to be seen to be believed – lots of new five-star hotels, giant by-passes, an Asiad village, beautification plans of all sorts. The money was not in short supply. More to the point, there were a great number of lucrative contracts to be handed out. Patronage was on a gigantic scale and Congress bosses grew richer and richer. Corruption was by now institutionalised in India. Sooner or later some enterprising publisher will need to produce *India: A Do-It-Yourself Guide to Corruption*, which explains the amount of bribes needed at different levels to get certain work done. India is not the only country where this exists. It happens everywhere, East and West. In India, however, it has reached new heights, is fairly open and, if the word can be used in this context, straightforward.

Some grew rich, while others slaved to build the new additions to an old city. Surely this was not the 'magic city' of which Jawaharlal Nehru had dreamed in his prison cell?

This was a living nightmare for those who were employed in the stone quarries of Faridabad outside New Delhi. Article 23 of the Indian constitution expressly forbade 'traffic in human beings and other similar forms of forced labour'. It did so because its founding-fathers regarded slave-labour as an evil, as something which destroyed the dignity of an individual. This article, like many others, challenged the right of the capitalist to *unconditionally* exploit labour. The Asiad could not have taken place without the work of these bonded labourers, most of whom had been kidnapped and brought to work in Delhi by unscrupulous contractors. They were illiterate. They were too frightened to protest. They were paid an appalling wage.

The Supreme Court of India finally intervened to safeguard these workers' rights, and under the influence of a number of radical judges, a new development took place in Indian law. This was known as 'social action legislation'. It marked a definitive break with Anglo-Saxon norms of jurisprudence, as practised in Britain today. These initiatives divided the lawyers, the judges and the politicians into two camps. The conservatives were for the judicial status quo, for maintaining unchanged the legal methods they had learnt from Britain. The radicals insisted that those methods were not particularly well-suited even to Britain, but in India they were a complete farce. A more activist, interventionist judiciary was required. If not People's Judges, then at least Judges for the People.

A historic precedent was set by a senior judge of the Supreme Court, H.N. Bhagwati, when he ruled that where the victims were incapable for whatever reason of making a direct habeas corpus appeal, it could be done on their behalf by a private citizen. The court would then investigate whether such a complaint was justified and act accordingly. The Supreme Court, in fact, established a precedent for courts everywhere, by financing and setting up a dozen social action groups in different parts of the country. 'I believe,' Justice Bhagwati told the author, 'that judges must develop an active approach and particularly in a developing economy, where the poor people are hardly acknowledged as human beings.' Justice Bhagwati heard the case of the quarry-workers versus the Union of India and others. These were the men and women whose labour produced the buildings for the circus called the Asiad. The story of their lives was one of eclipse, of desolation, of crushing defeat and total isolation, and they could not organise themselves because their bosses would not let them. The writ petition to the Supreme Court alleged that in addition to the iniquity of bonded labour, there were countless cases of deaths and serious injuries caused by the total lack of safety regulations:

> The stone-dust pollution near the stone crushers is so various that many valuable lives are lost due to tuberculosis while others are reduced to mere skeletons because of TB and other diseases. There is no medical care, leave alone any provision of compensation for injury or death. No cases are registered against the mine-owners or the lessees for violation of safety rules under the Mines Act . . .
>
> Almost 99 per cent of the workers are migrants from drought-prone areas of Rajasthan, Madhya Pradesh, Andhra Pradesh, Maharashtra and Bihar... the legislation is being flagrantly violated here in these mines. [The workers] are without any residential accommodation worth the name, not even a thatched roof to fend against the icy winds and winter rain or against the scorching heat of midsummer . . . [They have] scanty clothing, impure and polluted drinking water . . . no facilities for schooling or childcare . . . These thousands of sons and daughters of Mother India epitomise the 'wretched of the earth'.
>
> On top of all this exploitation is the totally illegal system of *'thekedars'* (middlemen), who extract 30 per cent of the poor miner's wages as their ill-gotten commission (Rs20 out of Rs60, wages per truckload of stone ballast). The trucks are often overloaded, but payment remains the same. The hills are dotted with liquor vendors, legal and illegal. Murder and molestation of women is very common.

This writ petition, from which we have quoted a small extract, is a solid piece of descriptive non-fiction. It could, however, be inserted without too much difficulty and with a few name-changes into a novel by Dickens or, even closer to the present day, Steinbeck or Dos Passos. The Supreme Court, fortunately, was not taken in by the Asiad circus. After a lengthy investigation it pronounced against the government and instructed the provincial administration of Haryana to transport all bonded labourers back to their provinces and drastically overhaul working conditions in the mines. It appointed a court ombudsman to supervise the carrying-out of the court's decision. The judgement, written by Justice H.N. Bhagwati, represented a savage attack on the socio-economic status quo. Amongst its opening paragraphs – the whole judgement consisted of 103 typewritten pages – the following passage conveys a flavour of an important new way of thinking in the upper reaches of the Indian judiciary:

> The appalling conditions in which bonded labourers live, not as humans but as serfs recall to the mind the following lines from *'Man With The Hoe'* which almost seem to have been written with reference to this neglected and forlorn species of Indian humanity:
>
> Bowed by the weight of centuries he leans
> Upon his hoe and gazes on the ground;
> The emptiness of ages on his face
> And on his back the burden of the world.
>
> They are non-beings, exiles of civilisation, living a life worse than that of animals. For animals are at least free to roam about as they like and they can plunder or grab food whenever they are hungry, but these outcasts of society are held in bondage, robbed of their freedom, and they are consigned to an existence where they have to live either in hovels or under the open sky and be satisfied with whatever little unwholesome food they can manage to get, inadequate though it be to fill their hungry stomachs. Not having any choice, they are driven by poverty and hunger into a life of bondage; a dark bottomless pit from which in a cruel exploitative society, they cannot hope to be rescued.

Here we have a flavour of Emile Zola's *Germinal*. Contemporary India is an extremely strange and unique mixture, which includes aspects of Victorian England, Second Empire France and the USA in the 1920s. The contrast between the splendours of the Asiad and the degrading lives of the quarry workers has not been provided to conjure moral outrage, but to explain the volatility of India and the diverse patterns which produce the explosions that happen every day throughout the length and breadth of this sub-continent. Caste wars in the north have pitted privileged Hindus against their poverty-stricken co-religionists. The Santhal villages amongst the wooded hillocks of West Bengal are still inhabited by tribespeople with their own ancient customs and traditions. Here old women and poor widows alike are branded as 'witches' and hounded out of society. The reformers of such a society have had to battle against the intimidation of the CP(M) which prefers to preserve the old order. In neighbouring Assam it is students versus the poorest of the poor immigrants from Bangladesh. In Maharashtra it is again the tribal people and those fighting to change their lives versus the CP(M) and others. Elsewhere the Congress presides over villages in which oppression and murder of the *harijans*/untouchables/*dalits* (the last is the name they prefer) is commonly practiced.

This is a sub-continent of contradictions. There was, however, a novel occurrence in the 1980s. The Indian economy, simultaneously advanced and retarded, has produced pockets of wealth in certain areas, and although this industrialisation has not succeeded in combatting rural destitution, it has given birth to a semi-privileged class in the towns and in the countryside. It is from within this stratum that the most frightening challenges have come. The three major upheavals which were noticed in 1980-84 throughout the country were not revolts by the dispossessed. It was not the pavement-dwellers of Bombay, the inhabitants of the Calcutta slums, the quarry workers from Delhi or the large armies of the famished around every city who rose and demanded their share, their right to work and live in peace. If it had been them, the phenomenon would hardly have been surprising or original, but the three movements – the Assam movement, the Sikh uprising and the Sharad Joshi campaign in Maharashtra – were essentially those of people with wealth, demanding a larger share.

The last of these events was, in many ways, the most important, for it possessed a symbolic value. Sharad Joshi, a former UN official, gave up his job and came back to his native land to campaign for better conditions in the countryside. Perhaps it was done with the best of intentions. The central demand of Joshi, however, was for raising the prices of primary products from the countryside. It was an old debate. To what extent should the countryside subsidise the towns, or vice versa? The movement developed a certain momentum and Joshi, on a trip to Britain, was interviewed on BBC television and presented as a dedicated social worker. Maybe he was, but 'his' movement was one of rich peasants and farmers and its demands were clear in this regard. There was no talk of distribution, let alone redistribution, but constant demands to raise the price, for instance, of milk. This would have reduced the nutritional content of the diet of workers and others in the towns still further, without even producing a corresponding rise in the living standards of the agricultural workers and poor peasants, because any price rise would certainly have led to increased profits for the farmers, but would have made life even more difficult for the rural poor. Yet this movement was backed by the opposition, received an amazing amount of publicity, and created a communal polarisation. The Chief Minister of Maharashtra, Abdul Rahman Antulay, was a Muslim and this fact was ruthlessly exploited by the farmers-turned-politicians. Antulay fell, not because of the Joshi agitation, but because his corrupt deals were exposed in a series of articles in the *Indian Express*. That he was involved in a number of shady deals was not in dispute, but many asked why only Antulay had been toppled on this charge, when the country was full of corrupt politicians. The stench of communalism had begun to pervade virtually every aspect of the country's politics. The Maharashtra movement for higher prices fizzled out somewhat rapidly after the fall of Antulay, but it was a clear sign of the times.

The Maharashtra affair looked very minor compared to what happened in India's north-eastern border province of Assam. This region contained one of the largest concentrations of tribal people in the country.

They were descended from some of the first inhabitants of the sub-continent. They pre-dated the arrival of Hinduism as well as that of the Indus Valley civilisation and their customs and traditions shared various common features with the native inhabitants of North America, Australia and New Zealand. The Indo-Aryan rulers as well as the Muslim conquerors had not treated them well, but there was no question of genocide. They were largely left to themselves, though their land and forests were reduced in size with every subsequent invasion.

From 1816 till 1824 the Burmese invaded Assam and unleashed a reign of terror. The tribes fought back, but would have collapsed had it not been for British support. In 1824-6 the British, aided by the local inhabitants, defeated the Burmese, but as they had done elsewhere, they usurped Assam and brought it under the aegis of the expanding *raj*. The missionaries soon arrived, bibles at the ready, to convert the pagans. In 1828 the Assam tribes united and fought against the British. They lost, but rose again in the following year. This time they succeeded, under the leadership of Teerat Singh, in massacring British officers, including a general, as well as hundreds of Indians in the British Army. This revolt was defeated only in 1833. The level of popular mobilisation during this period can be gauged by the fact that the Lushais began to organise guerrilla raids on British settlers once again in 1834 and were only defeated, this time permanently, in 1850. The missionaries were now given every facility to make converts and they did achieve some successes. With the defeat of every tribal rebellion, the new conquerors encroached on more and more land and forest, which were needed for the tea plantations.

The tribal peoples feared the upper-caste Hindus as much as they did the British. They retreated in every way, becoming an introverted community, but still preserving their old traditions – some of which, like head-hunting and cannibalism, were not designed to aid reform or modernisation. The changes after independence were slow. The British tea-planters had been cruel exploiters of labour, and they were replaced by Marwaris from southern India who were not much better. Some advances did take place over the years. For one thing, oil was discovered in the region, the largest reserves in India, and limited industrialisation created the need for cheap supplies of labour. At the beginning of the 1980s, Assam possessed four universities and an agricultural university. Literacy was rising. The population was 20 million, of which 17.4 per cent consisted of *adivasis* or tribals. More than half the people lived below the poverty line, which was determined by evaluating incomes below Rs65 per month and 2400 calories per day in the countryside and Rs75 per month and 2100 calories per day in the urban areas. There was a 60:40 ratio between country and town.

During the 1971 war in East Pakistan – which was about to become Bangladesh – a large number of Bengali refugees fled to the safety of West Bengal. A few returned to their homes, but many stayed behind. Since the job situation in West Bengal was extremely bleak, the refugees searched for areas where work was available. They were lured to Assam by middlemen and unscrupulous contractors on the look out for the cheapest possible labour to service the tea plantations. Native Assamese were subsequently to claim that there were eight million immigrants in all. Of these five million were supposedly 'illegal', although the word had little meaning when the border between India and Bangladesh was 1600 miles long and wound its way through villages and rice fields, taking in rivers and marshlands and streams and a lot else besides. The people on both sides of the border looked similar, wore the same clothes, often spoke the same dialects: it was, as a result, impossible to decide who was 'legal' or 'illegal'. Here one could observe the bitter fruits of the partition of 1947. It appeared in retrospect, much more so than it had even at the time, a crime against the millions who lived in the sub-continent.

Worse was yet to come. In Assam the students formed their union, AASU. Instead of a careful study of the overall situation in the country, they decided to make the poorest of the poor, the immigrant labourers whose only property, in the most literal sense of the phrase, was their labour-power, into a collective scapegoat for deep-seated fears and frustrations. Their politics were based on regional chauvinism. Given that a large proportion of the refugee-immigrant workers were Muslims, it was only a matter of time before communalism made an appearance. Almost 80 per cent of the population of Assam consists of Hindus. ASSU's political demands were defined as the four Ds: the centre should *detect* all the immigrants, *disenfranchise* them immediately, *deport* them to Bangladesh or *disperse* them to other parts of India. In addition to other grievances, the AASU leaders did not like the fact that the immigrants had become large vote-banks for the ruling Congress Party.

The reaction in New Delhi was a combination of panic and confusion. They did not know what to do. They tried to appease AASU by asking them to distinguish between legal settlers and 'illegal' immigrants. They promised a barbed wire frontier to separate Assam from Bangladesh. Very few actually asked whether AASU was correct in the first place and whether its political backwardness should be challenged or not. Congress was on the defensive. The opposition, with few exceptions, was delighted to discover yet another mass movement whose anger could be used to discredit the Congress. Journalists sympathetic to the right-wing opposition published numerous reports painting a picture that was totally sympathetic to the bigotry that was gaining ground in the province. It is an iron law of politics that making concessions to ideas or parties that should, in reality, be combatted always works to their advantage. It becomes difficult to fight a narrow-minded chauvinism on its own terrain.

The AASU took the opportunity to launch a full campaign against the 'foreigners'. The centre announced that Assam was a 'disturbed area', the state government resigned and President's Rule was imposed. Then Congress made a major blunder. Instead of pressing for a series of hard negotiations it sought to control the situation by a speedy election, imagining that a Congress government in the state would ease the situation. This was a disastrous mistake. Given that one of the major complaints of the Assamese was that Congress used the immigrants as vote-banks, it was an insensitive act but increasingly a typical Congress one. The paramilitary forces ruthlessly imposed order. The Gauhati High Court, sitting as a full bench, stated that, 'The forces of law and order behaved like forces of aggression.' The elections were a total farce. A large majority boycotted the polls. With the exception of one area, where the poll was 10.47 per cent, in all the other regions it was less than two per cent. Nonetheless a government was 'elected', but the problem was that it did not enjoy any legitimacy. The entire process was fraudulent.

The police were so busy supervising the polls that, despite repeated requests, they did not perform their duties of safeguarding life. The Assamese nationalists, too scared to confront the central state head-on in a military confrontation, unleashed their war against the scapegoats. The makeshift refugee villages were attacked and razed to the ground. On 20 February one of the worst massacres in recent Indian history took place in a small town called Nellie and another refugee township known as Darrang. Five thousand defenceless men, women and children were killed in cold blood, 16 villages were wiped out and half a million people were rendered homeless. All this in one of the smaller states of the Indian federation. The photographs of these helpless victims, lying next to each other in the fields were among the worst sights that I have seen. It was the My Lai massacre in Vietnam magnified by ten. The images of children young and old clinging to their parents in death as they had done during their last moments of life were a ghastly reminder of the world in which we live.

That the Congress Party could not be absolved from the disaster in Assam was obvious, but it was noticeable that few in India stood up and confronted the perpetrators of the bloodbath. Comments such as, 'it would be a gross simplification to attribute happenings in Assam to the RSS', 'the violence in Assam was not communal', etc., were common in the quality magazines and journals. Atal Behari Vajpayee, the leader of the old Jan Sangh in its new guise of the Bharitiya Janata Party (BJP) blamed those 'who had not only pushed through the elections, but openly sought Muslim votes'. The best way, according to this sort of twisted logic, of safeguarding Muslim lives would be to disenfranchise the minorities.

Once the fires of prejudice and communalism have been stoked it takes a very long time to cool the embers. When the AASU leaders were asked by *India Today* whether they would guarantee that there would not be another 'holocaust like Nellie', they replied: 'The government will be solely responsible if such a thing happens . . . We only want the foreigners to be disenfranchised and deported . . . We don't want bloodshed.'

When news of the Nellie massacre broke in the rest of India, the capital, was preparing for the Non-Aligned Summit at which Fidel Castro was due to relinquish the chairmanship and hand it over to Indira Gandhi. It was not being planned on the same scale as the Asiad circus, but was nonetheless seen as an important event for the electorate. Indira flew to Assam and appeared visibly shaken. She said: 'I can hardly find words to describe these horrors.'

The circuses did not succeed in distracting attention from these problems. Neither the Non-Aligned Summit meeting nor the Commonwealth Heads of State conference, which followed soon after, could hide the scale of the problems confronting Indira Gandhi. Assam was not the only province where evil was gathering strength. The Punjab, too, was preparing for disaster on a scale unforeseen by even the most pessimistic observers of Indian politics.

The context in which these eruptions took place, and backdrop to every political move from 1983 onwards, was the impending general elections. The last date for these was January 1985, but Indira Gandhi's opponents were undecided as to whether she would take them all by surprise and call elections at short notice or prepare a delay by creating a situation which necessitated a state of emergency. The most popular scenario amongst cynics was a war with Pakistan, which would both delay and ensure victory: an ideal combination. It was in such an atmosphere of uncertainty that the 77th plenary session of the All-India Congress Committee took place in December 1983 in the city of Calcutta.

Calcutta was the first capital of the *raj*. It was also the birthplace of Indian nationalism. It had elected a communist government to run the state and though there were many problems there is no evidence that the Chief Minister, Jyoti Basu or his Finance Minister, Ashok Mitra, were corrupt. Many other criticisms were made, but not the charge of corruption. That, in itself, is no mean achievement in Indian politics. Calcutta is the largest city in India. It has a population of over 10 million. The literacy rate is 66 per cent.

Many foreigners who visit this metropolis are scared by the sights. Poverty, the rush-hour crowds, the congested traffic, the slums . . . the list is a long one. Even when the worry is eloquently expressed it can not hide the simple fact of surprise that such a town exists. For instance, Günter Grass writes in *The Flounder*:

> There are no separate slums, or *bustees*, in Calcutta. The whole city is one *bustee* or slum, and neither the middle nor the upper classes can segregate themselves from it. High-school girls with their books can be seen plodding down the street among bundles of rags the same age as themselves, forming islands in the traffic, then merging again with the great, flowing mass. Wherever the traffic leaves a free space, there are people living in the roadway. Side by side with parks and rundown mansions one sees village-like groups of cardboard and sheet-metal shacks . . . Here the Stone Age is staging a comeback and has already made deep inroads.

This is where the Congress meeting took place and where Indira

Gandhi addressed a public rally attended by a quarter of a million people. The Congress session itself was a one-family show. I was there. Sitting on the floor of the wooden platform were Indira Gandhi and Rajiv, surrounded by provincial leaders. In the audience were 'delegates' from Congress branches in the country as a whole. 'Delegate' is perhaps a euphemism. They seemed like people picked up on the street and promised a good time, all expenses paid, in a large city. Some of them were constantly being rescued from police cells and brothels. These delegates were interested in many aspects of life, but politics was not among them. They listened to Indira, applauded her enthusiastically and then left the hall immediately, unless the speaker happened to be Rajiv. When a veteran cheerleader like V. C. Shukla shouted from the audience: *'Desh ka Neta?'* (Leader of our Nation?), they shouted lustily: 'Rajiv Gandhi'. Then they left. This posed some problems, as there were distinguished foreign visitors present from fraternal parties – the East Germans, the Tanzanians, the French Socialist Party and, as the star guest, a member of the Central Committee of the Communist Party of the Soviet Union. An interesting episode surrounds his speech. Mrs Gandhi, worried lest the delegates depart before hearing the esteemed delegate from the CPSU, gave the boys and girls a pep talk in Hindi (which the CPSU man's interpreter must have translated for him!): 'Look here,' she said, 'it looks very bad for foreigners when you all leave after I've spoken. Sit down! You near the door, sit down! Now listen to me.' Silence was temporarily restored. 'The next speaker is from the Soviet Union. He's come a long way to speak to us. The Soviet Union is an extremely friendly country and I am appealing to you to stay here for his speech and give him a warm welcome.' Then she reverted to English and introduced the visitor from the CPSU. The audience did not even wait for the well-dressed, portly figure to reach the microphone. There was a mad rush for the door. Mrs Gandhi was angry, but helpless. By the time the Russian had meandered to the half-way point in his speech, there were a hundred-odd people left and they looked like plainclothes policemen. The arena held several thousand people.

The impressions gained from this gathering were a confirmation of what many have said and it was something that Indira knew herself. The Congress was a party in an advanced state of political decay; which, bereft of a coherent ideology or programme, had developed pragmatism into an iron principle. The quality of its

MPs and MLAs had declined to such depths that it was difficult to visualise how they could be raised from the pit. Despite this fact, it was obvious that the most important sections of India's ruling classes preferred the Congress in power to the hurriedly confected cocktails of the opposition that were being prepared in the same city. They had found the Janata experience a painful business and did not relish the thought of a repeat performance. Nor were they alone in this belief.

It was clear that there were three components in the political make-up of India at the beginning of 1984. There was the Congress under Indira Gandhi; the Janata Party (minus the communalists), and the various splinter Congress groups, desperately looting the alphabet to find a separate identity. This alliance represented the old coalition painstakingly built up by Mahatama Gandhi, Jawaharlal Nehru and G. D. Birla. During Janata's period in power there had been no basic difference in the quantitative allocations in the proposals for planning. Congress and Janata budgets were similar in character. From the point of view of political stability and rationality a merger of these groups under the banner of a reformed Congress would undoubtedly have helped to clarify the existing confusion.

The main reason militating against such a possibility had been Indira's decision to establish a total monopoly of political patronage and her refusal to share power with a team of leaders. Once she had embarked upon this style of functioning then a return to the hereditary principle, a feudal characteristic, became important: a dynasty became virtually a necessity. Political retainers replaced elected politicians in determining the tactics for dealing with major problems, and any real possibility of a unified liberal or democratic party was excluded.

The second coherent pole of politics was undoubtedly provided by the communalist alliance of the BJP and the Lok Dal, led respectively by Vajpayee and Charan Singh. Their approach was based on an appeal to the northern Hindi-speaking belt on an unashamedly confessional platform. They set up a new coalition and called it the National Democratic Alliance. Inside the ranks of the opposition they were, in some ways, the best-organised core, but the Janata experience in office had soured relations with others and the parties of the left, in particular, were loath to enter into any new alliances with them.

The third factor in the situation was the left. Since the CPI's break with Mrs Gandhi, there appeared a new possibility of a merger between the two Communist Parties. Friendly relations were restored and discussions resumed, but with few concrete results. Neither party was able to re-establish the prestige it had enjoyed during the 1950s. The split was not the only reason. The experiences of the coalition politics encouraged by both parties had not been of a sort to inspire a new generation of militants. Neither organisation was encouraging the recruitment of newer, younger and more critical members. The atrophied state of the party apparatuses did not encourage any spontaneous movement of youth towards the CPI/CP(M). On the contrary the efforts of many dedicated ex-Maoists and others were concentrated on working in a very localised fashion: with miners, peasants, tribal peoples, Dalits and so on. The experience of the CP(M) in office had disillusioned many potential supporters, who retreated into purely local work and abandoned the concept of 'national politics' which became identified with corruption and electoral opportunism.

The CP(M)'s strategy was based on utilizing its regional strength in West Bengal and Kerala to win a position in national politics. Such an approach was not foolish, but was dependent on the success of their operation in the region where they were strong. The problems lay in the following contradiction with which they (and all opposition parties) were confronted. Once a left party wins power on a regional level, its choices of action are circumscribed by a series of objective political and economic realities. Either it functions as a 'normal' party and attempts to gain responsibility, while providing a reasonable administration and possibly a few reforms, or it embarks on a more daring and radical course. If it tries the first option, it leads to an unavoidable conservatism. The dialectic of partial conquests comes into play: let us preserve what we have got, even though it is very little, rather than risk its loss by an ambitious attempt to go too far. The logic is obvious. Struggles are discouraged. The party's traditional supporters become passive and cynical. In such a situation it becomes unnecessary for the centre to intervene and impose President's Rule. The party itself has started paving the way for its own defeat. The second option was attempted, partially in Kerala in 1956 by a united CPI. It was a limited experience. The centre had intervened, but the net result was an *increase* in support for the CPI. These lessons had been long forgotten. Both parties of the left, instead of offering a socialist alternative to the electorate, had embarked on a series of alliances with right-wing and centre parties, thus reducing their own credibility.

The fourth dimension in politics at this stage was a bizarre combination of comedy and tragedy. This was the entry of matinee idols on to the political stage. In Tamil Nadu and Andhra Pradesh, the hold of religion was not as strong as in the north; Brahmin domination had long been hated in these areas. Nonetheless they found themselves a new type of icon in the actors who played god in the cinema. The popular cinema in India, both on a regional and national level, is a powerful instrument for promoting a certain social stability. The Bombay movie (in Hindi) is probably the only populariser of a linguistic unity of sorts: the songs in these soap-operas are known throughout the country. In India, then, the cinema performs a role similar to that of television in the West. It both helps to individualise experiences and provide a release from the strains and tensions of everyday life. The escapist extravaganzas which dominate the screen are strongly reminiscent of the Hollywood musicals during the Depression in the 1920s – the difference being that in India there is a permanent depression and, as a result, a never-ending stream of films. In the south in particular, this cinematic opium has become the religion of the masses. The actors have larger followings than politicians (an interesting reflection on the political processes). 'Why,' Mrs Gandhi remarked to the author, at one stage, 'we even had actors running governments in our large states of Andhra Pradesh and Tamil Nadu, long before the Americans dreamed of Ronald Reagan.'

N. T. Rama Rao (NTR), was an actor who literally played god in the movies. No one ever told him, 'Darling, you were divine,' except the electorate of Andhra Pradesh, who treated him as a divinity and elected his hurriedly formed Telugu (the local language) Desam to office. Earlier the actor M. G. Ramachandran (MGR) had been swept to power as the leader of the regional DMK in Tamil Nadu. The first response of Congress and everyone else was laughter. That NTR was a semi-comic figure was beyond dispute: his nuttiness was well-known. In January 1984, Mrs Gandhi asked me whether I had met *all* the opposition leaders. I replied in the negative, and she then remarked that I should meet NTR to get a real flavour of the opposition. 'Did you know,' she asked with a twinkle in her eye, 'that he wears *saris* in bed?' I denied all knowledge of this, but observed mentally that this was another one-up for Indian democracy. She then continued: 'You know, according to Hindus, every person has fifty per cent male and fifty per cent female attributes and qualities. Don't you think that in NTR's case this ratio was altered to 60:40?'

Despite the jokes, however, the Congress machine began to search for pro-Congress actors in the same regions. In Tamil Nadu they found a rival for MGR, the actor Sivaji Ganesan, a veteran Congress supporter, and a protegé of the late Kamaraj, who had headed the Syndicate in days gone by. Ganesan declared that Mrs Gandhi was his *amma* (mother) (he meant it metaphorically), and offered his services:

> I have an advantage because of my cinema popularity. More crowds come when I address a public meeting. In Tamil Nadu politics, leaders must have a mass base and popularity. Because of my cinema popularity I have this mass base . . . I will not go against her in the smallest matter. If Amma asks me to die, I will die. If I question or doubt her, then I am not a true Congress worker.

When asked by journalists what acting had to do with politics in the first place, Ganesan replied: 'Everyone said that NTR and MGR know nothing except how to put on make-up. But today they are chief ministers of two large states. Crowds come because of film glamour. Out of every hundred who come to see and listen to me, at least ten will follow me.'

A few weeks after the Congress meeting in December 1983, the opposition leaders met in the same city for one of their 'conclaves'. The venue was the Great Eastern Hotel, once the pride of the *raj* with its elegant shops and its grand suites, but now replaced by the five-star monstrosities whose purpose is not comfort, but profit. The Great Eastern has become dilapidated and shabby, a museum-piece that has not been looked after too well. It was here that the opposition met to decide its strategy for fighting Indira Gandhi and her Congress. Not much happened at the actual conclave. The public rally was not much bigger than that of the Congress and one also got the feeling that many of the villagers and the big trucks that had transported them were the same in both cases. The speeches at the conclave were incredibly dull. Banality masqueraded as strategy, although the dreams were, of course, grandiose. They always are on such occasions. The ambitions were far more colourful than the seedy location of the conference. The real discussions were, as usual, taking place behind the scenes. The real question was whether the truncated Janata Party could present the electorate with an alternative. If the Janata leaders were incapable of breaking with their past, if they continued to be imprisoned by the images of yesterday, then their new challenge to an old opponent would fall and the party would stagger from defeat to extinction.

The Janata's President, Chandrasekhar, formerly a Young Turk in the Indira Congress, had completed a 2,500 mile march through the villages, which are rarely visited by politicians. He had actually walked all the way and had been appalled by the conditions he found. He favoured a complete break with the communalists of the BJP, but lacked the firmness to impose this view on the party. His two close colleagues, George Fernandes, one-time socialist and trade unionist, and Biju Patnaik, once Congress Chief Minister of Orissa, were reluctant to fight Indira without their old allies. Observing the Janata politicians in debate did not give one the impression that they could confront the Congress on a national level. There was something faintly ridiculous about an opposition which included both NTR and the CP(M) leader Jyoti Basu. The only common denominator here was an opposition to the Congress, but this was totally negative and unlikely to appeal to an increasingly desperate electorate. The discussions and squabbles within the ranks of the opposition seemed interminable.

Meanwhile, thousands of miles to the west of Calcutta, an opposition of an altogether more sinister variety was beginning to gather steam. Its headquarters were in Amritsar, the old religious capital of the Sikh set.

Nanak, the founder of the Sikh religion, was born in a small village near the Punjabi city of Lahore in 1469. He was greatly influenced by the mysticism of the Muslim *sufis*, whose unorthodox approach to their own religion had spread rapidly in the Punjab as well as the predominantly Hindu *bhakti* (devotional) movement. Both sufism and the *bhaktis* insisted upon an existentialist approach to religion. They denounced the exclusiveness of the Hindu Pandits and the Muslim mullahs and argued for harmony between all religions; one of the leaders of the *bhaktis* was a Muslim weaver, Kabir, whose poetry was recited by Hindus and Muslims. Nanak's parents were Hindus, but he was greatly influenced by the cultural ferment in the Punjab. India on the eve of the Mogul conquests was in a state of chaos. Religious communities became more entrenched. The Muslim rulers of

Northern India resorted to large-scale taxation of the 'infidel' traders; Hindus were retreating into religious orthodoxy.

In terms of literary output, there can be little doubt that Nanak's talents outshone those of his numerous predecessors, if one discounts the epics of Hinduism, which were the collective product of numerous minstrels in ancient India. Nanak's imagery is far more appealing than the fables of Moses and Jesus or even the inspired science-fiction of Mohammed. Gautama Buddha's mode of discourse was strictly oracular. This appeal is perhaps because Nanak is the closest to us in terms of time. He had assimilated the prevalent mysticism, heard his equivalent of the voices of God, who had given him a glass of nectar (*amrit*) to consume and instructed him to teach the world charity, cleanliness, prayer, service and a belief in the One-ness of God. He preached his message through his poetry, which is of a high quality and like the *sufis* who introduced the *pir-murid* (teacher-disciple) concept to India, he began to be regarded as a teacher to be followed, a *guru*. Hence he was called *Guru* Nanak, and hence the title *guru* was given to all his successors. Nanak himself attacked the caste system, refused to claim any divine status for himself and discouraged deification. The later *gurus* were not as tough-minded on these matters and did not raise many objections when they were treated as a form of the Supreme Being. In a sense this was inevitable. Nanak had gone one step beyond the *sufis* and *bhaktis*. He had institutionalised the role of the teacher, whose mediation was vital, he said, for salvation. Thus the *guru* became crucial to Sikhism. Nanak eschewed the hereditary method of selection. He did not regard his sons as worthy successors and so chose one from amongst his followers. In order to avoid confusion, Nanak had the second *guru* annointed, his forehead touched with saffron, while he himself was still alive. He died in 1539.

It was during the time of the fourth *guru*, Ram Das (1534–81), that the foundation of Amritsar was laid in the shape of a sacred pond. The land had been granted to the *guru*'s wife by the Emperor Akbar, the greatest of Mogul rulers, who was himself toying with the idea of a synthetic religion to unite Hindus and Muslims in India. Around the pond a settlement began to grow and was named Amritsar. It was thus, in a very real sense, the religious capital of Sikhism, joining Jerusalem, Mecca, Varanasi and Rome as one of the religious capitals of the world. The writings of Nanak and his successors were collected in the *Adi*

Granth, which became the holy book of Sikhism, but was intended essentially as a guide. The Sikhs were often in conflict with the Mogul rulers, though Dara Shikoh, the heretical son of the Emperor Shah Jahan (the man who placed the order for the Taj Mahal to be built), was an acknowledged *sufi* and had many conversations with the *guru* of the time. Unfortunately it was his more orthodox brother, Aurungzeb, who succeeded to the throne, and the *guru* had made an enemy of the new ruler because he had helped the defeated brother, Shikoh. What changed the character of the Sikhs from a peaceful sect which was neither Muslim nor Hindu, was the execution of the ninth *guru*, Tej Bahadur (1664–75), by the Emperor Aurungzeb. Bahadur's last message to his son, Gobind, was a plea to avenge his death because: 'My strength is exhausted, fetters have fallen upon me, there is no means of escape left.' It was Gobind, the last *guru*, who transformed Sikhism into a fighting force and took the name Singh (Lion). The new warriors were known as the *Khalsa* (special property of the *guru*) and every follower had to bear the same surname, Singh. The women, too, had a common surname: Kaur (lioness).

The last *guru*, Gobind Singh (1666–1708), was determined to erase inequality within the religion in order to make it a unified and identity-conscious battle unit. New vows were to be taken to stress the complete break with the remnants of Hindu tradition. These vows were *hukamnamas* (edicts) and were compulsory for believers: they were forbidden to cut off their hair or shave their beard; they must always carry a comb in the hair to keep it tidy; always wear breeches reaching to the knee as was the military tradition of the time, always wear a steel bracelet on the right wrist and be permanently armed with a sword. That was as far as dress was concerned. In order to discipline the troops, Sikhs were forbidden to smoke, chew tobacco, consume alcohol or rape Muslim women. Gobind ended these dramatic changes by a speech to the faithful:

> I wish you all to embrace one creed and follow one path, obliterating all differences of religion. Let the four Hindu castes, who have different rules laid down for them in the *sastras* abandon them altogether and, adopting the way of cooperation, mix freely with each other. Let no one deem himself superior to another. Do not follow the old scriptures. Let none pay heed to the Ganges and other places of pilgrimage which are considered holy in the Hindu religion, or adore the Hindu deities . . . but all should believe in Guru Nanak and his

successors. Let men of the four castes receive baptism, eat out of the same vessel, and feel no disgust or contempt for one another.

In this fashion was modern Sikhism born. It broke definitely with Hinduism and with Islam, but also with the style and the temperament of Nanak and the first seven *gurus*. Gobind Singh was murdered by two Pathans in the pay of a local potentate. As he was dying he told his followers that there were to be no more *gurus* after him and henceforth they should look to the holy book alone for guidance.

The Sikh *Adi Granth* is a remarkable collection of Punjabi folklore and poetry. It does not consist exclusively of the writings of Nanak or his successors. In fact it was a *sufi* poet, Shaikh Ibrahim Farid, who first used a spoken language, Punjabi, to communicate in verse. Punjabi literature proper begins with Farid and many of his compositions are present in the *Adi Granth*, which was only compiled by the fifth *guru*, Arjun (1581–1606). One of Farid's verses gives a flavour of the man:

> Farid, revile not the dust,
> There is nothing like it.
> When we are alive it is beneath our feet,
> When we are dead it is above us.

Another poet and mystic was the extraordinarily talented Husain. He was the son of a Muslim weaver and was born in Lahore. He became interested in mysticism and, in a widely-publicised gesture, he threw his copy of the Koran down a well. After this act he began to sing, dance and drink when he was not preaching or writing verse. Since he was always dressed in red *(lal)* during his wild dances, he became known as Lal Husain. He then fell madly in love with a young Brahmin boy, Madho, whom he pursued till the affair was consummated. His name then became Madho Lal Husain and his *urs* are celebrated even today with abandon in General Zia's Pakistan. Madho Lal Husain, the first gay poet to come out in such a fashion, was extremely popular. He was asked to recite his verse at the Court of Akbar, where Prince Salim and others drank and talked to him until the early hours. It was reported that 'when drunk, he would dance, sing his own poems and preach to the crowds gathered around him'. Among his recorded sayings is the following:

> Doubt has vanished and doubtlessness is established;
> Therefore I, devoid of qualities, dance.

If I play with the Beloved
I am ever the happy woman.
The liar's face has been blackened
The lover's word proved true.
Because doubt has vanished and doubtlessness is established,
Therefore I, devoid of qualities, dance.

The poetry and the cultural atmosphere created by Farid, Nanak, Husain and their successors, especially Waris Shah, has yet to be surpassed in the Punjab. The birth of Sikhism was part of this sea-change in religious attitudes that was taking place.

Sikh political power reached its apogee under their most gifted ruler, Ranjit Singh, who defeated his rivals from within the landowning classes and united the Punjab during the first decades of the 19th century. Ranjit Singh's court at Lahore was a lavish display of the advances made by the followers of Nanak, within a century of the death of the last *guru*. Ranjit Singh (1781–1839) entered Lahore in 1799, defeated other Sikh pretenders and established a confederacy, which he ruled with an iron hand till his death. The British had entered India and were gradually occupying the whole country, but the Sikh ruler kept the Punjab out of their reach by a combination of clever diplomacy and the maintenance of a strong cavalry. He hired foreigners to train his troops and made a point of employing known opponents of the British. In 1822 two former captains of Napoleon's defeated troops, Jean-Baptiste Ventura and Jean François Allard, found their way to Lahore and were given a high salary and luxurious quarters in return for educating Ranjit Singh's troops in the methods and discipline of the Grand Army. They did their best, but failed to point out to the Sikh ruler that a great deal of the success of Napoleon's soldiery had been the result of a strong ideological commitment to the man who, despite everything, was a product of the French Revolution of 1789. Ranjit Singh was aware that the British were waiting for him to die before striking at the Punjab and he was right. During the 1840s a number of rapid wars ended the independent political power of the Sikhs in the subcontinent.

Under Ranjit Singh, the power of religion declined considerably and angry priests often denounced the ruler and pronounced him to be acting in a fashion contrary to the tenets of Sikhism. Ranjit Singh had paid no attention to these people and, since he controlled the army, his will, rather than that of the priests, was law. The occupation of the Punjab was strategically vital for the British if they were to maintain their hold over this huge new colony. If the Punjab, and numerous Sikh and Muslim potentates, had not remained loyal during the 1857 Rebellion, it is possible that the British would have been defeated, though for how long remains a moot point.

Once the Punjab was firmly under their control and the rebellion definitively crushed, the *raj* decided to expend a large amount of money and care in cultivating the lands and the inhabitants of the Punjab. They did so by developing firm and lasting alliances with Muslim, Sikh and Hindu landlords and by creating the best possible conditions for the latter to remain on relatively good terms with their tenants. There were fewer famines and hardly any peasant struggles in the Punjab from the 1840s till the 1920s. Most of the rural uprisings took place in Bengal, the United Provinces (then Oudh, now Uttar Pradesh), Hyderabad (now Andhra Pradesh) and the Malabar Coast on the south-western edge of the sub-continent. The Punjab was to become the granary and the 'sword-arm' of British India. The *raj* was to encourage the theory of 'martial races' in India, which consisted of people who lived in the more backward parts of the country. The Bengalis, for instance, were definitely not thought to be a martial race and the Punjabi officers commanding the Pakistan Army which went to crush them in 1971 were seriously convinced that the weaklings in Bengal could not fight. They got a shock.

Once the Punjab was stabilised politically and economically, the Sikh and Muslim yeomen and peasants were to become the most valued cannon-fodder in the British Indian Army. In 1911, a senior British intelligence officer, Petrie, prepared a memorandum for English eyes alone. It was entitled *The Politics of the Sikh Community* and can now be read in full in the National Archives in Delhi. Its purpose was self-evident:

> At the present time one of the principal agencies for the preservation of the Sikh religion has been the practice of [British] military officers to send Sikh recruits to receive baptism according to the rites prescribed by Guru Gobind Singh. Sikh soldiers, too, are required to adhere rigidly to Sikh customs and ceremonies and every endeavour has been made to preserve them from the contagion of idolatry. Sikhs in the Indian Army have been studiously 'nationalised' or encouraged to regard themselves as a totally distinct and separate nation: their national pride has been fostered by every available means and the

granth sahib or Sikh scriptures are saluted by the British officers of Sikh regiments. The reason for this policy is not far to seek. With his relapse into Hinduism and re-adaptation of its superstitious and vicious social customs, it is notorious that the Sikh loses much of his martial instincts and greatly deteriorates as a fighting machine.

The policy pursued in the Indian Army has been directed and rightly directed to the maintenance of the Sikh faith in its pristine purity, for the reason that any falling off from orthodoxy not only detracts from the fighting value of the Sikh soldiers *but inevitably tends at the same time to affect adversely his whole attitude to British power.* [author's italics]

The Sikhs in the British Army fought in the First World War and many died. Those who were demobilised discovered a country feeling the effects of an economic crisis — India had been milked dry during the 'Great War' — and many of them migrated to North America. Here they experienced the most virulent racism, especially in towns such as Vancouver. In the Punjab itself the Non-Cooperation Movement radicalised many Sikhs in the towns and the countryside. The massacre at Jallianwalla Bagh was the single event that, for the first time since the 1840s, made a large proportion of Sikhs turn to nationalism, terrorism and communism. We have already referred to the execution of Bhagat Singh. Sikhs now joined the struggle to get rid of the British in large numbers. When arrested many of them would display an insolence coupled with a sense of humour, by changing their names in the dock. English magistrate: 'Your name?' Sikh prisoner: 'Bomb-London Singh, sir.'

Simultaneously the Sikhs decided to clear the corrupt *mahants* (priests and caretakers in charge of Sikh *gurdwaras* who collected the money paid by worshippers) out of their places of worship. In November 1920 a committee of 175 was set up to to take over responsibility for all Sikh shrines. The Central Gurdwara Management Committee (SGPC according to its initials in Gurmukhi) decided to petition the *raj* to let it establish control over all temples. A more militant group, while backing this initiative, decided that stronger tactics were necessary. They founded the Akali Dal (Organisation of Immortals) and they declared that their aim was to organise a corps of volunteers, to train them in the use of arms and to wrest control of the shrines from the *mahants*. A newspaper, *Akali*, was launched under the editorship of Mangal Singh and Hira Singh Dard. The first went on to become a leading supporter of the Congress and of Nehru during the 1930s, and the second joined the Communist Party. These facts are stressed to show that the Akali Dal, at the time of its formation, was composed of people whose politics were still in the process of formation. They were far removed from any form of religious fanatacism.

The Akali Dal gained mass support when the *mahants* organised vigilante squads to resist any democratisation of the temples. There were pitched battles, with the British often backing the established order. Gradually the keys of the temples began to be handed over to the SGPCs, though there was a deliberately provoked conflict by the British deputy commissioner over the keys to the Golden Temple in Amritsar, the most revered shrine for the Sikhs. Ultimately even that battle was won. There was no reason now for the Akali Dal to exist as a separate organisation, but the fight for control of the temples had strengthened communal feelings amongst some of the people. While Sikh nationalists and communists left the country in large numbers, those who remained began to contest elections to the SGPC and thus determine who controlled various *gurdwaras*. Since the whole purpose of the exercise was to preserve religion, the more radical Akalis were at a disadvantage. Communists were asked why they, who never went to pray, were so interested in contesting elections to win control of places of worship. The Congress wanted to be in on the act because the SGPC had a great deal of political influence and money. The Akalis realised that without the control of the *gurdwaras* they would have no reason to exist, so they made a superhuman effort to retain control, which they have succeeded in doing since the 1920s.

Since they had to fight the nationalists and the left, the Akalis began to build new alliances. In 1935, the Akali leader, Tara Singh, formed an alliance with the Maharaja of Patiala, who was the most powerful Sikh ruler of a princely state. His attitude to religion was somewhat ambigious. He was notorious throughout Northern India for his reckless extravagance, his consumption of the finest alcohol ('It is the nectar prescribed by my religion,' he used to joke) and his limitless sexual appetite. The orgies organised in Moti Bagh Palace in Patiala became the talk of all the princely states. The other rulers were plainly envious. His visit was an attempt by the Akalis to come closer to the British, like the *mahants* of old. In 1940, the Akali Dal blocked with the pro-

British Unionist Party and agreed to support the war effort, just like the Muslim League.

After the Second World War, partition loomed. The Akali Dal leaders never argued for a united Punjab. They now stated that they would never accept a Muslim majority in the Punjab and therefore the province should be divided. In their talks with the British, they stressed their loyalty in the past and appealed for more crumbs than they could possibly be given. The Sikhs represented only 14 per cent of the population in a united Punjab. If the province was divided along religious lines it was obvious that West Punjab would become Pakistan and East Punjab India. The Sikhs were spread all over the province. Their richest lands and 150 shrines were in West Punjab. But they wanted partition. Congress, partially under their pressure, argued strongly for dividing the Punjab. In 1947 any hopes that both states would remain multi-religious were shattered by communal bloodbaths. This period has been movingly remembered by the Sikh writer, Khushwant Singh in his novel, *Train to Pakistan*. There was blood everywhere as killings, rapes and looting paralysed the Punjab. The sub-continent was winning its independence.

The Sikh refugees from Pakistan were largely settled in Delhi and East Punjab. Countless Sikh shops and businesses and restaurants bear the name of towns and villages in what is now Pakistan, yet another vivid and eternal reminder of the tragedy of 1947. The demand for a separate Sikh state, Khalistan, was raised by the Akalis in 1946-7, but almost as a joke and largely as a ploy to bargain for more territory in the western regions. It was not taken seriously by anyone.

In India, the Congress had pledged to create linguistic states. Nehru, as we have seen, was personally opposed to the measure, for largely positive reasons, but he agreed that an old pledge should be honoured. The Akalis immediately demanded a separate Punjabi State. If the Congress Chief Minister had led the campaign for such a state Congress might well have outflanked the Akalis. But Pratap Singh Kairon was not particularly keen on the idea. A census was organised to ascertain how many people regarded Punjabi as their first language. The Punjabi Hindu communalists now began a campaign asking Hindus to register Hindi as their first language, which was blatantly false. The propaganda was successful and when the new states were being carved, the old Eastern Punjab was split once again into Punjab and Haryana, with the new city of Chandigarh, built in the 1950s by Le Corbusier, declared a Union territory but a capital city for both Haryana and Punjab. The Sikhs now dominated the Punjab, the Hindus Haryana, but there was hardly any movement in populations. Both provinces remained multi-religious. The prime minister who finally pushed through a Punjabi state was Indira Gandhi.

The population in the Punjab did not vote for the Akalis *en masse*. Both the Congress and the two Communist Parties obtained a large vote, though the fight between the Akalis and the Congress was the major dispute in any election. Except for 1977, the Akalis had only been getting 50 per cent of the Sikh vote. Underprivileged Sikhs rarely voted for them and had even established their own shrines. The Akalis were only able to win one seat in the Lok Sabha during the 1980 elections. The equation of an entire community (the Sikhs) with the Akali Dal was part of the latter's propaganda. Its acceptance by the Indian media and the Congress was to prove a disaster. In 1980, the Akalis began a new agitation against the centre to strengthen their political base and prepare a revenge for the next round. The demands in themselves were negotiable, but underlying them was an economic flexing of the muscles. Contrary to Akali mythology, there has been no *economic* discrimination whatsoever against the Sikhs — in fact the Punjab is the richest part of the country. The 'green revolution' did achieve some successes, though at the cost of a rapid class polarisation in the countryside. The key to the Akali agitation, and we should not forget that it is a party led by the more privileged sections of the Sikh community, lies in the fact that it resents the wealth accumulated by the monopolists of Indian capitalism. Having grown rich, the farmers of the Punjab want far greater control of the distribution networks. That is why the land-owning peasants of the Punjab have set up their own union, which agitates for higher prices of primary products and lower prices for services, such as electricity provided by the centre. Sucha Singh Gill commented astutely in the *Economic and Political Weekly* on 6 October 1984, that:

> The present struggle of the farmers indicates the true nature of crisis in the Punjab. The rich peasant class is demanding a larger share in power politics and is terribly conscious of its economic demands and contradictions with the monopoly bourgeoisie. It wants greater powers to the states so that it can use governmental power at a state level to

promote its interests, and make a better bargain with the monopolies. Unless this urge of the capitalist farmer is accommodated, the solution of the Punjab problem in terms of acceptance of regional demands will prove short-lived.

It is in this context that the Akali Dal agitation of 1981–2 needs to be seen. The Congress was not averse to many of the farmers' demands, since they too had support among the rural rich, but they would consider them seriously only if they had replaced the Akali Dal as a political obstacle in the Punjab. The process had started when Giani Zail Singh was Home Minister (he later became President of India) and the Congress was looking for allies to defeat the Akalis. Instead of doing so by combatting communalism and encouraging the reformist sects within the religion, Zail Singh and Sanjay Gandhi met a man called Jarnail Singh Bhindranwale, who was prepared to attack the Akalis for being too moderate. Almost every observer who is not a paid partisan of the Congress has stated that it was Zail Singh who encouraged Bhindranwale to take on the Akalis with covert backing by the Congress. He became their candidate for the Gurdwara committee, but lost badly. How long he remained under Congress control is a matter for speculation. What is beyond dispute is that he was rapidly becoming Jarnail Singh Frankenstein.

In April 1980, Bhindranwale was suspected of ordering the death of Baba Gurbachan Singh, a leader of the Nirankari sect of sikhs, who had been declared heretics by the Akalis. On 9 September 1981, Lala Jagat Narain, a journalist critical of the demand for Khalistan, was shot dead by terrorists. On 13 September a warrant was issued for Bhindranwale's arrest. He sought refuge in a *gurdwara* at Mehta Chowk, near Amritsar. His followers surrounded the area and fought the police. On 20 September 1981, Bhindranwale uncharacteristically gave himself up, but was released on 15 October 1981. Zail was then Indira's Home Minister. Bhindranwale was set free on his orders and not prosecuted. Why? The Congress leaders were never to answer this question, but the facts spoke for themselves. It was hoped that a free Bhindranwale would continue to damage the Akali Dal as an electoral force and thus, objectively, pave the way for Congress hegemony in the Punjab. It was a cynical display of real-politik which would prove costly. A few months later in early 1982 there were Hindu-Sikh riots after severed cows' heads were found outside two Hindu temples. A secessionist group called Dal Khalsa claimed responsibility.

As the Sikh fanatics began to be rounded up, it became clear to Bhindranwale that he could no longer avoid being arrested again. On 19 June 1982, the 'Sikh Khomeini', as some of his followers described him, sought refuge in the Golden Temple in Amritsar together with an armed band. It should be pointed out that various Sikh fundamentalists had, until now, killed more co-religionists than anyone else. Why was Bhindranwale permitted by the Sikh establishment to use the Golden Temple? And – an even more interesting question – why did the police who were pursuing him on charges of murder suddenly stop outside the Temple?

The answer to the first question lay in the changes which were taking place in the Punjab. The limited modernisation had created sharp polarisations between competing social groups. Marx had spoken of the French peasantry as a 'simple addition of homologous magnitudes, much as potatoes in a sack form a sack of potatoes'. In the Punjab during the 1970s, the potatoes were beginning to be differentiated from one another. They were no longer a shapeless or helpless mass. The richer, more choice variety could be seen in a separate sack from the large, misshapen, variety. However, the latter, too, were at least in one place. In both cases many were Sikhs. Sumanta Banerji, an Indian political analyst, stated that:

> The reassertion of fanatical loyalty to traditional rituals and symbols of Sikh religion does not stem from pure religious motives. It has a lot to do with the desire among certain sections to muffle emerging cultural and economic dissensions within the community. In spite of the original message of castelessness, Sikh religious institutions have become identified with the powerful Jat landlords and rich farmers. Those belonging to the lower castes in the community and who are also the poorest, have been moving towards reformist sects like the Nirankaris or the Radha Soamis which promise them a status of equality. To keep the religious community intact (necessary for the new rich class of Jat farmers to mobilise the Sikh masses behind them in any negotiations or fight with the centre) fundamentalists like Bhindranwale were found to be useful.

What Bhindranwale represented was a born-again Sikhism, a confessional zeal that could transform a militant minority into a moral majority. Violence and ritual were both important in this regard. This explains his attraction for many Sikh ex-Maoists in the Punjab, who joined his ranks. *Their* Maoism had also entailed a great deal of ritual, liturgy and violence. The fact that the police had treated them with the utmost brutality in the late 1960s and early 1970s had alienated them permanently from the system. Bhindranwale injected into these demoralised ex-Maoists a pride in their rustic environment and old Sikh values of collectivity, egalitarianism and militancy. He spoke of 'avenging all injustices' and of being able to provide protection against the law. Many ex-Naxalites joined his bandwagon and became amongst the most articulate defenders of Sikh chauvinism, helping to inculcate these newfound values in a younger generation of Sikh students.

Nonetheless, the practices of Bhindranwale's gangs included attacks on poor Sikhs attracted to reforming sects like the Nirankaris. The privileged group within the Sikh community found in Jarnail Singh Bhindranwale a warrior-priest who would preserve the established social order. Religious fundamentalism became a cloak which could be used by vested interests in order to continue exploiting their co-religionists. The one 'secular' part of the agitation designed to appeal to the broad masses was an economic chauvinism. The Punjab, this argument went, is doing very well and generating more wealth than its neighbouring states (such as Rajasthan and Himachal Pradesh). Why should it be forced to share this wealth with the poorer parts of Northern India? This was demagogy of the worst type, for it consciously sought to ignore the fact that the pocket of abundance (the Punjab) contained large-scale poverty as well. The Punjab contained the largest population of bonded labour in India. The wages of landless labourers had not gone up for almost twelve years in 1984. It was facts such as this that the Akali leaders and the rich farmers wanted to obscure from view. Bhindranwale was a useful and effective diversion.

But what about the government? Why had they not pursued the turbulent priest into the Temple and arrested him at the time? There were, after all, precedents for such an act in India and elsewhere. A famous Hindu temple had been entered by the police to arrest a corrupt priest. There had been no outcry. In the holy Muslim city of Mecca in Saudi Arabia, when a religious faction opposed to the medieval monarch in that country had occupied the *kaaba*, the Saudi rulers (themselves religious fundamentalists of the first order) sent in a commando team, which included Frenchmen, to flush their opponents out of the sanctuary. This was done after a bloody battle. Why then was Bhindranwale allowed to use the Golden Temple? How did he acquire the confidence to set up a medieval court in the confines of the Temple and receive journalists, visitors from all over the world and his own supporters without any problems whatsoever? How did Bhindranwale's men transform the Temple into a giant arsenal containing an incredible variety of weapons and bombs? There was a Congress government in power in the Punjab at the time. It did not act against the men in the Golden Temple, and Bhindranwale stayed in the Temple for two whole years! After a year of the occupation, the centre acted by imposing President's Rule on the Punjab because of the 'worsening law and order situation'. Then for another whole year they remained passive. It is difficult, in these circumstances, to refrain from drawing the conclusion that the Congress administration tolerated Bhindranwale in order to fulfil its old aim of destroying the Akalis. The longer Bhindranwale stayed in the Temple, the thinking went, the more divisions it would create within the Akalis. This was not an incorrect assumption. The Akalis were rent with divisions as Bhindranwale's appeal began to affect the electoral base of their party. It was, however, an extremely dangerous tactic on the part of the centre. In breaking up the Akalis they objectively encouraged the growth of a diehard and sinister Sikh nationalism which would transcend all the privately agreed rules of the game. Thus the Akali–Congress negotiations were permitted to drag on endlessly, till it was felt by Sikh extremists that the Akali leader Longowal was making too many compromises. The negotiations then ended abruptly. It was an extremely cynical political manoeuvre and it would soon lead to disaster.

In a lengthy discussion with the Bengali historian Nenai Sadhan Bose, in August 1984 (published in the Calcutta weekly *Sunday* on 4 November 1984), Indira Gandhi discussed the Punjab in some detail. What is staggering is that while making a number of interesting points on the Akalis and their opportunism, she did not make a single criticism of Bhindranwale. This may have been because he was, by then, dead, but what about his supporters?

> Today, I would say that the Punjab question is serious because never before was the integrity of the country challenged in this way. And this challenge has not come up in Punjab. It has come from outside. The cry for a separate state is not within our country. It is outside. It is raised in USA, it is raised in Canada, it is raised in West Germany. In

UK it is on a much lesser scale, but in Canada it is the most and USA is a close second . . .

Here the Punjab situation itself is very complex; the caste element has come in because within the Sikhs the *jat* Sikhs think they are superior to others. But again the Akali Dal feels that if you are not an Akali, you are not a Sikh . . . it is like in the old days the Hindu Mahasabha said if you are not with us you are not a real Hindu or the Muslim League that if you are a Muslim in the Congress then you are not a real Muslim. So, these are very dangerous theories, because they take us towards fundamentalism which has the seeds of destruction in it, of the same religion even, if you have become so narrow . . .

The situation in the Punjab deteriorated very sharply in 1982-3. Indira decided to appoint a Sikh as President of the Union. Accordingly Zail Singh, once Chief Minister of the Punjab, then Home Minister at the centre, the man who had discovered Sant Jarnail Singh Bhindranwale, was elected President of India by a large majority. (The electorate for Presidential elections consists of members of the provincial and central legislatures.) Zail Singh was the first Sikh to occupy this post. When asked by a journalist what he thought of his nomination, he replied: 'If my leader had said I should pick up a broom and be a sweeper, I would have done that. She chose me to be president.'

Zail Singh's accession to the Presidency did not have an effect on Bhindranwale's behaviour. He continued to mock the centre. His motorcycle squads continued to kill his opponents. The situation in the Punjab was approaching chaos. The local police force was reportedly extremely corrupt, and although a new police chief had been flown in with the imposition of President's Rule, he seemed to be waiting for orders from above. In effect the local administrative bosses claimed that they could not take any independent initiatives whatsoever without clearance from Delhi. In Delhi there was conflicting advice being given to Indira Gandhi. From December 1982 onwards her son, Rajiv Gandhi, recommended a change of course and the expulsion of Bhindranwale from the Temple. 'Tell him to come and try,' Bhindranwale retorted in his pure, village Punjabi. 'I'm not afraid of him or his mother. Who is she anyway? A Pandit's daughter. Tell her to come here if she wants to talk with me.'

The only explanation for the delay in confronting Bhindranwale could be that the central government still believed that they would be able to control him, while simultaneously splitting and weakening the Akalis. What this left out of account was that the forces unleashed by Bhindranwale developed their own momentum, and even if he had wanted to pull in the reins it would not have been an easy operation. As far as the Akalis were concerned the division that was taking place was not between those who favoured collaboration with the Congress and those who were for a more intransigent attitude. The breach within the Akalis divided militants from moderates, but the issue was 'separatism'. As a result, even the moderate wing of the Akalis were extremely anxious to show their followers that they were not Congress stooges or playing Indira Gandhi's game.

The decision by Delhi to let the situation drift, or what a British viceroy had referred to as a policy of 'masterly inactivity', had created a sharp communal polarisation in the Punjab. In response to Bhindranwale's excesses, Hindu communalists had taken to the streets and it was clear that blood would soon begin to flow. Indira Gandhi woke to find herself placed in an extremely difficult situation. Having rejected the possibility of pursuing Bhindranwale's gang into the Golden Temple at the outset of this drama, she had allowed the initiative to shift from Delhi to Amritsar. Concessions would only whet Bhindranwale's appetite. They were, nonetheless, made. On 25 November 1982, Indira proclaimed Amritsar to be a holy city (it had been an old religious demand of the Sikh elders). This meant that no sales of tobacco, alcohol or meat would be permitted in the Golden Temple area. In addition there would be a daily broadcast of Sikh religious services.

While this was taking place there were three simultaneous upheavals of one sort or another that required the personal attention of the Indian leader. In Kashmir the veteran nationalist Sheikh Abdullah died on 8 September 1982. Indira Gandhi attended his funeral and helped his family determine the succession. The Nehrus were not the only dynasty in Indian politics. There were others, and the Abdullahs in Kashmir were amongst the most prominent. Farooq Abdullah, the dead sheikh's son and a doctor of medicine, was the choice of the departed leader's widow. The only other candidate was the son-in-law, G.M. Shah. Farooq was chosen and became the leader of the Kashmir National Conference, a regional formation which had jealously preserved its independence in the post-1947 period. Relations between him and Mrs Gandhi soured rapidly after he defeated the Congress candidates in a provincial election, and in the summer of

1984 she engineered Farooq Abdullah's removal. Provincial members of the state assembly were bought cynically (for cash) and made to cross over to G. M. Shah's faction. Farooq fell. His stature had increased enormously in 1983–4 and he was acknowledged as one of the more articulate leaders of India's opposition. He defended secularism and democracy with great vigour at giant public rallies, where he also proclaimed: 'I was born an Indian and I will die an Indian.' This was to refute charges that he was aiding the miniscule pro-Pakistani elements in the Valley.

'She's getting too old,' Abdullah told the author in 1984 before he was toppled.

> Look at me. Who am I? In Indian terms a nobody. A provincial politician. If she had left me alone there would have been no problems. Her Congressmen in Kashmir were bitter at having been defeated so they began to agitate, but for what? For power, which the electorate had denied them. I met Mrs Gandhi a number of times to assure her that we were loyal, intended to remain so and wanted friendly relations with the centre. Her paranoia was such that she wanted one to be totally servile. That was impossible. So she gave the Kashmir Congress the green light to disrupt our government's functioning. It was she who made me a *national* leader. I would have been far happier left alone in our lovely Kashmir.

When I questioned Mrs Gandhi about this she said: 'Yes, yes, I know that is what he *says*. He said similar things to me, but he acts differently. He tells lies and we cannot trust him.' Kashmir kept her fairly busy for at least eighteen months.

Preoccupied with the Punjab, Kashmir, and India's foreign policy, Indira Gandhi confronted a domestic coup. Her daughter-in-law, Maneka Gandhi, widow of the dead Sanjay, left the joint family residence of 1 Safdarjung Road and declared a personal war on her mother-in-law and Rajiv. She announced her entry into politics and challenged Rajiv to a public electoral duel. This was avoided only because she was still under age and was legally barred from contesting elections. Rajiv won his by-election, but the spectre of his sister-in-law began to haunt him. Maneka claimed that she had been expelled from the family home. This was an untruth. As we shall see, Maneka's withdrawal was part of a carefully-laid political plot to cause maximum embarassment to Indira Gandhi at a time when she was confronted with crucial problems in the political arena. A great deal of soiled family linen was washed in public that year. Indira was grieved at the enforced departure of Sanjay's infant son, Feroze Varun, to whom she was deeply attached. She was paralysed for a moment by personal agony, but she could not let it distract her for too long. In order to ensure that Sanjay's widow could not use his name to enhance her political career, the personality cult of the younger son was abruptly brought to an end and the brick construction on which the funeral pyre had been lit was demolished. The fact that the cult did not survive official disapproval was the clearest indication of its superficiality.

While all this was taking place, Rajiv Gandhi and his advisers decided that the time had come to get rid of the elected regional government in the southern state of Andhra Pradesh. They would soon discover that money could not buy them love, but it was an expensive lesson in every respect. It gravely damaged Indira Gandhi's standing in the country. In fact the Andhra Pradesh affair was so badly mismanaged that it is difficult to believe that an experienced 'toppler' of provincial governments, in fact a pioneer of the process, like Indira could have been following events too closely.

The ailing actor, NTR, was becoming discredited by his own pursuits with every passing day. The civil liberties record of his government was appalling. NTR ran Andhra Pradesh like a dictator. He had personally abused trade unionists fighting for their jobs and turned a blind eye to attacks on *harijans*. Upper-caste supporters of NTR's politics had burnt 86 houses in one village alone. Four low-caste Hindus had been burnt alive. In another attack on a neighbouring village, two people had been killed and several women raped. There were three different reports of instances of police raping women prisoners while they were in custody. Police attacks on peasants were common. The Andhra Pradesh Civil Liberties Committee reported on a number of Special Armed Police Force raids on the poor:

> The dates change, the villages change, but the details of a raid remain the same. Destroyed houses, broken cots and utensils, ornaments lost, pulses and grains thrown into the well, men with broken arms and legs, molested women terrorised into silence, greet any visitor the morning after a raid . . . Altogether 250 villages were affected by such police raids in the last year.

This was NTR's record. When he had first stood for elections, people had tried to touch him since he was an actor-god. A woman had even fainted on one occasion after shouting, 'Here comes god!'. His unpopularity, however, had grown apace. Many observers hostile to Indira had concluded that Congress would win Andhra Pradesh the next time. It was at this crucial juncture that Rajiv and his friends had revived the old fraud's popularity by unseating his government. Their attempt, however, was a miserable failure. Telugu nationalism was offended. NTR marched his parliamentarians to Delhi and asked the President of India to determine who had the majority in the Andhra Pradesh legislature. Ultimately the Congress was forced to retreat and NTR was re-instated as chief minister. The whole escapade had proved to be a disaster. Given that the entire episode had been masterminded by Captain Rajiv and his new, clean crew, it did not augur well for the future of Indian democracy.

In the Punjab, in the Golden Temple there was a series of events that caused feverish excitement. The wild demagogy of the Sikh fundamentalists began to get a wider hearing in the Punjab. The longer the government delayed the more it appeared to the people that it was Delhi who was afraid. They commented on this weakness and it made them regard Bhindranwale not as the monster that he undoubtedly was, but as a superhuman hero in the tradition of the *gurus* of Sikhism. And the *guru* he was compared to the most was, of course, the martial Gobind. This is not to suggest that the entire Sikh population was ready to leap into the air and raise aloft the banner of Khalistan. The demand for an independent Sikh state did not and does not, even now, command the support of a majority of the Sikhs. Without determined opposition from within the Sikh community, however, it appeared that Bhindranwale ruled the roost, for the Akalis were obsessed with inner-party struggles. Their leaders had, of course, been imprisoned by Mrs Gandhi. The CP(M), the only party of the left with a base in the Punjab, saw its role as the mediator between the government and the Akalis, instead of unleashing an open frontal assault on the medieval nonsense that was being spouted in the Golden Temple. It was an old disease and its roots lay in a strange definition of secularism. Instead of seeing the latter as an opportunity to educate the new generations in a spirit of rationalism and encourage a self-critical awareness, most of the non-communal political groupings praised all religions. This was, to put it mildly, self-defeating. It made secularism into a totally negative concept and, in reality, preached the virtues of religion.

In February 1984 it had become clear to Indira Gandhi and her close circle of advisers that there could be no negotiated settlement with Bhindranwale. As late as April of that year, Rajiv stated that Bhindranwale was a 'religious leader' and not a politician. If this was intended as an attempt to mollify Bhindranwale, it was a dismal failure. The extent to which the Congress negotiated with Bhindranwale in 1982-4 is not known, though the truth will reveal itself sooner or later. India is not a secretive society. Until that time, however, any further speculation on the subject is pointless.

In May 1984 the government approved a plan to enter the Golden Temple. The task could not be entrusted to the police since the amount of weaponry possessed by the Bhindranwale gang was reported to be considerable. It had to be an army operation, and the involvement of Sikh officers and soldiers was crucial in order to preserve the secular fabric of the constitution. The situation had moved a long way since the occupation of the Temple first began. Few doubted the dedication and fanaticism of the Sikhs in the Temple – the photographs taken of the men inside were sufficient warning. Bhindranwale carried a sten-gun some of the time, but permanently wore a revolver and a shoulder-strap of bullets. Amrik Singh, his lieutenant, President of the Sikh Students Federation, carried a machine-gun and a revolver. The Sikhs who maintained a constant vigil were heavily armed. Their faces, old and young, displayed anger and puzzlement. Did most of them know why they were there and what was in store for them?

The Golden Temple consisted of three sections surrounding a giant pond which had a temple in the middle. This was Harmandir Sahib, the holiest shrine in the complex. The pavements surrounding the pond were pure marble and on one side were the residential quarters where the Akali leaders lived and worked. On the opposite bank there were more quarters, which also housed the *Akhal Takht* where the most powerful and authoritative body of the Sikh faith met to deliberate and pass judgement. Its *hukamnamas* (edicts) were holy writs that all Sikhs must obey; if they defied the edicts, the penalty was excommunication. It was in this part of the Temple that Bhindranwale established his headquarters. The Temple had been covered in gold during the reign of the Maharajah Ranjit Singh, who had also recovered looted remnants of the Temple from Ahmed Shah Abdali's raiders in Afghanistan and returned them to the shrine in Amritsar. It was here that the battle which had been delayed for far too long now took place.

May is one of the hottest months in the plains of the Punjab. Temperatures are known to reach unbearable heights, varying from 100 to 120 degrees Fahrenheit. There are often days when the heat begins to melt the tar on the roads. When the hot wind, the *looh*, blows, the streets are deserted, and everyone runs for shelter. On the night of 30 May 1984, the Indian Army began to surround the area. 70,000 troops were involved in the action. On 2 June, Indira Gandhi went on television to make a special broadcast to the nation. She stated that the government had decided to terminate the violence and terrorism in the Punjab and proposed a compromise settlement to the Akali leaders, pleading with them to call off their action. General Ranjit Singh Dayal, the Sikh officer in control of the western command was brought to Amritsar as a special adviser to the Governor. For three days the Army watched the Temple and other areas in the Punjab. On 3 June they realised that they were confronting a determined band of guerrillas, some of whom had been trained to fight a war. It was not an empty-headed rabble. A Sikh major-general, Shahbeg Singh, who had been dismissed from the Army for corruption a year earlier, had joined the Golden Temple brigade. On 4 and 5 June, the Army called on the armed bands of men inside the Temple to surrender peacefully. The response was bursts of machine-gun fire. On the night of 5 June, under cover of darkness, a team of commandos gained entry to the section of the Temple where the Akali leaders were based. Indira Gandhi had personally ordered them to bring out the Akalis who were unarmed, whatever the cost. The forty commandos rescued the principal leaders of the Akali Dal; Sant Longowal amongst them. Bhindranwale's snipers, however, got an old enemy, Gurcharan Singh, the former secretary of the Akalis, as well as Bagga Singh from the SPGC, who had openly mocked Bhindranwale's pretensions and his ambition to lead the Sikhs. Three commandoes were killed and fourteen wounded.

On the morning of 6 June the battle commenced. The Army was under orders to avoid too much damage to the Temple, and this gave their opponents a distinct advantage. Over a hundred soldiers were killed during the first assault. A senior officer told *India Today*: 'It was so utterly frustrating for the *jawans* (soldiers) who saw their comrades die under fire from the Temple and yet could not shoot back. Frankly even we never thought our men could have shown so much patience.' Towards the end of the day tanks and artillery were brought into play and the defences crumbled. Bhindranwale, Amrik Singh and Shabeg Singh died with their sten-guns in their hands, and the remainder surrendered over the next few days. 'Operation Bluestar' was over.

Among the first Sikhs to revisit the Temple was the President, Zail Singh. The casualties told their own story: 800 to 1000 of Bhindranwale's supporters and 200 to 300 soldiers of the Indian Army had been killed in the battle of the Golden Temple. On 11 June, Indira Gandhi told a public meeting: 'What has happened is a tragedy for India. It should not be celebrated as a victory.' In death Bhindranwale had been transformed for many Sikhs into a saint, a martyr in a community whose religion thrives on martyrdom. Many stories were spread about his last hours, most of them fanciful. Peasants claimed to have seen him with a falcon on his wrist. The flying falcon was seen by many people, at least in their imaginations. The falcon had been a favourite bird of the last *guru*, Gobind.

Indira Gandhi's decision was inevitable. There was no other way to end the reign of terror in the Punjab, which claimed hundreds of innocent lives. The only legitimate question is why it took Delhi three years before it moved into action – three crucial years during which a massive supply of arms were hoarded and training provided to Bhindranwale's men. That question has not yet been answered satisfactorily by Congress leaders or ideologues. Yet in the reply lies the future of the Punjab. In London, an old Akali rogue elephant, Jagjit Singh Chauhan, self-proclaimed leader of Khalistan, declared that Indira Gandhi's days were numbered. Chauhan is closely linked to various people in the United States. His closest contact is the senator from North Carolina, Jesse Helms, but he claims to have support from General Daniel Graham, co-chairman of the National Security Council. Chauhan has also, according to newspaper reports, developed contacts with the South African administration. His support in the Punjab itself, however, is somewhat limited. Until Operation Bluestar it was certain that the concept of Khalistan had more supporters outside India than inside. 'The best place for Chauhan's Khalistan is California,' a Sikh academic told the author in Delhi. 'Let the Americans give him some land and allow him to set up a Sikh state there, for we will never support it in the Punjab.' Whether this was still the case after 6 June 1984 remains to be seen. There was a mutiny by Sikh soldiers in Ramgarh in Bihar. They shot one of their officers, but the revolt was short-lived and rapidly quelled. It did, however, symbolise the distance many Sikhs had travelled since Bhindranwale had first entered the Golden Temple.

Negotiations about the repair of the Temple were conducted between the government and the Akalis. Problems arose, and the government short-circuited the entire process by ignoring the SPGC and asking Baba Santa Singh from the Nihang faction to take on the task of beginning *kar sewa* (voluntary labour) to repair the shrine. The Nihangs (the word means crocodile) are descended from a *kamikaze* cavalry unit organised by *Guru* Gobind. They had split in 1733 and Santa Singh belonged to the larger and older faction. The Nihangs began their work but Santa Singh kept up a barrage of attacks against the Akalis for having let Bhindranwale use the precinct in the first place: 'Why didn't the Akalis act when Bhindranwale's men were going about defecating and drying underwear on the balconies of the Akhal Takht? Why did they never approach me for help? I would have happily sent in my cavalry. What are all these gallant horsemen for if not for saving the shrines from desecration? It is because they did not ask their own Sikh armies that Mrs Gandhi had to send in hers.'

When the first repairs were completed the Temple was opened to the public. Thousands rushed to see the damage and pray, and many wept as they observed the bullet-scarred Akhal Takht. The Sikhs of the Punjab were in a state of deep shock. Whether time would soon have healed these emotional scars became a somewhat academic question, for in Delhi, three months later, a crime was perpetrated.

After the confrontation in the Punjab had ended, Indira Gandhi began her national tours, part of the forthcoming election campaign. She spent two extremely tiring days in Orissa. Like her father, she tended to disregard security precautions on these occasions. She returned to Delhi on 30 October. Her senior ministers were on tour in other parts of the country; Rajiv was in West Bengal trying to boost the morale of Congress supporters in the most important stronghold of the Indian left. On the morning of 31 October, Indira Gandhi talked to her grandchildren at 1 Safdarjung Road. She was then informed that the actor Peter Ustinov was waiting to interview her with a television unit in her office, a few minutes walk from the house. Two Sikh security men were on duty. One of them, sub-inspector Beant Singh, had been her bodyguard for several years, travelling abroad with her in that capacity. Her intelligence chiefs ordered his transfer after the Golden Temple incidents, but Beant Singh wept and begged her to override the order. She told a friend: 'How can we punish a whole community for what some minority has done?' and the order was countermanded by her in the interests of secularism.

As she walked from her home to the office on 31 October, Beant Singh and Constable Satwant Singh sprayed Indira Gandhi with bullets. Even after she lay immobile on the road, Satwant Singh kept pumping her with machine-gun bullets. She died shortly afterwards. The two assassins were apprehended. Beant Singh was shot dead by other security guards, but Satwant survived. Whether he will reveal the truth remains to be seen. The assassination had been carefully planned, the assassins carefully chosen – Beant Singh had known that on that fateful day she would not be wearing her bullet-proof vest. Both men had obviously been convinced that they had to kill her for the honour of their religion.

The continued strength of religion in the modern world is the most telling indictment of this century. India is not alone in this regard. What the novelist V.S. Naipaul referred to as 'the pull of the old barbarism', when writing about Mrs Gandhi's murder, is not something restricted to India. The members of the Klu Klux Klan in the United States are all firm believers in Christianity. Their symbol, after all, is a burning cross, and they pray before they go on their lynching expeditions. The Protestant-Catholic divide in Ireland, initially encouraged by London, has become a major problem for successive British governments.

Bhindranwale has his counterparts in the United States today as well as in Poland. The survival of religion from worlds which have, in other respects, long disappeared must be a response to some deeply felt psychological need. It must provide a feeling of identity in a world that encourages the atomisation of individual existence. For Marx it was not just the 'opium of the people', but equally 'the heart of a heartless world, the soul of soulless conditions'. It provided a feeling of collectivity and solidarity against a hostile world. These emotions are blind. Once aroused they spell the death of rational behaviour or thought. Satwant Singh and Beant Singh were instruments and victims of those who sought to harness religion to politics. They were used willingly, but the real murderers continue to stalk the land.

On the same evening that his mother had been so brutally murdered, Rajiv Gandhi was sworn in as Prime Minister, by President Zail Singh. The civil service and a tiny group of elected and non-elected advisers to the late Prime Minister carried out her wishes. A Nehru-Gandhi was still at 1 Safdarjung Road. Rajiv Gandhi's accession to the prime ministership of India marked the existence of a political dynasty unique in the post-war history of the democratic world.

When Mahatama Gandhi was assassinated, India had been stunned into silence. Shame was written on many Hindu faces, because his killer was a Brahmin. His funeral procession had been long, but silent, and after his death communal violence came to an end all over India. Indira was killed by two Sikhs, who were meant to protect her. The anger throughout the country was genuine. It was, however, immediately exploited by various Congress supporters in the neighbourhoods of Delhi and other cities. While Indira's body was burnt on the funeral pyre, near the spot where her father, her son and Gandhi were given their last farewells, the city in which she lived for most of her life was also on fire. Hindus intent on revenge began to attack Sikh families and burn their houses and shops and businesses. Delhi was red with blood, while the police watched impassively. M.J. Akbar, editor of *The Telegraph* in Calcutta sent his paper a despatch from the burning city:

> The frenzy of the Hindu mobs rampaging in the capital showed once again how human beings overrate themselves; no animal would have indulged in such brutality. Even now, sitting in front of a typewriter in an office, far away from the eerie, macabre glee of the young men who danced while they burned and looted, one breaks out into a cold sweat before surrendering to depression. If this is going to be the reality of India, what is the point of preserving it?

Young children were burnt to death by screaming adults. Women were raped. It reminded the older generation of 1947 and partition, when the same cries and burning houses had marked the first days of independence. Then and now there were people who gave shelter to the fleeing minority; then and now there were patrols formed by people who were decent and honourable and refused to sanction or tolerate or shut their eyes to the atrocities that were taking place.

What happened in Delhi was worse than anywhere else. The mob seized control. Elias Canetti's description, in *Crowds and Power*, of a rampaging mass, blinded by its own hatreds and traumas, is a powerful account of what was witnessed in Delhi after the assassination of Indira Gandhi:

> The baiting crowd forms with reference to a quickly attainable goal. The goal is known and clearly marked and also near. This crowd is out for killing and it knows whom it wants to kill. It heads for this goal with unique determination and cannot be cheated out of it. The proclaiming of the goal, the spreading about of who it is that is to perish, is enough to make the crowd form. This concentration on killing is of a special kind and of an unsurpassed intensity. Everyone wants to participate; everyone strikes a blow and, in order to do this, pushes as near as he can to the victim. If he cannot hit him himself, he wants to see others hit him. Every arm is thrust out as if they all belonged to one and the same creature . . .
>
> One important reason for the rapid growth of the baiting crowd is that there is no risk involved. There is no risk because the crowd have immense superiority on their side. The victim can do nothing to them. He is either bound or in flight, and cannot hit back; in his defencelessness he is victim only.

Canetti is talking about a *universal* phenomenon, but that does not help to exorcise the crimes that were committed collectively in Delhi. An entire community was punished for the death of Indira Gandhi. The new Prime Minister ordered the Army to stop the mobs, whatever the cost. He then went to the hurriedly organised refugee camps where the Sikhs of Delhi were seeking shelter from the firestorm and the killer-crowds. He wept, one is told, and shook numerous hands. 'If *you* had wanted to kill us,' a Sikh woman told him, 'I would have understood. After all it is your mother whom these two Sikhs have killed. But you are calm and *they* are killing us!' When Rajiv Gandhi's grandfather became prime minister, he too had visited refugee camps in Delhi and thundered against the inefficiency of the police in protecting innocent lives. Rajiv also cursed and swore at the police. While standing and watching his mother's dead body he must have been unable to keep his mind away from the other victims of the tragedy.

Indira was no more. Jawaharlal's daughter was dead, and with her an epoch ended. She was, in many ways, the last link between the old Congress and the new. She had grown up in a period when ideals still meant something, when there was everything to fight for and the future appeared rosy, when large numbers of Congress members believed that the magic city could be constructed in the years ahead. Indira had known all the veterans of the nationalist and socialist movements. What did she really feel about the decay of a once powerful political organisation? In the old days the money had come from G.D. Birla and his friends. It was capitalist money, but there was nothing underhand about it and everyone knew that India's capitalists were also nationalists in their own way. Birla had now been replaced by Haji Maastan, whose money was 'black' and tainted and illegal and evil and, what is more, he demanded returns and favours. His model was Marlon Brando in *The Godfather*, but he told interviewers that though he saw himself as Brando, the reality was more like *Godfather II* and the link between gangsterism and politics.

Sycophancy had, in the Indira years, become a national pastime. In the old days at Anand Bhavan, when some of Jawaharlal's supporters got carried away and started referring to him as the 'Jewel of India', he had been teased mercilessly by everyone at home: 'Would the Jewel of India mind passing the salt?' or 'Would the Jewel of India like something else to eat?' The whole family had roared with laughter, including the object of the humour. A friend reminded Indira of this and asked her how she reacted to the sycophancy. She replied: 'In my father's time we were new to such flowery language and so felt amused. Now superlatives are used so indiscriminately that I doubt if anyone can take them seriously. My family and I certainly do not.'

Indira had always known that she could be struck down by an assassin's bullet. If American presidents were not safe, then it was impossible to protect anyone. A few weeks before her death she confessed to an interviewer that she was prepared for anything, since she had lived a reasonable life – though not even she could have dreamt that her own guardians would slay her outside the front door of her residence. She was a strong and ruthless political leader, but in her private life she was an extremely warm and affectionate mother and grandmother. Were there then two different people? She tended to deny such an assertion. 'I am the same,' she would often repeat to those who asked her this question. But no person is the same in every sense. Individuals are many-sided, even though most of these sides remain hidden from public view. Her political legacy to the nation was twofold. She built on and strengthened the foreign policy laid down by Jawaharlal Nehru and Krishna Menon. Her success in this field was shown in the turn-out at her funeral.

On the domestic front, as we have attempted to explain, the country was beginning to disintegrate. Social polarisations had increased. Despite its rhetoric, Congress had become an instrument of the classes that ruled India, even though its appeal, increasingly tarnished, was directed at the underprivileged.

There was a division between her personal life and her politics. In Pirandello's play *Six Characters in Search of an Author* the father, laden with tragedy, says at one point:

> Each of us is many persons. Many persons, according to all the possibilities of being that there are within us. With some people we are one person, with others we are somebody quite different. And all the time we are under the illusion of always being one and the same person for everybody. We believe that we are always this one person in whatever it is we may be doing. But it's not true. It's not true. And we see this very clearly when by some tragic chance we are, as it were, caught up in the middle of doing something and find ourselves suspended in mid-air. And then we perceive that all of us was not in what we were doing, and that it would, therefore, be an atrocious injustice to us to judge us by that action alone. To keep us suspended like that, to keep us in a pillory throughout all existence, as if our whole life were completely summed up in that one deed.

It is a fitting epitaph for Indira Gandhi, who had been India's prime minister for 19 years.

THE BROTHERS GANDHI
Sanjay: 1946–1980
Rajiv: 1944–1991

1
The nation's grandchildren

Rajiv Gandhi was born in Allahabad in 1944. His brother Sanjay was born in Delhi in 1946.

Their mother's childhood had been, in her own words, 'an abnormal one, full of loneliness and insecurity'. This had made her determined to ensure that her children were never short of love, companionship and children their own age. Rajiv was given an enormous amount of attention during his first three years. They were still in Anand Bhavan. Feroze and Indira were on their own since Jawaharlal was in prison. Rajiv was a happy child, full of fun and laughter. In 1946 he suffered two concurrent blows: they had to leave Allahabad and move to Lucknow *and* Sanjay was born. His mother wrote: 'I was far from well and I found his tantrums very irritating. Scolding only made it worse. So I tried reasoning. I told him that much as I loved him, his shouting disturbed me.' The following conversation then took place between the three-year old and his mother:

Rajiv: What can I do? I don't want to cry, it just comes.

Indira: There is a nice fountain in the garden. When you want to cry or shout, go to the fountain and do it there.

Following on this experiment in child psychology, Indira explained that after this episode, 'at the first sign of tears, I would whisper "fountain" and away he went. In the garden there was much to distract his attention and he soon forgot his troubles.' Feroze for his part was a loving and playful parent, not in the least bit authoritarian. He was not, by temperament, a patriarch. Nor was he a hypocrite. He did not, therefore, play the part of a severe father. He was constantly making wooden toys for the children and joining in their games. It was hardly a secret that he had been unhappy when Indira took the boys to live with their grandfather in the palatial prime minister's residence in Delhi. What about the boys? Sanjay was still very little, but Rajiv was over four at the time. Whether or not he ever expressed any disquiet at the time, the second move from what had become home must have been an unsettling experience.

One of Rajiv's earliest memories of unpleasantness must have been the communal riots which shook Delhi in 1947, when Sikh and Hindu refugees from Pakistan massacred innocent Muslims in Delhi. Indira and the children had, at the time, been in Mussoorie, a hill resort. Feroze had cabled to say that under no circumstances should they return to Delhi. Indira was puzzled and 'Like all young wives, I began to get suspicious and I thought this was one reason why I should come immediately.' On the telephone Feroze described the horrors that had been taking place everyday and indicated that this was not the place for women and children. Indira's reaction was the exact opposite. She packed their suitcases and caught the next train back to Delhi. The two boys must have sensed the tension and then, as they neared Delhi, seen with their young eyes an awful scene. At a Delhi suburb, Shahdara, communal mobs were preparing to lynch a Muslim on the platform. Indira was outraged. Her Nehru temper became uncontrollable. Leaving her petrified sons in the train, she jumped out of the compartment and silenced the crowd by an effective display of oratory. The victim was saved and the train moved on. She later told an interviewer that she would have done a great deal more than just shout at them had it not been for the fact 'that I myself was in the process of dressing'. What effect did this incident have on Rajiv and Sanjay? Children are extraordinarily perceptive at this age and even though they may have repressed their feelings, the image must have stayed in Rajiv's head for some time. He would also have heard his mother describing it to other adults on numerous occasions.

In Teen Murti House, however, the outside world seemed very far away. The Prime Minister's house was enclosed on all sides, with gigantic lawns, huge rooms and lots of people coming and going. Jawaharlal loved animals and the house had acquired a little zoo, which consisted of animals presented to the Prime Minister on his travels throughout India. There were dogs (pedigrees and strays), parrots, birds, squirrels, rabbits and more exciting additions, which provided endless diversions for grandfather and grandchildren. In Assam, Nehru was presented with a red Himalayan panda. It was a cub. They had not seen one before and had to consult a book on Indian animals in an Assam library to recognize the tiny ball of fur. Rajiv named it Bhimsa and it occupied a corner in the boy's bathroom. Their mother was indulgent, but she complained that, 'I could not house-train him and he always climbed on to the towel-rack to do his business, besides racing all over the house.' He was ultimately banished to the garden, and in the summer, when Delhi became too hot, he went to the coolness of Nainital. The Assamese provided Bhimsa with a mate, Poma (lotus in Sikkimese). The two pandas immediately took to each other. It was love at first sight and they produced cubs, an unusual occurrence for captive pandas. Rajiv and Sanjay adored them. So did their grandfather. There was a small-scale rivalry for their affections. Jawaharlal spent time with them morning and evenings and Indira wrote that 'they miss him a lot when he is out of station'. When Nehru was unwell, his grandsons would take Bhimsa to his bedroom to see him, an event which always cheered him considerably.

The year before Rajiv and Sanjay were packed off to boarding school, the zoo at Teen Murti was enlarged. Three tiger cubs entered the house. Rajiv and Sanjay took to them at once. Before long they were frolicking with the tigers quite fearlessly. Neither of the boys was scared of them. They treated them as ordinary pets. Other children and adults were petrified of the cubs. They would not go near them, much to the amusement of Rajiv and Sanjay, who used these occasions to show off without inhibition. As the tigers began to grow, two were presented to the zoo at Lucknow. The third had caught the fancy of a visiting world leader, Marshal Tito of Yugoslavia. Nehru gave it to him as a present and it accompanied the Marshal back to Belgrade.

Life for the two boys was full of diversions, but the atmosphere was very different to the Anand Bhavan days in Allahabad. Jawaharlal and Indira had grown up at a time when India was engaged in struggles. The country was occupied by a foreign power. Indira's childhood was coloured by her never-ending visits to prison to see her father and grandfather, then her mother, and she had finally spent some time inside herself.

This had affected the intellectual and political formation of father and daughter. During her youth and in her student days, Indira had read Beatrice Webb, Harold Laski, Aneurin Bevan, Bernard Shaw and numerous autobiographies. Later she read Sartre, Camus and De Beauvoir in the original French. Her stay in Europe had made her an addict of Western classical music, Bach and Beethoven in particular, as well as the cinema. Her favourite European city was Florence. In later life her reading had become a little less highbrow. One of the favourites during her last years had been Barbara Cartland, symbolic perhaps of a more general decline in the country as a whole.

Rajiv and Sanjay, by contrast, were brought up in the shadow of power politics. Nehru was a popular political leader, but his period in office was hardly a golden age. The deterioration in political standards had began during his lifetime. Politics, in the India of the 1950s, as far as Rajiv and Sanjay were concerned, meant endless photographs with their mother and grandfather, accompanying the latter on odd state visits, being polite to visitors and dignitaries from abroad and observing the seamier side of politics when Congress bosses visited Teen Murti House to pay their respects. In short, the brothers Gandhi had become the nation's grandchildren. Whatever else this might have meant, it certainly did not encourage a critical view of India or the world. The ceremonies and rituals associated with power must have had some impact on two impressionable young boys. Their lives and their perceptions of reality might well have been very different if they had lived with their father in his modest MPs bungalow. Feroze Gandhi's lifestyle was markedly dissimilar in virtually every way to the domestic patterns of the Prime Minister's house.

Feroze was, in an environment of his own choosing, a totally relaxed individual. He hated protocol, state banquets, formality in any shape or form. He was at his best during family picnics, where he could laugh, joke and frolic to his heart's content. Equally important was his refusal to participate in cover-ups of any sort in order to maintain the unity of the Congress hierarchy. He was an iconoclast and extremely critical of the direction taken by the Congress governments under his father-in-law's stewardship. The children, under his care, would not have been so bedazzled by their proximity to power.

As Indira became more and more immersed in everyday politics a decision had to be taken about the boys. Rajiv was twelve. Sanjay was nine. Their education had become a major concern for Indira, Feroze and Jawaharlal. It was decided to send them to the country's leading public school in Dehra Dun, in the Himalayan foothills, where the air was fresh and where, it was hoped, they would find friends from a similar background and a good education. Dehra Dun was the site of India's first military academy and its most-sought-after Doon School, which had been established by an anglophile Indian in 1935.

Education in British India had been an upper-class affair, with certain institutions provided for the middle and lower-middle classes. The oldest schools had been set-up to educate the sons of the royal houses, the heirs to the large estates of the gentry in the countryside, and others who were owners of property and inheritors of wealth. The Chief's College in Lahore was, as its name suggested, designed to educate the chiefs of tomorrow. Most Indians were kept outside its boundaries, not in order to encourage rapid polarizations, but to ensure that it was the chiefs who became the leaders of the Indians and acted on their behalf *vis-à-vis* the British. Other schools were, of course, permitted for lesser mortals. The clerks and white-collar workers so vital to the Empire had to be produced from somewhere. As time had passed it was realised that the Chief's College syndrome was no longer sufficient. Polo, cricket and buggery might be sufficient to run a landed estate or a tiny despotism, but something else was needed to produce people who would manage industry and run the country after independence.

During the 1920s and 1930s, a number of schools were established in hill-stations throughout India. These were modelled on English public schools: they placed a great deal of emphasis on sports, but also provided a core curriculum, provided and taught by a set of efficient and relatively enlightened school teachers. There were St Paul's and St Joseph's in Darjeeling; Oak Grove in Mussoorie; Sherwood College in Nainital; Burn Hall in Abbotabad; Lawrence College in Ghora Gali; Bishops Cotton in Simla; St Edmund's in Shillong, and Doon School in Dehra Dun, to name but a few. A network of convents were provided to offer the same facilities to girls, but there were also the women's equivalents of Chief's Colleges, though very few in number. The prefix St was usually affixed to those schools which were run by Jesuits or Catholic brothers. These tended to be extremely strict, but maintained fairly rigorous educational standards. The Catholic brothers, descendants of the Inquisition, were great believers in torture. Beautifully oiled canes were kept on display and 'benders' were regularly administered to recalcitrant pupils. There were also numerous sexual incidents involving the Catholic brothers: 'Six benders now in front of the class or two in my room after school' usually meant that 'the two' would be applied to bare buttocks and in more than one case the petrified boy found that the object he was threatened with was not a well-oiled cane.

Doon School was established in the autumn of 1935 on a 70-acre estate in Dehra Dun. Its declared aim was to develop a rounded-out personality. The initial advertisement for the headmaster's job stated that: 'Though slavish imitation is to be avoided, the proposed school will attempt to develop in an atmosphere of Indian culture and social environment many of the best features of English public schools.' In fact 'slavish imitation' was not avoided. Nor could it be. The English public schools had become essential suppliers of army officers and civil servants to service the Empire. In India they were needed to continue the tradition, but with indigenous recruits. It was in some ways symbolic that the military academy and the school were both in Dehra Dun, the Indian Army and the Civil Service would require these and similar institutions throughout the country.

Rajiv and Sanjay arrived at the school in 1955. Everyone knew who they were, but nobody cared. That was one of the best things as far as the Gandhis were concerned. The school was full of young men from privileged families and the fact that Nehru's grandsons had joined this select band was not a big surprise. The friends that Sanjay, in particular, was to make here were to remain his 'buddies' for the rest of his life and their school nick-names 'Dumpy' and 'Roly-Poly' (applied to Akbar Ahmed and Kamal Nath respectively) were to be featured in the Indian press.

The principal of the school in 1955 was a legendary character called J.A.K. Martyn. He had taught at Harrow for ten years from 1924-34 and had then gone to India with Arthur Foot from Eton and helped start the Doon School. He had become the headmaster in 1948 and had stayed at his desk for another 18 years. He had been greatly influenced by the educational theories of Kurt Hahn and had incorporated many of his reforms. He was generally regarded as unassuming and friendly and integrated easily into post-independence Indian society. He loved the mountains, and the school's most arduous climbs were planned by him with great care and an incredible attention to every detail. He introduced countless young Indians to the joys of mountaineering. According to their contemporaries, Rajiv and Sanjay both enjoyed the school, though the younger brother was even then considered far more of an extrovert. Neither he nor Rajiv, however, were ever known to have boasted, or attempted to utilize their grandfather's standing in the country. Their contemporaries included the actor Roshan Seth, who would one day play Nehru in Richard Attenborough's cinema version of *Gandhi*, and Vivan Sunderam, who would become a Marxist and a painter of the Baroda School, the most exciting and innovative group of artists in India. Apart from them the overwhelming majority of Doscos (the name taken by the schools alumi) were civil servants, journalists, business executives and industrialists. There were also a sprinkling of men who had become senior army officers. *Imprint* magazine in Bombay published an article on the school in which the author was told by an old Doscovian, nicknamed 'Taggy' (short for Tagore) of an incident during the Indo-Pakistan war in Bengal: 'During the 1971 war on the Pakistan border, a famous commander of an Indian regiment took his foghorn and shouted over to the other side, "Any Doon students out there?" When the answer came back in the negative he said, "OK, then fire!" ' There is something grotesque about this story, but it is not apocryphal. There were other incidents of a similar sort which were reported at the time. Many senior Indian and Pakistani officers had been, if not to the same school, to the same military academy in Dehra Dun and after the surrender many old stories were exchanged over glasses filled with an amber liquid.

It should not be forgotten that Dehra Dun did not only accommodate a military academy and Doon School. It also had a prison. The two boys at Doon School had a grandfather, who had spent many years in Dehra Dun prison. Did they ever, during their long stay at the school, take an afternoon off and visit the prison? If they did it must have been a secret, for no one has written about or referred to it. All the indications are that they did not, which is hardly surprising. The colonial period may only have been eight or nine years away, but it already seemed distant. The new rulers were firmly embedded in the old soil and prisons were no longer symbols of respectability in the Congress milieu.

In 1960 Feroze had died. Both boys were extremely upset. Rajiv was the more reserved emotionally, but even he had not been able to hide the pain. Sanjay had been visibly upset. Their mother wrote to an old family friend, Mohammed Yunus:

> I don't know what to write. I am feeling so utterly desolate and miserable. You know more than anyone else how much Feroze and I disagreed and quarrelled over the years and yet instead of separating or slackening the bond of friendship, we were closer than ever before.

We had a wonderful holiday together, nearly a month in a houseboat in Srinagar, and we made so many plans for the future. The boys are of an age when they need a father more than a mother. I feel lost and empty and dead and yet life must go on.

Indira knew how much Feroze and his sons had been attached to each other. Any plans being made by their parents to live together, and it is obvious that this is what was being discussed, would have delighted both Rajiv and Sanjay. The death was a tragedy in more than just a personal sense. It is very unlikely that Feroze Gandhi would have encouraged any dynastic pretensions on the part of either son. Nor would there have been an excuse for Sanjay to become a pillar of support for his mother. Everything that is known about Feroze indicates that he would have found all talk related to the divine rights of the Nehru clan somewhat repulsive and would have been sarcastic, even brutal, at the expense of the sycophant who had suggested such a course. He had himself fastidiously avoided profiting from the fact that Nehru was his father-in-law. The sycophantic faction in the Lok Sabha had always avoided Feroze, whose biting humour was well-known. What could even have been in doubt was Indira's own position after the death of Shastri. We can not take speculation too far, but there is widespread agreement that if Feroze Gandhi had not died in 1960, India's political history – not in its essentials, but in relation to certain particular aspects – might have been very different.

After the death of their father, Indira confronted a dilemma. The Doon School days would soon be over. What should be done next? Neither Rajiv nor Sanjay displayed any interest in an academic career. Nor had they given too much thought to their futures. Indira discussed the problem with Jawaharlal. He was anxious that at least one of them follow in his footsteps at Cambridge. This was a period when the Indian government was discouraging Indian students from wasting precious foreign exchange by studying abroad. The decision to send Rajiv to Cambridge and Sanjay to study automobile engineering (his idea) was criticised by opposition politicians and the press. If restrictions were to be imposed on Indians wishing to complete their studies in Britain or the United States, then, it was argued, the nation's grandchildren should set an example. Indira's response was characteristically brusque: 'I couldn't care less what people say. I though it was necessary for my boys to go to England.' And

England is where her boys went. They had not shown the slightest interest in politics till that time. When a journalist later commented on this fact, Indira replied: 'I tried my best to keep them away from it.' That remark was made in 1973.

At Trinity College, Rajiv enjoyed himself. He was a quiet man, extemely modest and generally liked. Occasionally the odd English student would ask him: 'By the way are you related to *the* Gandhi. Are you his son or something?' Rajiv would smile and explain that all he shared with Gandhi was a name. He never went on to say that he was, however, a Nehru, and that his grandfather was Prime Minister of India. He was still at Cambridge in the summer of 1964, when Jawaharlal died. Friends recall him being extremely quiet and upset for a few days, but he did not discuss the event with too many people.

Cambridge had not managed to interest Rajiv in politics or any academic pursuits. He left without a degree. His most important discovery in this old English university town had been a young Italian woman, Sonia, with whom he fell in love in 1965. He returned to India soon afterwards and declared that he was going to learn to fly and become a pilot. Indira was not particularly pleased, but she had no serious alternative at the time, although she must have cursed inwardly at this hereditary passion for flying that had afflicted the Nehru men. As far as Sonia was concerned, Indira was initially less than enthusiastic and persuaded Rajiv to postpone the marriage for a while. She made no secret of the fact that she would have preferred her son to marry an Indian. Shades of old Motilal had coloured his grand-daughter's vision, but when she realized that Rajiv and Sonia were serious, she gave her consent. They were married in 1968, in Delhi, and Sonia was welcomed warmly into the Nehru-Gandhi family circle. Whereas Motilal had threatened Jawaharlal that if he had wed a foreigner the children would suffer since they would be deprived of grandparental affection, there was nothing remotely similar in Indira's response to her first grandchild, Rahul. The new addition became an instant favourite. Sonia and Indira became extremely fond of each other. It was a relationship that time would deepen still further. Rajiv got a job as a pilot with the state-owned domestic airline (Indian Airlines) and was both satisfied and happy. His voice was often heard in internal flights, but it was always, 'This is your Captain Rajiv . . .' The surname was never used. Life in Delhi for the new couple fell into an easy groove of parties (both diplomatic and business) and an aimless upper middle-class existence. Rajiv met old friends from Doon School and Cambridge, but that was all. He never cultivated the politicians or the gangster-businessmen who were often trailing behind them.

Meanwhile, Sanjay's life was taking a slightly different course, though equally removed from any involvement with day-to-day politics. Sanjay had not been able to stay at Doon School. It was not that he had been expelled, but his mother had been told that he would do better elsewhere. He had returned from Doon to Delhi and found a place in a day-school in the capital: St Columbus. When asked what interested him the most, he used to make no secret of his passion for cars. He declined the offer to go to a university in either Britain or the United States.

Instead he decided to work as an apprentice with Rolls-Royce in England for a period of three years. Once again he left without finishing his course. His name meant 'victory', but he had allowed himself to be defeated first by Doon School and then by Rolls-Royce. He returned home with an incomplete knowledge about the mechanics of motor-cars. His grandfather was dead, but so was Lal Bahadur Shastri. Indira was Prime Minister of India. Sanjay had never cared too much for his grandfather. He would later admit to a journalist that Jawaharlal had not influenced his thought in any way whatsoever. On his return to India, Sanjay could have obtained a job with the already existing car industry. It is unlikely that he would have been refused a place. Instead he began to agitate for a small manufacturing industry of his own. He said he wanted to make a small car for India, more compact and neat than the somewhat unwieldy Ambassadors. Foreign cars are not allowed into the country because of tariff barriers, designed to encourage local industry. Sanjay wanted to design and build his 'Maruti' (Son of the wind-god).

His request proved an embarrassment to virtually everyone. Prior to his return from Rolls-Royce in Crewe, a number of teams of experts had been nominated by the government to study the feasibility of a more economic and smaller car. There had been talk of a state-owned industry in collaboration with a leading European firm, but the matter had not been taken any further because of the undisguised hostility of the private sector's powerful lobby of motor manufacturers, which resented any thought of competition. There was a radical opposition to the project from economists who were opposed to allocating badly-needed resources to producing cars, when there was a desperate need in the countryside for bicycles and new buses for public transport. The issue had been shelved.

Then something not so amazing happened. Sanjay refused to be dissuaded from his beloved Maruti project and all the barriers were suddenly lifted, an indication that when bureaucrats and industrialists wanted to move quickly they could do so regardless of any red-tape. Sanjay obtained government approval, which meant that a project being discussed by the state was immediately transferred to the private sector. He then raised the necessary capital, bought land near Delhi (a difficult operation at the best of times) and set up the Maruti factory. Indira had obviously not asked that special favours be accorded to her son, but then this was not considered necessary. She did not oppose the Maruti plan either and that was sufficient for the sycophants. When the opposition attacked the Maruti affair as India's equivalent of Watergate, Indira was livid. She claimed that the opposition wanted to penalise Sanjay just because he was her son. 'What must I do,' she retorted, 'if my son does not happen to be a professor type?' Her opponents naturally remained unconvinced. They replied that Sanjay could do what he liked, but this was a case of the Prime Minister's position being indirectly used to give an inexperienced youth privileges, which would have been denied to the overwhelming bulk of his peers in India. The Maruti scandal continued to haunt Indira for a long time, but nothing illegal had been done. It was a straightforward case of nepotism. In Pakistan during the mid-1960s, the then military dictator's son had utilized his father's position to set-up a flourishing industry with the help of local businessmen. When questioned about the affair by foreign journalists, Field-Marshal Ayub had replied: 'I never knew that my son [he had previously been an army officer — *author*] had such a talent for business.' A more recent case of the same type has involved the British Prime Minister Margaret Thatcher and her son, Mark, who accompanied her on a state visit to the *de facto* British protectorate of Oman, during which visit contracts were signed by the Omani regime and the private company by whom Mark was employed. The resultant furore in the British press was short-lived; a number of MPs alleged many details remained covered. In other words the Sanjay phenomenon was by no means unique or original. Numerous other cases could be cited from virtually every other capitalist democracy.

Two further problems soon arose. The first was that the Maruti never materialised. Sanjay was good at driving cars and fixing his own, but his performance as an industrialist had merely created a set of problems for his mother. A large amount of money had been expended to build Sanjay's cheap, low-petrol-consumption automobile. People began to ask what had been done with the money. No replies were forthcoming. Sanjay had been defeated for the third time in his young life. To Doon School and Rolls-Royce could now be added the fiasco of Maruti. The second problem developed when Sanjay decided to abandon the small car and move into big politics. The catalyst was the famous judgement of the Allahabad High Court in 1975, which declared Mrs Gandhi's election from Rae Bareilly null and void and gave her a limited period of time to step down as the country's prime minister.

2
Sanjay and Maneka
1974–80

In the autumn of 1974 Sanjay had married a young Sikh woman, Maneka Anand. Her family had a long record of service to the *raj* in the Western part of the Punjab (which is now Pakistan).They had fled during the partition of the sub-continent and sought refuge in Delhi. Maneka's father was a retired army officer. Her mother had graduated in psychology and then did a post-graduate course at San Diego in the United States. When she was six, her father, Colonel Anand, had been posted to Britain for a special training course in signals. The family had accompanied him and they had settled in a tiny English village, Watchfield, near Swindon and not far from Cheltenham. For two years young Maneka studied at a NAAFI school, before returning to India.

During a long interview with Dhiren Bhagat in the *Illustrated Weekly of India,* she confessed that she had greatly enjoyed writing at school, especially children's poems, which 'I must have stopped as soon as I realised that they were bad'. This was not wholly true. She started writing poetry again after her marriage, though she only showed the poems to Sanjay. Her writing also included regular letters to her mother from school. One of these, written when she was fifteen, gives us an idea of her strong sense of loyalty: 'I hope Uncle Minna dies a gory death, I have run through all my schemes of kidnapping his children, poisoning his wife's food, etc., and now I give up.' The aforesaid Uncle Minna had been giving Mrs Anand a tough time!

Her reading, she confessed, consisted of 'studies on the mind'. This had startled her interviewer, who came back with: 'You mean things like Gilbert Ryle's *Concept of the Mind?*' Her reply was a quick denial: 'No, no, no. I'm talking about . . . training schedules. Memorex systems. How the mind can be sort of expanded. Do anything you want . . . At the moment I'm reading a book called *The Possibility of Impossibility* . . . [it's about] how they train psychics for warfare, and how they make them work in hospitals.'

When Maneka married Sanjay, she was not interested in politics. Her parents had not been too strongly in favour of the match. They thought that he was too old and a libertine. During the courtship, Mrs Anand used to insist that the eighteen-year-old Maneka was back home by 9.30 p.m. every evening. The couple had decided on a civil marriage, which was legalized in the house of a Muslim friend of the Nehru family, the ubiquitous Yunus:

> Around this time an exciting event took place in my house – the marriage of Sanjay Gandhi with Maneka Anand, on 29 September 1975 . . . Mrs Indira Gandhi, as well as the bridegroom himself, wanted austerity and neither any fuss nor advance publicity. Since the girl's people were known to me, they expressed a desire to use my place for the purpose. This fact was kept a well-guarded secret. The civil marriage and the signing of the documents were over in a few minutes. I was a witness along with the two mothers-in-law.

Maneka's arrival at 1 Safdarjung Road during the emergency further alienated Rajiv and Sonia. They found her enthusiasms irksome and her naïeveté painful. She later claimed that the emergency had not really bothered her in any way at all: 'You see, I was a new bride. All the time during the emergency the only thing I was aware of was that I was very much in love with Sanjay . . . My life really centred round Sanjay totally.' She was studying at India's famous post-graduate establishment, the Jawaharlal Nehru University in Delhi, during the emergency years. She claimed that she was oblivious to everything but the fact that her husband was being badly treated:

> I felt Sanjay was being made the scapegoat for everything. Ultimately, everything came back to Sanjay. The chief ministers shared no blame, the ministers shared no blame . . . all the people in charge were now on the other side accusing Sanjay . . . in those two years he was blamed for everything.

During these years a veteran Indian journalist, Khushwant Singh, had become a close friend of Sanjay and his mother. Khushwant once described himself to friends as the 'call-girl' of Indian journalism. His vices undoubtedly included political promiscuity and he was used by a wide variety of people, but always in return for favours of which he never made a secret. Thus in return for supporting the emergency he was the Nehru-Gandhi family's nominee for the editorship of the *Hindustan Times*, a paper owned by the Birla family and traditionally regarded as a government mouthpiece, like eighty per cent of the press in Britain. Khushwant was also presented with the Congress nomination to the Upper House of the Indian Parliament, a largely consultative chamber. He later became a non-favourite and then, as was his wont, revealed all. He helped Sanjay to start a weekly paper, *Surya*, so that Maneka could occupy herself at the editor's desk. He explained:

> Primarily he wanted to get her out. She was really getting into his hair the whole time. And he was getting very tired . . . After she got married, she was interfering in *everything*. She was very brash and she never really measures her words before she speaks. And he was getting a little tired and fed up. So *Surya* started. And the first half dozen issues were almost entirely rewritten by me.

On Sanjay, whom he met regularly during the emergency, Khushwant reported:

> He was obviously a very tough nut. He was very soft spoken. He never used any strong language. He was puritanical beyond belief . . . And he was quite ruthless. People who crossed his path were shown absolutely no mercy . . . He was really instrumental in my getting into the Rajya Sabha (upper house) and the *Hindustan Times*. He handed me a long list of *Hindustan Times* staff members and he said: 'These are communists. Watch out for them.' I had no intention of taking note of what he said – though I've preserved the list – but it surprised me that his information was absolutely correct. There were about 25 of them on this list and they were all members of the CPI or the CP(M).

Many other people who have written about Sanjay have commented on his semi-fascist streak. He was impatient with democracy, fed-up at the slow progress of industrialisation, hated nationalised industries and the trades unions. His Maruti plant had, on occasion, been disrupted by strikes and he had developed an obsessive hatred against the CPI for that reason, even though it had loyally supported the emergency. Sanjay had taken over the Youth Congress as his special instrument and inaugurated a four-point programme: slum clearance, mass sterilisation, tree planting and abolition of dowries.

All this had backfired after the killings near Turkman Gate. The stories of the crimes had spread throughout Northern India. In August–September 1975 casual labourers had virtually disappeared from Delhi. This was unheard of in a city where there is always a rush to find work. The labourers, it was discovered, had returned to their villages to avoid the fatal incision in their genitals. In November 1975, the Nehru birthday celebrations, which always included a large free picnic for hundreds of children, had to be cancelled. Mothers had refused to send their male children to the event in case 'Sanjay Gandhi's doctors' had them sterilized. Fear can create many diversions. What was clear was that the emergency regime could no longer be sustained. The parliamentary majority was slowly being whittled away. Sanjay Gandhi was, without doubt, the most hated man in the country.

Indira was not in favour of postponing elections indefinitely, despite Sanjay's pleas to the contrary. It was not that she was still Jawaharlal Nehru's daughter or that part of the old Congress tradition had rubbed off on her. She was the most astute political leader in India at the time. Sanjay was a novice. She had been aware of the change in mood. She knew that running trains on time did not mean much to the bulk of the country. Most important of all, she understood that if Congress did not quit voluntarily through an election, other methods might become popular and the legitimacy of the whole system, not just the Nehru–Gandhi heritage and the Congress, might be put at risk. Elections had been announced. Sanjay had sulked. His mother broadcast the following message to the nation:

> Every election is an act of faith. It is an opportunity to cleanse public life of confusion. So let us go to the polls with a resolve to reaffirm the power of the people and uphold the fair name of India.
>
> Change is the very law of life . . . This is a time of great fluidity in the world. Contemporary society is beset with dangers to which developing countries are specially vulnerable. Hence all change must be peaceful. This is the legacy of our freedom struggle, of Mahatama Gandhi and Jawaharlal Nehru.

It is difficult after reading the last paragraph to believe that the 1977 elections were a gross miscalculation on her part or that she had thought she would win. There had been too many writings on too many walls all over India for her to have harboured any illusions on this score. She knew Congress would not win even before the date was announced. One day into the campaigning and she had got a fairly good idea as to the size of her support.

Sanjay had now suffered his fourth defeat. He had lost Amethi, his constituency, despite the support of the local potentate, the Raja of Amethi. He declared, as the results came in from all over the country, that he was quitting politics. If Janata had offered any alternative, he might well have embarked on a new adventure, but observing their bizarre antics and mismanagement, Sanjay with his gang-leader's mentality, observed that this defeat could be transformed into a victory. He re-entered the battle and never left his mother's side during this period in her life. More to the point he began to build the Congress afresh, but on the lines we have already noted above. It was now that Akbar Ahmed (Dumpy from Doon) joined his ranks, a gesture Sanjay never forgot, for in India friends normally disappeared if you were no longer in office.

During the Janata years there had been a detailed enquiry into Sanjay's financial deals. The Maruti firm had, especially, been scrutinised in great detail, but there was no evidence to convict. Much of the money that Sanjay had gathered for the Congress had, in any event, been 'cash in hand' supplied by the godfathers of the smuggling industry in Bombay. This 'black money' was never registered anywhere in the first place, so evidence was not easy to obtain. Colonel Anand, Maneka's father, had been questioned about some of these matters during this period. He had been upset and had complained to his friends at the indignity.

Then one day he was found dead, with a revolver in his hand. Was it murder or suicide? He had left behind a cryptic note containing the words 'Pressure Sanjay Unbearable'. Every media commentator now became a temporary detective. Did the words indicate that Sanjay's pressure on the dead man had been unbearable? Was Sanjay preventing him from speaking the truth in court? In that case was the murderer engaged by Sanjay? Others argued that Colonel Anand had been depressed by the Janata government's pressure on his young son-in-law and that is why he had killed himself. The truth became a matter for conjecture, depending on the political views of those who engaged in speculation. No evidence was ever found to suggest that the colonel had been murdered, let alone by his son-in-law. The press, nonetheless, made sure that the incident left a murky impression. The very fact, however, that Sanjay's guilt was believed by large numbers of ordinary people requires no extensive commentary.

Sanjay was now portrayed as something of an enigma. He still had his supporters, but they were not large in number amongst the intelligentsia, a layer he loathed. It is easy to describe him as an assemblage of grotesque incongruities: perfidious and dedicated; selfish and generous; cruel and kind; crafty and simple-minded;

intelligent and stupid; villain and hero. The problem with this sort of description is that it could easily be applied to Hitler or Stalin. It is a mystification, but it was in wide circulation during the Nehru–Gandhi family's years in exile. In fact Sanjay's politics were coherent, logical, but marked a definitive break with the populist consensus projected by the Congress Party. What he wanted to do in India was the equivalent of what Thatcher did in Britain and Reagan in the United States. The problem was that such a sharp turn in Indian conditions might well have provoked a hydra-headed backlash, which would have weakened the Indian Federation and its political structures. Indira, in her own way, was aware of this fact, though she perceived the problem with which Sanjay was trying to grapple. Her own solutions were typically pragmatic and their outcome was a multiplication of tragedies throughout the sub-continent.

For the 1980 elections, Sanjay, had prepared his own complement of new, model Congressmen. He was determined to change the physiognomy of the Congress Parliamentary Party and prepare the way not simply for his own accession to office, but for a totally different Congress Party. His friend and colleague, Akbar Ahmed spelt this out very clearly after Sanjay's death. The word 'youth' is a code for the new congressman:

> Sanjay was one of the few people in India who really gave youth a chance. In 1980, in both the Parliamentary and Assembly elections, a substantial proportion of seats went to youth. In Uttar Pradesh over 200 seats out of 425 were given to youth. In today's politics nothing will get done till we get rid of the people who've been there for donkey's years . . . To build India we need a change. And only youth can change things . . .
>
> Sanjay was one person who wanted to liberate Indian industry from the strangleholds that there were. He wanted to lay emphasis on agriculture, on programmes that would be implemented and wouldn't just remain at the planning stage.

Sanjay's wife Maneka was a tiny bit more critical than Akbar Ahmed. In her picture book on her husband, she describes how she was sometimes forced to communicate with him via a set of poems. She would write one and leave it on his table. One of these was later reproduced by her and provides a glimpse of what life with him must have been like:

> Sanjay Gandhi, ferocious being
> Who never looks without seeing.

> Whose facts are almost always right.
> Whose judgements almost always bite.
> Who's so totally work-oriented,
> That he's driven his wife demented
> With his fact and figures and complete knowledge
> And his refusal to indulge in 'lollage'.
> Sanjay Gandhi computer man
> Why can't you be more human?

Sanjay's reply to this was not recorded, though he must have relented a bit, for Maneka bore him a son in 1979, Feroze Varuna. When asked by a reporter whether she had waited so long after her wedding to encourage birth-control, she confessed merrily: 'Rubbish – I wanted to wait ten years – this baby's not planned. I wanted to have my husband to myself.'

Sanjay remained extremely busy trying to re-organise the country's politics. He still had no official post in the government, but was behaving more and more as if he were the prime minister. He was planning a large scale purge of the civil service in order to replace senior administrators with his own tested loyalists. He was also busy ensuring that his new crop of Congress MPs were properly represented in the new government. One reason for Indira to wait a long time to stabilise her 1980 Cabinet was because of the relentless pressure from the 'Sanjay Caucus'. Soon she would be without Sanjay, and Maneka would not regret the lack of family planning that had given her young Feroze.

Just prior to the emergency, Sanjay had learnt how to fly and obtained his pilot's license. The Maruti disaster had cured him of the car-mania. From then on it was planes, like Rajiv and Jawaharlal. After the defeat of 1977, the Janata Government had taken away his license on the grounds that he might fly himself and his mother out of the country to escape retribution. He had now got it back. A close acquaintance of his, Karan Thapar, once accompanied him as a passenger in his two-seater. It was a terrifying experience as Thapar reported to a London magazine, the *Spectator*:

> I remember flying with him on one occasion in a single-engined plane, attempting every type of loop of which the little aircraft was capable. After exhausting the pleasures of aerial acrobatics, he set out to scare the local peasants working in their fields by aiming the aircraft straight at them, swerving dramatically upwards at the last minute. Whatever view one takes of such a sport, it requires nerves of steel and tremendous self-confidence.

On 23 June 1980, Sanjay Gandhi left 1 Safdarjung Road at 6.30 a.m. and drove to the Delhi Flying Club. It was early, but he wanted to avoid the heat that began to envelop the city soon after sunrise. He had an appointment with Captain Subhash Saxena, who was going to accompany him on the red Pitts S-2A, a light two-seater American plane. Saxena had not wanted to fly that day. He was due to have a hernia operation and was not feeling too well, but he allowed himself to be persuaded by Sanjay. The flying club's chief instructor advised Sanjay not to fly the Pitts, since it had only been used for the last few days and had not even been test-flown by the club's expert mechanics. 'I must take up this red bird today,' Sanjay had insisted. The discussion had ended.

The Pitts had been the centre of a long controversy. It had been despatched to Sanjay as a 'gift' during the emergency, courtesy of the British-Asian industrialist, Swaraj Paul. By the time it had arrived in India, the Congress had been defeated and Janata was in power. The new government decided to investigate the 'gift'. The American firm panicked and said they would happily withdraw the 'gift' and re-export the plane back from India. While the negotiations were taking place, the Indian electorate had returned Mrs Gandhi to office. The whole investigation was dropped and the firm was happy for the Pitts to become a 'gift' once again.

So on that warm summer's morning Sanjay and his less-than-enthusiastic passenger, Subhash Saxena, flew into the Delhi sky. Sanjay had clearly wanted to impress Saxena, who was an experienced pilot, with his flying skills. He flew the plane over Safdarjung Road and Willingdon Crescent. Then he started, at a thousand feet, to demonstrate a few somersaults. The Pitts never came out of a nose-dive. It crashed just behind Willingdon Crescent into some trees. Sanjay and Saxena died instantly. The once and future leader was no more. There was a great deal of sympathy for his young widow and his grief-stricken mother and the infant boy.

If the truth be told, there were many former victims of forced sterilization and 'slum-clearance' who made no secret of their belief that it had been an 'act of God'. It was these people who upheld Voltaire's dictum that: 'One owes respect to the living. To the dead one owes nothing but the truth.' This had been practised in the early years after independence. Indian communists, in particular, had declined to pay posthumous homage to their political enemies. During the late 1950s, CP members of the West

Bengal Assembly had refused to stand in silence and pay homage to dead Congress politicians. Apart from the press, there had been no outcry. In fact the West Bengal CPI had gained respect amongst the poor for not indulging in sentimental hypocrisy.

Times had changed. In 1980 it was much more than condolences for Sanjay's mother and wife. What took place was a grotesque act of hypocrisy. Men who had denounced Sanjay endlessly as a 'fascist', a 'Rasputin', 'a hooligan', who had demanded that Doon School should, in honour of Sanjay, be renamed Goon School, were now competing with each other to pay tribute to the departed Caesar. The devil was being transformed into a god. Charan Singh, who had launched a particularly nasty and vindictive witch-hunt against mother and son when they were out of office, said: 'It is a tragedy that a young man who dreamt about the greatness of this country is no more with us.' Atal Behari Vajpayee, supposedly a man of principle, albeit a communalist and at the helm of a semi-fascist party, declared: 'Mr Gandhi's death has brought darkness at noon.' The other Mr Gandhi had, it is worth remembering, been assassinated by men who were politically inspired by Vajpayee's own mentors. Indrajit Gupta of the CPI, a party which had been denounced as 'corrupt' by Sanjay declared that: 'All political controversies are still in the face of death'. The other Communist Party's Chief Minister of Tripura announced that Sanjay's loss was not just that of the Congress, but was shared by the country as a whole!

Given this barrage from his enemies, the courtiers had a hard task ahead of them, but old Khushwant Singh managed a personal tribute, which established a certain pattern:

> We bid farewell to our young departed leader with tears that will take an age to wipe off our eyes. His dying has made us rarer gifts than gold (sic). He has laid the world away and poured out the red wine of his youth, and given up the years that were to be his. The best tribute the nation can pay him is to create the India of his dreams: green with teeming forests, cleansed of all the filth in its cities; with small healthy families and smiling happy girls freed of worry over their dowries.

If some enterprising Indian magazine had instituted a 'Golden *Chamcha* of the Year Award', there is little doubt that the writer quoted above would have been a strong contender for the title in 1980.

Sanjay was embalmed for a day while Rajiv and Sonia returned from Italy for the funeral. Indira had wanted him cremated on the same spot as her father, but at this the opposition protested. For Sanjay's dead body to be set alight by Rajiv on the same spot where the dead man had lit his grandfather's funeral pyre? It was a sacrilege, said the opposition. Rajiv agreed. Sanjay was burned well behind the Nehru site. His ashes were sprinkled into the Ganges near Allahabad.

Maneka and her mother, Mrs Anand, felt that as Sanjay's wife, she should succeed him as MP for Amethi. When Indira asked Akbar Ahmed: 'Who do we put up in Amethi?' Sanjay's closest friend claims he replied: 'Put up Rajiv.' To be given the following answer: 'Don't be silly. His politics are not like ours. I don't trust him.' When he suggested Maneka's name the response was that she had fourteen months to go before she fulfilled the age requirement. All this changed the minute Rajiv was persuaded to give up flying and enter politics. Maneka felt humiliated. Sanjay's few close friends were also put out in the cold. Most of them had lost their influence overnight, but they had to adjust to the new situation.

Sanjay loyalist, Akbar 'Dumpy' Ahmed was angry at the defection. Even 'Roly Poly' had gone. 'I feel sorry for them,' declared Dumpy, 'because they are neither here nor there. Kamal Nath just chickened out, poor chap . . . He was close to Sanjay and should have stood up when Sanjay's people were being isolated and Sanjay's name was being wiped out. Now Jagdish Tytler is just another *chamcha* in the Congress set-up'.

Dumpy tended towards sentimentality. Most of the Sanjay intake of Congress MPs had been personally loyal to the dead man because of what he promised them in terms of politics and economics. Their fondness for Sanjay's style was not based on any aesthetic appreciation of the man, but because he promised to defend their material interests. That had been his main attraction. It was, of course, considered tasteless to say this aloud soon after his death, but it was said, though not by any mainstream publication. In a narrow, old Calcutta street, Mott Lane, an old Bengali Marxist intellectual and one-time poet, Samar Sen had his headquarters. All he did was to produce a weekly magazine, *Frontier*. He had been a sophisticated supporter of the Chinese in the years that immediately followed the Sino–Soviet split, and his magazine had always had to swim against the tide of public opinion. After Sanjay's death it was *Frontier* which printed an account that would outlive the mawkish banalities of almost everything else. It was entitled 'What Sanjay Meant'. Its author had preferred to remain anonymous. After describing how the streets of the city where he was had not betrayed any signs of emotion or distress at the news of the heir-apparent's death, the author described how as he was boarding a half-empty plane for Delhi he caught a glimpse of Sanjay's men. His account of these men remains the best description that I have so far read:

> The plane was getting ready when there was fresh activity. Suddenly new passengers started climbing up and pouring in an unending stream of dazzling white, freshly-pressed Sanjay suits, each with a jagged strip of black ribbon pinned either on the arm or the chest. There would be at least a hundred of them. There wasn't a seat left any more.

They were noisy, these late entrants to Congress politics and they talked a lot. *Frontier*'s anonymous correspondent observed them silently. As the plane went up, he started to pen the following despatch:

> It was then time to make a leisurely survey. This new group of a hundred and more Sanjay suits were all men – hardly a woman – of between 30 and 45, stout and gross, with a fullness of uncouth confidence, reeking of Old Spice, their stomachs round and tight as drums. These were the type I have seen in Andhra's districts, owning homes partly airconditioned and barns large as playgrounds, large and medium farms of tobacco, rice, oilseeds, new and neatly run agro-processing factories. These were the same men I had seen sitting on the boards of cooperative banks and other government financing institutions engaged in siphoning off money drawn in the name of hundreds of real or imaginary small beneficiaries, to profitable investments and shuffling them over a wide range of portfolios in and away from Andhra Pradesh. These were the men who owned most of the new medium and small-scale industries in town and struck profitable business and marriage alliances in the city, acquired themselves brides in the image of Telugu and Tamil films, each bound by ties of marriage, caste and inheritance with the older generation which had done well and completed the first and most crucial stage of primitive accumulation. They represented the new interacting triangle: the landed gentry in the village, the industrial entrepreneur in the city and the new intelligentsia that belonged to both. Few of them in the plane at all bothered to sidle up to Chenna Reddy or Narasimha Rao as is customary when such dignitaries travel. They kept their own company. Wiping out whole Harijan villages of an evening without batting an eyelid was as much in the day's work to them as buying off quietly and without fuss a hundred confirmed air passengers and dozens more on

the official waiting list at 9 o'clock any morning and taking their places on the plane to Delhi at 12.55. The point in either case was to do it efficiently, if need be ruthlessly, and without fuss. Network and understanding, understanding and network.

Sanjay was dead. His political project, however, was very much alive. And so was his wife.

3
The birth of a dynasty: Captain Rajiv

When Sanjay's death took place, his brother Rajiv had been sitting at the controls of a plane for fourteen years. His friends stated that he was happy. He showed no signs of wanting a change. He had not been particularly happy during the emergency years. He had little time for Sanjay's politics, but had been helpless to do much about it at the time. He told a friend later that he had not heard too much about the 'excesses of the emergency', but whatever he had been told, he had passed on to the other occupants of 1 Safdarjung Road, who had invariably refused to believe him.

It would be inaccurate to say that he was disinterested in politics. He had held certain views, which were traditional in his circle of friends. He was a liberal-democratic supporter of the Congress. Nonetheless both he and Sonia were totally opposed to his entering the cockpit of Indian politics. At one point Sonia told a friend that she would rather her children begged in the streets than that Rajiv entered politics. She, probably much more than him, regarded politics as filthy, corrupt and riddled with sycophants, whom she disliked intensely. There was, after all, no shortage of them at 1 Safdarjung Road. Whether or not she ever made the comparison between her native Italy and India is not known, but there were many similarities between the Indian Congress and the Italian Christian Democrats. Both parties were in the grip of venal politicians. Both were heavily dependent on both extending and receiving patronage. And then there was the link with the underworld. The Christian Democrats were linked to the Mafia. The Congress was financially in debt to its Indian counterparts. Political protectionism was practised in both instances.

Sonia had not yet exchanged her Italian passport for Indian nationality. After the electoral blow of 1977, Rajiv had informed his mother that he and his family wanted to leave India for a time and settle in Italy. This announcement had created a personal crisis in the household. Indira had pleaded with both of them not to leave her at this time. She had said that she could not bear being without her grandchildren. His mother's pleas had changed Rajiv's mind. Sanjay's cronies alleged that Rajiv and Sonia had regarded the post-emergency debacle as a catastrophe and had not believed that the family's political fortune could ever recover after such a stunning blow. Rajiv had not participated in the election campaign of 1980, which had been managed by Sanjay. This had been followed by the fatal plane crash. An argument had started over the succession and pressure was brought to bear on Rajiv. There had been two opposing factions. One led by Maneka and her mother, Mrs Anand, and backed by Dumpy which saw Maneka as Sanjay's heiress, who would keep the seat warm for her three-month old son, Feroze. It was hardly a secret that the two brothers and their families had not been on the best of terms. Sonia and Maneka, in particular, had not even attempted to conceal their mutual dislike. The struggle for the succcession with all its grotesque, medieval undertones had started even before Sanjay's cremation. The Maneka Caucus had met at Mrs Anand's house and discussed how to retain its hold on the large block of Sanjay MPs and use it as a wedge to press Maneka's claims.

Indira Gandhi and her close advisers opted for Rajiv. Once they had decided this question, then nothing was left to chance. In August 1980, barely two months after Sanjay's crash, 300 Congress MPs called on Rajiv to step into his brother's shoes and contest the by-election in Amethi. Rajiv hesitated. He was not even an ordinary card-carrying member of the Congress. His wife was still implacably hostile to the idea. Several months later, in April 1981, a respected conservative journalist, Sunanda Datta-Ray, wrote in the *The Statesman*: 'Leaders do not issue orders from behind their mother's skirts . . . They must operate within the constitutional framework, and be answerable to the people for all they do . . . Mr Gandhi should, therefore, either legitimise his position or be seen to surrender all claims to power . . . Will the real Rajiv Gandhi, therefore, please stand up and declare himself?'

The following month, Rajiv followed Datta-Ray's advice. He resigned his pilot's job with Indian Airlines and decided to contest Amethi. The seat had been unoccupied for one whole year, a constitutional impropriety since vacant seats need to be filled within six months. It had been Nehru's constituency and after his death it had been filled by his sister Vijayalakshmi, then Sanjay and now Rajiv. Sonia, reconciled to the new plans, quietly gave up her Italian nationality. The crown princess became an Indian citizen.

In June 1981, Rajiv was elected to Parliament in a landslide victory. When questioned about his political ideas he tended to be vague, saying that he supported the Congress manifesto. Yet his differences with Sanjay had not been on fundamentals, but on style. He favoured free-enterprise, foreign investments and modernisation. He disliked corruption, sycophants and gangsters. The problem was that they were not unrelated. Sanjay had discovered this at an early stage and attempted to harness the latter in order to enhance his politico-economic project. Rajiv would begin to discover these hard facts over the next few years. Sanjay's old friend, Dumpy, was enraged by the press descriptions of Rajiv as 'Mr Clean', though even he could not make a specific allegation about Rajiv. What he did say was that:

> During the emergency, Sonia was involved with Maruti Technical Services. If they didn't approve of Maruti as they later claimed then she shouldn't have become a shareholder. It wasn't just that they wanted to help Sanjay. Letters have shown that, during the emergency, Sonia's brother wanted a liquor contract in India for Italy. Sonia's family was involved in business in India, so how can they say they were not interested in politics?

In 1983, Rajiv took a step nearer to the throne when he was appointed one of the general-secretaries of the Congress Party by his mother. This was his first official post in the party and represented a phenomenal advance given that he had been a member for only three years. After winning Amethi, Rajiv had tasted the fruits of political victory. He confessed to Trevor Fishlock of *The Times*:

> Yes, I do feel excited about going into politics. But daunted, too. Look at the people in this constituency. They have so little and there is so much to be done. How do you begin to make improvements? It will be satisfying to make progress, but I have no illusions about the difficulties.

He told Ian Jack of the *Sunday Times* that he wanted to 'attract a new breed of person to politics — intelligent, westernised young men with non-feudal, non-criminal ideas, who want to make India prosper rather than merely themselves'.

Rajiv's politics may not have been too different from those of Sanjay's, but he rapidly made it clear that his brother's followers would not find much room in the new set-up. Instead he relied on a tightly-knit group of old friends, not too different from himself. Rajiv Dhar, the son of the late D. P. Dhar, a Kashmiri Brahmin, and one of the country's most distinguished post-1947 civil servants, had been a friend of Rajiv's for a long time. Then there was the Doon School/Cambridge connection. Arun Singh, was a scion of a princely family and a senior company executive with Reckitt and Colman. He had been a close personal friend at Cambridge, where he had imbibed his liberalism. 'Oh, we were the Beatles generation', he told an interviewer from Bombay's *Imprint* magazine. He also confessed that life as a business executive had become dull and boring. Rajiv's political turn had been an ideal moment for him, too, to change professions. Arun Singh became a political assistant to the future prime minister, but expressed the hope that he would soon end up in Parliament, which institution he regarded as 'being fundamental to democracy'. From the Nehru family, a cousin, Arun Nehru, had already been elected to Parliament from Rae Bareilly. Indira had told an acquaintance that: 'The people of Rae Bareilly are not happy without a Nehru.' Arun had been found and elected. He became another member of the charmed circle. It was the two Aruns who, more than anyone else, helped Rajiv to take important decisions such as the allocation of seats for the December 1984 general elections. Sanjay's advisers had included strongmen from the countryside. Rajiv's men were urban university-graduates, with a technocratic bent. Their affection for computer-predictions and television electoral campaigns did not endear them to the more cautious members of the A-team. The ethos of Rajiv Gandhi and his friends was spelt out by Arun Singh as follows:

> All the people I know have certain basic things in common. We're all Indians first; we are all secular Indians by any definition. Irrespective of what anybody might say, we operate on a very high level of integrity — personal integrity. I'm not only talking about money, for after all, money is only one of the aspects of personal integrity. Let's say we have a fairly high moral standard, and I think these are assets.

In December 1983, Rajiv was presented to the Congress delegates in Calcutta as the future leader of the country. The city itself had been festooned with pictures of Indira and Rajiv, which fought for space on the walls with the advertisements for Hindi movies. There was also a poster of Rajiv on his own, with the following caption underneath: *'Today's Leader, Tomorrow's Hope'*. One could not help feeling that the Congress's PR men had got this slightly wrong and it should have read: *'Today's Hope, Tomorrow's Leader'*.

The only irritant in this regard had been the public campaign launched by Maneka Gandhi, Sanjay's widow, against Rajiv. Maneka had left 1 Safdarjung Road in a blaze of publicity. She told the world that her mother-in-law had asked her to leave and she paraded herself and her son as the wronged members of the family. The truth was somewhat different. Ever since Rajiv's decision to enter politics, Maneka had been plotting her revenge. She had met leaders of certain opposition groups and had decided that she would try and break Sanjay's followers from the Indira-Rajiv Congress Party. It was widely known that she was out of favour, but Mrs Gandhi had not taken any decision to expel her from 1 Safdarjung Road. Maneka had been complaining bitterly to everyone who listened that she was being ill-treated and ignored by her mother-in-law. When she was asked why she did not leave the house and set up her own establishment, she used to reply that timing in such matters was crucial. In March 1982 she had finally walked out, after discussing the matter in some detail with members of the BJP (the former Jan Sangh). Immediately after her departure she announced the creation of the 'Sanjay Forum', which she said would work for 'socialism, secularism and democracy', none of which had been the strong points of her late husband. A year later she formed a political party and named it the *Rashtriya Sanjay Manch* (National Sanjay Organisation). She also announced that she, Maneka, would challenge the dynasty at Amethi. She would fight Rajiv bitterly for the succession. The Manchies gained a few successes. Dumpy was elected to Parliament in a by-election and the Congress began to take Maneka seriously. She also began to appear at the opposition conclaves and many opposition leaders saw in her a specialised instrument which could be used to damage Mrs Gandhi and her son. Certainly Rajiv and Sonia began to visit Amethi regularly after Maneka's challenge and a lot of money was poured into the constituency in the form of welfare projects. Maneka's main angle at political rallies was to present herself to the poor peasants as a wronged widow, cast out on to the streets by a tyrannical mother-in-law and under the cold eyes of her late husband's cruel elder brother and his foreign wife. This simplistic morality tale was largely fiction, but it did have an initial impact. The rows between Mrs Gandhi and Maneka over the share of Sanjay's estate and over Mrs Gandhi's legal rights to see her grandson, kept the dispute public. This was used with great effect by Maneka in her public campaigns. In her own way, Sanjay's widow did reveal a certain political flair and gutsiness, albeit of a somewhat undesirable variety. With her mother-in-law's assassination, she has lost the most important electoral card in her possession, but she still possesses the Gandhi name. If Indian politics were to continue for the rest of this decade in the same way as they have since 1980, Maneka might be able to exploit her dynastic connections far more blatantly than can be visualised at the present moment.

In the meantime the men of the Beatles generation were beginning to grasp the scale of the problems that confronted them. It was not just the massacres in Assam, the widespread outbreak of communal rioting in places like Bombay or the threatening clouds over the Punjab. It was the state of the Congress Party. The former US Ambassador to India, J. K. Galbraith, had during Nehru's lifetime referred affectionately to the Indian political system as an advanced form of 'organised anarchy'. The Congress Party had by now become an undisciplined anarchy. Sanjay's death had undoubtedly left a vacuum. One of the nastiest demonstrations of this was the conference of the NSUI (National Students Union of India), the student wing of the Congress, in Nagpur in September 1984. The Congress students had become well-known and well-feared since the late 1970s as hooligans without a leash. Sanjay had controlled them for a while, but not for long. The Nagpur gathering was scheduled for only 20,000 'students'. An extra fifteen thousand had turned up. Different groups within the Congress had mobilised their supporters in a show of strength designed to advance their claims for parliamentary representation.

These 'delegates' were not in the least bit interested in the speeches. They looted the shops, raided the liquor dens and fought each other in the brothels. The ordinary people of Nagpur were horrified. Young women were molested and there were a number of reported incidents of rape. The Bombay President of the NSUI, a decent young man, declared that he was extremely worried for the safety of the women delegates and sent them back home. The press reports were too detailed for any Congress leader to rebut the truth. Indira tried to blame the rowdyism on the opposition, by stating that the RSS had infiltrated the session to discredit the government. This was convenient, but false. What had happened was not so different from the AICC session of Congress adults in Calcutta in December 1983. Only the scale was much bigger.

The explosion finally came in the Punjab. 'Operation Bluestar' was successful, but the cost was heavy. India's Prime Minister was assassinated by her own Punjabi bodyguards.

Rajiv had been in Calcutta, helping the pre-election campaign of the Congress Unit in the province, when he received an urgent message from Delhi. He had been addressing a public meeting in Contai. All he was told was that his mother had been taken to hospital. His face did not betray any emotion. He wound up the meeting and headed for the nearest helicopter pad. 'She is tough,' he said to a journalist. He was clearly hoping that the worst would not happen. At 12.30 p.m. he listened to the BBC news bulletin. He said to nobody in particular: 'Inside our house and that too by her own security men?' Then he told journalists: 'Every morning I used to notice a young Sikh who was posted between 1 Safdarjung Road and Akbar Road and he looked very suspicious.' Rajiv had told his mother at the time that he did not trust the man. It was Beant Singh. She had laughed off his fears. All the reporters who spoke to him during those hours reported how he remained absolutely calm. He flew by helicopter to Calcutta's Dum-Dum airport, where a plane was waiting to fly him to Delhi.

Sonia had been at 1 Safdarjung Road. Around 9 a.m. she had rung up a friend to say that Mrs Gandhi wanted some cotton *saris* for the election campaign, which was due to be announced on 25 November. When Sonia had heard the shots she had rushed out to tell the servants to stop playing with *diwali* crackers. The festival of *diwali* had taken place on 24 October. When she saw what had happened she got into the car with her unconscious mother-in-law and drove straight to the Medical Institute. Sonia was still wearing her dressing-gown. She was still there when doctors pronounced the Prime Minister dead.

Rajiv went straight from the airport to the hospital. Meanwhile at 1 Safdarjung Road discussions on the succession had already started. The procedure normally followed is that the President appoints a caretaker prime minister, usually the senior minister in the Cabinet, till the Congress Parliamentary Party elects a new leader. Accordingly R. K. Dhavan, Mrs Gandhi's closest political adviser and a personal assistant of many years standing, suggested that Pranab Mukherji, the Finance Minister, was made caretaker prime minister. Arun Nehru, the family MP from Rae Bareilly, and V. S. Tripathi, another close adviser and civil servant, said that Rajiv should succeed her immediately. Both Dhawan and Kamal Nath ('Roly Poly'), an old friend of Sanjay's and an unofficial representative of the Sanjay levy of MPs, were kept in one room with Arun Nehru till the final decision was taken.

Zail Singh, the President, was on a state visit. Pranab Mukherji was flying back with Rajiv from Calcutta. The Home Minister, Narasimha Rao, one of the more capable leaders of the party, was touring his home state of Andhra Pradesh. The Defence Minister, Shankar Chavan, was in Moscow. An announcement of Mrs Gandhi's death was delayed by four hours in order for the succession to be clarified. Rajiv's first instincts were to state to his advisers that a senior minister should take over pending the CPP meeting. He was dissuaded by both Aruns. Others were discussing which senior minister should become the caretaker. Mukherjee was No 2, but he was a member of the Rajya Sabha (upper house) and this was thought by Narasimha Rao's supporters to be an unfortunate precedent, however brief. Rao, on the other hand was in the Lok Sabha. Someone else raised the question as to whether Rao as Home Minister should resign since his department had failed to protect the country's prime minister. The debate was ended by Vasant Sathe, Minister for Petroleum, who said bluntly that Mrs Gandhi had wanted Rajiv to succeed her, they all knew that and, in the interests of stability, they should follow their dead leader's advice. When Zail Singh returned to Delhi, angry crowds stoned his car, reminding him in a vivid fashion of his religion. He met Rajiv at the hospital and insisted that the latter accompany him to the President's House. The Congress Parliamentary Board had sent the President a formal letter asking for Rajiv to be appointed. There were five members of the CPB. One of them was dead. Two were absent. Two, Pranab Mukherjee and Narasimha Rao, had met and agreed on Rajiv Gandhi. Zail Singh administered the oath of office to Rajiv Gandhi the same evening. Outside Delhi was burning. The new Prime Minister went on to make a public broadcast appealing for peace and quiet. 'Indira Gandhi is dead,' he said in a sober and unemotional fashion. 'India is living. India's soul is living.' India was living, but Indira was dead. And many innocent lives were being claimed by the furies of communalism. For two whole days, the Sikhs of Delhi lived in fear of death. Then, the police having stood idly by, the Army was sent in to protect their lives. Rajiv visited the survivors and promised aid and support. It was to emerge a few weeks later that the violence was not a spontaneous show of anger, but had been led and encouraged by some Congress hoodlums. People not so different from the ones who terrorised Nagpur during the student convention. The 'law and order problem' was in this instance essentially a question of bringing the Congress and the heavily-communal police force under some control.

Once the funeral was over, the new Prime Minister decided on a quick election. He wanted a new bunch of MPs who would help him end the internal squabbling which had crippled the organisation. More importantly he wanted to acquire a popular legitimacy. This had to be done rapidly. Delay could prove self-defeating since the tragedy of Indira's death had united all the warring factions. They had accepted Rajiv because they thought they could not win with anyone else at the helm. That had been what they meant by 'stability'. The campaign went into top gear during the first week of December 1984. Rajiv's central theme was an old favourite of his mother's. The unity of the country was under threat. Only Congress could preserve the Indian federation. He admitted that mistakes had been made and pledged that they would be corrected. 'But,' he asked, 'what is at stake? It is not just Congress winning an election or Congress losing an election. What is at stake is the very integrity and unity of India. We have to fight for it.' Just in case the message did not get home, the Beatles generation hired the services of a much older (historically, though not in terms of age) and more experienced layer: the stars of the Bombay movies. Andhra had its NTR, Tamil Nadu its MGR. The appeal of these performers was basically regional. The Congress needed actors who were known throughout the country. Amitabh Bachan, the most popular actor in India, was a cross between Errol Flynn and Robert Redford. He was also, more to the point, a childhood friend of Rajiv Gandhi. He agreed to enter politics in order to help Rajiv, but it was said that he had set his sights on a Cabinet position. He stood in Allahabad, not far from Amethi. Congress election rallies in Uttar Pradesh featured two stars: Amitabh Bachan and Rajiv Gandhi. Bachan, whose screen performances included fantastic leaps into the sky, transferred this to politics: 'What India needs,' he told an interviewer, 'is a giant jump into the twenty-first century.' In Bombay, the Hollywood of India, the Congress was represented by another star, Sunil Dutt, who had the additional advantage of having been married to one of the first women stars of the screen, the legendary Nargis.

The election campaign would have become an Indian magical mystery tour, somewhat unrelated to the real problems of the country, had it not been for the grisly disaster that struck Bhopal in the state of Madhya Pradesh on the morning of 3 December 1984. A pesticide plant set-up by the giant multinational Union Carbide started leaking. The killer gas claimed over 3000 lives and blinded tens of thousands of citizens. It was the worst environmental disaster the world has ever known. The American one-man pressure group, Ralph Nader, had often accused Union Carbide of 'environmental blackmail'. *Fortune* magazine had once described the firm as 'a reactionary ogre obsessed with profits'. American environmentalists had been warning of 'double-standards' for some time. Ken Silver had constantly attacked the use of the Third World as 'pollution-havens'. It was stated in India that the storage arrangements in Bhopal were not up to the same standards as those followed by Union Carbide in the United States.

The location of the plant in a residential area in 1978 had resulted in a strong objection from the Administrator of the Municipal Corporation, M. N. Buch, a town-planner of some repute in India. He had issued a notice to the company asking that the plant be removed to an area where safety regulations could be observed. It was Buch who was transferred and not Union Carbide. There had been leaks in 1978, 1981 and 1983, but these had been covered-up by politicians on the pay-roll of the multinational. In 1982 the Congress Minister for Labour, that is the man meant to protect the interests of the workforce, told the Madhya Pradesh Assembly: 'The factory is not a small stone, which can be shifted elsewhere. There is no danger to Bhopal nor will there be.' As the Delhi weekly *Mainstream* commented on 8 December 1984:

> Conscience in politicians often turns to stone as they are exposed to allurements from the business world, particularly an affluent multinational corporation. The Union Carbide guest house at Bhopal has been playing host to many a minister, central and state-level, while a local Congress leader is reported to have been engaged as the company's legal adviser and its PRO is the nephew of a former Education Minister. There are many other beneficiaries, perhaps, less known.

The cloud of killer methyl-isocyanate gas (MIC) had exacted a heavy toll in the number of human beings and animals that perished. It had been like a scene from a horror movie. An eye-witness had stated: 'We were choking and our eyes were burning. We could barely see the road through the fog, and sirens were blaring. We didn't know which way to run. Mothers didn't know their children had died, children didn't know their mothers had died and men didn't know their entire families had been wiped out.' Bhopal had become a city of the blind.

Rajiv had arrived soon after the disaster. He was not blind. He could see what had taken place. He promised meagre compensation. Union Carbide had come to Bhopal because labour was cheap and plentiful. Lives, too, were cheap. There were no controls. Safety regulations were meaningless since most of the workforce was illiterate. If India's Prime Minister felt any outrage or anger at this brutal rape of a Third World town, he suppressed it perfectly. Then he washed his hands and flew back to continue the election campaign, leaving local Congressmen to supervise the mass cremations.

Some Western papers had written that casualties would have been lower if there had been no shanty-towns surrounding the plant. This was false as the factory was built in a residential area in the first place. The shanty-towns had been a later addition, designed to provide accommodation for the poor, unskilled and illiterate workers. They had nowhere else to live. On 12 December 1984, it was announced that the factory would soon resume the production of pesticides.

The Congress won the December 1984 elections. Rajiv was now an elected Prime Minister of India. The dynasty had now received a popular mandate. Some questions, however, refused to go away. Why had Indira developed an obsessive urge to have a son succeed her? Why had the Congress acquiesced to this display of lumpen-feudalism? Two Nehru Prime Ministers in South Block may have been a historical coincidence. Why did she press on for a third?

The dynastic project had faltered with Sanjay's unexpected death. His son had been too young, his wife unacceptable. Rajiv had agreed to the rescue operation. He had agreed to wear a soiled shirt, provided he could soon wash off its stains. He had his chance sooner than anyone had thought. The succession had contained an element of the grotesque, a reminder of days gone by.

Once upon a time the dynastic realm had been the most

accepted form of rule. Hereditary politics were taken for granted. Kings and queens had governed as they saw fit. Their populations had consisted of subjects, not citizens. All politics had been concentrated in the person of the ruler, who picked and discarded his advisers. The First World War had brought this phase to an end. The mighty Hapsburg Empire had fallen and the crash had liberated half of Europe. The Russian Revolution had removed the Tsars of All the Russias. The Allies had got rid of the German Kaiser. The Scandinavian monarchies had democratised themselves and stayed as titular rulers, bicycling to and from their palaces. The English monarch was still powerful, but mainly as an ideological totem for the established parliamentary order. Only Ethiopia and Thailand possessed emperors and kings of the old school: autocrats who both reigned and ruled. One had fallen. The other was weaker than ever before. Dynasties were definitely on the way out.

Political dynasties were, in any case, a rarity in the democratic world. The Roosevelt family, it is true had given the United States two Presidents, Teddy and Franklin, but they had belonged to different political parties for a start and had pushed through somewhat different policies. They had also not succeeded each other. The Kennedys had been a clan rather than a dynasty. The only cases where a family had inherited the political realm were Haiti and Nicaragua. Both had been family dictatorships. In Haiti, 'Papa Doc' Duvalier had utilized repression and primitive magic to ensure his son's succession. 'Baby Doc' Duvalier was carrying on the tradition on an island whose population felt totally crushed. In Nicaragua the Somoza family had made the mistake of extending its monopoly of politics to land. Its ownership of 40 per cent of Nicaragua's richest estates had created the conditions for a social revolution, which had come in 1979, sweeping aside the old order and instituting the Sandinistas as the new power. In Singapore, the Prime Minister, Lee Kuan Yew, a great favourite of the West, had brought his son, Brigadier-General Lee Hsien Loong, out of the army, where he was No 2, and inserted him into the People's Action Party and the Singapore parliament. The Brigadier told the press: 'In Singapore, you don't volunteer to go into politics — you are invited to enter.'

In the Democratic People's Republic of Korea, the 'Great and Beloved Leader', Kim Il Sung, had cleared the decks of the party so that his son could become the new 'Great and Beloved Leader', but since Kim is still alive it is not certain whether he has been successful. These were all, of course, special cases. Aberrations. They could not last for long. History was moving in different directions.

The dynastic realms of old had been designed to preserve the social order of that time, to resist encroachments from the newer and more unpredictable groups gaining strength in the cities, to utilise property as the cement to seal the loyalty of the rural hierarchy to the ruler of the day. Old dynasties were, in brief, the joint instrument of a propertied collective.

India does not fall into any of these categories, but it should be seen as part of a whole sub-continent. Nepal, Sikkim and Bhutan are monarchies of a sort. If Pakistan were not a military dictatorship, Bhutto's daughter, Benazir, would probably be prime minister at the head of the People's Party. In Sri Lanka, the ruling UNP (United National Party) has for many decades been known as the Uncle-Nephew Party. Its main opponent, the Sri Lanka Freedom Party (SLFP) has been divided into three warring factions: Mother Bandaranaike has watched her son battle against a daughter and her husband, who have been fighting against another daughter and all this to control a political party! In Bangladesh the Army regime is confronting two possible successors: the daughter of the murdered Sheikh Mujib or the wife of the assassinated President Zia-ur-Rehman.

It is too much to be a simple coincidence. In the countries already mentioned the reasons are diverse. In India they are related, in our view, to a number of connected facts. The majority of the population lives in the countryside where literacy levels (with the exception of Kerala) are extremely low. There is thus an equally low level of culture. Religion and other superstitions are rife. Belief in all sorts of religious individuals is strong. The owners of property are still masters of social life in the countryside. The personality cult that surrounds a leading political family is therefore a convenient way of preserving the electoral and social status quo. Two-thirds of Congress MPs in the 1980 Parliament were rural notables as compared to the urban lawyers, teachers and doctors who represented Congress in the years after 1947. This helps to explain Congress' ready acceptance of the Nehru-Gandhi dynasty. Then there was the argument that in a giant country, spanning almost a billion people of different creeds, castes and languages, it was not easy to find leaders who could 'unify the nation'. The Nehru-Gandhis, it was said, were crucial because they unified the country. This was to totally ignore the prime ministership of Lal Bahadur Shastri, who had succeeded Jawaharlal. His death had proved to be the dynasty's starting point. The sad fact was that Congress had declined as a *political* party. It had no real programme. It had become a coalition of competing economic interests, who needed a populist-type leader at the top to maintain a contact with the people. Indira's talents in this regard had been of enormous help to her party, but she had belonged to a different generation. Her sons were products of the post-independence period. Captain Rajiv had become Prime Minister in 1984, but there was still a great deal of turbulence in the country. How long would the people keep their seat-belts fastened? For that is where the ultimate power resides. It is the people of India who can make and explode dynasties. A large section of them may be illiterate, but they are not ignorant. They will have the last word. For despite all it is they who are modern India. It is they who suffer the rancid rhetoric of corrupt politicians. One day they will want their revenge.

4
The assassination of Rajiv Gandhi
The End of the Dynasty?

As has been stressed in previous chapters, the Congress Party over which Jawaharlal Nehru had presided had split after Indira Gandhi's rise to power. Rajiv's mother had remoulded the old party, but it was difficult, even if she had wanted, to make it as pliable as plasticine. Indian democracy and geography made such a prospect untenable. Nonetheless Indira Gandhi had transformed the internal functioning of the party. Before Indian independence was won in 1947, the party was often riven by lively strategic debates. This pattern was only marginally altered under Nehru's Prime Ministership. He tended to rule by the strength of his intellect and even though he was the dominant personality, he sometimes lost the argument to veterans such as Vallabhai Patel and Abul Kalam Azad. Indira ruled by diktat. She had removed the old power-brokers and brought in men she trusted, but even her supporters were careful about what they said at meetings of the Congress High Command. This pattern was further reinforced during the Emergency years, when constitutional government was temporarily suspended and dynastic politics were ruthlessly encouraged.

There were times when it appeared that the Congress was a totally spent force. The country's only national party gave the impression of complete exhaustion. At moments like this the enemies of Congress, left and right, old and new, stated in their different voices that the Congress Party had accomplished its mission in history and predicted that it would fall like empty husks. They had been invariably proved wrong.

Rajiv Gandhi's electoral triumph in December 1984 had been welcomed by many observers who believed that a dynastic succession on the governmental level would ensure the stability of the Indian Federation. This was, at best, a partial assessment. In reality, the continuity was largely symbolic, existing on the level of rhetoric. It was the elements of discontinuity – as evidenced by the abandonment of a populist approach – which were far more striking and which became a dominant feature of the new regime. In his first budget Rajiv presided over a reduction in personal income tax, a cut in corporate taxation and a liberalisation of import policies.

Nonetheless, Rajiv Gandhi's rise to power meant different things to different people. To the poor in town and country, whose votes had sent him back to South Block, he symbolised the virtues of decency and honesty. They viewed him as an innocent, orphaned by the tragic death of his mother and they felt that he would try to better their lot. These were modest expectations compared to the wild hopes which had been aroused by Indira Gandhi's populist campaigns of the Seventies when she had vowed to 'Remove Poverty', or the socialist pledges of her father in the decades following Independence.

Indira Gandhi, and to a much larger extent, her father, Jawaharlal Nehru, had been identified with a social-democratic concern for the welfare of the dispossessed. The 'mixed economy' had been the outcome of this concern, but even during the last years of Mrs Gandhi's government it was clear that the captains of industry wanted the removal of all domestic barriers. Initially, as has been argued in earlier chapters, the most astute members of India's bourgeoisie had, after independence, warmly welcomed state intervention, both on the level of protective tariffs against foreign competition and the creation of a state-capitalist sector to strengthen the economy as a whole.

The middle-classes envisioned Rajiv as their great white hope. They saw him as one of them. A man who understood their problems and would cater to their needs. Rajiv's promises of modernisation and computerisation were mistaken for a pledge to open the economy to the world market without any restrictions. This did not happen. In fact India succeeded in reducing its foreign debt and keeping the International Monetary Fund at bay.

The Indian civil service, a crucial artery of the political organism, was delighted by Rajiv's succession. For the first time in decades they felt they had a weak political leader at the helm, a person they could easily guide in the interests of the state. Rajiv's grandfather had been contemptuous of the fashion in which, during the first decades after Independence, politicians and politics in neighbouring Pakistan had been moulded by a bunch of corrupt civil servants, two of whom had risen to power through a combination of chicanery and political intrigue.

'Your country', Jawaharlal Nehru told an old friend who came to see him from Lahore, 'is run by *daftaris*! How can I negotiate with them?' The use of the word *daftaris* (which literally means office-boys or clerks) was used to show Nehru's scorn for an institution which had run British India and which was continuing to administer Pakistan. The message was clear. In India it was elected politicians who dominated the civil service. While both Nehru and Indira Gandhi relied on two or three top civil servants to prepare position papers and briefings, they always used their own skills as well as independent and unpaid advisers. In Nehru's case, for example, Krishna Menon was a greatly valued comrade whose advice was always taken seriously. In Indira's days there was a marked intellectual decline in the quality of the advisers, but she was careful not to let the civil service get the impression that they could ever be in command.

In the period which followed Indira Gandhi's assassination the Indian Administrative Service, for the first time since 1947, played a major role in the determination of domestic and foreign policy. It was not the case that Rajiv Gandhi was short of advisers. The fact was that a symbiotic relationship developed between his special advisers and the upper echelons of the civil service. In the old days disputes between the two were resolved by the Prime Minister of the day. Now there were very few serious disputes between the bureaucracy and the Prime Minister's office. Rajiv Gandhi was faced with three major challenges within the first year and a half of his Prime Ministership. Two of these were internal matters. The unrest in the Punjab and the disturbances in Assam required urgent attention. In the aftermath of the assassination of Mahatma Gandhi by a Hindu fanatic in 1948, the Congress government had succeeded in imposing its brand of secularism and nationalism on the country as a whole.

The killing of Mrs Gandhi by her own bodyguards had shocked the country. Could the new government utilise the tragedy to imprint a new political settlement with the disgruntled minority provinces on the Western and Eastern extremities of the Federation? In other words, was it possible to build a new, 'composite' national identity which could override ethnic, caste, cultural and religious differences in this sprawling subcontinent?

Within the Congress Party itself, Rajiv, whose political style was markedly different from that of his mother, realised that his will, however weak and flexible it might be, had to be imposed on the organisation. The two kingmakers, Arun Nehru and Arun Singh, were soon deprived of their posts. Rajiv's public image was constructed with the help of Amitabh Bachan, the popular film-star. Bachan, whose movies were watched by millions, was an Indian Superman. It was rumoured that, given a good director, he could act, but this supposition was never put to the test. He was popular. He was rich. And most important of all, he was a close personal friend of the new Prime Minister.

More serious matters, such as the internal functioning of the Congress Party, were, in the first phase of power, dealt with by Arun Nehru (a cousin) and Arun Singh, an old chum and scion of a princely family. The two Aruns were the men who had sat silently in Teen Murti House after Indira Gandhi's assassination as Congress hoodlums had gone on the rampage against New Delhi's Sikh community. They knew of the pogroms on the streets, but did not lift a finger to order a halt to the massacres. It was these two who were, in those early days, the advisers most trusted by the new Prime Minister. Indira's men had been removed by Rajiv in the first flush of his Prime Ministership, but the cumulative knowledge and experience of the old fixers was such that, within a few years, they had to be brought back into play as fully-fledged members of the kitchen-cabinet. To the two Aruns was added the urbane and sympathetic figure of Suman Dubay, a contemporary of Rajiv's at Cambridge and a former editor of the successful weekly, *India Today*. Patterned on the model of *Time* and *Newsweek*, it catered to the needs of India's burgeoning yuppies, offering a weekly digest of home and world news for those too busy maximising profits to keep in daily touch with anything but the stock exchange. Dubay was not simply a crucial link with the media. Together with Mani Shankar Aiyer, another Cambridge chum who was a Joint Secretary in the Prime Minister's office, he provided a solid bridge between Rajiv Gandhi and the bureaucracy.

On the external front, Rajiv Gandhi was confronted by a shrewd military dictator in Pakistan and a blatantly chauvinist Sinhala regime in Sri Lanka. The first was involved in aiding the Sikh insurgency in the Punjab. The second had presided over pogroms of the Tamil minority based in the north-east of the island and refused to consider the question of granting them an autonomous status. In both cases New Delhi felt that its interests were directly affected. Here the new Prime Minister, unlike his mother and grandfather, offered no distinctive policies. It had been widely rumoured in New Delhi that Mrs Gandhi had been the victim of a CIA destabilisation plan because Washington feared she might unleash a military attack on its favourite Asian despot, General Zia-ul-Haq. The latter's frontline role in the war against the pro-Soviet regime in Kabul had made him temporarily indispensable and the story went that to keep him in power they were prepared to despatch Mrs Gandhi.

Rajiv's platitudinous utterances on world politics were simply a bland echo of the Foreign Office. Despite the strong pro-Soviet and pro-American lobbies which proliferated in the ranks of the print media and the civil service, India had remained non-aligned since 1947.

The wave of sympathy generated by Mrs Gandhi's assassination, and garnered by the Congress machine to win votes in the general election of 1984, began to evaporate after a year. The country was tired of being ruled by a corrupt and hypocritical gerontocracy. Rajiv was not unaware of the depth of feeling on this issue and he chose the centenary celebrations of the Congress Party in the winter of eighty-five to launch his broadside. He referred to senior party leaders as 'the fence which had eaten the crop' and castigated 'their lifestyle, their thinking – or lack of it – their self-aggrandisement, their corrupt ways, their linkages with vested interests in society and their sanctimonious posturing'. In a rare peroration, he summed up his thinking in a memorably harsh sentence.

'We have government servants who do not serve, but oppress the poor and the helpless; police who do not uphold the law, but shield the guilty; tax collectors who do not collect taxes but connive with those who cheat the state.'

Every single word was true and the only response from the veterans was to grumble at the fact that this speech was made on an occasion to mark the centenary of the political party which had led the struggle for independence. A senior party leader and former member of Mrs Gandhi's cabinet told me some months after the event that 'it was an inappropriate speech. The boy has no sense of history. If I shut my eyes I can see his grandfather and hear the lofty sentiments that would have effortlessly tripped off his tongue. Even Mrs G. would have risen to the occasion.'

This was true, but it did not detract from the truth of Rajiv's speech and, in fact, made a much bigger impact on the general public, which felt that the new leader would not be held down by ties of sentimentality, but would clear the stinking stables of the Congress. The projection of the new leader as a Mr Clean, who was untainted and who had been upset by the Emergency regime his mother had imposed in the mid-seventies, had been accepted at face value. The Congress leaders needed Rajiv Gandhi. In a world where screen idols, realising that they were more popular than government leaders, were turning to politics, Rajiv appeared to his party as a symbol which offered a new sense of hope to a divided country.

As a Prime Minister elected with a gigantic majority – Congress won four hundred and one seats out of a total of five hundred and eight after two hundred and twenty million people had cast their votes – Rajiv Gandhi, in those first twelve months of office had a mandate to do what he pleased and he did, but the new policies did not lead to any concrete measures as far as the strictures contained in his speech at the Congress centenary celebrations were concerned. Life continued as before and Rajiv Gandhi was soon eased into the routine of an Indian Prime Minister.

In the days before the British began to rule India, the men who sat on the throne in Delhi used to permit access to their persons by the poorest in the land. A special room in the old Mogul palaces was designated as the arena where the monarch heard the complaints of the common people. This tradition had lapsed under British rule. It was revived by Jawaharlal Nehru and maintained by his daughter. It was thought that Rajiv might discontinue the practice given the sad fate of his mother, but he insisted that the durbar must continue on the agreed three mornings every week. In reality, these morning sessions had largely been of symbolic value. It was only rarely, even in the early days after Independence, that someone would slip through the net and harangue Jawaharlal Nehru, but it did happen once or twice. Mrs Gandhi used to listen patiently to the usually trivial complaints of village women, carefully selected by Congress Party organisers. For reasons of security, the selection was even more careful in the case of Rajiv, but the show had to go on and the Indian novelist Anita Desai, whose delicate fiction is known for its attention to detail, captured one such event for a profile of the new leader, published in a number of Indian publications as well as *The Times* in London:

> After passing through metal detectors and body checks, they are allowed on to the lawns of his residence for the morning durbar [the preferred word is *darshan* which has religious connotations, implying a blessing]. The Prime Minister arrives, with monarchial punctuality, at nine o'clock, beaming affably and dressed in dazzlingly white homespun which makes one wonder if this is the reason for his popular sobriquet, Mr Clean.
>
> It is a particularly colourful gathering this morning. Bharat Heavy Electricals Limited, one of the largest public sector enterprises in India, has sent colourful troupes of dancers from each of its units – Bhopal, Hyderabad, Bangalore and Punjab – to ask for the Prime Minister's blessings on their annual show and to give him a glimpse of it.
>
> Mr Gandhi watches with a kind of bemused pleasure and says that what he has just seen is exactly what the country is striving to achieve – the unity of diverse customs and traditions from which can be drawn mutual benefit. . . Then he moves between groups of petitioners instructing an aide to note their complaints and saying 'I'll see what I can do', before having to leave to meet a busy schedule. . .

When Rajiv and Sonia Gandhi arrived in the former Portuguese enclave of Goa to commemorate the centenary of the Mormugao port, they were warmly greeted by local dignitaries and a bravura display of bright colours by their female consorts. Later during a 'cultural performance' a Goanese crooner belted out a homemade tune dedicated to the new Prime Minister.

> 'Hullo Rajiv Gandhi! Hullo!
> How does it feel to be holding
> The reins of the nation?
> Do they feel like the chains of continuation?
> Hullo Rajiv Gandhi! Hullo!'

The Goanese philosopher-poet deserved a reply, but did not receive one. Four years later the nation would give its answer to the question posed by the pop-singer in Goa, but 1989 and the general elections seemed very distant in those early days of the honeymoon. Rajiv Gandhi had a great deal of support from the Indian press, which had rubbished his mother with a venom rarely displayed towards a serving Prime Minister by the Western media. Liberal political analysts stated in writing that under Rajiv there would be a more collective, more decentralised way found to run the Congress and the Federation. The abrasive and arbitrary tests of loyalty which Indira Gandhi imposed on her closest Cabinet colleagues were regarded as dead and gone.

Within two years Rajiv was being pilloried in the press as an ineffectual and weak leader, incapable of controlling the corruption with which he was surrounded. A wave of disillusionment swept the country. Those who had harboured the greatest illusions felt the most betrayed. And yet, as the Indian political analyst, Achin Vanaik, points out in *The Painful Transition*, an acute and stimulating study of Indian democracy and its discontents, the reasons for the crisis which engulfed Rajiv Gandhi were not brought about by a mass upheaval from below as a result of declining living standards. The actors in the process were not poor peasants, workers, the unemployed in town and country, the 'low-caste' Hindus, etc. It was rather a case of 'shifting tensions within the ruling coalition, or, even more narrowly, of conflicts within and between the ruling political institutions of civil bureaucracy, political executive, judiciary and party. . . By mid 1987 an acute conjunctural crisis had emerged, one of whose essential components was a constitutional conflict between President and Prime Minister. It was alleged that the former was trying to dismiss the latter in the context of corruption scandals surrounding defence deals and the possibility of those close to or within the Gandhi family being involved in them.'

How did a government with an overwhelming popular mandate and a modern Prime Minister become so paralysed in such a short space of time? After all, Mrs Gandhi, however unpopular some of her actions may have been, never permitted the impression that she was out of control to gain ground in the country. Some of Rajiv's supporters argued that his critics wanted it both ways. They did not want him to mimic his mother and when he did not do so, they attacked him for being weak and indecisive. There may be a tiny grain of truth in this assertion, but the problem went much deeper.

The fact was that Mrs Gandhi's hegemonic victory against her opponents in the inner-party struggle during the late Sixties and Seventies, had set the party on a particular course and fractured the centre of Indian politics. Many politicians and their followers were driven out of the new party by dynastic factionalism. Was the split irrevocable? And, if not, could it be healed? These questions dominated the Indian political scene after Mrs Gandhi's assassination.

The haste with which Rajiv had been catapulted into his mother's office in South Block was an indication that the Congress leaders were not prepared for any real alteration to the status quo. In retrospect this was a tragically short-sighted perspective. Intoxicated by their electoral successes the Congress High Command ignored the very real social polarisations taking place in the country and failed to analyse their likely political impact. There was very little that divided the socio-political policies of the Congress from the various bourgeois factions of the political centre. It had become clear after Mrs Gandhi's post-Emergency defeat at the polls that there was no stable *national* alternative to the Congress. The ramshackle Janata coalition had destroyed itself within a year and a distraught nation had sent the architect of the Emergency back into the South Block.

The Indian electorate, despite the level of illiteracy in the country and despite the level of manipulation in the countryside, has often shown a far greater degree of political consciousness, astuteness and responsibility than its educated counterpart in, for instance, the United States of America. Perhaps it is easier to notice this from a distance, but the Congress strategists should have been aware that much more was expected from them on a political level.

The attraction of the Congress for the most downtrodden strata in Indian society has, in recent decades, had very little to do with any real expectations on the material level. It has been seen more as a measure of self-defence by a mass which feels itself permanently under siege. The French historian of the middle ages Marc Bloch described a nobleman as a man who initially owned a horse. If the peasantry defended his castle, accepting in the process the constraints of serfdom, forced labour and the communal kitchen, this was because the peasant wanted the nobleman to defend him with force against the force of nature in a world dominated by scarcity. In a curious sort of a way the Congress is seen as a nobleman with a horse by its electorate. People depend on this party to defend it against the outrages of caste, class and communal violence.

A serious effort to unite the political centre and weld it into an effective secular bloc could have stymied the advance of fascistic political formations which donned the mantle of Hindu fundamentalism. This would have entailed a concerted attempt to bring those politicians who had left the party during and after the Emergency, as well as men like Chandrashekhar, back into the Congress fold. Since the differences between those who had deserted or been driven out of the Congress rarely involved any fundamental principles, a compromise could have been reached if the political will to do so had existed inside the Congress. Such a choice would have, of necessity, compelled the Congress to revert to a more collegiate structure and prevented further divisions, which began to loom large after Rajiv's first year in office.

In brief, it was the failure of Rajiv Gandhi to ditch dynastic politics and embark on a new political course, in which pride of place was given to the concept of power-sharing with politicians of like-minded views, which prepared the basis for what was about to happen to him. Dynasticism has an ugly logic. If the dynast refuses to share real power with those who are in general agreement with his politics, but happen to be outside the party for a series of contingent reasons, it follows that he or she can never really accept a division of power and responsibility inside the party and government.

It would be foolish to see this simply as a defect of hereditary politics. Margaret Thatcher, during her last five years as Prime Minister of Britain, behaved in a similarly abrasive and authoritarian fashion, brooking no dissent from her colleagues and surrounding herself with sycophantic advisers. The difference, however, lies in the fact that in the case of the Congress it appeared as if dynasticism had been institutionalised and de facto enshrined in the party's constitution.

By the middle of 1987 the Congress government was confronted by a set of crises on the level of both internal and external politics. Externally the Indian Army had been sent into Sri Lanka to defend the Tamil population, concentrated in the north-eastern part of the island, against the pogroms unleashed by the security forces of the Sri Lankan government. Initially the intervention was welcomed both in India and by the Sri Lankan Tamil population, but, inevitably, the Indian troops got bogged down in intra-Tamil disputes, with disastrous results.

On 15 August 1987, India had celebrated the fortieth anniversary of Independence with the traditional display of pomp and ceremony. Rajiv had addressed the faithful outside the Red Fort in Delhi and warned neighbouring Pakistan to stop interfering in the Punjab. He was not a great public speaker and his weak command of Hindi did not help, but the advent of the electronic media meant that old-style oratory was no longer considered a major asset. The speech was not a total disaster, though it lacked the authority of his grandfather and the effective populism of his mother.

The very next day there was a damaging broadcast on Swedish Radio, which alleged that Bofors of Sweden, a firm with a distinguished pedigree in manufacturing weapons of destruction, had paid bribes to senior Indian politicians to win a contract for the sale of four hundred howitzer guns. The Government of India responded with alacrity and declared that the item broadcast was, 'false, baseless and mischievous'. It went on to ascribe political motives to Swedish Radio:

> The report is one more link in the chain of denigration and destabilisation of our political system. The government and people are determined to defeat this sinister design with all their might.

It was an odd response. After all this was not the first occasion on which a giant firm had attempted to bribe a government. One only has to recall the Lockheed scandal which led to the fall of the then Japanese Prime Minister Tanaka and involved leading figures in most of Western Europe. There was in that first reply no mention in the Indian government statement which indicated that they would conduct their own inquiry and if there were guilty parties in India, they would be punished.

The Swedish government, irritated by the foolish charges of 'destabilisation' levelled against them, ordered their own investigation. The Swedish National Audit Bureau confirmed that payments worth Rs. 64 crores (i.e. 640 million rupees) had indeed been made. This made further prevarication in New Delhi impossible. Rajiv set up a Joint Parliamentary Committee to investigate the scandal, but the resignation of his onetime Finance and Defence Minister a few months before the eruption of this scandal made Rajiv's belated decision to conduct a parliamentary inquiry untenable.

V. P. Singh, a veteran leader of the Congress, had been a loyal and quiescent supporter of Indira Gandhi. He clearly felt that the new Prime Minister was a lightweight, but instead of a frontal assault he had decided to put the new leader's rhetoric into practice. As Finance Minister, he took the cleaning-up campaigns – whose intended function was largely cosmetic – way beyond the prescribed limits. In the process he antagonized India's powerful capitalist entrepreneurs, who were amazed by his political audacity. Under pressure, Rajiv transferred his portfolio from Finance to Defence. Within a few months of the change-over, V. P. Singh began to investigate an important submarine deal with a West German firm in the course of which, as is usual in these affairs, a great deal of money had clandestinely exchanged banks.

In retrospect, veteran observers of the Indian political scene claimed that behind V. P. Singh's campaigns lay a shamelessly opportunist plan to outflank Rajiv Gandhi as the Mr Clean of India politics. In other words V. P. Singh was deliberately making demands which could not be met by any government managing a capitalist state. Perhaps the campaigns were cynical, but what is beyond doubt is that their audacity was greatly appreciated by the ordinary citizens of the country. V. P. Singh described his meeting with Rajiv in the following way:

> One day I got a telex from our embassy in West Germany. A senior West German government official had told us that a seven per cent commission had been paid on the submarine deal. I immediately ordered an inquiry and informed the company in question. The Prime Minister sent for me and asked me a number of questions, the first of which was how I knew whether the telex was correct. I replied that I had been informed of the existence of a 'corpse' and it was my duty to discover the 'murderer'. Then he said 'This company gives commissions to several heads of state. If they revealed the names in our case, they would suffer as a company as their confidentiality would have been breached.' I replied that my duty was to uphold the laws of our country and I was not concerned with the affairs of the West German company. It was during this conversation that I felt I could not continue as a member of his Cabinet.

When, despite repeated warnings, V. P. Singh refused to back down, Rajiv dismissed him from the government and expelled him from the Congress Party. Within a fortnight after his expulsion V. P. Singh was addressing large crowds throughout the country on behalf of the his new party the Jan Morcha [Peoples Front] and pledging to wipe out corruption.

It was against this backdrop that the Bofors scandal hit Rajiv Gandhi. A government already weakened by the defection of a senior Minister who alleged corruption in high places and by Congress defeats in the states of Kerala and West Bengal had no option but to ease public fears of corruption at the very highest level.

The Opposition boycotted the parliamentary inquiry into the Bofors allegations on the grounds that the composition of the committee was rigged. Nobody was surprised when the Inquiry exonerated the government completely. What had happened to the millions referred to by the Swedish government? For some months the Indian press was engulfed by a set of wild speculations. The name most frequently mentioned was that of matinee-idol Amitabh Bachan's brother, but it soon became clear that the Bofors 'commission' was one that he had definitely not received. Within the country at large the image of Rajiv Gandhi became tainted. Few suspected him of being personally corrupt, but rumours began to circulate about Sonia Gandhi's entourage of sycophants and hangers-on, whose behaviour was the cause of adverse comments in the press and social circles in the capital.

When I questioned Rajiv Gandhi in relation to the dissension inside the Congress and the allegations of corruption, his complacency was astounding.

> I think they're storms in a tea-cup. They'll pass over. . . Corruption is a problem, but our government has done more to fight it than any other and we are continuing that process. There are two aspects of fighting corruption. One is direct policing, if you want to call it that. That means that the organisations really looking at the problem should be geared up and take action and they're doing that. Equally important, perhaps even more important, is to get at the roots of why it happens. That means the destruction of a value system where the making of a quick buck seems to be more important than how you make it. Unless you fight that attitude off in society the other battle will be endless.

These were noble sentiments, if slightly utopian in the context of August 1987 when the discussion took place, for when I asked him whether corruption would be a central issue in the forthcoming general elections he stated calmly: 'Oh, if anything it will be our issue!'

In reality the Government found it impossible to bury the Bofors issue because the Indian press, more vigorous and alert than its counterpart in Britain, refused to let the matter die. The government organised a cover-up. It failed. They attempted to gag the press through the hasty passage of a Defamation Bill through Parliament. The country's journalists went on strike. The government withdrew the bill. At the height of the press campaign there was a sensational new development. The Comptroller and Auditor-General of India reported that the evaluation of the Bofors guns was seriously flawed. Then the man who had initially recommended the gun, retired Chief of Staff, General Sundarji, in a rare public pronouncement, stated that he had also recommended that the government cancel the contract, but that his advice had been ignored and he had been asked to 'modify' his views. The Opposition parties, scenting victory, demanded the resignation of the Government and immediate elections. Rajiv refused upon which the Opposition walked out of Parliament and called a general strike against corruption. The country ground to a halt. Rajiv survived the onslaught, but his reputation as Mr Clean was now in tatters. Madhu Dandavate, one of the Opposition Members of Parliament summed up the sorry trajectory of the case in an interview with *Bandung File* on Channel Four television.

> The story can be summed up as follows on the basis of statements made by Rajiv Gandhi in parliament and to the newspapers. In the beginning he stated that there were no middlemen involved in the Bofors deal. When we produced the middlemen he said the middlemen might be there, but they were not paid any money. When we proved that money had been paid to them he said it was a winding-up charge and not a commission. When we proved that a commission had been paid he said a commission might have been paid, but not to Indian agents. When we proved it had been paid to Indian agents, he said it might have been paid to Indian agents, but they had no links with the government. When we proved that the Indians who had been paid did have links with politicians he said 'Well, what's wrong if a commission is paid for a genuine cause'.

Soon after his election victory of 1984, Rajiv had declared that he had an A-team which consisted of the two Aruns and V. P. Singh. Since every member of the team had by now decamped he brought back two veteran fixers from his mother's B-team. Makhan Lal Fotedar and R. K. Dhavan were installed in his private office. Fotedar had been a clever fixer, good at carrying out orders. Dhavan had started as Mrs Gandhi's stenographer and progressed upwards by his incredible photographic memory. He never forgot a face or a document. He was the sewer, who also provided most of the sewage. Since, in his capacity as her private secretary, he controlled access to Mrs Gandhi he was courted most assiduously by Congress MPs and leaders from the provinces. He thus acquired certain talents in dealing with courtiers, businessmen, journalists and the like. These skills were now put in the service of Rajiv Gandhi, but it was already too late.

A demoralised and disparate Opposition had found a cause (corruption) and a leader (V. P. Singh). The opposition National Front was a new version of the Janata alliance which had defeated Mrs Gandhi in the post-Emergency elections in 1977. At the heart of the coalition was the disaffected centre of Indian politics, symbolised in the person of V. P. Singh, who drew the largest crowds.

On the extreme right there was the Bharatiya Janata Party [BJP], whose 'cultural' extension, the Vishwa Hindu Parishad (VHP) was campaigning shamelessly for Hindu votes under slogans such as 'Victory to Hinduism', 'Swear an oath to Lord Ram', 'In today's India, Hindus are as oppressed as they were under the Mughal kings and the British.' The BJP leader, L. K. Advani, a shrewd and artful manipulator, attempted to distance himself from the more crazed antics of his VHP extension, but few were deceived. The fact was that the main target was perceived to be the Congress rather than the cancer of communalism which was spreading throughout Northern India and in parts of the South.

Thus the Left Front, whose main constituents were the two Communist Parties, argued that the overthrow of a corrupt Congress was the main target. Jyoti Basu, the Communist Chief Minister of West Bengal stated: 'I am aware of the danger of Hindu and Muslim fundamentalism, but the Congress is the main enemy.' In a sense Rajiv was now reaping the bitter fruits of his decision to keep the Congress in a dynastic grip, but that cannot excuse the failure of the Left Front to campaign effectively against the confessional excesses of their coalition partners.

The rise of communalist politics in India has to be perceived on two levels. First, there is the specifically Indian dimension. Hindu ultra-nationalism, as we have seen in earlier chapters, existed in India from the very beginning of the rise of Indian nationalism. Mahatma Gandhi was killed by an RSS assassin, but Gandhi himself had imbued nationalist politics with an aura of Hinduism. The ideological basis of the RSS, the Jan Sangh and the BJP, was provided by men who were not gifted Sanskrit scholars, but had imbibed their Hinduism from texts translated and explained by the British Orientalists. It was Warren Hastings who took the first initiative to codify Hinduism. Under his instructions a simple code of Hindu law was put together and translated into English in 1776. Ten years later, a Hastings protégé, Charles Wilkins, who had been urged to master Sanskrit, published the first translation of the *Bhagavadgita*. Their aim, of course, was to acquaint themselves with the religious precepts of the majority of Indians in order to be better able to rule over them, but a crucial side-effect was that this version of Hinduism became the dogma of ultra-nationalists. It was the irruption of modernity, in the shape of British imperialism, which laid the ground for the variety of Hindu nationalism, currently in vogue.

Romilla Thapar, author of a classic ancient History of India has argued that:

> 'The notion of a Hindu community as it is defined today became necessary when there was a competition for political power and access to economic resources between various groups in a colonial situation. There was need to change from a segmental identity to a community which cut across caste, sect and region. This social need also required a reformulation of Hinduism which was attempted in various socio-economic reform movements of the nineteenth century.'

In reality the midwife of modern Hinduism was the East India Company. Prior to 1800, even though three-quarters of those who inhabited the peninsula were Hindus of one description or another, they were divided into two major sects: those who, while recognising other divinities in the pantheon, believed in Vishnu as the one God and those who worshipped Siva as the major God, but also recognised the others. The Vishnuites and Sivaites, both worshipped idols, but amongst the latter the worship of phallic images was more usual than pleasing the gods. Despite the fact that Muslim rulers had governed large tracts of the sub-continent since the year 1200, the preponderance of Hinduism is a testimony to the fact that, apart from odd aberrations, the Muslim kings did not go in for mass conversions and genocide on the pattern of, for instance, the Spaniards in Latin America. If they had, there is little doubt that they could have subjugated a large majority spiritually as well as militarily.

The reconstruction of Hinduism by the Orientalists would, of its own, have had very little impact. It was coupled with what was to become the ideological cornerstone of British policy in India and be institutionalised in the practice of the Empire. The British, like the Mogul Empire which preceded them, decided against any large-scale conversions to Christianity. The Protestant Missions were never impeded, but their guide-lines were clear. Conversions must be voluntary. The repressed lower orders of Hinduism, the so-called 'untouchables', did migrate to Christianity in large numbers as did their equivalents in parts of South India, but it was, relatively speaking, a small scale affair.

The reason for this restraint had nothing to do with tolerance. It was necessitated by geography and demography. The East India Company had won its territory with a predominantly Indian army, which consisted largely of high-caste Hindus. It was in the interests of the Company to preserve caste divisions both in order to retain the loyalty of their sepoys, and also to maintain an institutional barrier against unity between the Hindu castes which could have proved dangerous. A religion which atomised its own followers into castes which ruled and others whose lot in this life was to be permanently enslaved, was a blessing to any invader.

In the nineteenth century, Hindu reformers tried to build a reformed and modernised Hinduism through new societies such as the Brahmo Samaj in Bengal. They achieved successes in the towns, but their heretical teachings polarised matters and a new orthodoxy arose which defended the Hinduism reconstructed by the Orientalists against the reformers. But reformist propaganda did gain ground and prepared the basis for the promulgation of laws which forbade suttee – the self-immolation of widows on the funeral pyre of their husbands – and permitted the remarriage of widows.

Even though there have been recent instances of Hindu fundamentalists reviving the practice of suttee and organising demonstrations in support of a family who pressured a young widow to burn herself with her husband's body, it is unlikely that the ideologues of the BJP would ever enshrine these traditional atrocities of their culture in the statute book. Like many other modern fundamentalisms the BJP utilises religion to win support, but if it were ever to come to power or head a coalition in which it was the largest component it would, like fundamentalists elsewhere in the world, abandon much of the demagogy. Its nastiness would use religion as a cloak, but underneath it would lurk the more traditional symbols of authoritarian rule to be found in most other continents. For any secular politicians to align with such a force is a self-defeating exercise. For the avatars of Indian communism to justify a coalition with the BJP on the grounds that 'anything is better than the Congress' is a grotesque display of electoral opportunism.

Yet such a coalition did exist and its combined forces fought a pitched battle against the Congress in 1989. A Congress leader had boasted that the peasant masses were not interested in all this city talk of corruption. 'In the poor villages', he insisted, 'they know only three things. The voice of Lata Mangeshkar, the location of the post-office and the Congress Party.' This sort of complacency was totally routed in the country's ninth general elections, which were held in November 1989 and led to the formation of a new minority government under the Prime Ministership of V. P. Singh. The latter's own party, the Janata Dal, secured 141 seats as opposed to 193 won by the Congress. But the Left Front had 55 and the BJP's victory in 88 constituencies marked a tremendous leap forward for the consolidation of Hindu politics. The elections had not revealed any major difference between the two main rivals. What India had experienced was a referendum on the question of who should be Prime Minister and the majority had voted against Rajiv Gandhi. Within the space of five years the Congress had lost 222 parliamentary constituencies.

How did Rajiv view this humiliation? In time-honoured fashion everything was explained away by the mistakes of his advisers. Twelve hundred years ago, the Sanskrit dramatist, Visakhadatta, had already dealt with the problem of dynastic incompetence in his play, *Rakshasa's Ring*:

> It is the minister's fault
> If the king acts ill.
> And it is the driver's incompetence
> That makes a rogue elephant.

This would have been a good moment for Rajiv Gandhi to retire from politics and return to more congenial pursuits, but there is no evidence that such an early retirement was ever on the agenda. He had tasted the elixir of power and become a hopeless addict. Instead of withdrawing from the arena, he decided on a policy of sitting back and watching the victors fight each other over the spoils. It did not require a political genius to understand that a government dependent on the parliamentary support of the two Communist Parties on one hand and the BJP on the other, would not be able to survive for too long.

The one issue which had been smouldering away in the background for several years had been the Hindu revivalist campaign spearheaded by the Vishwa Hindu Parishad and backed by the BJP to reclaim a sixteenth-century mosque for Hinduism. The Babri Masjid [Babar's mosque] dated from the time of Babar, the founding-Emperor of the Mogul dynasty. The VHP alleged that the mosque had been constructed on the site which was the original birthplace of Rama, a revered Hindu divinity. They stated that there had been on this site a temple dedicated to Rama, but it had been razed to the ground by the Mogul conquerors and on its foundations had been constructed the Babri Masjid. The VHP 'volunteers' mobilised thousands of Hindus in regular marches to the site to demand that the mosque be torn down brick by brick. Hindu fanatics in the service of the VHP then stoked the fires of the faithful with incendiary remarks, such as the following remarks made by Sadhvi Ritambhara, who regularly preaches the fundamentalist message:

> 'Muslims are like a lemon dipped into cream. They turn it sour. What do we do with the lemon? We cut it up, squeeze out the pips and throw it away!'

Hindu-Muslim riots in the year which followed V. P. Singh's election were the worst since the Partition of the sub-continent. Nearly four thousand people, largely Muslims, were killed in a spate of intolerance which swept the country. The saffron caps of the Shiv Sena, the self-proclaimed storm-troopers in the army of Shiva [the Hindu god of destruction], have terrorised Muslims, Sikhs and low-caste Hindus in Maharashtra.

From the first day in office, V. P. Singh realised that the antics of the BJP and its allies would pose a serious threat to his administration. For the first few months he toured Northern India preaching peace and reconciliation. Then in August 1990 the new government decided to preserve 27 per cent of public-sector employment for the 'backward castes'. This was in addition to the 22.5 per cent guaranteed by the Indian constitution to tribals and 'untouchables'. It was a well-meaning gesture, but it brought all the caste polarisations out into the open. Public-sector professionals came out on to the streets to protect their jobs and were backed by the BJP, which defended casteism to the hilt. Three months later V. P. Singh decided that the BJP-VHP assault on the Babri Masjid could not be permitted. Tens of thousands of saffron fascists were arrested on 30 October 1990 when they assaulted the mosque.

Riots followed in hundreds of towns and a curfew was imposed.

Chandrashekar, an old rival of V. P. Singh's who had been desperate to become Prime Minister after the defeat of the Congress, now saw his chance and withdrew his support from the Government. He was backed by fifty-eight MPs. Simultaneously the BJP withdrew its support and V. P. Singh was left with his own eighty-two MPs together with the fifty-two Communist members.

Rajiv Gandhi and his supporters were delighted. They had always believed that the anti-Congress coalition could not last for more than two years. They had been unduly pessimistic. Eleven months after he took office, the new Prime Minister was brought down by a vote of no-confidence in the government. India's President, Ramaswamy Venkataraman, wanted an interim national government pending the elections and he wanted it to be headed by a figure acceptable to all the major parties. Failing this he was prepared to ask the Congress to form a new government. Rajiv Gandhi, who had the support of the single largest party in Parliament, refused both to participate in any national government or to form his own government. He offered to support a minority government led by Chandrashekhar, knowing full well that Congress could force a general election at any time. Rajiv Gandhi hoped that the new government would make such a mess that within months the people would be desperate for a return to the Congress and stability. These were not empty hopes. Chandrashekhar was not best known as a man whose conscience was stable. He had changed parties four times over the last twelve years. His first cabinet announced in November 1990 was the rogues gallery of Indian politics. William Dalrymple, reporting from New Delhi, captured the new mood accurately in a pre-Christmas despatch to *The Spectator* a few weeks later:

> The ministers form a depressing line-up even by the worst Third World standards: an extraordinary collection of the most ruthless and unprincipled backstabbers and opportunists ever to enter India's political arena. Included among their ranks is at least one man who has faced murder investigations. The country which produced Mahatama Gandhi and the principles of non-violence now finds itself under *goonda raj* – the rule of the thug.

In addition to Hindu revivalism, there was an escalation of violence in the Punjab and an extremely serious crisis in Kashmir, which had been at boiling-point ever since the rigged state elections in 1987. The opposition had taken up arms, and guerrilla groups on the Lebanese model and backed by Muslim fundamentalist regimes had begun a terrorist campaign against Indian soldiers as well as their co-religionists whom they accused of 'collaborating' with India. In January 1990, the Chief Minister, Farooq Abdullah, had resigned and paramilitary units had embarked on a campaign of brutalising and humiliating the Muslim inhabitants of the state. Innocent civilians were subjected to the most brutal tortures. Women, young and old, were raped by Indian paratroopers. A teenager described how he had been suspended from a rotating ceiling fan. An old peasant told of how he had been hung from a tree and beaten with clubs. And the sad tales of inhumanity and barbarism began to multiply. The Hezb-e-Mujahideen, a Kashmiri variant of the Afghan model, began a campaign of intimidation against Muslim officials and traders, introducing their own protection rackets and driving an already tormented population to near despair. Many Kashmiris felt that the choice between the Mujahideen and the paratroopers was only a choice between being drowned in the waters of the Dal lake in Srinagar or being parched to death in a Rajasthan desert.

As the crisis grew worse, Rajiv Gandhi became more and more confident that the Congress would be returned to power. The tension that surrounded him during his Prime Ministership seemed to disappear. He appeared to be disregarding the most elementary security precautions as he waded into crowds to press the flesh. He tended to do this much more in South India than in the North where there were still too many obvious enemies. His oratory, which had been stilted and unconvincing in 1984 and 1989 had also improved and he enjoyed attacking the political brothel which ruled in Delhi. And yet something was lacking. Few expected anything radical from the Congress, even on the level of rhetoric, but it was the failure to understand that secular politics were under very serious threat and, therefore, what was needed above all was a centre-left coalition against the revivalists.

Secularism for the Congress leaders from Mahatama Gandhi onwards has always meant equality for all religions. Gandhi was assassinated by RSS men for daring to implement that equality. Jawaharlal Nehru understood the necessity of modernisation even in his prison cell as he was writing *The Discovery of India*:

We have to come to grips with the present, this life, this world, this nature which surrounds us in its infinite variety. Some Hindus talk of going back to the Vedas; some Muslims dream of an Islamic theocracy. Idle fancies, for there is no going back to the past; there is no turning back even if this was thought desirable. There is only one-way traffic in Time.

But Nehru in power could not impose modernity on the Indian countryside and, as a result, the political forces advocating a two-way traffic in Time are gaining ground as we approach the twenty-first century.

Nehru, like Gandhi before him, saw secularism as a form of peaceful co-existence between religions, but this was always a utopian ideal in a country where one religion was so heavily dominant. Only a secularism based on a rigid division between state and religion would have stood a chance of success. This would have meant laws applicable to all regardless of caste or creed. It would have meant antagonising Hindu as well as Muslim orthodoxy and dragging the post-independence generations towards a new synthesis. Once such a project had been rejected it was only a matter of time before religious revivalism gained ground.

During the election campaign which began in earnest in March 1991, Rajiv Gandhi, a strong adherent of the old vision of secularism, offered prayers in temples as well as mosques. Given the BJP-VHP-Shiva Sena nexus, this was a brave and well-intentioned gesture, but it was futile. That style of secularism had failed, its bitter fruits were littered all over India in the shape of corpses.

Rajiv had been campaigning effectively and had even begun to draw large crowds, but the overall mood of the country was despairing and cynical. People would continue to vote since it was the only way they could make some impact on the country's politics, but they expected very little from the politicians. The general feeling was that the politicians ruled in their own interests and those alone. During his period in office, Rajiv had antagonised a section of the Tamil population in India by the actions of the Indian Army in Sri Lanka in the period 1986–88. Indian troops had initially been despatched at the formal request of the former Sri Lankan President, Junius Jayewardene to act as a peacekeeping force between the Tamils in the north-east and Sri Lankan state forces. Rajiv had sent in the Indian army to defend the Tamil enclaves against the brutalities of the Sinhala soldiers. His civil servants, however, could not bring the ultra-nationalist Tamil Tigers to heel and were in the end compelled to fight them. The Tigers had embarked on a campaign to polarise the Tamil quarter of the island. The Tamil moderates, and India, favoured a solution which gave the Tamil province total autonomy, but within a Sri Lankan federal framework. The Tigers wanted a separate Tamil state. As the Tamil moderates began to discuss a political solution, the Tigers became Tamil-eaters. Supporters of a settlement were killed, kidnapped, blackmailed and subjected to intimidations of every sort. Clashes between the Tigers and Indian troops developed into large-scale bloodbaths. Before the Indian troops were withdrawn, they gave as good as they got and the man who sent them there became a target for the vengeance of the Tigers.

The election campaign was virtually over and the first day of voting had ended on the previous day as Rajiv's plane touched down at Madras airport on 21 May 1991. He was in a cheerful mood, confident that he would soon be back in office as Prime Minister. From Madras he was driven to address a public meeting at Sriperumbudur, twenty-five miles south of the city. His wife Sonia had loyally accompanied him on his tours of his own constituency and elsewhere, but he travelled to the South alone. Within minutes of his mounting the dais to address the crowds, there was an explosion. Rajiv Gandhi died on the spot. History, with an impassive hand, had inscribed a new chapter in the tragedy of the Nehru-Gandhi family and the country over which they had presided for so many years. Like his mother before him, Rajiv Gandhi had been killed by hired assassins. She had been killed by Sikhs. In Rajiv's case, all the indications were that Tamil separatists had been involved in the conspiracy. Once again the parched and cracked lips of India were moist with blood and vultures were at the zenith.

The crowds that turned out for his funeral were not as large as expected and, after his remains had been burnt to ashes, a large section of the crowd mobbed the film star Amitabh Bachan. It was a surreal occasion. Some Congress leaders decided to highlight their political bankruptcy by asking Sonia Gandhi to become the President of the party in place of her husband. Fortunately she refused and the tragedy did not degenerate into a farce. A veteran politician, Narasimha Rao, agreed to lead the Congress over the next period.

The dynasty, unlike the kings of old, had always been elected to office. It was seen by many as the principal stabiliser of the Indian state machine. And yet India could not be further removed from the dreams of Jawaharlal Nehru as it is today. Instead of a modernised democracy where religion takes a back seat, the country has become a battlefield of warring fundamentalisms. Sonia was not the only widow in India in 1991. Thousands had been widowed and orphaned in communal massacres. Rajiv's tragic end had highlighted the true scale of a tragedy which continues to unfold.

Many wondered whether the Nehru–Gandhi dynasty had come to an end. The answer perhaps lies in an unreported exchange between Rajiv Gandhi and Benazir Bhutto in 1989. Both were then Prime Ministers, of India and Pakistan respectively. They were attending the bicentenary celebrations of the French Revolution as guests of the French President François Mitterand in Paris. Rajiv confided to Benazir that his daughter Priyanka was obsessive about politics. 'Please try and talk her out of it', he asked Benazir, whose own father, Pakistan's first elected Prime Minister, had been judicially assassinated on the orders of a military dictator. 'She doesn't realise', Rajiv continued, 'what a dangerous occupation it is.'

Books and magazines consulted

This is not a complete list of the works consulted for this book over a period of eighteen months, but is, in the absence of footnotes, a reference to the most important magazines and books I have read.

Magazines
Economic and Political Weekly, Illustrated Weekly of India, Sunday Observer and *Imprint* (Bombay); *Sunday, Frontier* and *The Telegraph* (Calcutta); *India Today* and *Mainstream* (Delhi).

Books
Benedict Anderson, *Imagined Communities,* London, 1983
Abul Kalam Azad: *India Wins Freedom,* Delhi, 1959
Krishan Bhatia: *Indira Gandhi,* New York, 1974
Bertolt Brecht: *Poems* (three vols), London, 1976
Judith Brown: *Gandhi's Rise to Power,* Cambridge, 1972
Elias Canetti: *Crowds and Power,* London, 1973
Bipan Chandra: (ed): *The Indian Left,* Delhi, 1983
M. N. Das: *The Political Philosophy of Jawaharlal Nehru,* London, 1961
R. Duncan (ed): *Selected Writings of Mahatama Gandhi,* London, 1951
Indira Gandhi: *Speeches and Reminiscences,* London, 1975
Sarvepalli Gopal: *Jawaharlal Nehru: 1947–56,* London, 1979
A. Gorev and V. Zimyanin: *Jawaharlal Nehru,* Moscow, 1982
Selig Harrison: *India: The Most Dangerous Decades,* Oxford, 1960
D. D. Kosambi: *An Introduction to Indian History,* Bombay, 1956
Zareer Masani: *Indira Gandhi: A Biography,* London, 1975
Ved Mehta: *A Family Affair,* New York, 1982
Dom Moraes: *Mrs Gandhi,* London, 1980
M. Mujeeb: *The Indian Muslims,* London, 1967
B.N. Mullick: *My Years with Nehru,* Delhi, 1971
Jawaharlal Nehru: *An Autobiography,* London, 1936
— *The Unity of India,* London, 1941
— *The Discovery of India,* Calcutta, 1946
— *Glimpses of World History,* Delhi, 1951
— *A Bunch Of Old Letters,* Bombay, 1958
B.N. Pandey: *Nehru,* London, 1976
Anil Seal: *The Emergence Of Indian Nationalism,* Cambridge, 1978
David Selbourne: *An Eye to India,* London, 1977
Khushwant Singh: *A History of the Sikhs* (2 vols), Delhi, 1977
Mary Tyler: *My Years In An Indian Prison,* London, 1977

Index

Abdali, Ahmed Shah, 252
Abdullah, Farooq, 248–49, 301
Abdullah, Sheikh, 79, 191, 248, 301
Act of India (1935), 51–54, 56, 60, 63, 85
Advani, L. K., 315
Ahir, Bhagwan, 27
Ahmed, Akbar ('Dumpy'), 268, 279, 280, 284, 288, 289, 291
Ahmed, Fakhrudin Ali, 185
Aiyer, Mani Shankar, 304
Akali Dal, 155, 239–43, 245–48, 251–55
Akbar, Emperor, 3, 70, 80, 234, 236
Akbar, M. J., 257
Akbar of Allahabad, 114
Alexander the Great, 3
Allard, Jean François, 237
All-Assam Students Union (AASU), 215, 224–26
Allende, Salvador, 186
All-India Congress Committee (AICC), 167, 168, 227, 293
Amethi, Raja of, 278
Amin, Idi, 204
Anand, Colonel, 275, 279
Andhra Pradesh Civil Liberties Committee, 250
Antulay, Abdul Rahman, 222–23
Arjun, Guru, 236
Assam, 303
Assam movement, 222–27
Associated Chambers of Commerce and Industry (ACCI), 169
Atlantic charter, 69
Attenborough, Richard, 269

Attlee, C. R. 33, 74
Aurungzeb, Emperor, 235
Awami League, 172, 173
Ayub Khan, 106, 149, 150, 171, 183, 273
Azad, Maulana Abul Kazam, 64, 71, 74, 80–81, 191

Babar, Emperor, 101
Babri Masjid mosque, 319
Bachan, Amitabh, 295, 304, 313, 323
Badminton School, 120
Bahadur, Tej, 235
Bahuguna, H. N., 206, 208
Baker, Beatrice, 120–21
Balkan Wars, 19
Bandaranaike, Srimavo, 175, 177, 299
Bandung Conference, 100–101
Banerji, Sumanta, 244
Bangladesh War, 171–75, 183, 185, 224, 269
Baroda School, 269
Basu, Jyoti, 162, 227, 233, 315
Besant, Annie, 6, 20, 21
Bevan, Aneurin, 218
Bhagat, Dhiren, 275
Bhagavadgita, 316
Bhagwati, H. N. 219–20
Bhandari, S. S. 198
Bharatiya Jan Sangh, 92
Bharatiya Janata Party (BJP), 226, 229, 233, 291, 315, 316, 318, 319, 320, 322
Bharatiya Lok Dal, 199
Bhindranwale, Jarnail Singh, 243–48, 251–56

Bhopal disaster, 296–97
Bhutto, Benazir, 299, 324
Bhutto, Zulfiqar Ali, 172, 174, 175, 177, 202–3, 299, 324
Bibi, Chand, 70
Birkenhead, 1st Earl of (Frederick Edwin Smith), 20
Birla, G. D., 57, 85, 88, 90, 98, 145, 180, 229, 259, 277
Birman, Professor, 88
Blavatsky, Madame, 6
Bloch, Marc, 309
Boer War, 37
Bofors company, Sweden, 311, 312–13
Borooah (politician), 205
Bose, Nenai Sadhan, 245
Bose, Subhas Chandra, 53, 62, 64, 65, 69–71, 82, 140
Bowles, Chester, 158
Bradlaugh, Charles, 6
Brahmo Samaj society, 317
Brando, Marlon, 259
Brecht, Bertolt, 109
Brezhnev, Leonid, 217
British, in India, 315–16
Brooks, F. T. 6–7, 11
Buch, M. N., 296
Burke, Edmund, 132

Calcutta University, 13
Callaghan, James, 155*n*
Cambridge University, 14, 15, 41, 49, 114, 134, 270–72, 290
Canetti, Elias, 258
Castro, Fidel, 226
Catholics, 103, 267
Central Gurdwara Management Committee (SGPC), 239, 240, 253, 255
Central Intelligence Agency (CIA), 104, 106, 208, 305
Chakravarty, Nikhil, 189
Chamar, Rampati, 27
Chamberlain, Neville, 62
Chandra Gupta, 3
Chandrashekhar, 163, 165, 207, 233, 310, 319, 320

Chattopadhyaya, Virendranath (Chatto), 31, 35
Chauhan, Jagjit Singh, 254
Chavan, Shankar, 294
Chavan, Y. B., 160, 165, 166, 188, 200, 205
Chen Yi, 105
Chiang Ching, 195
Chiang Kai Shek, 63, 64, 99
Chief's College, 267
Chinese Revolution, 84, 90, 93, 94, 105–6
Chou en Lai, 98–100, 105–7
Christian Democratic Party, Italian, 287
Chu Teh, 99
Churchill, Winston, 36, 55, 68, 69, 136–37, 142, 145, 218
Cold War, 90, 91, 93, 104
Comintern, 32, 51
Commonwealth Heads of State conference, 266
Commonwealth Prime Ministers' Conference (1964), 149
Communist parties 315
Communist Party (Marxist) (CP[M]), 82, 154, 157, 161–63, 166, 167, 171, 178, 180, 188, 195, 196, 208, 210–11, 221, 230, 233, 242, 251, 277
Communist Party of India (CPI), 50–51, 82, 90–93, 102–3, 105, 128, 139–41, 154, 157, 161–63, 166, 167, 180, 186, 195, 208, 210, 212, 215, 217–18, 229–30, 240, 242, 277, 282–83
Communist Party of India (Marxist-Leninist) (CPI[M-L]), 179
Communist Party of the Soviet Union (CPSU), 228
Companies Act (1956), 87
Congress, *see* Indian National Congress
Congress for Democracy (CFD), 193, 196
Congress Socialist Party, 91
Conservative Party, British, 218
Constituent Assembly, 76

Cripps, Sir Stafford, 69, 126, 127
Curie, Eve, 126
Curie, Marie, 127
Curzon, George, Lord, 12–13, 19, 56

Dal Khalsa, 244
Daladier, Edouard, 62
Dalmia (capitalist) 98
Dalmia-Sahu (company), 88
Dalrymple, William, 320
Damodaran, K., 91, 105
Dandarate, Madhu, 314
Dange (politician), 180
Dard, Hira Singh, 239
Das, C.R., 24
Datta-Ray, Sunanda, 288
Dayal, General Ranjit Singh, 253
de Gaulle, Charles, 145
Defence of India Regulations (DIR), 181, 187
Delhi Development Authority, 191
Deng Xiaoping, 179
Desai, Anita, 306
Desai, Bhulabhai, 69
Desai, Kantibhai, 165
Desai, Morarji, 138, 143, 146–47, 150–52, 158, 160, 162, 163, 165–68, 185, 199–200, 203–4, 206–8, 212
Devi, Phoolan, 216–17
Dhar, D. P., 290
Dhar, Rajiv, 290
Dhavan, R.K., 293, 294, 314
Dhebar, U.N., 137
Discovery of India, The (Nehru), 321-2
Dong, Pham van, 100
Doon School, 189, 267–70, 272, 274, 283, 290
Dravida Munnetra Kazhagam (DMK), 162, 168, 187, 231
Dubay, Suman, 304
Dulles, John Foster, 98
Dutt, Batukeshwera, 34
Dutt, Sunil, 296
Duvalier, 'Baby Doc', 298
Duvalier, 'Papa Doc', 298
Dyer, General Reginald, 24–25, 63

East India Company, 33, 316, 317
Eden, Anthony, 104, 142, 145
Edward, Prince of Wales, 27
Einstein, Albert, 156
Eisenhower, Dwight D., 98
Elizabeth I (Queen of England), 154
Ellis, Havelock, 15
Epstein, Jacob, 96

Fabian Society, 6
Faiz, Faiz Ahmed, 77
Farid, Shaikh Ibrahim 236, 237
Farrukhsiar, Prince, 4
Federation of Indian Chambers of Commerce and Industry (FICCI), 84–85, 87
Fernandes, George, 181, 199, 206, 207, 233
First World War, 19, 37, 70, 84, 239, 298
Fishlock, Trevor, 289
Five-Year Plans, 86, 154
Foot, Arthur, 268
Foot, Michael, 55
Ford, Gerald, 193
Foreign Service, 95
Forward Bloc, 82
Fotedar, Makhan Lal, 314
Franco, Francisco, 50, 63
French Revolution, 237
Friedan, Betty, 136
Frost, Robert, 108, 153

Galbraith, John Kenneth, 292
Gandhi, Feroze, 120, 122–29, 131–35, 141–43, 159, 161, 213, 263, 264, 266, 269–70
Gandhi, Feroze Varun, 215, 250, 281, 288
Gandhi, Indira (*née* Nehru), 63, 81, 94–95, 103, 108, 311, 314; and Assam movement, 226, 227; assassination of, 255–60, 291, 293–95, 303, 304, 305, 323; during Bangladesh War, 171–75; becomes Prime Minister, 151–55; birth of, 22, 113; birth of children of, 129, 130,

263; childhood of, 30, 113–18; and designation of Rajiv as successor, 290, 297; and economic crisis, 176–78, 210–12, 215; education of, 31, 52, 62, 117–22; elected President of Congress, 102, 138–39; emergency declared by, 185–88, 190–93, 276, 278, 301, 306, 309; foreign policy of, 156–59, 217; found guilty of electoral malpractice, 184–85, 188–89, 274; and Janata Government, 199–207; and Kashmir power struggle, 248–49; Maneka's hostility toward, 249–50, 291–92; marriage of, 75, 122–28; as mother, 131, 263–66; during Nehru regime, 131–44; in 1967 elections, 159–65; and 1969 Congress Party split, 165–69, 301; in 1971 elections, 170–72; in 1977 elections, 193–96, 309, 315; and preparations for 1985 elections, 227–33; press and, 307; as Prime Minister, 301, 302, 306, 307, 308; and railway strike, 181–83; returned to power, 207–10, 280–82; and Sanjay's death, 213–14, 283–84, 288; scandals involving, 176–77; during Second World War, 128–29; in Shastri government, 147–49; and Sikhs, 155, 242, 243, 246–48, 251–55

Gandhi, Karamchand, 36

Gandhi, Kasturbai, 43

Gandhi, Maneka (*née* Anand), 203, 215, 249–50, 275–77, 279–81, 284, 286, 288, 291–92

Gandhi, Mohandas K. (Mahatma), 23, 24, 26, 28, 30–62, 64, 65, 68–72, 74, 75, 79–82, 85, 92, 95, 114, 115, 117, 124–26, 133, 152, 183, 185, 190, 196, 197, 218, 229, 257, 283, 303, 315, 321, 322

Gandhi, Priyanka, 324

Gandhi, Rahul, 271

Gandhi, Rajiv, 153, 228, 249, 255, 276, 302, 320; as airline pilot, 8, 271–72, 281, 287, 288; and Andhra Pradesh affair, 250–51; assassination of, 323; birth of, 129, 263; childhood of, 131, 133–35, 143, 263–66; and Congress Party, 303–4, 305–6, 310, 313, 315; in constitutional conflict, 308; defence deal scandal, 308, 311–14 *passim*; designated as future leader, 290–91; education of, 266–71; foreign policy, 305; Maneka's hostility toward, 291–92; marriage of, 201, 271; in 1989 elections, 307, 318; in 1991 election campaign, 322, 323; in opposition, 320, 321; as Prime Minister, 257, 258, 293–97, 300, 301–307 *passim*, 309, 310, 322, 324; and Sanjay's death, 213–15, 283–84, 287–88; and Sikhs, 247, 252

Gandhi, Sanjay, 177, 200, 201, 203, 205, 206, 211; birth of, 130, 263; childhood of, 131, 133–35, 143, 263–66; death of, 8, 213–15, 281–88, 292; education of, 266–70, 272; elected to Parliament, 288–89; during emergency, 188–93, 195, 276–78; marriage of, 275–77; and Maruti affair, 177, 188, 189, 272–74, 277, 279, 281; in 1977 election, 195, 278; in 1980 election, 208, 280; in Parliament, 209, 289; and Sikhs, 243

Gandhi, Sonia (*née* Maino), 201, 271, 276, 283, 287–89, 291, 293, 307, 313, 323

Gandhi, Tehmina, 124

Ganesan, Sivaji, 232

Gang of Four, 179

George V (King of England), 114

Ghosh, Atulya, 143, 162

Gill, Sucha Singh, 242

Giri, V. V., 164–66

Godfrey, Admiral, 72

Gokhale, G. K., 7, 12

Gopalin, A. K., 91

Gowan, Jean, 96

Graham, General Daniel, 254

Grass, Günter, 227

Gupta, C. B., 162

Gupta, Indrajit, 283

Hahn, Kurt, 268
Haksar, P. N., 156, 191
Hansraji (Congress member), 137
Hapsburg Empire, 298
Harrow, 10–11, 41, 134, 268
Hastings, Warren, 132, 315
Heber, Bishop, 48
Hedgewar (founder of RSS), 197
Helms, Jesse, 254
Hersh, Seymour, 208
Hezb-e-Mujahideen, 321
Hindu fundamentalism, 309, 315, 317, 320
Hindu ultranationalism, 315, 316
Hindu-Muslim riots, 1989, 319
Hindus, 12, 35, 40, 54, 56, 58, 61, 71, 77, 80, 82–83, 88, 92, 103, 125, 135, 155, 196–97, 206, 223, 224, 233, 234, 241, 243–44, 248, 257, 264, 316, 317, 318–19, 322
Hitler, Adolf, 50, 55, 62–65
Ho Chi Minh, 32, 159
Ho Lung, 99
Home Rule Leagues, 20–21
Hooper, Cecilia, 114
House of Commons, British, 132
Hunter Committee, 24, 25
Husain, Madho Lal, 236–37
Hussein, Zakir, 164, 165
Hutheesing, Krishna (*née* Nehru), 18, 21, 31, 114, 116, 123, 124, 127, 129, 133, 148

Iltutmish, Shamsuddin, 153
India League, 55, 159
India Today, 304
Indian Airlines, 271, 288
Indian Army, 78, 174, 175, 253, 295, 322, 323
Indian Civil Service, 14, 78, 103, 268, 302, 303
Indian Constitution, 83, 84, 90, 146, 219
Indian High Command, 173, 175
Indian National Army (INA), 71, 72
Indian National Congress, 5, 7, 12, 15, 19–21, 23, 24, 26–36, 38, 40, 43–58, 60–70, 72–74, 76, 80, 82, 83, 85–88, 90–93, 95, 101–3, 107–9, 115, 117, 118, 120, 122, 134, 135, 137–43, 146, 150–55, 157–71, 183–85, 187–90, 192–200, 203, 205–15, 217–18, 221, 225–29, 231–33, 239–43, 246, 248, 251, 252, 254, 255, 257–60, 266, 276, 278–85, 287–301, 303–306 *passim*, 309–10, 312, 315, 318, 319–20, 323

Indian Trades Union Congress (INTUC), 181, 210
Indo-American Education Foundation, 156–58
Indo-Pakistani War (1965), 149
Indo-Soviet Treaty (1971), 173
Industries Act (1951), 87
Inner Temple, 15
Inquiry Commission, 88
International School (Geneva), 118
Irwin, Lord (Edward Frederick Lindley Wood), 45, 46
Islam, *see* Muslims
Italo-Turkish War, 19

Jack, Ian, 289
Jahan, Shah, 235
Jaipur, Maharani of, 160
Jalib, Habib, 180
Jan Morcha (People's Front) party, 312
Jan Sangh, 93, 155, 162, 163, 166, 167, 169, 171, 184, 185, 196–98, 206–8, 226, 291, 315
Janata coalition, 309, 315
Janata Dal party, 318
Janata Party, 194–96, 198–210, 212, 215, 217, 229, 233, 234, 278–79, 281, 282
Jawaharlal Nehru University, 276
Jayewardene, Junius, 322
Jinnah, Mohammed Ali, 26, 56, 57, 61, 65, 73, 76, 79, 171, 172, 174
Johnson, Lyndon Baines, 156, 158
Joshi, Sharad, 222
JP Movement, 184
Julaha, Abdullah, 27

Kabir, 233
Kairon, Pratap Singh, 241
Kamaraj, Kumaraswamy, 142–43, 147, 150–52, 158, 160, 162, 164, 165, 168, 232
Kant, Immanuel, 45*n*
Karunanidhi, M., 187
Kashmir, crisis in, 320–21
Kashmir National Conference, 248
Kaul, Kamala, *see* Nehru, Kamala
Kaul, Raj, 4
Kaul, T. N., 191
Kennedy, John F., 156, 298
Khilafat Movement, 23
Khrushchev, Nikita, 101, 149
Kidwai, Rafi Ahmed, 74, 81
Kim Il Sung, 298–99
King, Commander, 71
Kipling, Rudyard, 59
Kissinger, Henry, 173, 193, 208
Korean War, 93–94, 97
Kosygin, Alexei, 157, 158
Kripalani, 83
Krishnamachari, T. T., 141
Ku Klux Klan, 256

Labour Party, British, 33, 69, 97, 121, 218
Lajpat Rai, Lala, 34
Lall, Bansi, 189, 195, 200–201, 209
Lane, Allen, 55
League Against Imperialism, 32
League of Nations, 121
Le Corbusier, 242
Lee Hsien Loong, Brigadier-General, 298
Lee Kuan Yew, 298
Left Front party, 315, 318
Lenin, V. I., 9, 22, 34, 106, 157
Liberal Party, British, 12
Licensing Commission, 87
Lin Piao, 99, 179
Linlithgow, 2nd Marquis of (Victor Alexander John Hope), 65
Lohia, Ram Manohar, 155
Lok Dal, 229
Lok Sabha, 92, 161–64, 209, 242, 270, 294
London School of Economics, 120, 301, 302
Long March, 63, 99
Longowal, Sant, 246, 253
Lothian, 11th Marquis of (Philip Henry Kerr), 54
Ludhianvi, Sahir, 72–73

Maastan, Haji, 259
MacArthur, General Douglas, 94
Macaulay, Thomas, Lord, 41, 42
McMahon Line, 105, 107
Mafia, 287
Mahasabha, Hindu, 38, 80, 82, 92, 196–98
Mahatab, Harekrishna, 176–77
Maintenance of Internal Security Act (MISA), 187
Malhotra, Inder, 200
Malraux, André, 99
Maneckshaw, General, 174, 175
Mao Zedong, 63, 64, 84, 98–100, 106, 107
Maoists, 179, 188, 244–45
Martin Burn (company), 88
Martyn, J. A. K., 268
Maruti (automobile), 177, 188, 189, 272–74, 277, 279, 281, 289
Marx, Karl, 41, 43, 54, 154, 244, 256
Masani, Zareer, 169
Mathai (Nehru's personal assistant), 137
Menon, Krishna, 55, 62, 81, 107, 121, 145–47, 157–60, 260, 303
Michaelis, Arnold, 163
Mill, John Stuart, 41
Minto, 4th Earl of (Gilbert John Elliot-Murray-Kynynmond), 13
Mishra, L. N., 182–83
Mitra, Ashok, 227
Mitterand, François, 324
Modern School, Allahabad, 117, 118
Mogul Empire, 3, 4, 70, 101, 234, 235, 306, 316, 319
Mohan, Inder, 192
Mohan, Jag, 191, 192

Mollet, Guy, 104
Molotov-Ribbentrop agreement, 68
Montagu-Chelmsford Report, 23
Mookerji, S. P., 83, 92, 197, 199
Moraes, Dom, 213
Morley, John, Lord, 13
Mountbatten, Edwina, Lady, 76, 78, 81, 95–97, 102, 159
Mountbatten, Louis, Lord, 73–76, 78, 81, 95–96
Mujib, Sheikh, 299
Mukherjee, Pranab, 294
Munich Accords, 62
Murdoch, Iris, 121
Muslim League, 26, 56–58, 60–61, 65–66, 72–74, 76, 79, 80, 103, 141, 241
Muslims, 12, 13, 19, 20, 23, 35, 40, 54, 56, 58, 61, 65–67, 71, 77, 79–81, 83, 89, 135, 149, 164, 174, 190–92, 196–98, 206, 208, 224, 226, 233, 234, 241, 264, 316, 319, 320–21, 322
Mussolini, Benito, 50, 55

Nader, Ralph, 296
Naidu, Sarojini, 38, 61
Naipaul, V. S., 256
Namboodiripad, E. M. S., 91, 102, 103
Nanak, Guru, 233–37
Nanda, Gulzarlal, 109, 146, 147, 151, 153
Naoroji, Dadabhai, 7
Napoleon, 237
Narain, Lala Jagat, 243
Narain, Raj, 184, 194, 203–4
Narayan, Jayaprakash (J. P.), 82, 183–85, 195, 199, 205
Nargis, 296
Nasser, Gamal Abdel, 97, 100, 104, 156, 158
Nath, Kamal ('Roly Poly'), 268, 284, 294
National Co-Ordinating Committee for Railwaymen's Struggle (NCCRS), 181
National Democratic Alliance, 229
National Front, 315

National Railway Workers Union, 182
National Security Council, US, 254
National Students Union of India (NSUI), 292
Naval Strike Committee, 72
Naxalite movement, 179, 180
Nehru, Arun, 290, 294, 304, 314
Nehru, Brijlal, 14–15
Nehru, Jawaharlal, 152, 153, 161, 168, 170, 178, 183, 185, 190, 191, 195, 201, 218, 229, 259, 260, 281, 289, 292, 301, 321, 323; and achievement of independence, 73–77, 129–30; anti-fascism of, 62–63; birth of, 4, 5; and Chauri Chaura incidents, 27–28; childhood of, 5–9; conflicts with Gandhi, 28, 30–59; death of, 108–9, 143–46, 199, 213; education of, 10–18; family background of, 4–5; during First World War, 19–22; as grandfather, 264–66, 268–72; during Indira's childhood, 113–22; and Indira's marriage, 120, 122–28; law practice of, 18–19, 23; marriage of, 16–17, 21–22, 115, 271; and 1937 elections, 60–62; in Non-Cooperation Movement, 26; on Pakistan, 303; as Prime Minister, 78–108, 131–43, 156, 159, 197, 210, 214, 241, 300, 301, 302, 303, 306, 322; and Rowlatt Acts protests, 23–26; during Second World War, 64–71, 128–29; and Sikhs, 239
Nehru, Kamala (*née* Kaul), 21–22, 30, 31, 45–47, 52, 75, 113–20, 122, 127, 129, 133, 134, 138
Nehru, Krishna, *see* Hutheesing, Krishna
Nehru, Motilal, 5–10, 12, 14–19, 21, 23, 24, 26–29, 31–33, 41, 43, 44, 46, 47, 108, 113–15, 117–18, 123, 124, 126, 127, 136, 195, 213, 271
Nehru, Swaruprani, 5–10, 16, 49, 62, 75, 113, 116, 124, 127
Nehru, Vijaylakshmi, *see* Pandit, Vijaylakshmi
Nijalingappa, S., 143, 162, 165, 167–68

Nirankari sect, 243–45
Nixon, Richard M., 193
Non-Aligned Summit, 226
Non-Cooperation Movement, 26, 239

Operation Bluestar, 254, 293
Outram, General James, 132
Oxford University, 52, 62, 121, 122

Painful Transition, The (Vanaik), 308
Pakistan, 302–3, 304
Pakistan Air Force, 173
Pakistan Army, 149, 172–74, 210, 238
Pakistan Civil Service, 172, 302–3
Pakistan People's Party (PPP), 172, 299
Pandit, Vijaylakshmi (*née* Nehru), 9, 60, 90, 114–16, 124, 128, 152, 289
Pant, Pandit Govindvallabh, 137, 138
Parliament, British, 51, 52
Parliament, Indian, 93, 102, 159, 170, 184, 188, 196, 205–7, 209, 214, 291; *see also* Lok Sabha; Rajya Sabha
Parsis, 120, 124, 126
Patel, Vallabhai, 49, 57, 64, 69, 72, 73, 80–83, 88, 95, 153, 301
Patiala, Maharaja of, 240
Patil, S. K., 143, 162
Patnaik, Biju, 143, 233
Paul, Swaraj, 282
Pearl Harbor, 69
Pelican Books, 55
People's Action Party, Singapore, 298
Petrie (British intelligence officer), 238
Pillai, Kirshna, 91
Pirandello, Luigi, 260
Planning Commission, 86, 94
Pompidou, Georges, 145
Prasad, Rajendra, 57, 64, 88
Punjab, unrest in, 303, 304, 310, 320
Purshottamdas (FICCI President), 85

'Quit India' movement, 128

Radha Soami sect, 244
Radhakrishnan, C., 182
Radhakrishnan, Sarvapelli, 146, 164, 303
Radio Tokyo, 70
Rajya Sabha, 277, 294
Rakshasa's Ring (Visakhadatta), 318
Ram, Jagjivan, 143, 152, 165, 193, 196, 199, 203, 207, 208
Ram Das, Guru, 234
Ramachandran, M. G., 231, 232, 295
Ramarao, N. T., 231–33, 250–51, 295
Ranadive, B. T., 82
Rao, K. Subha, 164
Rao, Narasimha, 214, 285, 294, 323
Rao, Rajeshwar, 218
Rashtriya Sanjay Manch, 291
Rashtriya Swayamsevak Sangh (RSS), 80–82, 92, 185, 196–98, 206–8, 215, 226, 293, 315, 321
Rattray, Admiral, 72
Ray, Satyajit, 89n, 132n, 178
Razia, 153, 154
Reading, 1st Marquis of (Rufus Daniel Isaacs), 39
Reagan, Ronald, 231, 280
Reddy, Sanjiva, 143, 162, 165, 166, 205, 285
Rehman, Mujibur, 172, 173, 175, 177, 193, 299
Ritambhara, Sadhvi, 319
Rolls-Royce, 272, 274
Roosevelt, Franklin D., 69, 104, 145, 156, 298
Roosevelt, Theodore, 298
Round Table Conference, 48
Rowlatt Acts, 23, 24
Royal Indian Navy, 71–72
Russell, Bertrand, 19, 42, 108
Russian Revolution, 22, 33, 34, 106, 157, 298
Russo-Japanese War, 9

Sadiq, Ghulam, 149
St Cecilia's School, 117–18
St Columbus School, 272
St Mary's Convent School, 118
Salim, Prince, 236
Salt Act, 45
Sanjay Forum, 291

Santa Singh, Baba, 255
Santiniketan academy, 119
Sathe, Vasant, 294
Savarkar, V. D., 197
Saxena, Captain Subhash, 282
Scott, Paul, 66–67
Second World War, 64–71, 84, 240–41
Sen, Samar, 284
Seth, Roshan, 269
Shah, G. M., 248, 249
Shah, Waris, 237
Shah Commission Report on the Emergency, 186
Shastri, Lal Bahadur, 109, 137, 143, 145–51, 155–57, 214, 270, 272
Shaw, George Bernard, 6, 15
Shih Huang Ti, 100
Shikoh, Dara, 235
Shiv Sena, Hindu 'stormtrooper', 319, 322
Shukla, Vidya Charan, 189–91, 195, 200–201, 209, 228
Sikh Students Federation, 252
Sikhs, 40, 58, 71, 77, 80, 88, 155, 168, 222, 233–48, 251–60, 264, 295, 304, 323
Silver, Ken, 296
Simon Commission, 33–35
Singh, Amrik, 252, 254
Singh, Arun, 290, 304, 314
Singh, Baba Gurbachan, 243
Singh, Bagga, 253
Singh, Beant, 256, 293
Singh, Bhagat, 34, 239
Singh, Charan, 199, 204–8, 218, 229, 283
Singh, Gobind, 235–236, 238, 251, 254, 255
Singh, Gurcharan, 253
Singh, Khushwant, 241, 276–77, 283
Singh, Mangal, 239
Singh, Ranjit, 237, 252
Singh, Sant Fateh, 155
Singh, Satwant, 256
Singh, Shabeg, 253, 254
Singh, Swaran, 149
Singh, Tara, 240

Singh, Teerat, 223
Singh, V. P., 311–12, 314, 315, 318, 319–20
Sinn Fein, 15
Sino-Indian War, 104–7, 159
Slave Dynasty, 153
Socialist Party, French, 228
Socialist Party of India, 141, 183, 199
Somoza family, 298
South-East Asia Treaty Organisation (SEATO), 101
Soviet invasion of Afghanistan, 210
Spanish Civil War, 55
Special Armed Police Force, 250
Sri Lanka, 304, 310, 322–3
Sri Lanka Freedom Party (SLFP), 299
Stalin, Joseph, 55, 97, 99
Sundarji, General, 314
Sunderam, Vivan, 269
Supreme Court of India, 164, 219–20
Swatantra Party, 160, 162, 163, 166, 167, 169, 171, 199
Swedish National Audit Bureau, 311
Syndicate, 143, 146, 150–53, 155, 159, 160, 162, 163, 165–68, 232

Tagore, Rabindranath, 89, 101, 119, 189, 190
Tamils, 304, 310, 322–3
Tanaka, Japanese prime minister, 311
Tandon, P. D., 82–83
Tashkent Peace Treaty, 171
Tata, Jamshedjee, 20
Tata, J. R. D., 85, 88, 90, 98, 180, 187
Telugu Desam, 231
Thant, U., 158, 159
Thapar, Karan, 281
Thapar, Romilla, 316
Thatcher, Margaret, 155n, 273, 280
Thatcher, Mark, 273
Thimmaya, General, 107
Thorner, Alice, 86–87
Thorner, Daniel, 86–87
Tilak, Bal Gangadhar, 7, 12, 19–21
Tito, Josip Broz, 97, 156, 158, 265
Tolstoy, Leo, 36
Tripathi, V. S., 294

Trotsky, Leon, 9, 22, 34, 63
Truman, Harry S., 91, 94, 97, 145
Tytler, Jagdish, 284

Union Carbide, 296–97
Union of India, 220
Unionist Party, 40, 58, 241
United National Party (UNP), Sri Lanka, 299
'untouchables', 317, 319
Urs, Devraj, 206
US Seventh Fleet, 174
Ustinov, Peter, 255

Vajpayee, Atal Behari, 198, 205, 226, 229, 283
Vanaik, Achin, 308
Venkataraman, Ramaswamy, 320
Ventura, Jean-Baptiste, 237
Vietnam War, 156–58
Vietnamese Communist Party, 105
Visakhadatta, 318

Vishwa Hindu Parishad (VHP) party, 315, 318, 319, 322
Voltaire, 282

War Cabinet, British, 69
Wilde, Oscar, 49
Wilkins, Charles, 315
Williams, Rushbrook, 79
Willingdon, Lady, 38
Willingdon, 1st Marquis of (Freeman Freeman-Thomas), 38

Yahya Khan, General, 171–75
Youth Congress, 192, 277
Yunus, Mohammed, 201, 269, 276

Zail Singh, Giani, 243, 247, 254, 257, 294
Zeppelin, Count, 8
Zia-ul-Haq, General, 175, 202, 210, 236, 305
Zulu revolt, 37